THE STEEL OF THE DLI

THE STEEL OF THE DLI

2nd Battalion of
the Durham Light Infantry

1914 – 1918

John Sheen

Pen & Sword
MILITARY

This book is dedicated to the memory of the Officers, Warrant Officers, Non Commissioned Officers and men of the

2nd Battalion Durham Light Infantry 1914 – 1918

Just ask them down at Armentières,
At Arras, at Neuve Chapelle,
Inquire of the Germans at Ypres and Hooge,
Inquire down below in Hell,
And ask where the shrapnel bursts and screams
And the whiz-bangs crack and fly
You'll find the Germans don't forget
The steel of the DLI;
Yes, especially well you'll find in Hell,
They remember the DLI.

First published in Great Britain in 2009 by
Pen & Sword Military
an imprint of
Pen & Sword Books Ltd
47 Church Street
Barnsley
South Yorkshire
S70 2AS

ISBN 9781848841437

A CIP catalogue record for this book is
available from the British Library.

Typeset in Palatino 10pt

Printed and bound in the United Kingdom by CPI

Pen & Sword Books Ltd incorporates the imprints of Pen & Sword Aviation, Pen & Sword
Maritime, Pen & Sword Military, Wharncliffe Local History, Pen and Sword Select, Pen and
Sword Military Classics and Leo Cooper.
For a complete list of Pen & Sword titles, please contact
Pen & Sword Books Limited
47 Church Street, Barnsley, South Yorkshire, S70 2AS, England
E-mail: enquiries@pen-and-sword.co.uk
Website: www.pen-and-sword.co.uk

CONTENTS

Foreword

In 1881 The 106th Bombay European Light Infantry became the 2nd Battalion, "The Durham Light Infantry" and during the following years served in Ireland and Gibraltar. Then in 1885 they saw active service in the Sudan before moving to Burma. They sent a Company of Mounted Infantry to South Africa to take part in the Boer War, but their real test came in September 1914 when they embarked for France.

After the First World War, the battalion was one of the few regular battalions that did not have its war time history published and this left a gap in the history of The Durham Light Infantry. With the writing of this new book, John Sheen has filled this gap using unpublished diary entries and letters from the Regimental archives as well as many photographs from the regimental collection and battalion war time diaries.

As well as a complete list of the officers that served with the battalion, the author has included a nominal roll of the regular soldiers, regular reservists and special reservists that were awarded the 1914 Star whilst serving with the battalion.

This book is a tribute to the "Faithful" service of The 2nd Battalion of The Durham Light Infantry which was the only regular battalion of the regiment to remain in theatre throughout the full period of The Great War from 1914 to 1918.

Major Chris Lawton, MBE
The Rifles Regimental Secretary,
The Rifles Office, Durham,
24 March 2009

Acknowledgements

Thanks are due to many people, and this work could not have been completed without the support of the Trustees of The Durham Light Infantry Museum and Major (Retd) Chris Lawton, The Rifles Secretary, Durham Office.

Also Steve Shannon at The Durham Light Infantry Museum, his help and advice as always has been greatly appreciated.

The staff at Durham City Library, Darlington Library, Hartlepool Library and Gateshead Library.

The Staff at the Durham County Record Office. In particular Gill Parkes and the County Archivist Liz Bregazzi.

The late Mr Malcolm MacGregor for assistance with Honours and Gallantry Awards to members of the 2nd Battalion.

Malcolm Anderson, Clive Dunn, Andrew Brookes, Fred Bromilow, David Thompson, who loaned material from their collections.

Sean Godfrey of The Teesside Branch of the WFA who helped with obtaining photographs.

Last but not least those relatives, who loaned photographs of the soldiers:

Dave Armstrong	Bugler Thomas Armstrong MM
Steve Cuthbert	Private Billy Renton
Steve Dance	L/Cpl Charles Dance
Geoff Fox	Private James Henry Fox
Tony Freeman	Private John McDonald
John Malcolm	Private Walter Galloway
Dale McGall	Private J. McGall DCM
Jean Riding	Private J. H. Pattison
Mr Rowland	L/Cpl John William Wrathmall
Barry Thornton	Sergeant Arthur Clark

Bibliography

The Regimental Archives of the Durham Light Infantry are now held at Durham County Record Office.

Becke, Major A.F., *Order of Battle of Divisions: Part 1 – The Regular British Divisions*

James, Brigadier E.A., OBE, TD, *British Regiments, 1914-18* (Samson Books Ltd. 1978).

Plews, Sergeant Isaac diary and description of the Hooge action, and the poem 'The Steel of the DLI', the first verse only is reproduced.

Maxwell, Second Lieutenant Claude, letters

McBain Lieutenant Hubert , diary & letters.

McGregor, Malcolm, *Officers of the Durham Light Infantry, 1758 to 1968* (Volume 1 – Regulars). Courtesy of Steve Shannon, DLI Museum.

Military Operations, France and Belgium, 1914, 1915, 1916, 1917, 1918.

Moore, William, The Durham Light Infantry (Leo Cooper Ltd. 1975).

Unknown reservist, transcript of a diary.

Vane, Colonel W.L. The Vane Papers', draft manuscript of 2/DLI History and rolls of officers that served.

Local newspapers: The *Durham Chronicle*, The *Durham Advertiser*, The *North Star*, *The Chester Le Street Chronicle*, *The Consett and Stanley Chronicle*.

Personal photographs – from collectors, family, authors' collection or Regimental Archives.

MAPS

Chapter One

The Bombay European Regiment

T he forerunner of the 2nd Battalion of The Durham Light Infantry came into being in 1839 and was known as the 2nd Bombay European Regiment; the regiment was raised by order of the British East India Company. In 1840 Headquarters of the new regiment was established at Poona and drafts were received from England, which by the end of the year had brought the regiment up to full strength. At that time, the uniform was red and facings were in pale buff, and command of the new regiment was given to Lieutenant Colonel G. Brooks.

Glengarry Badge of the 106th Bombay Light Infantry.

In April of 1842, part of the regiment marched to Bombay to form part of the garrison of that station, and around this time the colour of the facings was changed to white. It was later that year that the regiment was ordered to join Sir Charles Napier, in Sind Province. However, owing to the victories gained by Sir Charles in the actions against the Indian forces, the war was brought to a close before the 2nd Bombay European Regiment could actively engage the enemy. In 1844, the regiment returned to Western India and went into the garrison at Belguam, where they received a message thanking them for their efforts from Sir Charles Napier. The regiment was now ordered to send a detachment of nine officers and 200 other ranks to join the forces operating in Kholapore territory and it was here that they suffered their first casualties in action when the detachment lost five officers and thirty-seven other ranks killed or wounded. At the end of the campaign a number of the men were mentioned for gallantry in action. When the fighting was over, the remainder of the detachment returned to Belguam. In 1846, after the presentation of the first colours, the regiment moved to Aden, where two uncomfortable years were spent in the heat and dust.

In 1848, the regiment returned to India and over a period of several years moved to various garrisons throughout the country. In 1855, the name of the regiment was altered to the 2nd European Regiment, Bombay Light Infantry. In November 1856 the regiment was ordered to Persia and left with 929 all ranks under command. They formed part of the 2nd Brigade of the 1st Division, and were present at the actions of Reshire, Bushire and Kooshab. The last named was the final action of a short war and for the three actions, the regiment received three battle honours. With the war over the regiment returned to India once more. In July 1862, the forces of the Honourable East India Company were amalgamated with the forces of the Crown and when the regiment was brought on to the strength of the British Army, they became the 106th Bombay Light Infantry. During the next ten years the regiment served in many Indian garrison towns, until in 1873, on 12 December they were embarked for England. When the ship carrying the 106th landed in England, the regiment was quartered at Parkhurst on the Isle of Wight.

Throughout the next several years, they moved to various English garrison towns: Aldershot, Chester, Manchester, Preston, and then in 1880 to Athlone and from there to The Curragh. It was in the year 1881 when they were stationed at Royal Barracks in Dublin that the Cardwell reforms took hold of the British Army and reorganised the infantry of the line. These reforms linked the 68th Durham Light Infantry and the 106th Bombay Light Infantry and brought them together as the 1st and 2nd Battalions of the Durham Light Infantry. At the time of the amalgamation the Durham Light Infantry was serving in India, and the Bombay Light Infantry, as we have seen, were in Ireland.

In August 1882, the battalion left The Curragh and embarked for the

In 1881 a new bad was taken into us The Durham Ligh Infantry with the palm leaves representing the 106th, described a 'A Bugle with str taken up into the base of a Victoria Crown'.

The Band and Colours of the 106th Light Infantry at Umballa circa 1869. In 1881 this Regiment became the 2nd Battalion Durham Light Infantry.

Lieutenant, later,
Lieutenant General Sir
Henry De Beauvoir De
Lisle, led the Battalion
Polo team to the final of
the Army Polo Cup. He
later commanded 1st
Cavalry Division, 29th
Division and eventually
XVIII Corps and then XV
Corps.

Mediterranean. Half of the battalion was stationed at Malta and the other half at Gibraltar. Whilst the battalion was overseas the regimental depot moved from Sunderland to Fenham Barracks in Newcastle. Here, they formed part of the 5th/68th regimental district with the Northumberland Fusiliers, an association that was to last for many years.

In 1885 the battalion was ordered to Egypt to strengthen the garrison there after the fall of Khartoum and the death of General Gordon. Initially, they moved to Abyssinia, and then to Wadi Halfa in Upper Egypt. Whilst here the battalion supplied a detachment of mounted infantry, commanded by Lieutenant de Lisle: this detachment engaged with the enemy in December of 1885, when Lieutenant de Lisle and Sergeant Stuart earned the award of the DSO and the DCM respectively for their gallantry in action.

On 30 December the whole of the battalion took part in the Battle of Ginnis, where for the first time the Dervish hordes were met by troops in line instead of squares, bringing four times the volume of fire to bear; the result was a disaster for the Dervishes and they were completely defeated.

Lieutenant de Lisle told of his part in the battle in the November 1896 issue of *The Bugle*, a battalion magazine:

The Nile runs from South to North and Kosheh is placed on the bank about a mile north of Ginnis. Long before daylight the troops marched up in line of quarter columns with cavalry and mounted infantry echeloned on the exposed flank, till a long rocky spur was reached overlooking the camp of the enemy. Before daylight they became aware of the impending attack and began to collect in the cold dawn of this December morning. Forced back by the British rifle fire, they retreated to a deep nullah between two hills; the line advanced taking up a second position in the same order, and then we saw something of the undaunted courage of the followers of the Mahdi as a few hundred, in spite of the steady fire from the brigade in front as well as flanking fire from the men of the mounted infantry, charged up to the very bayonets of the steady British line. It was their last rush and directly afterwards they retreated as rapidly as possible towards the South.

The following day a pursuing party under Major Smith-Dorrien was sent to follow them. After a march of forty miles – we were all mounted – we came to a village at a bend in the river. There on interviewing one of the villagers he informed me that one of the enemy's cargo boats was tied up on the bank about four miles further on. After some difficulty I obtained permission to push on with ten or twelve men after assuring my Commanding Officer that my men were, 'as fresh as paint'. We pushed on rapidly for some miles and then in the dusk we saw the outlines of the masts of the barge: and soon after came on the party of about thirty pulling her upstream.

Muhammad Ahmad al Mahdi, the leader of the Dervish fighters again the British.

The Last Stand at Abu Klea. An incident during the Sudan campaign in 1885.

...y James Francis ...ham, an abandoned ...b baby found after ...Battle of Ginnis. He ...s rescued and brought ...by the battalion ...ch he eventually ...ed.

Not knowing how many might have been there, we decided to creep up on foot, discharge two volleys and then charge with as much noise as possible. These tactics were highly successful for as soon as we set up a yell the Dervishes fled dismayed we ran up to the boat and seized the towline; and there standing on the bank of the stream alone was a small curly haired child under two years of age, dressed in the full war paint of a Sudanese warrior. As he held up his arms for me to take him up I did so and threw him to Sergeant Stuart to look after along with the barge, while the remainder of us pressed on in pursuit for a few hundred yards.

The child was rescued and adopted by the regiment and given the name James Francis Durham. His real name was Mustafa and he was brought up in the battalion and when he came of age was enlisted as a boy in the regimental band. Jimmy Durham, as he was known, died at Fermoy in Ireland on 8 August 1910.

By February the war was over and the battalion had lost one officer and fifty-five other ranks. With the return of peace 2/Durham Light Infantry were now ordered back to India, and in 1887 they arrived in Poona. Twelve pleasant years were spent serving in Indian garrisons, until in 1899 orders were received to move to Mandalay in Burma.

During this period of service in India the regimental polo team had a number of great success's winning the infantry cup and the cavalry cup, and in 1896 they won the Regimental Polo Cup which was open to all infantry, cavalry and artillery units serving in India.

When the Boer war broke out battalions from the home-based forces were quickly sent out to South Africa; 1/Durham Light Infantry were sent out and soon followed by men from 3 and 4 Militia Battalions. However 2/Durham Light Infantry did not serve in South Africa as a unit, but a number of officers, non-commissioned officers and men served in with the Burmah Mounted Infantry Company under the command of Captain Luard. This company, with a strength of three officers and around 100 men, served with the Burmese Mounted Infantry Contingent. The Durham Company was in action with the enemy twenty-eight times between Bloemfontein and Pretoria, and they distinguished themselves at Sanna's Post, where they assisted with the withdrawal of the guns of Q Battery, Royal Horse Artillery, under heavy fire. The action at Sanna;s Post, or Koorn Spruit as it was also known, began on 30 March 1900, when a British convoy consisting of ninety-two wagons, two horse artillery batteries and 1,700 men under the command of Major General Broadwood was retreating from Thaba Nchu in the direction of Bloemfontein. Broadwoods force consisted of Q and U Batteries of the Royal Horse Artillery, a composite regiment of the Household Cavalry, the 10th Hussars, the New Zealand and Burmah Mounted Infantry, in which was serving the company from 2/Durham LI as well as Roberts Horse and Rimingtons Guides.

A typical mounted infantryman of the period.

The Boer Commander, Generaal Christiaan De Wet had sent 1,600 of his men, under, the command of his brother Piet, to attack Broadwood from the north, while he himself occupied Sanna's Post to intercept their retreat. During the darkness De Wet infiltrated a force of riflemen into the ravine created by the Modder River, setting the kill zone of the ambush. At first light on 31 March, Piet De Wets artillery opened fire from a set of small hills to the north as the British troops were striking camp for the morning. Tactical surprise was complete and all were sent into a state of confusion. The British force began to retreat as expected, in the direction of the ravine where the blocking force awaited with orders from De Wet to hold their fire. The civilian wagon drivers preceding the soldiers were seized by the Boers and told if they warned the British they would be shot. Therefore the British soldiers suspected nothing and approached the river in small groups. As they did so De Wet's

Commandant de Wet, the Boer commander and his sons pictured in With The Flag to Pretoria a magazine of the time.

16

An artist's impression of the guns being saved at Sanna's Post; the Burmah Mounted Infantry cheer as the guns come through their lines.

troops ordered them to surrender, and approximately 200 were captured, along with the six guns of U Battery.

Major Taylor and a sergeant major managed to get away and alert the rest of the column, by shouting, 'Files About', the command to retire, whereupon a fearful fire broke out from the hidden Boers. Under this fire the gunners and drivers of Q Battery managed to get their guns away, and galloped away across the veldt under fire. At the same time one gun team from U Battery managed to break away in the confusion and join up with Q Battery. When they reached the site of Koorn Spruit Station, the guns were wheeled about and came into action. A way out was found, by crossing the river to the south and the Household Cavalry and 10th Hussars went off that way, only to be met by a withering hail of fire and they were unable to charge home.

The Mounted Infantry in the meantime covered the retreat of the guns; they remained in position and beat off a number of Boer attacks with steadfastness and courage. A number of them were killed where they stood, because they refused to fall back and give up ground until the guns had got away. The gunners showed much heroism in bringing the guns out of action and as they passed through the lines of the Mounted Infantry they were given a rousing cheer.

At about noon, threatened by a British mounted brigade to his flank, De Wet decided on a policy of disengagement and withdrew eastwards across the Modder River, taking the captured British guns, ammunition and prisoners with him. The day's action drew to a close with the approach of the Ninth Division.

So the Mounted Infantry contingent served on until the end of the war, for which the following awards for gallantry were made to the unit for their part in the campaign. Lieutenants Ainsworth and Way received the DSO, whilst Privates Pickford and Horton and Lance Corporal Steele were awarded the DCM.

With the war over and almost twenty years, service in the Far East, 2/Durham Light Infantry were now ordered back to England, and in 1902 were posted to Aldershot. During the 1904 manoeuvres the battalion spent some time under canvas at Ripon, in fields near the cathedral from where Private Gilbert Furry sent a card to Miss Lena Hewitson in Rowland's Gill, County Durham. This was followed in October 1905 by a move to Cork in Southern Ireland. In 1906 the new .303 Lee Enfield rifle was taken into service and that year the battalion shooting team won the Queen Victorias Cup of the Army Rifle Association at Bisley against all comers. After three years in Cork the battalion moved to Fermoy and here they were re-equipped with the 1908 web equipment. In September 1910 the battalion took part in the Irish Command manoeuvres as part of 'Blue

With the death of Queen Victoria th regimental badge was changed to a 'King's' Crown.

Card sent from Private Furry to Miss Lena Hewitson of Rowland's Gill, County Durham in 1904.

Colour Sergeant J. Baugh with his shooting trophies; in 1904 he 'swept the board' at Bisley.

Colour Sergeants in Cork.

The Sergeants of 'G' Company, with trophies for football, shooting; and rugby, taken at Cork, Ireland, 1908, Back row: Sergeant G. Shaw, Sergeant F.B. Gaire, Sergeant J. Kilgour, Lance Sergeant R. Smith, Sergeant Bugler J. Lazzari. Front row, seated: Captain A.E. Irvine, Colour Sergeant T. Heslop.

Men of E Company, including two in bayonet fighting kit, taken at Cork, Ireland, 1906. Named soldiers are: Tate, Harrison, Purvis, Captain F.G. Maughan, Campion, Jones, and Lister.

The Band in Cork.

The Colour Party: Second Lieutenant Norton, left: Colour Sergeant Black, centre; Second Lieutenant Parke, right; Colchester, Essex, 9 July 1912.

In the 1912/13 season 2/Durham LI won the Army Football Cup.

In the same season they also won the Army Hockey Cup.

Force'. Each day the battalion marched and counter-marched across the Irish countryside. Mail arrangements were poor to say the least, but 10140 Private William Craig managed to get a photograph of the tented camp at Moore Park away to his girlfriend Miss Lizzie Rix, who resided in Tyne Street, Jarrow, County Durham.

> *Pte W Craig No 10140*
> *E Coy 2/DLI*
> *Blue Force*
> *Irish Command Manoeuvres*
> *Ireland*
>
> *Dear Lizzie, just a line in answer to your letter that I received all right. I have had no time to write a letter as we are on the move to a different camp every night. My address for the next week, I will write a letter when I get time. Yours Will.*

After several years in Irish Command a move was made in 1911, to Colchester. Here the battalion was particularly successful on the sporting front, winning the Army Hockey Cup and were runners-up in the Army Football Cup. On 19 July 1912 the battalion paraded in Colchester for the presentation of new colours by Lord Durham. In his address at the end of the parade Lord Durham spoke of his family connections with the regiment and of the smartness of the battalion on parade. Later that year on 24 October, this was followed by the laying-up of the colours of the first, second and third battalions of the regiment in Durham Cathedral and during this parade detachments of the Territorial battalions took part in the ceremony.

During the winter season of 1912/13 the battalion football team won the Army Football Cup for the first time in the history of the regiment, and after the completion of army manoeuvres in September 1913 the battalion moved to Lichfield in Staffordshire. It was here in January 1914 that the team was accused of misconduct during a match and the following small article appeared in the Colchester Telegraph on 7 February:

> *As a result of a commission appointed by the Army Association to inquire into misconduct at a match in which 2/Durham Light Infantry, formerly of Colchester, but now stationed at Lichfield, were concerned it was decided to suspend Sergeant Johnston for six weeks and remove the captaincy of the DLI Club until reinstated by the Army F.A.. Private Read was suspended for six weeks. The referee was ordered to withdraw a charge against an officer in plain clothes and the expenses of the commission to be born by the regiment.*

In June 1914 the battalion went to camp in Wales with the rest of 18 Brigade, but the events in Europe would bring an end to the pleasant occupation of peacetime soldiering.

B Company taken at Whittington Barracks Lichfield 1913.

D Company taken at Whittington Barracks Lichfield 1913.

The Outbreak of War – The Call to Arms

On the bright sunny morning of Sunday 28 June 1914, the visit of the Archduke Franz Ferdinand and his wife, the Duchess Sophie, to Sarajevo, the capital of the Austrian province of Bosnia-Herzegovina was to set Europe alight. It was a National Fête Day and the streets were decked with

The assassination of the Austrian Archduke Franz Ferdinand and his wife the Duchess Sophie by Gavrilo Princip plunged Europe into a war that lasted over four years.

flags and thronged with people as the royal train arrived at the station. Security arrangements began to go wrong almost immediately: when the royal cars left the railway station, the security detectives were left behind and only three local policemen were present with the royal party. The Archduke with General Oskar Piotorek the Military Governor, travelled in an open-top sports car, which, at the Archduke's request, travelled slowly so he could have a good look at the town.

As the car drove along the Appel Quay, near the Central Police Station a tall young man named Cabrinovic threw a hand grenade at the car. The grenade bounced off the folded roof and exploded under the following car wounding several officers. Despite the threat, Archduke Ferdinand ordered a halt to find out who had been injured and it was now that it was discovered that a grenade fragment had grazed the Duchess. Archduke Franz Ferdinand arrived at the town hall in an outrage and decided to visit one of the wounded officers who had been taken to a nearby military hospital; he would then continue with the visit to a local museum as arranged. The cars left the town hall and went back along the Appel Quay this time at high speed, but the drivers had not been told of the unplanned visit to the military hospital. The first two cars turned right at the corner of Appel Quay and Franz Josef Street but General Potiorek shouted at the driver of the third car that he was making a mistake. The driver, obviously confused, braked sharply and brought the car to a halt, in the worst possible place. Standing right at the spot was a young Bosnian, Gavrilo Princip, who emerged from the crowd only some three or four paces from the Archduke's vehicle. Drawing a pistol he fired two shots into the car; the first mortally wounded the Archduke and the second struck the Duchess Sophie in the abdomen. The car raced to the Governor's official residence but the bumpy ride only made matters worse and the royal couple were pronounced dead shortly after arrival. If Austria-Hungary was to continue as a world power this outrage could not go unchallenged.

If Austria-Hungary declared war on Serbia, this would bring in the Russians, but Austria was allied to Germany and as early as the beginning of July the Kaiser, who was a personal friend of the Archduke, is reported to have said 'The Serbs must be disposed of.' Then on 23 July the Austrian Government sent a strong memorandum to the Serbs listing ten demands, the strongest of which was that Serbia allow Austria to suppress local agitation and subversion directed against Austria. Although the Serbs accepted most of Austria's conditions Austria deemed it inadequate and declared war. The nations of Europe rushed to mobilise: the Tsar, Nicholas II of Russia tried to maintain peace but the Russian Army mobilised on 31 July. To counter this Germany declared war on Russia, having first offered France the chance to stay out of the conflict and remain neutral. The French, however, remained true to their treaties and refused the German offer; the Germans therefore declared war on France. Having declared war on France, on 3 August the Imperial German Army crossed the border into Luxembourg and threatened to move into Belgium. Belgium had mobilised on 2 August and the Germans sent an ultimatum on the pretext that the French had crossed the border into Belgium. The French in fact had retired so that they could not give any cause for such an accusation. The note said that if the Belgian Army could not stop the French the Germans would, and if the Belgians resisted then it would be considered an act of war. The Belgian border with Germany was covered by a line of forts and the key to these was the fort at Liege on the river Meuse. The main invasion of Belgium began on 4 August, although a cavalry patrol had crossed on 3 August. The German cavalry moved quickly through the frontier towns and villages, their task to capture the bridges over the Meuse before the defenders could blow them up. They also had the task of providing a screen in front of the advancing infantry and carrying out advance reconnaissance.

Meanwhile in England mobilisation had been ordered. On 30 July, more by luck than planning, the majority of the Territorial Army were on their annual camp and were quickly moved to their war stations guarding vulnerable points on the coast and along railway lines and docks. The Belgians had a treaty with England and when the German Army crossed the frontier, Britain sent an ultimatum to Berlin. No reply was received so the British Empire declared war on Germany on 4 August 1914. The British Army at home in England and Ireland had been organised as an Expeditionary Force of six infantry and one cavalry divisions and at a meeting of the principal Ministers, including Lord Kitchener, who became Secretary of State for War on 6 August, the decision was taken to send four infantry divisions and the cavalry division to France on 9 August. The other decision taken by Kitchener was to raise New Armies, each army of six more divisions of civilian volunteers and on 7 August, he appealed for the 100,000. He launched his poster 'Your Country Needs You' and the recruiting offices were packed with recruits, over 10,000 men enlisting in five days

The Germans attacked France by marching through Belgium; here a German Cavalry patrol, part of the advance guard, is seen in a Belgian border village.

Chapter Two

Tipperary Days, 1914, The Aisne and Armentières

With war so close 2/Durham LI received orders to move to certain critical points. A detachment moved from Headquarters at Lichfield to South Shields under the command of Major D'Arcy Wentworth Mander, who had been commissioned into the regiment as a second lieutenant in 1892. When the order to mobilise came, the various detachments were in place and ready to deploy. At 1800 hours on 4 August 1914 the telegram ordering mobilisation was received at Battalion Headquarters in Lichfield and the telegraph wires hummed as the word was passed to the South Shields detachment that they were to move out to their allotted places. The detachment, 400 strong, of whom 137 were attached from 1/West Yorkshire Regiment deployed as follows:

Captain Ernest William Birt and twenty-one men to Hebburn Dock, Lieutenant H. Taylor and twenty-five men reported for duty at South Shields oil depot. Lieutenant Leopold Norton and twenty-five men went to Frenchman's Battery and Lieutenant William Grey-Wilson, who had recently rejoined the battalion after a tour with the West African Regiment, took twenty men to Palmer's Dock. The remainder stood by in a supporting role.

On the night of 4 August immediately after war was declared, Major

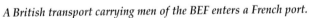

A British transport carrying men of the BEF enters a French port.

Men of the BEF march down the gangway to land on French soil.

Mander assisted by Captain Harry Hare and Lieutenant Victor Yate with a detachment of men boarded a German merchant ship lying in the Tyne and arrested the crew and seized the ship. This action was reported in *The North Star* in the following way:

Eight German seamen who had formed the crew of the German steamer Albert Clement which was seized at Tyne Dock on Wednesday were arrested by the military authorities at South Shields yesterday and were taken to the Central Police Station at South Shields, where they were detained pending instructions from the military authorities. At the same time Pastor Singer of the German Sailors Home was arrested and was escorted to the police station by a party of soldiers.

He was marched through the town under escort and the paper reported the incident created great excitement throughout the town.

During the summer of 1914 the orders for mobilisation, which had been worked out over many years, were refined so that every officer and man at the depot knew exactly what was required of them. At the depot each reservist had a pigeonhole with all his required equipment in place, so that

Very soon the German Army were at the heart of Belgium; here a German supply column enters Brussels the Belgian capital.

At a railway station in a French port, British soldiers watch as another train loaded with men moves off inland.

on arrival the business of kitting the men out proceeded very quickly and smoothly. Regular reservists began to arrive as early as 0600 hours on 5 August and the arrangements for feeding and billeting worked admirably. Throughout the day men were medically examined and when passed fit were issued with their kit, nominal rolls were filled in and the men prepared for dispatch to join 2/Durham LI. It is interesting to note that the officers at the depot recorded that the regular reservists nearly all reported sober and on time; whilst those of the special reserve battalions, i.e. 3/Durham LI and 4/Durham LI, were mainly late and in many cases under the influence of drink, many having to follow on behind the main party after it had deployed.

Meanwhile back at Lichfield things were moving at quite a pace. At 0400 hours on 6 August, the first party of 301 regular reservists, under the command of Major Alexander K. Robb, arrived from the Regimental Depot at Fenham Barracks, Newcastle.

Later on the morning of 6 August, the South Shields detachment rejoined the battalion. All day the men were busy checking kit and inoculating the new men and preparing to leave for the war station. On 7 August at 0400 hours another train carrying 384 reservists under the command of Lieutenant Nigel Conant, who had served with the 4th Special Reserve Battalion prior to being commissioned into the battalion in December 1910, arrived at Lichfield. This officer had been detailed to take the battalion colours to the Regimental Depot where they would be kept safely until the battalion returned from active service, and on his way back had been given command of the party heading for Lichfield. At 2025 hours another telegram arrived ordering the battalion to move to its war station. At 2200 the battalion paraded ready to march to the station, however, harness for the horses which had been indented for some months earlier had still not arrived. This didn't stop the Durhams though and the wagons were hauled to the station by men detailed for the task instead of the battalion horses.

This period of mobilisation is recorded by an unknown reservist of C

Company, in a manuscript of his diary held in the Regimental Museum.

Mobilised on the 4th of August and proceeded to Newcastle on the night of the 5th , arriving about 9pm. Went through the ordeal of passing the Doctor and drawing my kit and other equipment. I was now ready to march off. The order we received at 6.30pm on 6th August not knowing where we were bound for. We had a great send off from the barracks to the station where we entrained. Our destination was supposed to be Belgium, but it turned out to be Lichfield, arriving there at 3.30am on the 7th of August, having passed a good time on the train. From the station we marched to barracks a distance of about 3½ miles.

By the next afternoon Battalion Headquarters along with A and B Companies had arrived in Dunfermline. Upon arrival the Commanding Officer carried out a reconnaissance of the local area, whilst the men moved into their allotted billets.

Meanwhile back in Whittington Barracks in Lichfield, on 8 August 1914, the battalion suffered its first death of the war, when one of the rear party, 8968 Private Robert Archer Ferguson, a Londoner, who had joined the Durhams in Aldershot, killed himself. The suicide was reported in the local press in the following way:

Two of the reservists that rejoined the regiment, seen here in a 1st Battalion photograph of 1911; Sergeants Bleackley and Fellingham reported to the Depot at Fenham and were sent to 2/Durham LI at Lichfield.

Soldier's suicide at Whittington Barracks

A regrettable incident took place at Whittington Barracks on Saturday morning, Robert Archer Ferguson (24) a bandsman in the 2nd Battalion Durham Light Infantry, shot himself because (it was believed) he was unable to go with his battalion on active service.

On Friday night an order was issued by the officer in charge to prepare to depart to Trent Valley Station. All the men who obtained permission to be absent for an hour or so were called up, but Ferguson was nowhere to be found. It was ascertained that he had borrowed a bicycle from one of his comrades and had left the barracks. On Saturday morning about 8 o'clock he was seen, by James Wealleans, who is in the same battalion, racing across the Barracks Square towards the bathhouse. He was carrying a rifle. Wealleans noticed there was something very strange about the deceased's manner, and followed him. Ferguson entered into the bathhouse and locked the door. Being unable to gain admittance Wealleans went for assistance and when the door was forced open Ferguson was found with a gun in his mouth. He was quite dead.

The grave of 8968 Private Robert Ferguson in Whittingham Churchyard, Litchfield, Staffordshire; he committed suicide on 8 August 1914.

On the following Monday morning an inquest was held on the circumstances surrounding the death by Dr Auden (the coroner) of Burton upon Trent Captain Birt, Durham Light Infantry, gave evidence of identification and said the deceased had been in the battalion for several years.11529 Private James Wealleans gave evidence and said:

I saw the deceased, who was an intimate friend of mine go across the square towards the bathhouse, carrying a rifle. As he appeared strange in manner I followed him, but the deceased had locked himself in by the time I arrived. I went for help and with the help of several others forced the door open and we found the deceased with his rifle in his mouth. He was quite dead.

The deceased told me that both his parents had committed suicide and it was generally known that the deceased had tried to commit suicide whilst stationed at Colchester. Private Ferguson joined the battalion from an industrial school in London.

The jury returned a verdict of 'suicide whilst temporarily insane'.

The deceased soldier was interred in St Giles, Churchyard in Whittington, Staffordshire: the funeral took place on the Wednesday following the incident; the coffin was carried on a gun carriage, but owing to the war there were no horses available to pull the carriage, which was drawn by a party of men from the battalion.

As the other companies arrived at Dunfermline, they too took up quarters in local houses and municipal buildings until on 11 August the battalion went into camp. With so many reservists having been recalled to the colours, route marching and breaking in army boots became a priority. At that time men were enlisted for seven years with the colours and five on the reserve or five with the colours and seven on the reserve, so some of the men could have left the army as long ago as 1908, whilst others could have only been out of the army a matter of months. The one thing they all had in common was the fact that they had, as infantrymen, the ability to fire fifteen aimed shots in one minute, and although there must have been some musketry practised in order to zero personal weapons, there is, however, no recorded evidence of this activity.

The unknown reservist wrote the following of Dunfermline:

[After two days in Lichfield], we left for Dunfermline in Scotland arriving there about mid-day in a downpour of rain and we received our water proof sheets. We then marched to our billet, which was one of the Carnegie libraries. Here the people were very nice to us, giving us everything we required. We stayed here until Tuesday the 11th when we went into camp at Pittengrief, in the park. As nice a place as one could wish for to be camped. We had very good weather and an easy time of it, doing very little drill.

In France the first five divisions of the British Expeditionary Force had met the German Army at Mons, in Belgium and had started to fall back towards Le Cateau. It was now that the 6th Division was called upon to assemble and the various units began to move to the divisional assembly area. 18 Brigade moved south, 1/East Yorkshire Regiment from Edinburgh, 1/West Yorkshire Regiment and 2/Durham LI from Dunfermline and 2/Sherwood Foresters came from Sheffield. When the order for mobilisation came 16 Brigade which was based in Cork and 17 Brigade, based in Fermoy, and the supporting engineers and artillery also came over from Ireland where they too had been stationed. On 13 August 2/Durham LI along with the other battalions of 18 Brigade arrived in Cambridge where the 6th Division was concentrating. Here they went under canvas in a brigade camp on Jesus Common and divisional training commenced. Although the men went under canvas, the dining hall and common room of Jesus College were made available to the officers of 2/Durham LI and 18 Infantry Brigade Headquarters as an Officers' Mess.

The manuscript of the reservist's diary records:

> We left on the night of 13 August about 11pm then en-routed for Cambridge arriving about 3pm on the 14th and marched about 2 miles to camp. There we stayed until our Division the 6th was formed which lasted about a month. We having done a great amount of work in the meantime. Having very hot weather the whole of the time.

It was in Cambridge on 18 August that 9094 Private John Pringle, a Gateshead man, passed away and was buried by the battalion with full military honours in Cambridge City Cemetery. Later in the month on Sunday 23 August the Dean of Durham visited the battalion and held a service prior to the battalion leaving for France. Two weeks later on 8 September 2/Durham LI, under the command of Lieutenant Colonel Bernard W. L. McMahon marched out of Cambridge enroute for Newmarket where they entrained in two trains. On the first train, Battalion Headquarters and Captain William Northey's A Company and Major D'Arcy Mander's B Company were followed on the second train by Major Edward Blake's C Company and Major Alexander Robb's D

An open-air Church Parade; it was at a similar service that the Dean of Durham said farewell to the battalion.

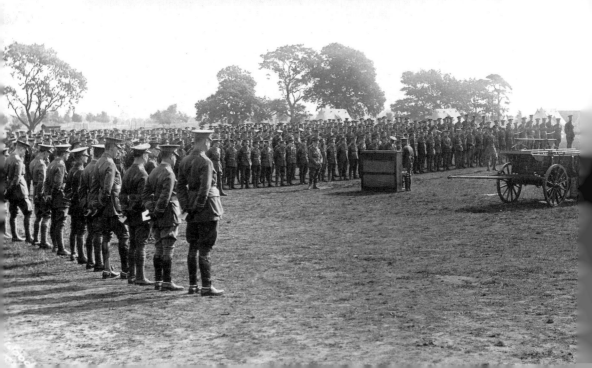

The Staff Officers of 18 Brigade Headquarters and 2/Durham LI taken at Jesus College, Cambridge prior to embarkation for France, September 1914.

Company, which as soon as they were loaded left for Southampton docks.

The march to Newmarket was recorded in his diary by 10994 Corporal Frederick Stone, 'Left Cambridge to march to Newmarket, very hot march, Lance Sergeant Ross died on the road from the heat. Bivouacked on the common until entrained for Southampton.' [No trace of Lance Sergeant Ross has been found.]

The trains arrived in Southampton the following morning and the troops were embarked as soon as possible. The men off the first train embarked on the City of Benares and those of the second train went aboard the *Bellarophon*.

Another few lines in the reservist's diary manuscript tell of the march from Jesus Common into Newmarket and eventually to the port of embarkation:

> *We then left for Newmarket on the morning of the 7th September which was a very trying march on account of the heat and not being used to the new equipment. Arriving there about 3.30pm on the same day we rested until 1.30am on the 8th September. Then we entrained for Southampton where we arrived about 8.30am and embarked about 11am on the troop ship Bellarophon. We set sail about noon for St Nazaire, France.*

An unidentified group of sergeants of the battalion in the camp on Jesus Common prior to embarkation. sent from Bob, at Cambridge, to Mrs. Dawson, 22 Galgate, Barnard Castle, postmark 24 August 1914.

At the time of embarkation the senior positions of Warrant Officers and Quartermaster Sergeants were held as follows:

Regimental Sergeant Major		6402 Joseph Watson
Regimental Quarter Master Sergeant		5824 Ernest Black
Orderly Room Quarter Master Sergeant		5492 Augustus Monks
Orderly Room Sergeant		10539 Sidney Jiggins
A Company	CSM	7279 Robert Haylett
	CQMS	6739 Charles Couchman
B Company	CSM	6997 Henry Vaughan
	CQMS	5508 Percy Harrison
C Company	CSM	5617 James Jones
	CQMS	5829 Thomas Heslop
D Company	CSM	5558 Charles Kent
	CQMS	5286 Harry Storey

Within weeks four of the above had been sent back to England, where they were commissioned and returned to the battalion and by the end of the war, a further three had been commissioned and they would have amassed an impressive record between all twelve of them.

The two transports sailed and proceeded to the French port of St Nazaire; this was owing to the fact that the British Base Depot had been forced to fall back from Le Havre owing to the retreat of the BEF. On arrival in France the companies of 2/Durham LI disembarked and marched to a rest camp; Fred Stone recorded the events in this way:

> At about 6 p.m. arrived at St Nazaire but took some time to get into the river mouth, but we were eventually landed by means of a very rickety ladder. My Platoon, Number 11, was detailed to unload guns and horses. We marched up to a rest camp and next day did a little musketry, then mooned about until the evening, when although it wasn't allowed, managed to slip out and had a couple of bottles of vin rouge and went into what appeared to be a pork butchers shop. The people were very kind and wouldn't let us pay. We had coffee with milk and returned to the camp.

Major Crosthwaite who was born in Australia and educated at Bath College and Sandhurst and had served with the Durham Light Infantry since 1886, also went into town and gave his impression in one sentence:

'Remained at rest camp all day – walked into town with Robb in afternoon, nothing of interest in it.'

At 1030 hours the following morning orders arrived for the battalion to march to the station to entrain at 1200 hours. They duly paraded and marched to the railway station where they arrived in pouring rain only to find there was no train. Eventually at 1630 hours the first train arrived and the first half-battalion entrained; the companies proceeded in the same order, by train to Coulommiers, east of Paris, where once the battalion detrained they went into billets at St Germain. 'Here I was detailed with six men to guard a barricaded road during the night. It

Taken before the war in 1913, Company Sergeant Major James Jones, C Company CSM, and CSM Fraser who by the outbreak of war was time-expired; he did, however, re-enlist in the Seaforth Highlanders.

37

poured the whole night and we were soaked,' wrote Fred Stone in his diary.

The 6th Division arrived in the area behind III Corps and was temporarily broken up as the brigades were allotted to different corps. 17 and 18 Brigades were placed under command of I Corps and 16 Brigade came under orders of II Corps. The battalion now began an approach march to the Aisne Front; on 15 September a 25-mile hike took them to Chateau Thierry where they went into billets at midnight.

The march was recorded in his diary by Major Crosthwaite:

> *Long march to Chateau Thierry, motor lorries with our wounded on board passed us on the march, many signs of war along the road, trenches, shell holes and broken telegraph wires. Marched into Chateau Thierry after dark, a large town all in darkness, very few people about – a great deal of wilful damage done to the houses by the Germans and all left in a very dirty state – billets very uncomfortable.*

The next day, with an early start before daybreak, saw them trudge another 18 footsore miles to the village of Tigny, it was raining and wet when they started but soon cleared up after an hour or so. Here they were billeted in a very large farm which held the whole battalion. The officers were able to buy fresh eggs from the farmer and also only two or three bottles of red wine, as the Germans had taken most of what the farmer had. Then on 17 September the battalion marched to Chacrise where they spent the night. The next afternoon the march continued through Braine to Bourg where they arrived at midnight and went into billets. It was in this village that the manuscript of the unknown reservist reveals a small mystery! His diary records the movements in the following words:

> *We landed on the night of the 9th after a very pleasant voyage and received a great reception. We then marched to camp where we stayed until the 11th when we entrained for Paris, but we landed in Coulommiers on the morning of 13th September, here we had breakfast and dinner, then marched to a place called St Germans[sic], where we stayed until the other half of the battalion joined us on the night of 14th September. We then started our rough time, marching 75 miles in 4 days. We passed through Chateau Thierry where a great deal of fighting had taken place, but our battalion had taken no part in that. We arrived in the town of Braine and bivouacked in heavy rain. Here one of our men died of exhaustion. We left at 3.30am on the 19th September wet through to the skin and marched to Bourg.*

Who was the unknown soldier that died of exhaustion? No man has been traced to this date, to the battalion – was he included in the casualty list of two days later when a number of men fell in action? Or was the unknown reservist mistaken in date and location? Could he have been referring to Lance Sergeant Ross mentioned in similar circumstances earlier?

Meanwhile in the County Durham village of Annfield Plain a picture postcard and a letter arrived from a West Stanley policeman on the reserve, 9210 Lance Corporal Tom Armin, a keen local footballer, serving with A Company of the newly-landed battalion. The card stated:

I received the cigarettes safely, but no safety matches. I am in the best of health and am having a lively time with the Germans. We are progressing splendidly up to now. From the official news the war will not last long; but we will have to be careful. We have done some splendid marching and all our troops are quite happy under the circumstances. Yours Tom.

The letter was written just after the battalion had landed and must have been in the post for some days – written on a number of scraps of paper, it read as follows:

I received your letter of the 5th on the 18th. I expect you have received some of the postcards I have sent you. We are on top of the Germans now and are hoping to come out successfully after a few hours are over. We had a very good wash last night – it simply rained in torrents: But we are still very happy and are all sure of success in the next big engagement. Not one of our battalion have made goalkeepers yet, meaning none of them have stopped an enemy shot. We all expect to be home before the year is out. In a few days time you will be reading in the daily newspapers of our troops taking all before them, we are on the tide of a big battle, which will be over before you get this letter. Our Engineers have done well for us and built six bridges in a week. We are all in the best of spirits and thankful we are fighting for a good cause.

A few days later another letter arrived from Lance Corporal Tom Armin this recalled in some detail the march up to the front:

A considerable portion of time was occupied in marching and preparing us for the severities of the front. One day, we started out on the march at seven in the morning and continued until about 1030 at night. The distance covered would be something like thirty miles; it rained in torrents all the time. Next morning we were up again and by four o'clock we were marching, this time doing about 10 miles. Whilst on this route we met one of our supply columns deadbeat to the world, the men lying asleep on the wagons. The stiffest march was that which lasted two days during which time they traversed over fifty-four miles. We were under the constant guard of the British aeroplanes.

On 16 September they had what he termed the first good nights sleep in France.

We were only about five miles from the firing line, being kept as reserves in case of emergency. These long marches, which we indulged in did not dampen the spirit of our troops, though it rained continuously and made them look more like drowned rats than anything else.

On 19 September for the first time in France, the battalion took over the front line; every man of the battalion was in the trenches north of Troyon, having relieved units of 2nd Brigade. Major Crosthwaite wrote at length

Second Lieutenant Charles Stanuell was Killed in action 20 September 1914. He has no known grave and is commemorated on the La Ferte-sous-Jouarre Memorial to the Missing in France.

Second Lieutenant Roger Marshal was killed in action 20 September 1914. He has no known grave and is commemorated on the La Ferte-sous-Jouarre Memorial to the Missing in France.

about this period:

> Saturday 19 September, started from bivouac before daybreak and marched to Bourg, halted there, had breakfast and a wash and tried to dry our things in a very uncomfortable little house. I thought that Arthur [possibly his brother] was with the 1st Division to which our Brigade had been temporarily attached, so I sent word to him through our supply officer. He turned up during the morning looking very fit and jolly. I was very pleased to see him. Bourg had been badly knocked about by shells and the bridge destroyed, so we had to cross the Aisne by a pontoon to get in. We were ordered out of Bourg about 1000 hours on account of risk of the shelling being repeated. We marched a mile outside to the north under the cover of a big hill. About 1400 hours I was sent with the Officers Commanding Company's to Troyon to see the Officers Commanding, Northamptonshire and Gloucestershire Regiments, about taking over trenches from these regiments. We had our first shelling experience as a portion of the road was being shelled, but none of them went near us. We passed a good many dead horses and for the first time saw the large holes made in the ground by the big German percussion shells known in the British Army as 'Coal Boxes' or 'Black Maria's'. When we arrived at the trenches North of Troyon, we found officers with beards and plastered all over with yellow clay living in dugouts scooped out on the safe side of big banks, these were the battalion and brigade headquarters and nearby the reserve or supporting companies. The actual trenches about two hundred yards in front were very different to those we had dug in training and they had to protect men from the big shells and shrapnel which the enemy periodically poured into them. We marched through Troyon after dark and relieved the above named regiments in the trenches in the centre of the line occupied by their brigade. The East Yorkshires took over on our left and the West Yorkshires on our right with the Sherwood Foresters in reserve in the rear.

Having taken over the line, the first night for the battalion was quiet but Fred Stone wrote about it in

Major William Northey was badly wounded on 20 September 1914; although he reached a hospital on the French coast the same day, he died from his wounds and is buried in Boulogne.

Major Edward Blak was killed in action 20 September 1914. He has no known grave and is commemorated on the Ploegsteert memorial to the Missing in France.

40

Major D'Arcy Mander was killed in action on 20 September 1914 and is buried in Vendresse British Cemetery.

Major Alexander Cobb was wounded on 20 September 1914; although he was rescued by Private Warwick, he died from his wounds and is buried in Vendresse British Cemetery.

his diary:

> *A Corporal and four men were posted out in front of our company to give notice of any German movement and being 'Jumpy' imagined that they saw something and commenced firing. Before they had time to retire, the company, also 'jumpy', fired. The result was four men killed, the Corporal managed to get back.*

On the following afternoon a strange incident occurred when the Germans launched an attack by the whole of the VII Reserve Corps. It was a very cold day and there were occasional heavy showers of rain. The Moroccans on the British right came under heavy attack from the Germans and were forced back. The Officer Commanding 1/West Yorkshire Regiment, which was the right-hand battalion of the British Army, moved one of his companies to cover his exposed flank. However, the Moroccans were rallied by their officers and came back forward and not knowing that they British had moved into their position, they opened fire on the men of the West Yorkshire Battalion, who suffered around thirty casualties. Things settled down a little, although the Germans kept up heavy artillery and rifle fire. Around 1000 hours the Germans again launched another attack, but this was checked by a stubborn defence by the West Yorkshires. At noon a third attack came on, under the cover of a heavy rainstorm and once again the Moroccans fell back. Yet once more the gallant West Yorkshire men moved eastward to cover the vacated ground and at the same time their Commanding Officer requested assistance from 2 Cavalry Brigade. Before reinforcements could arrive the Germans had occupied part of the Moroccan position and were able to bring enfilade fire on the British, inflicting heavy casualties; they charged and captured most of the right-hand company. Within half an hour, working down the front line, they had taken prisoner most of the two front-line companies.

This exposed 2/Durham LI to a withering enfilading fire. According to reports in the local press the fall back of the West Yorkshire battalion occurred because the Germans showed a white flag and came forward to surrender and then opened fire with a

Private William Toole from Shotley Bridge, County Durham was one of those men taken prisoner by the Germans in September 1914.

Sergeant Creber from Stanley, County Durham was one of those men taken prisoner by the Germans in September 1914. In 1919 he re-enlisted and served for many years in the Durham Light Infantry, he then became a Chelsea Pensioner until he died.

machine gun. This incident was well recorded by Lance Corporal Armin:

> They had been firing for a good while, and in the end the white flag started to wave in the distance. A host of Germans advanced towards the English trenches to surrender. The West Yorks, were ordered to disarm them and proceeded to take the Germans as prisoners. Instantly the Yorkshire men put their rifles down and made towards the enemy, the Germans in the front ranks fell down and behold! In the rear were no fewer than six machine guns, which opened a terrible fire on the West Yorks. They had no guns, but oh no! They were not to be denied and against overwhelming odds went at them with natures weapons, their big fists. They suffered heavily at that time this happened about the 20th of September.

> Our lads were not far away, but were under the impression that the Germans had been taken prisoners by the West Yorks. Suddenly an enfilading fire commenced along the ranks, the enemy had turned their machine guns upon us now. Our officer on the left was amazed at the situation and required a signalman. I had to go from the right to the left of the firing line amidst a hail of bullets. How I got there, I do not know, but I managed safely. As soon as the situation was explained to the officer, we were ordered to retire.

Soon however B Squadron of the 18/Hussars came up and rallied the West Yorks. The 9/Lancers dug in behind the Moroccans and eventually the front was stabilised. The news of the arrival of the cavalry spread like wildfire through the infantry ranks and morale was raised immediately. The lost trenches were regained by a dashing charge of the Sherwood Foresters. But the whole of the brigade had suffered terrible casualties.

When the Foresters were ordered to counter-attack, the Durhams also received orders to drive the Germans out of their entrenched position on the side of a hill. They were subjected to a terrible ordeal of bullets and shells and the losses, trying to take a position where the Germans were, at least twelve to one. But the men fought grandly, led by Major Robb. A dashing attempt to lead a company into action led to Lieutenant Twist being shot down. 8757 Private Jackie Warwick courageously went to the rescue and brought him back into the British trenches escaping miraculously. 7544 Private Joseph Howson, a Darlington man also engaged in rescue work, fell wounded and Warwick succeeded in getting him back; at a third attempt, he rescued Private Maughan, but his crowning feat was to rescue Major Robb. To do that he had to dash over the crest of a hill to within 30 yards of the German trenches.

> He crawled along and succeeded in getting him back, to use his own words, 'right under their very noses of the Germans. It was hard job to get him in, and in my effort I was shot in the back and fell.

A somewhat different version of events is recorded in Major Crosthwaite's diary which is well worth recording in full, and whilst Major Robb is mentioned there is nothing about Private Warwick.

During the morning there was considerable amount of shelling by the Germans, replied to by our guns. About noon the Colonel, Godsal and I were standing talking outside our dugout when a shrapnel shell burst just over us. We all dived under cover but a bullet caught Godsal in the calf of his leg. I put a dressing on the wound and gave him some brandy; he was then taken off on a stretcher. About 13:30 after the Colonel and I had had some lunch, I happened to look towards the rising ground on our right where the West Yorkshires were holding the trenches. I saw some men standing in close order on the top of the rise. I looked through my glasses but could not tell for certain whether they were our men or not – they were holding their hands up. Realising something was wrong I told the Colonel and as all of our companies were in the trenches I got together the men belonging to Headquarters, pioneers, signallers, cooks and orderlies and took them away to the right and lined them up along a bank from which we could fire to the right. The men on the top of the rise disappeared and a line of men commenced to advance towards us from the high ground. We opened fire on them with the few men we had and some time afterwards the Sherwood Foresters came up and sent forward a company to attack. This company was checked but when supported by others they advanced and retook the trenches. While this was going on the right our companies in the trenches found themselves exposed to artillery, machine gun and rifle fire from their right. The companies were from left to right Mander's,, Northey's, Blake's and Robb's. After the attack developed on the right Robb ordered his company out of the trenches and took them forward to the crest in front – we do not know why he did this, but suppose it was with the idea of finding out what was in front of him! Hare followed with half of Blake's company and also companies of the East Yorkshires on the left. Parke who had his machine guns in Robb's trenches took them forward also. In this forward position a good many men were hit by fire from the right, and the companies of the battalion on the right retired back to

For his bravery in rescuing the wounded and bringing in Major Robb, 8757 Private Jackie Warwick was recommended for the Victoria Cross but only received the Distinguished Conduct Medal.

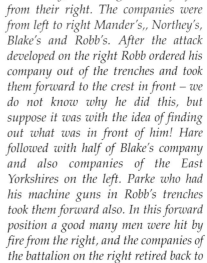

An artist's impression of the tactics used by the Germans to hide the machine guns that cut down the West Yorkshire Regiment and allowed the enemy to enfilade the Durham Light Infantry.

43

their trenches. Our company and a half also retired to theirs, Parke was unable to get back as quickly as the others with his guns, but he got them back all right. Robb was hit when he was out in front of the trenches and was being helped back by two men when he was hit again, the men also. Hare and Stanuel were also shot dead out in front. Stanuel being found after dusk but Hare was not. Twist was also hit at the same time. Mander was killed in the trenches. I think Grey-Wilson and Marshall were hit in the trenches too. I believe this is a fairly accurate account of what happened but I cannot vouch for all of it.

One of those engaged in collecting the wounded was 6742 Private George W. Harrington, a native of Walsall, Staffordshire, who voluntarily went out twice under heavy fire to bring in wounded men.

On arrival at hospital in England, Private Warwick wrote to his wife at Grasmere Road, Darlington, and described the incident:

> We were entrenched just eighty yards from the Germans. Shells were dropping in hundreds night and day. It was a perfect hell, I shudder when I think of it. We went into action, 1121 men of the regiment, and 86 came out of it. The German used the support of a white flag, and when we went out to bring them in, they shot us down. It was on Sunday at six o'clock

> that I was shot down. I volunteered to bring Major Robb from in front of the German trenches. He was shot down, when we made the bayonet charge, and he was lying 40 yards in front of the Germans, who were waiting for anyone who attempted to rescue him. I do not know what made me do it, but I went out to bring him back. I got him on his feet and started to run with him. A poor young chap, belonging to Bishop Auckland called Nevison [11653 Private John Nevison] rushed to help me. We got within 50 yards of our trenches, when all were shot down. He was shot through the brain so they told me, and also I believe our major died shortly afterwards. They call our trenches, Hells Gate, it a proper name for them too. We were outnumbered by the Germans, fifteen Germans to one Englishman.

Lance Corporal Armin also recalled the incident, and in a much more dramatic fashion:

> When we got back far enough it was found that the major was missing. It was Major Robb; he had been wounded. One private volunteered to rescue him from the danger zone. He was shot. Another man went out and he was shot too, a third volunteered and met a similar fate. But Jacky Warwick was in the crowd. 'To hell with this,' he said, 'I'm going to chance my lot and get him.' He went and under our instructions, for we could see the enemy, and his position, he got to the major and gradually by dragging him along the ground; he got into a place where he was capable of carrying him. He did not do this brave act without injury; but as

he came back, he was given a rousing cheer from the boys. It was a cheer that a real British Hero most thoroughly deserved. Private Howson also did some brave deeds by carrying his comrades back into safety.

About two hours later, we were all most agreeably surprised to see the form of Colour Sergeant Kent, on the skyline, with Private Bootes on his back. The boys laughed at the sight, but as he came nearer they accorded him a rousing cheer and he was justly welcomed into the line again. He had proved himself a real hero that day. We lost heavily, the enemy must have been at least twenty to one and we lost a good number but the enemy losses must have been twice as many.

Private Warwick was recommended for the award of the Victoria Cross; however, he did not receive that medal. For his gallantry in action, he was awarded the Distinguished Conduct Medal. Colour Sergeant Kent also received the same decoration.

Another among the wounded that day was Sergeant Arthur Hudson, whose story was told under the heading of:

A remarkable experience

Sergeant A Hudson, Durham Light Infantry, who is a patient at Stobhill Hospital, Glasgow, had a remarkable experience at the front. The Durhams were entrenched at Soissons and were only eighty yards from the German trenches. Along with others, Hudson rushed a German trench, where nine Germans were working three Maxims. After accounting for two of the Germans he lunged his bayonet through a third; but as the man fell dead his rifle went off, the bullet entering Hudson's left arm. One of the privates accompanying him killed four Germans and then was killed himself. When

0 Private William
lairs from Sunderland
s killed in action 20
tember 1914. He has
known grave and is
memorated on the La
e-sous-Jouarre
norial to the Missing
rance

a support position; the men have dug a rudimentary ench against the German shell-fire. However, it is one ng line; without the fire bays developed later, enemy fire d shrapnel can sweep straight along the trench.

Infantry in an early fire position, at this stage of the war they have not started digging the deep trenches that came later.

running back Hudson fell in a gulley and lay beside a dead German who had had his head blown off by a shell. The sergeant heard his comrades saying, 'Sergeant Hudson is killed.' For thirty yards he crawled along with bullets flying overhead and eventually making a dash for it reached the British lines.

One story attributed to the battalion, which appeared in the local press at this time. was about an Irishman in the Durhams ranks, who was sick to death of being harassed in his quiet moments by a big German who was in a trench about 30 yards away. This German was in the habit of constantly popping his head up and having a shot at the English trenches, when it was night-time. 'Indeed!' said Pat, 'I will stand this no longer, but if I have a shot at him and then we will have some peace.' Pat was informed that he had not to open fire until he had orders. However, he did not wait and the next time the German appeared he fired one and the German was surprised as he had never had a bullet in his head before. Pats rest that night was assured.

The Durhams could not get the Germans to come out and fight in the open and one story that went about was that one of the Durhams shouted 'Waiter!' and a host of German heads appeared above their trenches, to be met by a hail of Geordie bullets.

In this first action the battalion had many casualties. Major D'Arcy Mander, Captain Harry Hare, Lieutenant Roger Marshall and Lieutenant Charles Stanuell were all killed, and Major Alexander Robb died of his wounds, whilst Lieutenants Wilfred Twist, William Grey-Wilson, John Gales, Colin Mearns and Charles Baker were all wounded. Of Captain Harry Hare, the Colonel wrote:

He was one of the very best – a very gallant gentleman – a good soldier. He was dearly loved by officers and men and his death has been a grievous loss to the regiment. Long will little "Bunny" Hare be affectionately remembered by the Durhams.

Casualties in the ranks too were heavy thirty-six men killed and ninety-two wounded.

Overnight the battalion rested where possible and in the early dawn a request was made for a volunteer to go out and find out where the enemy was and what they were up to. Having bravely rescued men under fire the previous day, 6742 Private George W. Harrington stepped up to the mark and said he would go. Just before dawn broke he went out into No Man's Land and found where the enemy had dug in. He gathered some very useful intelligence and came safely back to the battalion's lines. The information he brought back proved to be of great value to the British gunners.

His exploits over the last two days brought him promotion and later on 10 March 1915 he received the Distinguished Conduct Medal. The word of his deeds reached his home town and the Lord Mayor of Walsall, Alderman J. W. Cotterell, wrote the following letter to him:

Second Lieutenant Victor Yate was wounded and evacuated on 20 September 1914.

Second Lieutenant Colin Mearns was wounded and evacuated on 20 September 1914.

Lieutenant, later Major Hugh Go. was wounded 20 September 1914. became a Staff C and was killed i action on 26 Ma 1918 whilst ser on the staff of X Corps.

I have read with much interest and pleasure the account of your heroic conduct at the front and in the name of the town I wish to congratulate you most heartily on the decoration of your bravery. Walsall feels proud of you and will not forget what she owes her soldier sons. Wishing you every success, good health and a victorious, safe and speedy home coming.

It was now that the letters started arriving from the War Office, in the colliery villages of County Durham. The lists in The *Durham Chronicle* started a sad story that would last longer than the war itself. The following articles appeared in the local press relating to men of 2/Durham LI killed in action on 21 September 1914.

Mrs A Hewick of Duke Street, Low Spennymoor, has been notified by the War Office of the death of her husband, Private Louis Henry Hewick, who is connected with the Durham Light Infantry, who was killed in action on 21 September. Hewick who was 28 years of age was a native of Ferryhill village.

Word has been received at Coxhoe that Private Robert Barker of the 2nd Durham Light Infantry has been killed in action. No particulars were furnished. The deceased who was a reservist resided at Front Street, Coxhoe, and was employed at East Hetton Colliery. He leaves a widow and two children.

Mrs Flowers of Brasside, near this city, has received intimation from the War Office that her husband has been killed in action. Private Flowers served with the Durham Light Infantry in India for seven years which expired three years ago. During the last three years he has been employed at Kimblesworth Colliery, and immediately war broke out he was called up to join his regiment. Private Flowers was widely known and much respected; he leaves a widow and one child. Private Flowers was a well known boxer and whilst in India won the middle weight championship. After his return he engaged at some contests at the Durham grounds and was on the whole, very successful. He has only been married about eighteen months and much sympathy has been expressed with his widow.

A further story appeared in *The Consett and Stanley Chronicle* relating to Private Flowers, narrated by a comrade, 9693 Private Robert Wainwright, a regular reservist who had already served seven years on the North-West Frontier: discharged in 1913, he had just completed about nine months of his five years, reserve service when called up. He had gained employment as a porter at the railway station in his home village of Lanchester. However, it is very easy to see why he has the dates and actions muddled owing to the fog of war, as the events took place a week later than the date given.

Private Robert Wainwright of Lanchester had an interesting story to tell a representative who interviewed him, about Private Flowers who is in 2/Durham LI, and served with his regiment for five years on the North-West Frontier of India and was on the reserve when he was called to the

47

colours again in August. Landing at St Nazaire, the Durhams, according to the young soldier soon saw evidence of German 'Kultur'. Passing on their way up country, they passed the graves covered with straw, of two young women who had been subjected to ill-treatment by the Huns. Passing on to the Aisne. Sunday 13 September is a day I will not forget. Four hundred Germans came over on the right flank and the white flag was displayed. The Yorks and Durhams went out to take them prisoners, but the advancing body opened out at the rear and too late the discovery was made that the white flag had been abused for it was seen that they were carrying what appeared to be stretchers with machine guns and a heavy fire was opened upon the 'Tommies'. Amongst the victims of the treacherous act was Private Flowers of Brasside. Relief came to the Durhams and Yorks and the former afterwards went down country to Armentières.

> When reconnoitring, a small party of which I was one suddenly came upon a number of Germans who were entrenched beside a gravel path, near a gentleman's country estate. An enfilading fire was directed upon the reconnoitring party and an officer was shot through the head and I was shot through the lower part of the arm. The wounded were removed to field hospitals and later in motor ambulances to the base. From there I made the journey to Boulogne and the Yacht Albion took us to Folkestone. The wounded soldier was in Cambridge Military Hospital, at Aldershot for five weeks before he was fit to return home. Asked what his feelings were when a 'Jack Johnson' came in the proximity of the lines, Private Wainwright replied that at first he had a scared feeling but after a time that feeling passed and like others he joined in timing them out 'That's gone west.' In the trenches many a dull hour is whiled away by talking and speculating upon football. For that reason he hopes that football will be continued to be played. Referring to the trenches Private Wainwright said it was easy for a British soldier to whistle over to the enemy's trenches and a German reply. He also told how an Englishman who was wounded in danger of being captured asked his comrades to 'finish him' rather than he should fall into the hands of the Germans.

Another Stanley man writing home at this time was 8770 Private Joseph Turnbull writing on 21 September he said:

> I am writing these very few lines under very trying circumstances. We have been in the trenches since Saturday night and on Sunday afternoon we had a very hot time of it and lost a lot of our chaps. I had a bullet through the heel of my boot; it passed right through without making the slightest scratch on my skin. I therefore consider myself quite lucky. I hope you received my letter quite safe as I sent one off on Saturday last. Tell May I will bring her a big present from France, if I am spared, as I hope to be. Hoping to hear from you soon, – Yours Joe.

On 25 September, the battalion was relieved in the trenches by men of 2

Brigade. Once the relief was complete the battalion marched to Peargnon arriving shortly after midnight. The next day at 0900 hrs, the march continued and they marched to a wood north of Bourg and became the reserve to 3 Brigade. That evening at dusk, they moved forward, and went into support trenches at Vendresse. The next evening 1 Brigade arrived and relieved 3 Brigade in the trenches. The battalion left the trenches at 2230 hours and marched to Vauxtin. They spent two days here. The Battalion Headquarters were located in the house of the village priest, and although heavy shells were falling nearby most of the battalion fell asleep and didn't hear the noise until they awoke in the morning. Then at 1900 hours on 2 October they marched to Ciry and took over in the line from the 4/Divisional Cyclist Company. The cyclists had gone into the line during the day and taken over from the Duke of Wellingtons Regiment and the Kings Own Scottish Borderers in order that the relief by the Durhams could be made later in the evening. The cyclists gave a warning that the village was not a healthy place during the hours of daylight, although many of the inhabitants were still there and the battalion was able to buy chicken, eggs, coffee and milk. In the evening of 3 October Second Lieutenant F. J. Gilbertson arrived with ninety-eight men from 3 and 4/Durham LI. The following morning the Reverend Day came over to the battalion from the Brigade Field Ambulance and held a service in the field. The next couple of days were very quiet so they had an easy time of things.

Meanwhile in Stanley another letter was received from Lance Corporal Tom Armin, dated 24 September, which read as follows:

I have had some of my letters and parcels sent back, as I have been reported missing. However, if you see in the newspapers that I am missing, don't believe it, as now I am strong and happy and full of life, and still ready to fight for King and country and for God above. The reason I was reported missing was that when my goods arrived at the firing line, I happened to be further along the line signalling; consequently, the material for me was returned to the base. We stood as the 'Faithful Durhams' always do. The word 'Faithful' is very sacred to the Durhams. The General gave us great praise for our conduct in the field. There would have been a few V.C.s if there had been any high officials present.

Be of good cheer for there is plenty of fighting in the 'Faithful Durhams' yet and with God's help we shall return home safe and sound, what is left of us. I hope you will put this short note in a newspaper and let the people of Durham know of the deeds of their county regiment. I hope I shall return to read it but if not send a copy on. Tom.

On 7 October the Lancashire Fusiliers arrived to relieve 2/Durham LI who rejoined 18 Brigade. Major Crosthwaite recalled this in his diary:

The relieving battalion was very late in arriving and we did not get away until 0400 hours! We marched to rejoin our brigade at St Remy arriving there about 0900 hours and went into billets. We had breakfast and a rest, the Colonel and I had one of the cleanest rooms we had seen in this country. At 1800 the brigade paraded and marched to Largny.

The period of the war known as 'The race for the sea' began, and there now followed a series of route marches: 18 Brigade, along with the rest of 6th Division began moving north. The march route took the battalion via St Remy, where C Company stayed in an infant school and then they moved to Largny where the night was spent. The next day the column didn't start until 1400 hours when they left for St Saveur (Oise), followed by a further move at 1700 hours to Le Meux where they entrained in a train of cattle trucks of the French railways. The train carried them through the night via Etaples, Amiens, Abbeville and Desbres to Arcques and here they detrained and went into billets.

We detrained and stayed in a Brewery all night, marching to a farm the next day. The farm was only 2 miles away and here we had Sunday and part of Monday to ourselves. We then marched to a place near by and were supposed to be met by motor lorries but they did not arrive, for a considerable time.

This was how the unknown reservist wrote of this period of movement.

The next move was to Wardrecques where they arrived around 0900 hours on 11 October. The day was spent resting in the fields waiting for a unit to leave the billets and then at night the battalion moved into the newly vacated premises. The next morning a convoy of motor lorries of the French army arrived and the battalion en-bussed and were transported to Hazebrouck where they arrived at 1500 hours.

Upon their arrival we got onboard and proceeded to a place called Hazebrouck, here the whole Brigade formed up in the Market Square and from there we marched to an old factory were we stayed the night. The next day we went another 5 miles and halted for 2 hours on the road side as the division formed up.

So wrote the unknown reservist in his diary about this period of the war.

Another unknown soldier was quoted in the *North Star* on 10 October: the reporter put several questions to the Tommy and their conversation was printed on page 3

Motor lorries of t Army Service Cor were used to mov men quickly up t the front. Here at rest halt men try converse with the local population.

under the heading of 'What it feels like.' Impressions of a soldier in battle'

"I have suffered and will suffer again", remarked the private who is attached to the Durham Light Infantry. "What does it feel like to be in the fighting line?" "Well it is difficult to express one's feelings. Indeed, there is no time for thought, deeds speak not words. Tucked away in our trenches which are not so cleverly constructed as those of the Germans, we just waited until the target presented itself and then – well the bullet did the rest." The private's diffidence was remarkable in the extreme and he was reluctant to talk about what he had seen in the Battle of the Aisne, in which he was wounded. "Have you participated in a bayonet charge," "Ugh it was terrible. When we were ordered to fix bayonets, I felt a queer sensation go through me, for, while I had done plenty of drill exercise, yet when it came to it on human beings it was horrible. But! It had to be done, and my mate remarked," "If you do not do it to them, they will do it to you." That advice made me see blood, it was no use; it had to be me or the enemy, but I will not forget pushing my bayonet into the body of a German. He squealed at the sight of the steel, but he had to have it, and after I accounted for my first man the rest was plain sailing. It was like sticking sheep. Still when it comes to every man for himself in a matter of this kind you just do your best, never knowing when your own turn will come. The German soldier does not like the bayonet; he will advance in the face of the most terrible artillery and rifle fire with the utmost bravery and they do drop in the hundreds, but they still come on. At the sight of cold steel however they showed a faint.

It was in this region that III Corps were concentrating, covered by 2nd Cavalry Division. The plan was a general advance and III Corps advanced with both its divisions in line. The 6th Division moved forward in three columns towards the line Vieux Berquin–Merris, some 5 miles to the east of Hazebrouck. At 1400 hours on 13 October, 2/Durham LI advanced to the attack against Les Fermes, which was successful despite losing Lieutenant Walter E. Parke, who after his death was mentioned in dispatches by Sir John French, and Second Lieutenant Harry H. Storey, who was also killed in action. Harry Storey was a native of Shildon, County Durham and had worked his way up the ranks to Company Quarter Master Sergeant; he had served over eighteen years in India prior to returning to England in January 1914 before being commissioned on 1 October. He fell to an enemy sniper, with a bullet in the head as he led his platoon forward, bayonets fixed, on 13 October 1914. Another officer Second Lieutenant Cecil Evans Smith was wounded along with around sixty other ranks killed, wounded or missing. The unknown reservist continued:

The next three days were a series of skirmishes, we seeing the novel sight of two aeroplanes fighting in the air on the 15th, the French machine bringing the German to earth. We then received the orders to prevent the enemy from blowing a big bridge up. But we were too late as they had

Many of the walking wounded had a quick field dressing placed on their wounds and made their way back to the Field Ambulance from where they were evacuated to a CCS and then on to a hospital on the coast.

> *nearly completed their task. When we arrived they were retiring in great haste after setting fire to a beautiful chapel in the village of Sailly sur Lys, we then took up an outpost position, where we captured one German and found another dead on the road side. His name was Krup and he had a wife and two children living in London. We buried him on the following morning.*

In mid October, it was reported in the *North Star* that Mr and Mrs J. W. Smith, of 44 Beaconsfield Street, Norton-on-Tees, received a letter from their son, 10285 Sergeant Harold Smith in which he said:

> *The Valley of The Aisne the poor old Durhams struck a proper death trap, I took my platoon up on the left and was met by a perfect hail of bullets and shrapnel and the men went down on both sides of me. We made the beggars run though, our attack being fine. When the time came not a man hesitated.*

Sergeant Smith was wounded in the arm during the attack and was evacuated and ended up in the War Hospital in Bromley, Kent. Later after the formation of the Machine Gun Corps he was transferred to that corps and promoted to Company Quarter Master Sergeant.

The same edition of the paper carried a small report from Private Edmund Clegg, a resident of Close House, in which the story of the white flag attack on the Sherwood Foresters was retold and also the fact that he reported seeing the mutilated bodies of two young girls.

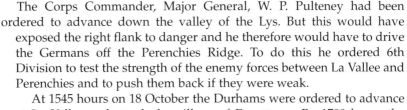

The Corps Commander, Major General, W. P. Pulteney had been ordered to advance down the valley of the Lys. But this would have exposed the right flank to danger and he therefore would have to drive the Germans off the Perenchies Ridge. To do this he ordered 6th Division to test the strength of the enemy forces between La Vallee and Perenchies and to push them back if they were weak.

At 1545 hours on 18 October the Durhams were ordered to advance at La Vallee and attack the village of Ennetteres. By 1700 hours the attack was successful but two officers, Captain William Northey and Lieutenant Nigel Conant, were wounded and amongst the men, four were killed, seventy-four wounded and twenty-nine missing. One of the wounded was 10156 Lance Corporal Henry Oxley, from Coundon Gate near Bishop Auckland. He spoke to a reporter from The *Durham Chronicle*, who recorded his words:

When given the order to attack the Durhams had to go through bogs, sometimes almost up to the waist and then we got into ploughed fields, which we had to go through at a quick pace. It was whilst going through

Second Lieutenant Parke was given a hasty field burial; here two young French girls put flowers on his grave. His remains were later moved to Outersteene Communal Cemetery Extension in Bailleul.

Les petites Françaises n'oublient pas les braves Anglais morts au champ d'honneur

Little French girls keep green the memory of brave Englishmen dead on the field of honour

these fields that I was wounded and after evacuation was admitted to hospital, where not having had my clothes off for seven weeks they had to be cut from me.

The reporter also recorded that Lance Corporal Oxley spoke in high regard in praise of the officers of the battalion, stating that they always shared their cigarettes etc with the men and seeing that they were splendidly fed.

7507 Lance Corporal John Watson, a regular reservist, writing to his former colleagues at South Shields Police Station, had this to say:

I am thankful to say I must be a lucky man. We have had two more fights and are getting quite used to it. On 13 October I am sorry to say we lost a lot of men and officers, some fine fellows amongst them. One poor fellow who had just got his commission from Quarter Master Sergeant was killed and our Machine Gun Officer was also killed lifting the gun over a hedge. What a terrible thing is war to see the dead and wounded lying about after a battle, the wounded crying out in pain. We are very busy chasing the Germans who are on the run, our lads have got a lot to wipe off and the sooner the better.

Second Lieutenant Cecil Smith was wounded and evacuated on 13 October 1914.

Another man who recorded the attack in some detail was 10994 Corporal Fred Stone,

Advanced in extended order to about one hundred yards to our front, when suddenly a hail of bullets began coming from right, left and in front. Dropped flat and shrapnel began to burst over us. Rushed forward over turnip fields with no cover what so ever. Drop again, bullets so thick that it was almost impossible to lift head from the ground. I risked a look over the turnip tops and was hit in the shoulder by a piece of spent shrapnel, sore, but alright. We remained here for about two hours, but we were unable to get forward bullets so thick. Just before dusk I was struck by a bullet in the calf. Sergeant Harrington on my left was struck in the foot, so when it was dark enough we both hobbled back. Before leaving I reported to Second Lieutenant Bradford, sort of 'Permission to fall out Sir, wounded. and I remember he expressed his regret. We met the C.O. and Major Blake and explained where the troops were in front. Sergeant Barber of B Company bound my leg up and I hobbled down to a village where I found the R.A.M.C. in a cottage. After a short time a horse ambulance of the Lancashire Territorial R.A.M.C. took me away to Ennetteres.

From here Fred was evacuated by motor ambulance and eventually wound up back in England.

Another soldier, 9639 Private George Snaith of A Company, was interviewed by a reporter from *The Consett and Stanley Gazette.* The article covered his service right from the start and was similar in content to the others already drawn on; however his view of the fighting in October is worth quoting:

The trenches that they had dug were like being at home; they had fitted

them up with beds and almost everything that was needed to make one really comfortable. When we took them over we found a respectable quantity of empty wine bottles the Germans evidently having had a good time. We kept them on the run until we came to a place between Armentières and Lille. Here we were ordered to take a village, a river had to be crossed but the bridges had been destroyed. We managed to get across by means of planks. On approaching the houses we found that the village was barricaded with household furniture. We pushed our way through that obstacle and got inside the village. There was a large church burning – it was a complete furnace. The Germans were good at picking up their dead on the field but as we got into this place we came upon half-a-dozen French Dragoons who, the previous night had been out patrolling. Their eyes had been cut out their ears were off as well as their noses. It was a most horrible sight! Further on in a house we found a Frenchman standing as though he was keeping the enemy at bay. His eyes were out and his ears and nose cut off as well as one of his legs. What a deliberate barbarity.

Describing how he sustained his wound Private Snaith stated that in the course of one very hot action he stopped behind to bandage a wounded comrade:

I bandaged the fellow, but was unable to carry him back to the lines owing to the deadly fire. I hid him behind a hedge from where he was rescued later. Having completed the bandaging proceeded to get my rifle which was lying on the ground. When in the act of picking it up I got 'one gentle reminder' in the forearm. I fell into a hole and soon another bullet came and fell close to my head the dust going into my eyes and partially blinding me. When things became quieter I made my way back to safety.

After being wounded Private Snaith was picked up by stretcher-bearers and eventually wound up in a hospital in Swansea from where he was sent home to Catchgate near Stanley to recuperate.

Also involved in the action was the unknown reservist of C Company, who wrote in his diary:

Marched about a mile and a half and commenced an attack. A Company formed the firing line, D Company the supports, these were however reinforced. Although nothing being done until later in the day, then a general advance was made at about 4pm. Our losses were pretty heavy about 126 killed and wounded. Here Captain Northey was shot in the leg. We having taken a village in Armentières, about 8pm our section went to search a house in the main street and an appalling sight met our gaze. On going into the cellar we could see nothing else but arms, legs and heads lying about the floor. In one corner an old man and woman lay terribly shattered by a shell. The old man dying as soon as we got to him. Here the Notts and Derbys came up to relieve us.

After the action 2/Durham LI were withdrawn to the village of Fetus into reserve positions on 19 October, but C Company were left behind

as a reserve to 2/Sherwood Foresters. On 20 October the German Army launched an attack in strength all along the British Front from Ypres to Armentières. At 0830 hours 2/Durham LI were ordered forward to La Vallee, and shortly afterwards B Company under the command of Captain John Wood and D Company under the command of Captain William Birt were sent up to support 1/East Yorkshire Regiment at Paradis. By 1100 hours a gap had opened at Paradis, between 1/East Yorkshire Regiment and 1/North Staffordshire Regiment of 17 Brigade; consequently the Commanding Officer of 2/Durham LI was ordered to take up the remaining company, 'A', under the command of Captain Henry Taylor. The gap was closed by B Company assisted by one platoon from A Company under Second Lieutenant Charles W. Beart, who would later have a distinguished career in the regiment. At around 1530 hours, in drizzling rain, Captain Taylor was ordered to move to the right flank and support 1/West Yorkshires as the Germans resumed their attack against that flank, but once again with the assistance of the Durhams the enemy was repulsed. In order to secure the right flank the remaining half company of 2/Durham LI was moved to a farm in the rear of the right flank to prevent any further advance of the enemy on that flank.

Second Lieutenant Charles Baker was wounded and evacuated on 20 October 1914.

The Germans came on again and no one will ever know for certain what happened to the Durham Light Infantry platoons supporting the West Yorkshire Regiment. From some survivors, statements it would appear that Major Blake took two platoons of his company into a factory and from the upper stories brought effective overhead fire onto the Germans attacking the Sherwood Foresters. However, this attracted heavy shellfire from the German gunners supporting their attack. The shells poured into the factory and Major Blake was killed and many of his men were either killed or wounded and only a few returned to the British lines. The other two platoons of C Company under the command of Lieutenant Norton went to try to protect the right flank of the Foresters as they retired, but during the action the officer was wounded and taken prisoner. When the fighting was over only twenty-three NCOs and men of C Company were accounted for and it was presumed at that time that those not killed had been taken prisoner. The survivors rallied on XXXVIII Brigade, Royal Field Artillery near the windmill at the north-west of La Valleee. The Official History records that it was little wonder the line had been overcome, for it was not until the publication of the official German records that the actual forces against 18 Brigade became known. The German records show that on 20 October 1914 the Germans employed the whole of 25th Reserve Division and 52nd Infantry Brigade, almost three quarters of the German XIII Corps opposing the British 6th Division.

Second Lieutenant Charles Beart was wounded and evacuated on 20 October 1914; he eventually became a Brigade Major.

Once again the diary of the reservist sheds light upon what happened

Sergeant Thomas
...op; CQMS of C Company,
...as posted as an instructor
...e Officer cadet Battalion
...hen transferred to the
...ur Corps.

...tain Leopold
...ton was killed
...ction 20
...ober 1914.

...enant Edmund
...enham joined the
...lion on 26
...ber and was
... on 27 October
...he is commemo-
...on the
...steert Memorial.

from the private soldier's point of view:

This was the beginning of a day of great bloodshed for all concerned and although our casualties numbered about two hundred of which Major Blake and Lieutenants Norton and Gilbertson are shot, those of Notts and Derbys must have been far greater. Our line was now on the verge of retirement for our position had become desperate as we were completely outnumbered. Time after time the enemy advanced only to be driven back, their shells never ceasing the whole of the day. At last well on dusk our position became unbearable. Just then I was hit by a piece of shell which tore my pack almost from my back and then I fell from the end of the trench. Just then my pal, Private Halse [8909 Private John Halse] came up and took off my equipment and then managed to get back into the trench again. There was very little hope of getting to our headquarters and we were thinking of our artillery and what could be the matter as they had stopped firing for a while. But our Artillery who were quite insufficient to cope with the enemy was endangered and with the Headquarter Staff commenced their retirement. Our task now was to shield them, which we did, with great losses to our side and terrible mutilation to theirs. Just before dusk a platoon of ours was sent to reinforce the Notts and Derbys who held a position on the right and were severely pressed. The enemy here were forced back with great loss just as the day closed. The party on our right had in the meantime retired and unknowingly we were surrounded. About 5pm the enemy again crossed our front to charge the ridge. This they carried out with great loss. But they succeeded in capturing 760 men of various units. After leaving the trenches we were ordered to lay down our arms by Captain Drury–Lowe of the Notts and Derbys who told us our retreat was completely cut off. This order was taken with mixed feelings.

The surviving Durhams were collected and pulled back then marched back, from Fetus to Bois Grenier. However, they were only out of the line one night. The following day saw them take over the front line from the Leicestershire Regiment at Rue du Bois. This position was held for over ten days. Throughout the whole period the enemy provided a continuous bombardment by day and often at night: the main problem was the enemy snipers, who accounted for two officers killed and two wounded. While they were here the third batch of reinforcements arrived – twelve officers, Captains, Bowers, Turner, Legard, Meldon, Streatfield and Lieutenants, Swetenham, Newstead, Vane, Mortimer, Cruickshanks, with Second Lieutenants, Neal and Lavery, accompanied by ninety-eight NCOs and men. The following morning the officers reported to their allotted companies. Lieutenant Swetenham had been posted to B Company which was holding the line and he went up into the trenches to join them. During the day the Germans made an attack which was easily repulsed but, Swetenham and Vaughan were both killed by a German sniper during the morning.

On 28 October the enemy put over a very heavy bombardment and followed it up with an infantry attack on the barricades at the Rue du Bois. Some Germans managed to get round the flanks, some even into the battalion positions forcing the Durhams outpost positions to fall back on the East Yorkshire Regiment; here the enemy advance was checked. Then a company of the Lancashire Fusiliers and some thirty men of 2/Durham LI came up and with the assistance of 1/East Yorkshire Regiment and the surviving Durhams, retook the lost trenches. It was noted that the machine-gun section of 2/Durham LI had done great execution amongst the enemy as they came over, and again when they were exposed as they withdrew.

Major Joseph A. Crosthwaite assumed command of the battalion when Lieutenant Colonel McMahon was posted. Promoted to Lieutenant Colonel he took over 1/Somerset LI and then 8/York and Lancaster Regiment.

Captain John Wood : wounded and evacua on 28 October 1914.

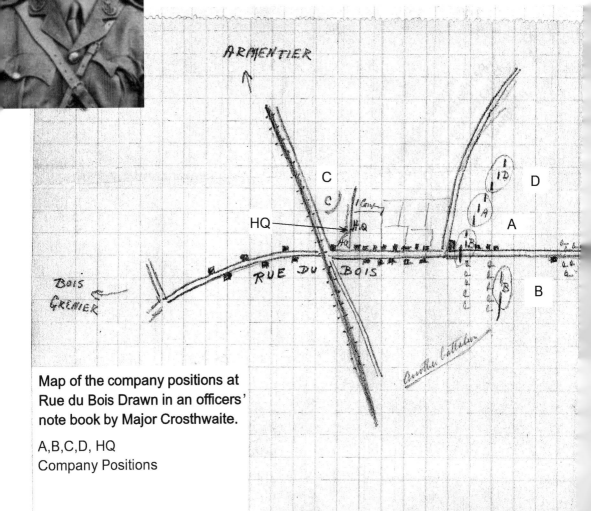

Map of the company positions at Rue du Bois Drawn in an officers' note book by Major Crosthwaite.

A,B,C,D, HQ
Company Positions

After the action 9074 Private Joseph Fleetham wrote to his wife, who was residing at 9 Dyke Street, West Hartlepool. In the letter he explained they had been in the trenches six days and then he told her how his chum 8986 Private James Matthews of Stainton Street in the town had met his death. 'We had just finished breakfast and Matthews had got up to look out when he was hit by a bullet.'

Private Charles Alderson writing to his sister, Mrs Pettinger, who resided at North Road, Durham, the letter bearing the date, Saturday, 28 October says:

I am in the trenches again. Hardly a minute to spare. We had an awful day on Thursday. I am sorry to say we suffered a good deal. All our officers are nearly gone and all the men who were in India with me are also gone. I have had many narrow escapes. It is an awful sight seeing your comrades knocked down right and left and you cannot stay behind to assist them.

We have had to keep going on amid a rain of bullets and shell and I think it will be a marvel if I ever get out of this. But up to present I am all right. At the time of writing we have had a young fellow killed with shrapnel in the next trench to us. Of course his death was instantaneous. We are burying him now. I have not heard of M Hopper for three days and I don't know where he is. You have heard me talk of a Durham man. He is badly wounded and when I spoke to him he did not know me. There are several cases just the same. Sunday last we were in action but did not lose so heavily, though it was pretty hot. There were four of us messing together but one has got wounded in the foot and that leaves three. One is Private Howson, a Darlington man who has been mentioned in the papers in connection with Private Warwick, who was in my section. I don't really know what part of France we are in, but wherever we are, we are amongst it. One would wonder where all the Germans come from. They are thick, but they have been mowed down like chaff by our fellows. The weather is beginning to get very cold rainy and damp. We get plenty to eat when we get a chance.

It was for his bravery during these actions in October 1914 that Second Lieutenant Roland Bradford, who would later win the Victoria Cross and went on to become the army's youngest brigadier, received his first award for gallantry when a Mention in Despatches was recorded in The London Gazette on 17 February 1915. Then the following day the same journal recorded that he had been awarded the Military Cross for 'services in the field'.

Sometime during 29 October a small patrol of 2/Durham LI and two men of the Divisional Cyclists went out in front of the barrier to examine the houses in front of the Durhams. It was from these houses that the German snipers had been causing casualties among the battalion. The patrol shot two Germans that ran out from one of the houses. Afterwards six more men of the battalion went out to assist the patrol and on their return they reported that they had shot a further ten German soldiers.

On 31 October 1/King's Shropshire LI arrived and took over the trenches, allowing 2/Durham LI to march back to billets some 2 miles back in divisional reserve in the village of L'Armee. Casualties had once again been fairly heavy: two officers killed, three wounded and fifteen other ranks killed, forty wounded and seven missing. Many of these men had only arrived on a draft a few days earlier: three drafts, totalling thirteen officers and 262 other ranks having arrived between 25–31 October. The heavy shelling had caused a strain on the nerves of all ranks even though little actual damage had been done, indeed more cause for concern were the German snipers who were very active and hit quite a few men: they had got into the houses in front of the battalion position and loopholed the walls from where they shot anyone who exposed themselves.

Lieutenant Congreve was awarded the Distinguished Servic Order for rescuing Captain Wallace un fire on 28 October 19

One of the officers who arrived at this time was Lieutenant John Harter, who wrote a long letter home to Lieutenant Colonel H. H. S. Morant commanding 10/Durham LI:

My Dear Colonel,

Our train journey lasted two days. We moved very slowly and very comfortably. At one time there were 2000 men onboard the train and in Picardy somewhere the couplings of the Durham LI carriages gave way, the engine driver spotted the absence of half of his load luckily and backed into the still moving second half thereby causing the carriage to be smashed, however none were hurt and we eventually arrived at the railhead. There we were billeted in a school our men were in the chapel and I was above in a classroom upstairs. The next day we were taken by motor bus along with the rations and parcels to the Divisional headquarters. Shells were bursting all around us as we buzzed along all on top to see the fun. We were showered with apples bread and wines in bottles, so pleased are the inhabitants to see us.

Lieutenant, later Captain John Harte wrote long letters to his former CO, Col Morant. On 3 April 1915, when he was Brigade Major of 1 (DLI) Brigade, he w badly wounded wh German barrage hi Brigade Headquart dug-outs at Zillebe he died from his wounds the follow day.

At the railhead a poor old peasant told me that the Germans had stayed there nine days and that they had stolen all the blankets from the people and the barber said that they had taken all his razors. We remained at divisional Headquarters all day and came up to the trenches at dark. All moving about is done at night as by day shells buzz about in all directions. Blake has been killed. Northey is at the base severely wounded. Wood was hit in the thigh the day I got here by one of his own sentries who had the jumps and he is very bad I am afraid to say. Swetenham was hit in the head by a sniper and Birt in the arm by a sniper. Storey was killed by shrapnel. Parke was looking for a site for his machine gun when he was killed by a random bullet in the neck. Everyone speaks highly of him. Colonel McMahon is naturally rather worn out and worried at seeing all his officers go down, but those who remain are very cheerful and we are confident of giving the Germans beans. Congreve is Adjutant and Crosthwaite Second in Command, Bowers,

Turner, Taylor, Bradford, Neil and myself are the only other regular officers here, the others are Special Reserve. My Captain is Legard Special Reserve; we only have eighteen of the original men left as the company was decimated on the way here and are now reforming with my new men. Norton is a prisoner and Corporal Ball I am sorry to say is killed. Please tell his brother and say that he died fighting hard so I am told at Soissons.

Our fire trenches are 500 yards away from the support trenches and the battalion headquarters. Some men have been in the fire trenches for ten days or more and we can't make out why we haven't been relieved. A, B and D are in the fire trenches, about 250 yards from the Germans who swarm like bees. All the trenches have scooped out cover and no head cover, we have no blankets and just sleep in overcoats, if it rains, as it did last night we spread our oil sheets over the top of the trenches. All day we are shelled by the 'Coal Boxes' and all last night too. The effect of two days and two nights continual shelling on our battalion (500 men) is one man killed and one man wounded. So you see that as long as one keeps cheerful and is well entrenched there is no fear, but 'Coal Boxes' are very nerve racking I must say. I have got used to them now and slept like a top last night in spite of shells bursting ten feet off the trench.

The Durham LI have done marvellously, there have been no regrettable incidents and the casualties only show that we have attacked again and again and driven the Germans back to their present positions. There is a row of cottages twenty yards from my trench and this is the mark for several hundred German shells daily. It is in ruins and the last occupant but one rabbit had a rude awakening this morning when a shell landed on its hutch. The other is a poor little dog which won't leave. I have a Grandfather clock and a shutter as a bomb proof shelter. We had stewed rabbit and onions for lunch today as we are entrenched in an onion field. The Germans advance every few days and mostly at night, when they do this we mow them down. They can't get through our lines and they won't. We are now in a large town which has the same class of inhabitants as where the depot is situated. Morton managed to kill a man before he was wounded and caught [9580 Pte Edward Morton?]. Five hundred dead bodies are supposed to be drying out in front of our line. They advance in bunches and never attempt to shoot. One man was found last night among the dead. He told me in French that he had been there for three days and was wounded in four places. I gave him my rum and assured him that we would look after him. I doubt if he will live but he will be well looked after I know. He said that every shell went over him all day long. Our men are very good to the wounded Germans and I am very glad to say it. One of our Company went off to fetch water from the farm and as he was at it we saw a 'Coal Box' burst two yards from him. He jumped like a frightened cat but was not hurt. One has plenty of time to take cover as one can hear the shells coming. The signallers have not used their flags since they came out. They are used as orderlies and they *also have a telephone. Our Brigade gunners are doing splendid work and although they do not fire as many shells as the Germans, yet they shoot more accurately and do less damage to houses and more to men. The battalion transport, Shea etc, are all out of shellfire by day. They bring us our rations by night. The great secret I am told by Colonel Linden Bell whom I met en-route is:-*

1 Train Officers and men to march themselves silly with 150 rounds pack and rifle.

2 To have good Officers who take an interest in their men.

3 Train the men not to mind 'Coal Boxes' and shrapnel.

4 To train men not to get the wind up in a tight corner.

5 To make every man look after his rifle and to fire rapid.

Many rifles get sand logged in the trenches and I would strongly recommend linen covers which can be slipped off quickly. One always has a canvas cover when big game shooting. I carry web equipment, a bayonet and rifle also a revolver and now I must say goodbye. I am in my little burrow lying on straw and shells are buzzing over my head. Please remember me kindly to all my friends and especially to C Company 10th D.L.I.

Yours sincerely
John Harter Lieutenant.

As Lieutenant Harter had stated, the battalion transport brought the rations up to the rear line at Desplanques Farm. From there they were cross-loaded onto a small railway truck and manhandled up to the reserve line, before being carried up to the front line by a ration party found by the platoon in the support line.

A letter now appeared in the Police Gazette, sent to the Chief Constable in South Shields by Captain Ernest Birt:

One of your men, Watson, was a member of our Ambulance Brigade and went through a proper course of ambulance training in France; he has put this to excellent use. Until wounded three days ago I was commanding D Company 2nd DLI at the front, in which Lance Corporal Watson is serving. On my being hit Watson got me to shelter and with what was afterwards called by medical authorities, really expert knowledge, applied my first field dressing and took me to the Dressing Station and then to the Field Ambulance. He was most thoughtful and considerate in every way, his promptitude and skill undoubtedly saved me much agony and I am extremely grateful. My wife is sending him a parcel of warm underclothing as good as she would have sent to me and I am sending a memento to his wife.

By the beginning of November the whole of III Corps was so exhausted that General Pulteney had to inform GHQ that his line was so extended he doubted whether a serious attack could be stopped. Meanwhile

2/Durham LI had been into support positions at La Chapêlle d'Armentières behind 12 Brigade, 4th Division and then on 4 November they marched to Rue de Lettere and became the support for 16 Brigade of their own 6th Division. They remained in billets here and nightly two companies went up into the support trenches. The other two companies went out to dig trenches. As the phase of what was to be later known as The Battle of Armentières drew to a close the enemy kept up shelling and sniping and although the Germans ceased any offensive in force the casualties mounted.

Another short piece from 7507 Lance Corporal John Watson appeared in the Police Gazette after he had written to friends at South Shields Police Station:

> We had another fight a day or two ago and I believe young Brew is among the missing [10886 Private H. D. Brew, brother of a South Shields policeman, he was in fact a prisoner of war] I got a bullet through my coat sleeve, just grazing the skin, a narrow escape for which I am thankful. We are in the trenches again and fighting is going on around us. The weather is fine but coming cold at night. Nights are the worst waiting and watching.

It was now that mining operations started and the early attempts to go underneath the German line were recorded in a letter, published in the *Durham Chronicle* by 8744 Private William Ewart, who before the war had been employed as a miner at Harraton Colliery:

> We were in the trenches near Armentières and an attempt was being made to mine those of the Germans, which were just about twenty-four yards away. I and another miner, James Smith of Wheatley Hill had volunteered to carry out this dangerous operation. We had progressed nineteen yards in four days and had only five yards to go before we went off to the right to carry a branch, with the object of making the mine more effective and blowing up a larger number of Germans. The company to which we belonged was relieved by a company from another regiment. The men were interested in the work that was going on, having never seen anything like it before. They went and stood round the entrance to the shaft and apparently the Germans could see their caps, for they immediately sent over a few shells. One bomb went right into the mine. One man was killed and seven wounded. Smith the man who was with me received eight wounds. As a result of my injuries I am often quite deaf for thirty or forty minutes at a time. I believe if we had been successful we would have got the Victoria Cross.

Later in January 1915 the same newspaper carried the news that Private James Smith of Pyman Street, Wheatley Hill, one of five brothers in the forces, was now at home recovering from his several wounds.

On 14 November the battalion marched back to Rue du Bois and took over the trenches from the KSLI, After four days there was a readjustment of the line and the left-hand company of the Durham Light Infantry, B Company, moved across to the right flank and occupied the trenches facing south between the poplar trees and the railway line. They remained in these trenches until 25 November. The enemy was fairly quiet and there was only a little shelling. On Sunday 15 November before their move B Company had a few shells explode in their trenches and then after they had moved, on Wednesday 18 November they came under heavy shellfire and had one man, 8728 Private Walter Mason, killed. As before the German snipers were at work both night and day and where the British trench formed an angle their fire came from several different directions. The trenches were very close together and at one point the Germans were seen to be sapping towards the British line. The artillery was contacted and they put several good shots onto the position which halted the work. The best shots in the battalion did a good deal of sniping at the Germans and two of them were positioned in the upper floor of a house in Rue du Bois from where they had a good view of the enemy trenches, which probably caused the Germans much discomfort. Two more batches of reinforcements arrived, 100 men came on 15 November and the next day 165 men under the command of Captain W. Gibson joined the battalion. Rifle grenades were now supplied to one of the companies and after a little practice they were able to drop them into the enemy trenches. During this tour a lot of work was done improving the trenches and digging communication trenches.

In another long letter, dated 15 November but written over a few days, Lieutenant John Harter informed Lieutenant Colonel Morant about the officers of 2/Durham LI and the routine goings-on of a battalion at the front:

> *Dear Colonel,*
>
> *My Special Reserve Captain has gone sick and I am now in command of C Company. Turner commands another, Bowers another and Taylor the fourth company. I am alone in C Company at present as my subaltern Vane (Lord Barnard's son) is indisposed as well as the Captain.*
>
> *We are nominally resting but we spend every day and night in the mud and cold either digging for five hours or else in reserve in a ditch. It is far from pleasant but everyone sticks to it, for we have to. C Company is to spend tonight in a donga.*
>
> *Later, we spent last night in a donga and it pelted down all night long. We got drenched – luckily I carried my rum out with me which revived us. We were in reserve for the brigade but as this was not broken we were not wanted. We just sat in the wet and listened to the shells and bullets and dreamed of feather beds and Good Old England.*
>
> *Tonight we return to our old trenches and will be fighting day and night for the next fortnight. It is damp work as one is never off one's legs; if one tries to be brave and silly one gets a bullet from a German sniper.*

Swords are not carried by officers who have to footslog; only mounted officers carry them on saddles. The Sirhind entrenching tools are most useful, and everyone knows it too. We prevent individuals from creeping up at night by our rapid fire; the Germans don't like it. The German snipers bother us considerably but we are now sniping them; they apparently have some good shots; the bulk are hopeless and don't attempt to shoot straight.

Bobs inspected us a few days ago well within 'Coal Box' fire; he had come to cheer on the Queen's Westminsters; we lined the streets of a small town near by and he walked between the lines. I had to practise 'Present Arms' before I left my farm house with C Company as they are all D Section and Special reserve; there are only eighteen left of the original company. Bobs saw us and was nice and cheerful. Shells were falling just over the rise, which was not far off; however he pushed off in his motor when he had done his job and is now safe from 'Whizz then Bang'.

My QMS said to me 'Why do they call them Allemans? Silly I call it; they should call them Germans'. Several of the officers who came out on the same ship as me have been killed. The casualties seem enormous, but, believe me; the Germans have suffered far more heavily. We have swarms opposed to us and are fighting as we always have done from Crecy downwards, against long odds. The native troops left their trenches the other day on purpose; when the fat Germans flopped in they were all blown up by our sappers who had mined them...

The last I heard of Sergeant Bell's brother is that he was seen to be staggering back to hospital with a wound in his face; he was walking with assistance and held a German helmet in his left hand; he repeated to his chums en-route; 'I've got the bugger's helmet at all events'.

There are many more as stout-hearted as he was and I wish he was with us now.

We are all very sorry to be leaving our farm house; the men are great pals with the French dairy maids and we have comfortable meals and sleep in the best parlour.

Yours in haste,
John Harter

During this tour of the line the battalion had fourteen men killed and thirty-nine wounded, the majority of whom fell to German snipers. Then on 27 November the battalion was relieved and moved to billets at L'Armee, where they remained until 1 December. The time was spent cleaning up and new clothing was issued. Major Crosthwaite wrote of this:

All the men were fitted out with clean shirts and many of them with thick drawers. During the months of October and November a large quantity of warm underclothing, mufflers, helmets, mitts, tobacco and cigarettes collected by the people of County Durham were received from

ptain William
ldon was wounded
d evacuated 12
vember 1914.

Lady Londonderry, also many more things collected by the wives of officers of the regiment. More things were received than were required at the time and these were stored.

Out at rest the men found time to relax and write home. 9257 Charles Alderson, now a Lance Corporal, wrote another letter to his sister, which was published in the *Durham Chronicle*;

I have been unable to write to you until now as we have been back again in the trenches for fourteen days. I am keeping well. We have had a very quiet time in the trenches although the Germans were quite near, they were only about eighty yards from us and we could see their trenches quite plainly. We have to be very careful on account of snipers, as they keep sniping at us every chance they get. We had a man drawing water from a pump the other day when he was shot through the head. So you see how careful we have to be. We have had a cover of snow here and it has been quite frosty. It comes in very handy for instance whilst in the trenches there was a hole made by a shell, 'Coal Boxes' we call them. It was frozen, so we got some ice, melted it and made tea for our breakfast. The trenches we have just slept in are not so bad. There are little places dug out at the back for two and you can make yourself quite comfortable. We are now staying in a farm, but I don't know for how long. We have had clean shirts issued to us and it was a treat to get one also a wash and brush up – the first for fourteen days. I don't mind telling you we needed one badly. I see from the papers that M Hopper [6895 Private Mark Hopper of 22 Neville Street, Durham City] is a prisoner. There are a good many of his company prisoners. We have just had a church service in the farmyard just in a simple form.

Love Charles

Owing to the men standing in wet muddy conditions their feet were not in the best condition and many suffered from sore feet. Time was spent route marching to harden the feet before relieving 1/West Yorkshire Regiment in the trenches south-east of La Chapelle d'Armentières. When 2/Durham LI took over they extended the line and the section they held ran from the Lille–Boulogne road to a point 400 yards north-west of the village of Wez Marquar where they joined the section that they had previously held. Three companies, Taylor's (A), Gibson's (C), and Turner's (D) held the front trenches and Bower's (B) was in reserve with the Battalion Headquarters located in the nearby farm of Du Bie. As C Company were making their way up the very muddy communication trenches they came under a sudden burst of artillery fire and had to lie flat in the mud until it was over; fortunately it only lasted ten minutes. In this sector the trenches were further apart with an average of 400 yards. Even at that range the enemy was able to inflict fatalities and two Sunderland men, who had arrived with the draft on 1 November, were killed. On 5 December, a man from 4/Durham LI, 4/7725 Private John Farrer, who was

CSM Robert Haylett in the trenches, he was sent back to England and commissioned into the Durham Light Infantry and rejoined the battalion in France.

standing guard at the Battalion Headquarters, was killed by a stray bullet and then the next day 8211 Private William Smailes was killed in action.

The battalion War Diary records that at first the trenches were very comfortable but then torrential rain fell until the battalion was relieved by 1/Queen's Westminster Rifles, who as we have already seen were inspected by Field Marshal Lord Roberts earlier. This unit of the Territorial Force had been quickly mobilised in 1914 and with other units considered fit enough had been sent out to France. A number of Territorial battalions had arrived at the front in November 1914 and were allotted to various brigades; the 1/Queen's Westminster Rifles had been allotted to 18 Brigade as its fifth battalion. Captain Godsal described the state of the trenches:

> It had rained considerably on Saturday afternoon and Saturday night; consequently the trenches were in places ankle deep in water, while the mud made walking hard work. The battalion that had originally took up this line of trenches was no doubt pressed for time and placed their trenches in the ditches, utilising existing ditches saved time and is probably alright in dry weather but any such advantage was outweighed by the discomfort of occupying them after wet weather. The Colonel went round the trenches in the morning as usual and complained frequently of the size of his feet which picked up so much clay it impeded his progress.

It was now that a newspaper cutting, taken from the *Morning Post* arrived at Battalion Headquarters. This was a report of a speech made by Lady Jellicoe. In a speech made at the opening of the National Schools in St John's Wood, she said:

> I have heard from Lady Eileen Roberts today. Lord Roberts went over to France on Wednesday… On Friday he was again in the trenches and when he left them on the way back he met the Durham Light Infantry who were going towards the trenches! He was very surprised at the light hearted way in which they were marching, singing 'Tipperary' they saluted him and he stopped and saluted them. It was his last salute.

After the relief was completed the battalion marched back to billets in L'Armee ready to go back into the line in the Rue du Bois sector on 13 December. However the programme was changed and 2/Durham LI remained in support until 18 December when they moved further back to billets in Pont de Nieppe and became the reserve battalion for III Corps. This allowed time for the men to have a bath and over 600 of them went through the divisional baths at Erquinghem.

Another man mentioned in the newspapers at this time was Private S. Robson of Murton Colliery, who was home on leave having been wounded. Prior to the war he had been a reservist and was employed as a hewer at Murton Pit. A highly exaggerated account has him in the thick of the battles of Ypres and after thrilling escapades was shot through the leg at Soissons. He was in the trenches for twenty-three days without a change of clothes and in the last of these became separated from his regiment. Twice reported missing he wandered many miles before he was able to regain his regiment. Yet no trace of a Private S. Robson serving with the battalion at this time has been found.

Yet another man who had a letter printed in the local press was 7695 Private George Hobson of Langley Moor. Mrs Hobson received the news that her husband was lying wounded in hospital at Coventry Hospital in Warwickshire. Hobson, a reservist, had gone out with 2/Durham LI to France where he had some very trying times. At the Battle of the Yser on 31 October he was in the trenches and shells were flying all around, when a splinter struck him in the ankle. He lay wounded from 0730 hours until 1730 hours before he could be attended to by Red Cross men, who were fired upon by the Germans and it was midnight before he was clear of the fighting. Mrs Hobson said her husband spoke highly of Captain Norey [Northey] who was killed in action. He led his men about 1,500 in number over about two miles of open ground with just his cane in his hand. The lieutenant that replaced him was also wounded. Part of Private Hobson's ankle has been taken out and the doctors are using all their skill to try and save his foot.

The same edition carried a small report from 8771 Private Robert Fleming who was serving in B Company. Writing to his sister and brother, in Brandon, he said that the Germans have smashed the railway line and station up. He thought they were part of the main German Army which was scattered. There are plenty of aeroplanes dodging about trying to find the British artillery positions. Everybody wishes the war was over. The Durhams have lost many of their officers and men.

Another policeman among the battalion reservists was 8915 Sergeant Joseph Turton in a letter to PC Hamilton at Newfield Police Station he wrote:

> We are now in the firing line and we have been for ten days. The weather is wet and things are in an awful state as the earth falls away, and sometimes men get buried with the trench falling in. I wish you could see us, we all get as black as coal as we haven't the opportunity to wash or shave until we come out of the firing line for a day or so.

As was indicated earlier, back in Durham the people of the county were very active in collecting comforts and clothing for the men of the regiment fighting in France. The Marchioness of Londonderry headed a committee and a weekly list appeared in the local press, listing items sent out to the front. All types of clothing, shirts, socks, underwear, vests, gloves, handkerchiefs, were parcelled up and sent along with pipes, tobacco, cigarettes and matches. Other useful items sent were bootlaces, soap, foot powder, sweets and chocolate. The men were really pleased to receive items such as these and many wrote to Lady Londonderry expressing their thanks. Second Lieutenant Neal wrote,

'Dear Lady Londonderry: – Very many thanks for the presents received. I really cannot fully express the gratitude of the men of my platoon for the noble work you are carrying out. You appear to know exactly what our brave fellows are most urgently in need of – again thanking you, yours very sincerely A Neal, Second Lieutenant The Durham LI.' 'I received your parcel and was very delighted. It is a pleasure to know that someone thinks of the soldiers out at the front and hope that others follow your example. I wish you good luck – Yours Truly' wrote one anonymous Tommy. 'Received tobacco and cigarettes. The non coms and men thank you and the county very much indeed for your kindness B. McMahon, Colonel, 2nd Battalion The Durham Light Infantry.' 'A thousand thanks from Corporal Sullivan and a chum for gifts of shirts etc. Best Wishes.' These were just a few of the many letters of thanks received by Lady Londonderry.

On 20 December along with 2/Sherwood Foresters, 2/Durham LI moved forward to Le Bizet in case they were required to support an attack planned by 11 Brigade. However this was cancelled and they returned to the billets in Pont de Nieppe. Here they remained and absorbed two drafts, one arriving on 13 December and another four days later, a total of eighty-four all ranks. Then on 23 December they moved into Armentières. The next day Lieutenant J. N. Armstrong, Royal Army Medical Corps, arrived to relieve the Battalion Medical Officer, Captain G. P. Bracken who had embarked with the battalion three months earlier and had looked after the battalion wounded throughout the fighting up until now.

They remained in Armentières throughout Christmas Eve and Christmas Day and Lance Corporal Charles Alderson described the rest period to his sister:

We had a service in a factory, very simple but it brought back old memories and I thought it was a very nice service. The rest of the day was spent as well as could be expected under the circumstances. We are billeted in a school room. Rather a nice place and on Christmas night we had a concert. There was a piano and I had no music so I did the best I could. Raine and Casey gave a turn and they were very good. We had cards distributed among us. I think we are going back to the trenches tonight but so long as we had Christmas out of the trenches that is all we care about.

Corporal Alderson was right, for on Boxing Day they moved up to the trenches near Frelinghien and took over trenches from the Royal Welch Fusiliers of 19 Brigade. This was a very quiet tour of duty, the rain was very heavy and except for New Year's Eve the enemy were not at all active or aggressive. Indeed one German stood on top of his trench and began using his arms to send semaphore signals. One of the Durhams started to do the same but was quickly ordered back into the trench. The left company, D, commanded by Captain Turner was cut off from the rest of the battalion and to reach them you had to go 70 yards along a wet ditch behind a low sandbag wall, then through a tunnel under a road. Their

Men of 2/Durham LI manning trenches opposite the village of Freilinghien north-east of Armentières December 1914.

trench had been all boarded out by the Royal Engineers and a stream flowed along it under the duckboards. But Captain Turner was forced to abandon the last 10 yards of his trench and build a dam to prevent the rising water level flooding them out completely.

During the time in the line only one man, 11570 Private Robert Cuthbert from Sunderland, was killed on 28 December and another four were also wounded but their names are not recorded. Then during the following day, Second Lieutenant William Oliver arrived from the base bringing with him a draft of eighty-three other ranks.

Charles Alderson recorded the passing of the year in another letter to his sister:

> *On New Years Day we were in the trenches. We welcomed New Year by bailing water out of the trenches. They run close to the river and we kept bailing water out night and day. The Germans are very close to us; in fact on New Years Eve they gave us a reception, just on twelve they fired a*

*volley or two. They were blowing trumpets and singing and kicking up a
devil of a noise right along the line. I still have my Princess Mary gift, and
I prize it very much, I do wish I could get it home.*

Robert Fleming was writing to Brandon in similar vein and although there
had been a Christmas truce whilst the Durhams were out of the line,
Robert tells of a New Year's truce in this letter published in the *Durham
Chronicle.*

*I wish you a happy and prosperous New Year, but I am having a sorry
time of it here nothing but rain and mud. It is a bit quiet at present. The
Germans gave us a surprise last night when they fired off a few volleys at
twelve o'clock. On Wednesday morning we got on top of the trenches and
were talking to them. The Germans got on top of theirs as well. You will
hardly believe it, I know but it is true. They shouted and waved to us to go
over for a drink. They are all sick of the war. They are only young lads and
old men here. Singing and shouting went on all last night and it seemed as
if we were not at war. We shall be trying to shift them from here shortly. I
wish we could start now and get it over with as it's awful weather.*

Mrs McGuire in Stanley received a short letter from her son 9715 Private
Peter McGuire, who was in hospital in Aberdeen, in which he informed
her he had been wounded in the hand by a bullet and that he was
progressing as well as could be expected. He also gave her the news that
his brother Thomas was in the best of health when he left him.

At Battalion Headquarters Major Crosthwaite and Captain Godsal saw
in the New Year with a toast 'Peace and absent friends' drunk in issue rum
and hot water.

So the first period of the war came to a close; it hadn't ended by
Christmas as many had hoped for. The men of the old regular army had
in the main been killed, wounded or taken prisoner as had many of the
regular reservists and men of the reserve and special reserve battalions.
New men would be needed to bring the battalion up to strength to
continue the struggle in 1915.

Chapter Three

1915, The Hell of Hooge

On the night of 1 January 1915 the 1/Queen's Westminster Rifles came up to the line and relieved 2/Durham LI, who in their turn marched back to billets in Houplines where three companies were in a factory and one in a large disused house. Battalion Headquarters was located in another large house which had been the home of the factory manager. Time was spent route marching and Major Crosthwaite and Captain Godsal found time to go shopping for the officer's mess.

Three days later the Commanding Officer, Lieutenant Colonel B. McMahon received the news that he had been appointed to the command of the Hythe School of Musketry and he left the battalion for England the same night. A two seat-car was sent from Brigade and his packing case was strapped on the back and his saddle and harness was shoved under his legs on the passenger side. It was a very dark night and no lights were allowed, but the men turned out and lined the street and gave him a cheer as he left. Command now passed to Major Joseph A. Crosthwaite, who had originally been commissioned into 3/Manchester Regiment in 1889. On 6 January they moved back up into the trenches near L'Epinette. During the time spent in the line the weather was atrocious; it rained for most of the time and the trenches became rivers of mud.

utenant Colonel Bernard Mahon commanded the talion until posted to mand the School of sketry at Hythe.

The communication trench between Battalion Headquarters and the front line was over 800 yards long and in places was over 3 feet deep in water. Whilst in the left section held by C Company, the trenches were full of water and all the dugouts were under water.

On 7 January two new officers, Lieutenants, John Robinson Hill and James Maddison Kent arrived from 3/Durham LI, and that night word came in from the OC, A Company on the right, that the water was starting to rise in his section and in C Company lines it appeared as if a dam, had broken the water was rushing in so fast. By constant bailing they managed to keep the level manageable. Soon the water started to affect B Company also, and to give the men some respite the reserve company sent up its platoons to relieve a platoon from each of the front-line companies.

Suddenly at 1000 hours on 9 January word came that they were to be relieved that night and the Commanding Officer of 3/Rifle Brigade arrived to take over. Later his battalion came up and 2/Durham LI

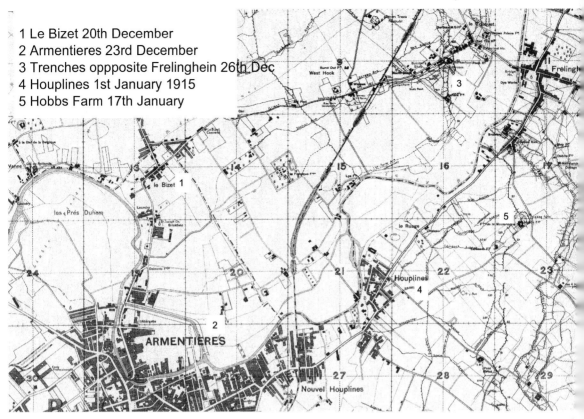

1 Le Bizet 20th December
2 Armentieres 23rd December
3 Trenches oppposite Frelinghein 26th Dec
4 Houplines 1st January 1915
5 Hobbs Farm 17th January

returned to billets in the eastern end of Armentières; here two companies were in a factory and two in schools. Two days later, Lieutenant G. Weyman arrived from the base with a draft of sixty-five NCOs and men, among them was 7012 Private Walter Galloway from Cassop Colliery. He had already seen eight years, service with 1/Durham LI in South Africa and India, having enlisted in December 1899 at the age of eighteen, and when he was discharged in 1908, he completed his Class A Reserve Service and then remained on Class D of the reserve and extended his service in December 1911 for a further four years. He attended annual musketry camps to keep his proficiency pay as a marksman and when war was declared he had rejoined the Regimental Depot in Newcastle on 5 August, but had not been included in the early drafts to the second battalion. In September he had spent a week absent without leave, which probably meant he missed the drafts that left the depot at the end of September.

Meanwhile in the billets in Armentières, the usual drying out, cleaning up and training took place. Working parties were provided building breastworks and digging trenches at night. A new arrangement came into use at this time, whereby two battalions worked together – one holding the line and one out at rest, for a four day period. 2/Durham LI were

paired up with 2/Sherwood Foresters and they relieved each other in the same sector near Pont Ballot north-east of Houplines. In the line on 17 January, Captain Samuel Rowlandson was wounded, and then on 14 January, a dull day with not much rain, conditions in the trenches improved a little, with not so much water about. At about 1400 hours the British Artillery opened fire on a village on the battalion's left front and a great number of high explosive and shrapnel shells hit the target; the fire lasted until 1600 hours and the gunners managed to set fire to the brewery from where German snipers had been particularly active. To this British fire the German Artillery soon replied and they sent over about forty shells; most of these were directed at a disused farm some 300 north of the Battalion Headquarters. Going round the line on 15 January Major Crosthwaite noted the improvements to the drainage and the parapets' many of which had been shored up. When he reached A Company, the Officer Commanding that section of the line pointed out a sap that ran out towards the German line, which he called a listening post. He called out to see if the sentry posted in it was on the alert: no reply, he called out again, still no reply. Then a voice came up from a dugout, 'Private Jones is up there Sir, he is very deaf!' The Major also wrote of two men of B Company who were lying in a dugout and when asked how they were, replied that they were 'quite comfortable'. It was noted that they were lying in two inches of water.

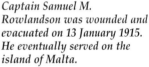

Captain Samuel M. Rowlandson was wounded and evacuated on 13 January 1915. He eventually served on the island of Malta.

On 21 January, owing to the wet and waterlogged ground a dugout collapsed and trapped 8605 Private Henry Burn, a West Hartlepool man; although they dug him out as fast as they could, sadly by the time the rescuers reached him he was dead. The next time the battalion was out of the line they were inspected by Major General John L. Keir, late Royal Artillery, who was commanding the 6th Division. After the inspection he expressed his satisfaction at the turn-out of the battalion.

It was at this time that one of the 4th Battalion Reservists, Private James Henry Fox, died at home in England. He had gone out with the draft that joined 2/Durham LI on 1 November, so had only been at the front a short time when he fell sick. The Durham Advertiser carried a lengthy report and description of the funeral proceedings under the heading:

Military funeral at Durham

With military honours the funeral of Private James Henry Fox of the 4/Durham LI took place at St. Oswald's Cemetery on Friday afternoon. As stated in our last issue, the deceased was a reservist working at the patent coke ovens at New Brancepeth and was among the first units of the British Expeditionary Force sent to France. He saw considerable fighting, and following 23 successive days in the trenches near Armentières, he fell a victim to frostbite and other ailments and was invalided home, where he died from pneumonia last week. The Deceased was unmarried.

The service on Friday was timed to commence at 2.30 p.m. and a quarter of an hour before then a large number of people had congregated in New Elvet. In Court Lane the firing party, consisting of twelve khaki clad soldiers from the 16th Battalion of the DLI, were drawn up near the house of the widowed mother of the deceased and as the coffin was being borne down the stairs the party stood to attention. 'Slope arms' and 'Present arms' were the ensuing orders, and whilst they were being executed the six under bearers, also connected with the Battalion and dressed in the familiar blue uniforms, placed the coffin on two chairs, where the Union Jack was laid over it. Had one been available a gun carriage would have been used, but instead the under bearers carried the coffin. At a slow march with arms reversed the firing party proceeded towards the church, six buglers immediately following them. Near the coffin walked a relay of under bearers and then came the widowed mother and her two sons. Mrs Fox carried a floral token composed of chrysanthemums. There were many mourners in the procession, and the Battalion with which Private Fox was connected was represented by Corporal Collinson. At the church gates the vicar (Rev C R J Loxley) met the cortege. He conducted the short service in the church, where the hymn 'O God our help in ages...' was sung.

The military funeral had its attractions for the curious minded was plainly evidenced at the cemetery. With the opening of the gate there was an unseemly rush to obtain places of vantage, and there were also a large number of people on the grassy slopes overlooking the cemetery. At the graveside the vicar pronounced the committal sentences and the firing party fired three volleys. The sounding of the 'Last Post' by the buglers concluded the sad proceedings. The coffin which was of plain character bore on the breast plate the deceased name, date of death, and age. Mr C Richardson was the undertaker.

The soldier named in the article, 4/8964 Corporal Charles Collinson representing 4/Durham LI eventually went out to France and served with 14/Durham LI.

Prior to the next tour of the front line for the battalion, it was again inspected at 1030 hours on 29 January by Major General Kier. The General said he was pleased with the turn-out of the battalion and that they appeared to be well looked after. The battalion formed up with

5948 Pte James H. Fo: was evacuated with frostbite and pneumonia after only few weeks at the fron Sadly he died at hom in Durham City in January 1915.

Second Lieutenant A Neal was commissic from the ranks after sixteen years service was evacuated sick January 1915. By 19 he was serving in France with a Servi Battalion of the regiment.

76

040 Private
exander Whitelaw
m North Leith
ived in France on 4
cember 1914; too late
the 1914 Star, he
s killed in action on
January 1915.

e view from the
nt of my Dugout,
. 2 Platoon, A
mpany', showing
bankment and
dbags at the moat
e, at Hobbs Farm
s series of
tographs were taken
Second Lieutenant
ver.

twenty-four officers and 957 men on parade and of these five officers and 311 men had come out with the battalion in September 1914. Of these originals one officer and 110 other ranks had been away sick or wounded and returned to the front.

The next stint in the line covered the period from 29 January to 1 February during which Captain Robert Turner was wounded and two men were killed in action: 4/8367 Private John Watson, a native of South Shields, and 9040 Private Alexander Whitelaw, who came from North Leith, with a further four men wounded. The Brigade Commander and the Brigade Major came up on 30 January and went round the battalion trenches, probably owing to the fact there was a rumour of a German offensive that would take place in the neighbourhood very shortly.

Inside the roof at Hobbs Farm showing the damage caused by a German shell; this position was held by A Company.

The weather started to improve and the ground began to dry out as the level of the River Lys, which had risen by over 7 feet, dropped. With the system of relief adopted the battalion was able to set up various workshops in the rear area. The battalion tailors and the bootmaker were able to repair clothing and boots for the men, whilst the battalion pioneer section was busily employed making duckboards for the front-line trenches.

On 31 January and again on 1 February the Germans shelled Houplines and the majority of the shells fell around the 'Marie'. Among the casualties was a twelve-year old French girl who died from her wounds later in the day. Major Crosthwaite recorded that after the bombardment Captains Godsal and Congreve went out to look for souvenirs and found a few pieces of metal which they seemed to think worth keeping. However the two captains added a note to his diary entry: 'The Major forgets to add that he implored us

Hobbs Farm was surrounded by a moat; here a German shell explodes in the moat, having missed its target the farmhouse.

to bring him some of the above mentioned pieces of metal but we wouldn't give him any.' Signed WHG & CMC.

The following day the Commanding Officer was inspecting the battalion transport, which was very well turned out. Just as the inspection came to its close, the Brigade Commander, Brigadier General W. N. Congreve, VC, was passing and stopped to have a look for himself, at the end of which he complimented the Transport Sergeant on both horses and men. On the night of 6 February Major Crosthwaite accompanied by

Captain David Brereton set off to inspect the companies, and he recalled:

> On the right of C Company trenches we had to cross a plank over a small stream and climb up a bank. Brereton was leading and used his electric torch to cross the plank and as he climbed on top of the bank the Germans opened a heavy fire. He fell flat – thinking he was hit I called out to him; he was all right and crawled back to me. When the shooting commenced, C Company turned out, they were ordered to stand down when the firing ceased. I heard one man ask another what it was all about; the reply was 'only the CO with his b....y searchlight'.

Over the next month the front went very quiet and there was little to report; the Canadian Division had arrived at the front and two officers and four NCOs were sent to the rear area to act as instructors for 3/Canadian Battalion (Toronto Regiment).

At this time, however, the *Durham Chronicle* reported that the news had

The view over the parapet about 100 yards in front of the farmhouse.

Lieutenant Scott Scott RFA and Second Lieutenants Hill and Harter (in the white), find time to play with a raft on the moat of Hobbs Farm.

been received in Cassop Colliery that Walter Galloway had been killed in action on 30 January. His family had received a similar letter when he was in South Africa, but two days after the latest communication had arrived his parents received a letter from the soldier dated 2 February, three days after he was supposedly killed. In the letter he gave some idea of the conditions at the front:

> The weather is very cold and it is very monotonous in the trenches day in and day out and there is nothing but the continuous rattle of the guns both day and night. We cannot get much sleep as we have to be constantly on watch especially at night time. But we can stick it as we know that we are in the right and fighting for our home and children. It might last a bit yet, but we will win in the long run and we cannot grumble when we think about the poor Belgians and what they are suffering. It was raining part of the time we were in the trenches and I can tell you things were a bit thick – up to the knees in mud and the enemy firing all the time at you when you are bailing out the water. There is only one thing for it – stick it to the end.

Lieutenant Scott Scott RFA and Second Lieutenants Hill and Harter (in the white); well afloat, they paddle up and down the moat ignoring the war.

RENE COTTAGE

2 CLUMPS VILLA

LONG FARM

FARM de la Vache

OUR LIN

A view from the roof with Rene Cottage, 2 Clumps Villa and Long Farm marked.

A view from the roof with Fme de la Vacherie and the British and German lines marked.

> *We gave the Germans a good dose before we came out of the trenches and I can tell you I would not have liked to be there where they were.*

Various drafts arrived during the next few weeks; Lieutenant Walter D. Potts with thirty men on 20 February and Lieutenant Frederick L. Newstead and thirty men on 16 March.

Writing home at this time was 8908 Private Thomas Blakey, another of those who had arrived in France on 5 January. In a letter to Miss G. Charlton, he told a vivid story of life at the front:

> *I received your parcel all right while in the trenches. We have had a very hard time of it as we are up to our knees in mud and water. Some of our fellows have been knocked up with frost-bitten feet. You have no idea what it is like, but we shall just have to put up with it.*
>
> *On the night of the Kaisers Birthday we went out on patrol to the German trenches, as far as we could get without being seen or heard. When we got there we could hear the Germans singing and having a good time of*

*The view from A Company farm, showing
damaged interior, barricades and position of
Quatre Hallot Farm, marked.*

*it, but when we got back to our trenches they were shelled by our men – and
they didn't forget them. One moonlight night I was going for rations over
a field and when I was coming back I was seen by German snipers. I
dropped the box and lay behind it till they went away and then got up and
ran for the trenches. It is very dangerous going out during the day, as it is
very open and the German sniper is always waiting for our men coming. If
once they catch you, you are a dead man. They are splendid shots. They have
a powerful searchlight. It shows for miles around and they are always
trying to find our guns at night time.*

*I am just coming out of the trenches today, never had a wash for five
days. You couldn't see my face or clothes for mud. The Germans tried to
shell the place where we were at rest last night. They were about 100 yards
from us. They set fire to a church and houses and we had to turn out and
try and put the fires out.*

Meanwhile in North Road, Durham City, Mrs Pettinger, had another letter from her brother, Lance Corporal Charles Alderson, dated 18 February, in which he said:

> I am quite all right except for a cold which pretty nearly we all have got. The weather continues to be very nasty. We have had rain all the time in the trenches with the exception of one day. It makes such a beastly job of things when it is so wet. We are in billets in houses and the people are Belgians. There are four of us to one house and now and again we have a sing song. They are very nice people. We have a good many Canadian soldiers here quite fresh and fit. Several NCOs are on furlough for a few days – not long but very acceptable. We have been supplied with gum boots and waterproof coats and they are very useful. There is no change in the situation here, heavy firing on our right and left, in front very quiet, just a few flares up now and again.

In the middle of February the III Corps Intelligence Officer, Second Lieutenant Arthur Ladenburg, stayed with the battalion for three or four days and on the night of 15 February accompanied Second Lieutenants Oliver and Cruickshank on a patrol in No Man's Land as far as the German wire despite remaining in position for over an hour no sounds were heard and the patrol returned unscathed to the British lines. The

Captain F G Mau

Lieutenant V.A.C. Yate and Second Lieutenant Layng beside a wooden footbridge in trenches connecting No.2 Platoon (Second-Lieutenant Oliver) and No.1 Platoon (Lieutenant Cruickshank), February 1915

battalion was starting to get wise to the enemy and Second Lieutenant Bradford started constructing booby-traps to be placed in the open ground in front of his company. The traps consisted of jam tins filled with explosive and metal and a tripwire constructed so that anyone touching the wire would explode the bomb, however, no German was caught. Another trick they tried, in an effort to take a prisoner, was putting a dummy disguised as a dead British soldier out in No Man's Land. Snipers were set to watch for any Germans coming to have a look, but no German came out to examine it so no prisoners were taken.

During February Lord Londonderry had died and Major Crosthwaite sent the condolences of the battalion to Lady Londonderry, 'All ranks of 2nd Durham Light Infantry express deepest sympathy.' To which Lady Londonderry replied, 'Thousand thanks for your deep sympathy for me on the death of Lord Londonderry. Trust all is well with the Second Battalion.'

During March several units were attached to the battalion for training in trench warfare: first came the Canadians of 3/Canadian Infantry Battalion, a Toronto-based unit, and they were followed by men of 15/Canadian Infantry Battalion. This unit was raised in Ontario and Quebec, from men of the 48th Highlanders, a Canadian Militia Regiment.

Officers and men of D Company at a farm in the Houplines sector in front of Armentières; unfortunately the actual location is unknown.

Four soldiers of A Company, in a trench in the Armentières sector, France, February 1915. Left to right: Jackson, Fenwick, Mason, Tynan

The company that joined 2/Durham LI was split up, one platoon to each Durham Company; they were described as 'a good lot of men, very keen and very pleased to be in the trenches'. Indeed one of their officers was heard to say, 'Guess this is the best stunt I've struck since I left Canada.' After the Canadians, up the line came 5/North Staffordshire Regiment and then 7/Royal Warwickshire Regiment; these latter two battalions were part of the 46th (North Midland) Division, one of the Territorial Force Divisions which were now arriving in France to reinforce the regular divisions of the BEF.

In keeping with the best traditions of the British Army the 6th Division held a horse show when out at rest, 'A very good show of horses and some fine jumping,' wrote Major Crosthwaite. The prize for the best charger went to an officer of the 19/Hussars but 2/Durham LI managed a creditable second place in the Small Ammunition cart and pair.

March passed into April and the same routine was maintained, manning the trenches in the same sector and then resting in billets in Armentières. From here 7507 Lance Corporal John Watson wrote again to his friends at South Shields Police Station and they had his letter published in the *Police Gazette*.

I am keeping well, and the weather is A1. We are out of the trenches for our usual four days' rest, the trenches were nice and dry and we were sorry to leave them. We had a small trench dug behind the firing line and being out of sight of German snipers some of us used to pass the time during the day sitting in this trench looking across the open country watching the big shells bursting in the distance.

Lieutenants Walter Potts, Gerald Sopwith and Roland Bradford outside their billet in Armentières. Only Potts would survive the war.

Bullets keep whizzing over you, spent ones, they make a buzzing sound. Some pass right over you, others just drop around and throw the dust up. It makes you duck sometimes when you hear them coming. We had a busy time last time in the trenches; we fairly had the wind up. We used to man the firing line and give a few volleys in the early morning and night. Of course the Germans thinking we were going to attack put up a lot of star shells, all to no purpose. We have been in this place a long time now. The Germans found one of our regiment's billets with a shell the other day, the lads were playing cards I believe. It burst in the middle of them, killing eight and wounding about fifteen. Isn't it rotten, spies I suppose? Very little news, nothing doing.

On 6 April, 9661 Sergeant John Drummond, a Gateshead man, was killed and two men wounded and during each tour there was a steady trickle of fatalities and men wounded. At the end of the month Mrs Golightly of Douglas Street, Stanley, County Durham, received a letter from her brother-in-law, 9925 Private Edward

Golightly, who was one of her five relatives serving at the front:

I was down the base for four weeks for a rest, but am now back again at the firing line. We are having fine weather here it is very hot; I am pleased to hear Jim has enlisted. You folks in England do not know what a sight it is here. What a lot of people there are without homes. Their homes have been blown away with shells and it would make you cry to see them sometimes. But when the boys get the Germans on the run, you would laugh to see them. They do not like steel and we are the boys who know how to use it.

I might tell you I have had a narrow squeak, as I had my boot heel taken off by a bit of shrapnel, but then God meant that it was not my time then. God is the only one that us poor fellows have to look to. You will laugh at what I am going to tell you, but it is true. Last Sunday I and my mate were just getting breakfast when Mr Kaiser's men sent us over a coalbox. Of course our meal got tossed about. He is very kind you know and he would like to murder us all, but he got a shock last week. He sent some gas on us, but the boys knew that it was coming over, so they put on their gags and stood still for a bit and the

Privates Fenwick and Mason of A Company in the trenches; they were possibly officers' batmen as they feature in three photographs of this period.

Germans thought that they were all dead, so they crept up to our trenches to kill what was left of us. Oh my! What a surprise they got! Our boys just let them get about forty yards off them, then they put in about 7,000 bullets. And next morning you could not see anything but dead Germans.

I don't want to be sleepy to go on my post, for that is a bad crime. I will do my best to send you a bit of shell for a keepsake, and in memory of the greatest war ever known. Tell father to keep his heart up because I hope to have a drink with him again at 'The Clock', God watch over you all in dear old England.

Your loving brother, Ed Golightly.

During the month the new Lord Londonderry came out to France and visited the battalion in the line and went up to Captain Hutchinson's company. He presented the battalion with a rifle with telescopic sights to be used in sniping the enemy and they promised to give it back at the end

When he visited the battalion in the field, Lord Durham presented them with a hunting rifle for the Sniper Section. Here Second Lieutenant Oliver of No. 2 Platoon, A Company, poses in a trench with the rifle. Today the rifle is on display in the Regimental Museum.

of the war with a score card. Meanwhile the battalion was providing digging parties of over 200 men every night as the condition of the ground improved with the warmer weather.

On 26 April the battalion went back into the line relieving 2/Sherwood Foresters; during the relief the enemy put a number of shells into Taylor's Farm which slightly wounded three men of the battalion machine-gun section. Then the next day the twenty-second reinforcements reached the battalion in the shape of forty-one other ranks. During the day Major Crosthwaite wrote that:

The enemy had the impertinence to shell our Battalion Headquarters Chateau, about 15 shells from a field battery two of which actually hit the house in an upper room, a small piece of it and a lot of dust coming down into the room in which Godsal and self were. We immediately sent a request to 53rd Field Battery asking them to deal with the matter; they promptly shelled a farm in the enemy lines which was evidently used as a headquarters house.

The weather had changed during April and the ground had dried up, so much so that Battalion Headquarters was linked to the Company Headquarters by communication trenches. This was achieved by large parties working at night assisted by smaller parties during the hours of daylight. During this latest tour in the line, Lieutenant Thomas Garfit, who was only twenty-two years of age and had only been with the battalion since January, was killed in action. Also killed at the same time was 4/7895 Private John Murphy of Gateshead, whilst a Middlesbrough man, 4/9029 Private Patrick Maloney, died from his wounds.

At the end of the month Private Robert Fleming wrote again to his relatives in Brandon:

I am keeping well and have just come out of the trenches for four days. We lost one man in my Company; you never know your luck. We will probably be making an advance soon as you will see by the papers how the British are going about their work. We had another man shot by a sniper, one of my school. It knocks me up when they get shot like that as you never know who will be next. Our artillery are doing fine work now, we have been lucky up to now the Germans have not shelled us for a bit. They dropped two or three near our billets a day or two ago, but no damage was done, they only smashed a house up. They generally drop a few in the town now and again and they shelled the 'Yorks' billets last week, seven being killed and forty wounded. Hard luck; they are the unluckiest regiment here, I blame spies for it. They are quite used to it now but they scatter for the cellars when the shells come over.

    All for now

    Bob

Four soldiers of A Company, three holding rum jars, in a trench in the Armentières sector; Back row, left to right: Mason, Fenwick, Jackson. Front, seated: Allsop.

Behind the line the battalion machine-gun section carried out training; many of them were transferred to the newly-formed Machine Gun Corps and served with the 18th Machine Gun Company.

Having left the front line the battalion moved back to scattered but comfortable billets near Le Bizet. It was here that Captains William Hutchinson and Henry Taylor along with Lieutenant Sidney Streatfield were evacuated to the field ambulance sick. Those employed on working parties came under shellfire and three men lost their lives, 8736 Private John Craddock, 4/9027 Private Nicholas Seaton and 4/8246 Private Michael O'Halleron, and a further two men were reported as being wounded.

An unnamed private of the battalion, who came from Blackhill, near Consett, told several stories in letters home to his family, which were published in *The Consett & Stanley Gazette*:

> One day we were standing facing front on look-out; I got my baccy out and filled my pipe, when the lad beside me asked me to pass my pouch along so he could get a fill. I did so but, after a few minutes I thought he was taking a long time to pass it back. I turned round and looked at my mate to find the poor chap had lost his hand in the act of passing the pouch back to me. Another time I was passing by a friend when he was shot in the arm to which I must add, 'I am as lucky as a black cat'.

In another letter he wrote:

> The weather is very hot out here just now, and we get terribly thirsty.

The Battalion Transport Section was well behind the line; here the horses are lined up for inspection.

We were this way the other day, when I decided to take two water bottles and try to get some water at a well a short distance away. There was a wall on the far side of this well and I thought if I could only reach that wall I would be all right. I set off and reached the wall and then moved on to the well. I had filled the water bottles with the precious fluid and was just putting the top back on one of the bottles when a shell burst on the other side of the wall and partly buried the well and myself. When I pulled myself together and found I had no bones broken, I drank to my own health and then went back to the trenches.

You would laugh if you could see us shaving sometimes. Half a pot of cocoa, coffee or tea is sufficient to leave for one to get lather on the face. I got a laugh at a Welshman the other day, a man called Davis. It seems there is a common occurrence for a few men to fall sick and get a few days rest through it. Davis told me he was going to fall sick, thinking about his problem he said he had 'Floating Kidneys' caused by the amount of beer he couldn't get.

In the early evening on 6 May the battalion moved back into the front line and relieved 1/East Yorkshire Regiment near Le Touquet. In this sector the battalion held a stretch of trench 900 yards long; this meant placing three companies in the line and only one in support. On the right the trenches were only 25 yards from those held by the Germans and as the line stretched away northwards the gap gradually opened until in the centre the gap was 200 yards, but then the lines came back together until on the battalion's left flank the trenches were 35 yards apart. These were much poorer trenches than those previously held and a lot of energy was spent trying to improve them. Mining operations were carried out in the battalion's sector in an effort to plant mines under the enemy trenches and blow up their front-line positions. Another novelty was the use of catapults to throw bombs over to the enemy and early trench mortars were making their appearance. Further north at Ypres the Germans had used gas and a great battle had been fought in April. Involved in this had been the Northumberland, Durham and Yorkshire battalions of the Northumbrian Territorial Division. Their casualties had been very heavy and there was a requirement for experienced regular officers to help rebuild the battalions. When 2/Durham LI moved back into billets at Le Bizet, orders were received that Lieutenants Roland Bradford and Victor Yate were to proceed to the Northumbrian Division and take up the post of Adjutant of 7/Durham LI and 5/Northumberland Fusiliers respectively. Lieutenant Bradford handed his company over to Captain Legard on 1 May, leaving the battalion the same day. Early in the morning of 3 May the Germans fired a barrage on the north end of Le Bizet where Captain Bowers' Company was billeted This shelling wounded four men and killed 8736 Private John Craddock from Sunderland later a Haswell man, 4/9027 Private Nicholas Seaton, died from his wounds. Both men had been out with the battalion since the previous September. Practically the whole battalion was marched to the divisional baths and when they returned Major Crosthwaite found a signal waiting for him from the Divisional Commander. 'Colonel Shea and I have just been round your old line and must congratulate and thank you all very much for the extraordinary fine results of your labours.'

One of the few NCOs to be mounted in an Infantry Battalion, the Transport Sergeant is seen here seated on his horse

On 16 May the battalion commenced their next tour of the line when they relieved 2/Sherwood Foresters in the Le Touquet sector. Here they remained for eight days and during the tour on 20 May A Company, 12/Royal Scots, newly out from England with the 9th (Scottish) Division, spent twenty-four hours in the line with the battalion. They were followed, the next day, by the Commanding Officer and several officers of 8/Black Watch. Next the Durhams hosted A Company of 10/Highland Light Infantry, who were treated to about fifteen big shells from the German gunners.

Whilst the battalion was in the trenches Captains

The bivouacs at the Transport lines, rough but certainly more comfortable than a front-line trench.

Gilbert Coddington and Robert Turner joined along with four subalterns. After being relieved the battalion returned yet again to Le Bizet and spent four days cleaning up and resting. However they did not return to the line. On 28 May they marched into Bailleul and went into billets. For the first time since the battalion arrived in France they were led on the march by the Battalion Bugle Band; the buglers had been reorganised by Captain Godsal and over the last few weeks had been practising under Sergeant Spray. They played very well on the march and were much appreciated by all ranks.

The next day the battalion paraded in the Square and were inspected and addressed by Field Marshal Sir John French. At 0500 hours the following morning, in column of route the battalion crossed the border into Belgium and marched to Wippenhoek near Poperinghe and found billets in the scattered farms of the district. The next day as the battalion rested, the Company Commanders and an advance party went forward to Potijze to carry out a reconnaissance of the trenches to be taken over from the Royal Fusiliers. This was recalled by Major Crosthwaite:

Captain W. R. C. Hutchinson was wounded and evacue 18 May 1915.

> Our new Brigadier, General Carlisle, late commanding 5th Fusiliers, (1/Northumberland Fusiliers), joined us. In the evening the Brigadier, Commanding Officers and Company Commanders of 2/Durham LI, 1/East Yorkshire, and 1/Queen's Westminster Rifles were conveyed in motor buses to the Asylum just west of Ypres, from there we walked through Ypres to inspect our new section of trenches, which were between the Ypres–Verlorenhoek road and the Ypres-Rouliers railway, east of Potijze. We were all much impressed with this our first sight of the ruins of Ypres.

That same evening the battalion met a convoy of motor buses and were transported to Vlamertinghe where they debussed. As the shades of night came down they marched up through the eerie ruins of Ypres and eventually arrived at the front line. The front taken over was from Verlorenhoek on the left to a point about 750 yards south of the Ypres–Zonnenbeeke road. The battalion was well up to strength in other ranks but was short of two captains. The line was held with three companies and one in support.

B Company, under the command of Captain Bowers was on the right, Captain Coddrington with C Company held the centre, whilst on the left Captain Turner took charge with D Company. In support was A Company under Second Lieutenant T. M. Layng, temporarily attached from the Indian Army. The Battalion Headquarters was located in a large dugout near Potijze, which they shared with the Queen's Westminsters. In front of the left company a post was established 150 yards in front of the fire trench, to cover the front of some houses along the road. It was in this post on the evening of 2 June that Second Lieutenant John R. Hill of B Company and six men were killed and fifteen wounded. All day the enemy had shelled the British lines with over 100 shells falling on B Company.

Lieutenant John Robertson Hill was a Scot, born at Helmsdale and an Old Watsonian who had distinguished himself at sport: in his time at the school he had shone at athletics and represented the school rugby XV, the soccer XI and the shooting VIII as well as being the secretary of the Literary Club. He had gone on to Edinburgh University where he had gained an MA in 1911. Commissioned into 3/Durham LI, his death was a great loss to the battalion and the regiment.

Also serving with B Company was 8771 Private Robert Fleming who wrote to his relatives in Brandon Colliery from a hospital on the coast, where he had been evacuated with shell shock:

enant John R. Hill
killed in action 2
1915; he was buried
•tijze Burial Ground
•tery.

> *I suppose you will be surprised when you get a letter from this letter from a place like this, but I am sorry to tell you I have been sent down to the base, as my nerves have all gone to pieces, and I am a bit sick with pains. The first three days of June were awful, worse than hell. I went into the trenches at Ypres on Monday night and our section was picked off for the listening post 200 yards in advance of the others and only 15 yards from the Huns. We lost a man in the first five minutes and we were told by the men we relieved that we would likely leave the trench at two in the morning and go into reserve, but we did not – better for us if we had. About two o'clock on the Tuesday the corporal had a look through a hole to see if there was anything on and he was instantly shot in the head, which must have sent him dotty for the time being, poor fellow as he shouted out to us about some gas and that we had to retire. He went and another four men followed, but they were instantly shot on the parapet of the trench. I never saw them go,*

but stopped to see if the gas was coming; as there was none, I told the other three men who were with me it was a false alarm. We had to lie on our bellies in the trench until nine o'clock at night. They shelled us all day, blew the parapets down and were sniping as well and then the 'sods' turned the machine-guns on those that they had killed, and were lying on top of the trench, and riddled them. It was horrible for us; God knows how we got out of it: and I was sent sick at once that put the finish to me as they shelled us day and night. I could not eat or sleep or eat, and I am only hoping they will give me a spell out of this at home, as it would do me a world of good to see you again.

Thank God I have done my duty since I came out here – nine months now of hell. It is like Heaven here with clean white beds and the nursing sisters walking about. I am only hoping I may get properly better to have another go at them, as we need all the men we can get. It will be a hard struggle for us yet, but if they would only fight fair the same as we do it would be over in a short time, and they know that too. Tell the young men who are dodging it to list at once, as they want to remember we are fighting for our homes and liberty and if they could only see the poor Belgian people's homes it would make them wild. They want to think of us too and get back to work and get some shells made as we will want them when we get on the move.

Both the War Diary and Robert Fleming over estimated the number of men killed at this time as the Official records show that on 1 June, 3/9303 Corporal Michael Coleman, and Privates 3/9474 John Atcheson and 4/8272 Michael Usher, all from Sunderland were killed in action. The following day 7556 Corporal Archibald Cummings and 3/9423 Lance Corporal Sidney Bailey were also killed.

There was a readjustment of the line and instead of two battalions holding the front, it was now held by three.

The unnamed private from Blackhill continued his letters:

We have changes in weather out here just the same as at home. The last two days we have had some heavy rains with the result that the trenches got into a filthy state, halfway up to the knees in mud and water. The other day four of us were bailing water out of the trench when a shell burst above us and knocked the pipe out of my mouth. The other poor chaps were not so fortunate one being killed and one wounded in five places, the other being wounded in the right arm. I had to write home for some new underclothing. I was obliged to burn what I had on, they nearly walked out of the fire. There is a heavy battle going on to my right and it makes me wish I could go and help them, but I have no doubt they will give a good account of themselves as they are a Scottish Regiment. I have just had a breakfast of sardines, bread and butter and smokeless tea made with pure water. I have many a time washed the back yard with better water than we have here for making tea.

*74 Private John
...eson, a Sunderland
...who arrived in
...ce on 5 January
...: was killed in
...n 1 June 1915, he
...o known grave and
...nmemorated on the
...n Gate Memorial to
...Iissing in Ypres..*

*'rivate Quinn of B
...any from
...rland 4 June 1915;
...s buried in Potijze
Ground Cemetery.*

By midnight on 5 June 2/Sherwood Foresters had relieved 2/Durham LI who went back to billets 2 miles west of Ypres and began cleaning up and bathing and the like.

In keeping with the battalion tradition five officers managed to get a game of polo, although their opponents or the final score are not recorded. In the afternoon the battalion football eleven played against the 1/East Yorkshire Regiment, the team they had defeated in the Army Cup in 1913. Although some of the best players of both teams were now dead, the Durhams managed to repeat the victory by winning five goals to three.

The rest period was short though, and by 2130 hours on 9 June they were back in the line. This time the line held was a little shorter than that held on the previous occasion; they were on the northern side of the Ypres–Zonnenbeeke road running to a point 250 yards south of Wieltje on the battalion's left flank. Two companies commanded by Captains Coddington and Turner held the front line with Lieutenant Beart now commanding A Company and Captain Bowers' companies in support.

It was around this time that a letter was received in South Moor, Stanley from Private Thomas McGuire who had before the war been employed as a barman at 'The South Moor Hotel'; he had previously seen service in India and when war broke out was still on the reserve. He wrote:

Up to present things have been O.K. You may think it strange having this letter written with pen and ink but, from this you can see things are working to our hand now, which makes everyone pleased to be a British. I think we have got a good grip of them now. Judging from the appearance of their prisoners, whom we managed to get hold of, they seem to be in a half starved condition and look very down hearted. So they well might for lately their progress has been 'NIL'. They sprang on Belgium like a bull-dog on a little mouse. Nevertheless the Belgians put up a great fight. The Germans come to us with all sorts of raggy clothes on, some of them wearing our own khaki trousers and jackets, which they manage to get hold of somehow, some of them are almost barefooted. They are only too pleased when they fall into the hands of the British, in spite of the bitter hatred they have for the English people. I am sure South Moor will be a very quiet place now, as I hear all the young fellows have joined Kitchener's Army. I only wish I was back again enjoying the life of peace once more.

With best wishes to Mr Oxley,

Yours Thomas McGuire.

On 11 June there was very heavy rain and the trenches became very wet and muddy and within a short time there was a number of casualties to 'trench foot'. It was on this day that Lieutenant Colonel Michael Goring-Jones arrived and took over command of the battalion from Major Crosthwaite. The same day a number of men who had been attached to the Royal Engineers Tunnelling companies as miners returned to the battalion as with all battalions of the regiment the Durham miners were always in demand for their skill with the pick and the shovel.

It was on 13 June Lieutenant William Mortimer who was observing the shooting of a British Artillery Battery was killed, being shot in the head by a German sniper. However, another report states that his position came under retaliatory fire from the enemy and he was hit in the head by a piece of shrapnel and killed outright. He had originally been commissioned into 3/Durham LI in 1897 but had resigned the following year. During the Boer War he had been commissioned into the Ceylon Mounted Infantry. On the outbreak of war in 1914 he had immediately applied for a commission in 4/Durham LI and he was sent out with the second batch of reinforcements at the end of September 1914. The previous month his brother Edmund had been killed at Ypres with 6/Northumberland Fusiliers. The German Artillery was most effective during this spell in the trenches and six men were killed in action and a further forty-five wounded, of which two died from their wounds.

1915.Lieutenant Col: Michael Goring-Jon: seen here when a Captain in India wit 1/Durham LI, assum: command of the battalion on 11 June 1915.

But the events taking place in another sector of the Ypres Salient were in the coming months to have a great affect on 2/Durham LI.

At the end of May as the Second Battle of Ypres came to its official end the ruins of Hooge had fallen back into British hands. The line here was held by V Corps and it was a dangerously weak position and the fighting there had not died down as in other sectors. The line ran north from Kemmel to Hooge and then turned back and ran to the north-west corner of Zouave Wood and then turned north again to Railway Wood. The ruins of Hooge village, Hooge Chateau and the stables were at the apex of a salient. On 2 June this part of the line was held by dismounted regiments of 3rd Cavalry Division, commanded by Major General C. J. Briggs. At 0500 hours the enemy started a severe bombardment that lasted until noon. With most of the buildings totally destroyed and only two walls of the Chateau still standing the enemy attacked from the north and drove out the surviving cavalry men and succeeded in taking the Chateau and stables, although they were unsuccessful along the other parts of the line they attacked. Men of 1/Lincolnshire Regiment and 4/Royal Fusiliers of 9 Brigade went up in support and managed to recover the stables but failed to take the Chateau.

Between 18 and 25 June the whole of 18 Brigade was out of the line together; this was the first time since October 1914 that at least one of the battalions hadn't been in the line. 2/Durham LI were billeted in farms around Poperinghe, until 23 June when two companies moved forward to billets in Ypres. Whilst the battalion had been out at rest a draft had arrived from 3/Durham LI in South Shields; they had left

Lieutenant Willian Mortimer was kill: action on 13 June 1 he was buried in P Burial Ground Cen

South Shields on 4 May and on arrival at 35 Infantry Base Depot they spent a month training and learning the tactics and drills of trench warfare. One of the NCOs among them was 10963 Sergeant Isaac Plews; the son of a regular soldier who had served in the Egyptian Campaign of 1884–1885, Isaac had enlisted into the regiment in July 1910.

He kept a diary of his time at the front; this recorded the move up to join the battalion.

ant Isaac Plews kept a diary of the 's leading up to the e.

Left Rouen on June 18th to join the Batt, who were just out of the trenches for eight days, I was posted to B Company.

June 23rd, my Company were sent to Ypres and billeted in broken down houses for one night. The next night back again to the old billet near to Poperinghe.

June 25th again went to Ypres and did some digging at night against the firing line.

June 26th same thing again but a bit nearer the firing line and a few shells were sent over but nobody hurt.

When 18 Brigade went back into the line they moved into the Yser Canal sector, the other three battalions went into the front line and 2/Durham LI were in support trenches along the canal bank. This too was recorded by Sergeant Isaac Plews who wrote:

June 27th No work but joined Batt and proceeded to dug-outs by the side of the canal; I think it is called the Yser, outside of Ypres Town. Here we stayed for nine days and lost one or two men with shells a lot were sent over and we were digging six nights out of nine.

During this period another two drafts amounting to 102 men joined the battalion; along with them came Lieutenant Robert Purvis who was rejoining after being evacuated the previous November. Commissioned from the rank of Colour Sergeant he had served seventeen years and 111 days in the ranks, seeing much service in South Africa during the Boer War. These two drafts brought the battalion almost back up to strength, the figures in the War Diary being thirty two officers and 1,050 other ranks. However, out of them only 180 remained who had come out with the original battalion, less than 20%.

'rivate Edward 's, died from 's 2 July 1915.

On 30 June Major Crosthwaite received a message which asked if he was willing to take temporary command of another battalion in the Army Corps. He sent a message back in the affirmative and the following day received word that he had been given command of 1/Somerset Light Infantry and that he was to report to Headquarters 4th Division, where he was told he had been given the rank of Brevet Lieutenant Colonel. Although he continued his diary, none of the contents now tell the story of 2/Durham LI and it is here we must leave his excellent story.

For four days the battalion remained in support and then on 4 July they relieved 1/West Yorkshire Regiment in the front line at La Brique.

The position taken over was a sector between View Farm on the right and Algerian Cottage on the left. The casualties during this tour were light: two killed in action, Captain Hubert Coddington, who had originally been commissioned into a militia battalion of the Leinster Regiment and had served in South Africa with the 23/Mounted Infantry with whom he had been wounded, and at the same time 3/8611 Private John Waters fell. Also Lieutenant Robert Hill and eighteen men were wounded, before the battalion was relieved by a battalion of the King's Shropshire Light Infantry, after which they went back to a hutted camp near Poperinghe. These events were also mentioned by Isaac Plews in this way:

July 5th I was on Gas Guard when some gas shells sent over and it was most painful for the eyes. July 6th Proceeded to the trenches on the left of Ypres – lost Captain Coddington with a shell and a few men. I came out after being in five days, with a bad knee. I was detained at the dressing station for two days. The battalion had relieved the West Yorks and the trenches, parapets and wire were all in a very bad state. Mr Hill was badly wounded last night in the advanced post.

Captain Hubert Coddington was Kill in action on 7 July 1 and buried in La Bri Military Cemetery N

On 19 July, after spending a week in rest the battalion moved back to the line and took over trenches from 1/Royal Fusiliers between the Verlorenhoek Road and Wieltje. Two companies were in the line commanded by Captain Robert Turner and Captain Arthur Bowers with two in support commanded by Lieutenant James Kent and Lieutenant Walter Potts. But nearby at Hooge a dangerous situation was developing. Opposite the British position at Hooge was an enclosed German work said by enemy prisoners to be manned by at least a company. In spite of all the difficulties encountered with the high water table and the subsoil, 175 Tunnelling Company, Royal Engineers had constructed a mine under this German position. Commanded by Major S. H. Cowan, the company had driven a gallery 190 feet long and laid a charge of 3,500 pounds of ammonal. This had been laid in a chamber above the gallery owing to the water level which was some 6 inches deep in the bottom of the gallery.

At 1900 hours on 19 July the mine was exploded. It blew a crater 120 feet wide by 20 feet deep, with a lip 15 feet high. Immediately, two companies of 4/Middlesex Regiment occupied the crater. The attack was a complete surprise to the Germans, and bombing parties of 4/Middlesex Regiment and 1/Gordon Highlanders drove the enemy back for over 300 yards. However, they had to retire owing to the fact that they had run out of grenades, and as they had advanced so fast they had outrun the British barrage and the German counter-barrage was quite intense. On 22 July two other attempts to take portions of the German line met with failure.

Although five drafts arrived at 2/Durham LI during July, these only amounted to 132 other ranks and scarcely replaced the daily wastage. On 21 July, Second Lieutenant Miles Coverdale, who had been commissioned into 4/Durham LI on 17 February, arrived at the front to join the battalion.

Despite rumours of an expected German attack against Hooge on 26 July it did not take place. The crater was untenable and the front-line trenches, which were dry but in poor condition, ran up to, but not round the lip of the crater. The sector had a very bad reputation, for as well as constant shelling and mortar fire it was subject to lots of accurate sniper fire. On the night 29/30 July 8/Rifle Brigade relieved 7/Rifle Brigade and 7/KRRC relieved 8/KRRC. The German lines went very quiet and even bombs thrown by the new battalions didn't get a reply. Then very suddenly at 0315 hours the site of the stables was blown up and on the front of 8/Rifle Brigade on either side of the crater, a strange hissing sound was heard. The whole scene was turned red as a bright crimson flame shot across the front trenches manned by 8/Rifle Brigade. It was as if the Germans were using a fire hose but spraying flames instead of water. Immediately the whole area was hit by a mass of artillery fire. Close up to the crater the enemy used mortars and hand grenades and the front line was subject to machine-gun and rifle fire. The support lines in Sanctuary Wood and Zouave Wood and the open ground in between came under a rain of high explosive. Further back all the routes out of Ypres up to the front line were subjected to an intense heavy bombardment. Any part of the line subject to such a barrage would have fallen; 8/Rifle Brigade did their best to hold on but with so many casualties, they were forced back to the support line. The enemy did not follow up his gains but paused to consolidate the position and then attacked 7/KRRC, from the front, the flank and the rear. They tried to bring up the flame-throwers but the KRRC opened rapid fire on the men carrying the equipment and the enemy were unable to use them. However, eventually despite a gallant defence the enemy took all but a small section of the trenches held by 7/KRRC. The lost ground would have to be retaken and the staff at VI Corps Headquarters began the planning. It was obvious that the counter-attack would have to be thoroughly prepared and the 6th Division was chosen for the task.

Later, after the successful counter-attack intelligence, was gathered from prisoners and captured documents. A prisoner of the 126th Infantry Regiment, when he was interrogated stated,

On 29 July the 1st Battalion of my regiment were inspected by the Corps Commander General von Deimling, accompanied by a large staff. In his address he told us that we were to attack the English position next day and he said that it was of the utmost importance that this position should be taken. To assist us in our attack, use was to be made of a new form of weapon, the *flammenwerfer*. The General concluded his address by stating that he was sure the battalion would uphold the highest traditions of the German Army.

This prisoner also stated that he had not seen the *flammenwerfer* apparatus close but a friend of his who had used it had had his two hands almost burnt off.

On 1 August, 126 Infantry Regiment (8th Wurttembergische) issued the following regimental order:

> On 30 July the Regiment attained a brilliant success, which will take a high place in its history. The attack was carried out with great bravery and the English counter attacks on the same day, in the morning and the evening of 31 July were repulsed with incomparable tenacity. His Majesty, The King of Wurttemberg, His Royal Highness, The Grand Duke of Baden, Colonel in Chief of the Regiment, His Royal Highness, Duke Albrecht of Wurttemberg, the Army Commander and all Corps, Division and Brigade Commanders have congratulated the regiment on its conspicuous services and have expressed their satisfaction and appreciation. His Royal Highness, The Grand Duke of Baden has conferred on me the Knight Commandership of the Charles Henry Order and I express to all Officers, NCOs and men my warmest thanks for their loyal devotion to the high cause of our fatherland.
>
> It is my hope that in the future as in the past we may continue to live up to the Regimental Motto Fearless and True.
>
> Von Gluck

On the night of 2 August 2/Durham LI were relieved and moved back to billets in Poperinghe; during the last tour they had lost one officer and forty-four other ranks wounded and six other ranks killed.

Writing home at this time was 12867 Private Daniel Connor who was serving with D Company: whilst out at rest, he sat and penned a letter to Mr John Fleming, the miners' secretary at Thornley Colliery, where prior to the outbreak of war Private Connor had been employed. He gave this description of life at the front:

> We are now finishing our time in the trenches. We have been in for sixteen days, and it has been the roughest sixteen days I have ever had. A battle has been raging for four days. The Germans have lost a good position and they have been attacking and counter attacking ever since. The shells from both sides are creating a terrible din; some are bursting high up in the air, and others are bursting on the ground. As it is night time there are thousands of star shells being thrown up, making everything as light as day. It is not warfare, but murder, and if the young men in England who are standing idly by, could see and taste what is happening here – everybody on the qui vive, and with nerves strung to the highest tension – they would no longer wait, but besiege the recruiting offices in their eagerness to come out here and help their comrades.
>
> It is awful to think that men could be so callous as to go on strike at a time when they are endangering their brothers' lives out here as well as their own. They are as surely killing men out here as are the German guns, but I am convinced that it is only for the want of thought, as they don't

know what their conduct at home means to the men out here. If they did know they would not have the cheek to go on strike, but would do their level best to deliver the goods.

You have heard about the Germans doing all the difficult work about sinking shafts – such as freezing and so on – but they can sink a shaft out here with one turn of the handle. They just shoot what is commonly known as a 'coal box' or a 'Jack Johnson'. These shells make good places for men in thick 'ramble' places. They can get stowing for months. [A Durham miners' dialect reference]

When we went up country on 2 May we had four officers. There is only one left now, Captain Turner. Two are killed and one is back in England again and it was his second time out.

Regards

Daniel

Daniel Connor was eventually promoted to Sergeant and after being wounded was transferred to the 2/Garrison Battalion of the King's Own Yorkshire Light Infantry.

As in almost all infantry attacks a reconnaissance of the ground to be fought over had to be carried out. For some reason the task was allotted, not to an officer of 2/Durham LI, but to an officer of 10/Durham LI, Lieutenant C. E. Pumphrey, this officer carried out a detailed reconnaissance of part of the area to be attacked and reported back as follows:

Report of reconnaissance of the STRAND Communication Trench

August 4th, 1915

4.55 am.

About 40 yards on our side of the junction of FLEET STREET and THE STRAND, the Germans have built a barricade, two sandbags thick, with large sandbag loophole. There was no sentry on this barricade. At all points above our barricade our shells have damaged the trench, and for the last 30 yards before the junction the parapet is mostly gone. There is a very strong barricade at the junction.

The defences are;

The lower barricade already named. Presumably this is manned at night, though I could see no evidence of this.

The trench is filled in, 4 yards in length, thus cutting off a traverse which might shelter an attacking party.

There is a small loophole on the left side of the barricade. I saw the sentry behind this loophole.

Three yards to the right is a large steel plate – possibly 3 ft by 2 ft. It is so placed that a gun behind it will command the maximum length of trench. Presumably it shelters a   machine gun.

I did not see any wire – but there may have been some. There is a general mix up of sandbags etc. which would slightly delay a rush.

An intensive bombardment of the junction of THE STRAND and FLEET STREET would be of great help to an attack. From the appearance of the parapet, I suspect that a second machine gun is at the left corner, covering the open field to the left of the communication trench.

Sd.C. E. Pumphrey. Lieut.

10th DLI

Meanwhile the battalion rested and reorganised and on 5 August began moving back into the line. This time, however, they took over from units of the 14th (Light) Division in the support lines near Hooge. On the way in they came under fire and Captain David Beresford and Lieutenants, James Kent and Walter Potts were wounded; Lieutenant Kent died from his wounds later in the day. Another man wounded at the same time was 7012 Private Walter Galloway who received a gunshot wound in the abdomen. He was evacuated initially to 15/Field Ambulance, RAMC; here his condition was stabilised and he was moved after a day or so to 10/Casualty Clearing Station which was located in the village of Abeele, close to the Franco-Belgian border. Unfortunately his condition worsened and sadly on 10 August, as many

14878 Lance Corpora. William G. Burns fro. Wallsend had only b. in France since 23 Ju. when he was killed i. action on 5 August 1.

7012 Private Wal. Galloway from Cassop, County Durham, marked had served in Sou. Africa with 1/Du. LI. He died of wo. 10 August 1915.

of his comrades were falling at Hooge, he died of his wounds in the Casualty Clearing Station.

The days of the hasty attack 1914-style when every man knew what he had to do had come to an end and now for the first time the Commanding Officer of 2/Durham LI, Lieutenant Colonel Michael Goring-Jones, issued written orders for the attack, with the issue of Operation Order Number 1.

To the north of Hooge the 49th Division and the French to their left started to make preparations as though they were going to make an attack, to deceive the Germans as to where the actual attack would take place. Whilst to the south, to prevent Hill 60 from being used for observation purposes, the 46th Division was to make a diversionary attack, and if the conditions were right, with a favourable wind it was planned they would use liquid fire. Another diversionary tactic employed was that the artillery early each morning fired a heavy barrage against the German trenches. The timing of the barrage varied each day so that the German front line soldier grew used to it and took cover instead of standing- to.

The 2/Sherwood Foresters were to work along the trench G1, G2, G3 to protect the flank from an attack from that direction. It was the GOC 6th Division's intention to attack Hooge between the Q19 & P7 including the Crater. To do this he chose to use 18 Brigade, which was to establish a line continuing trench G3 across the Menin Road, north of the houses to the Crater and 16 Brigade on the left. 18 Brigade was temporarily under command of Lieutenant Colonel F. W. Towsey, West Yorkshire Regiment, who selected 2/Durham LI to lead the advance north of the Menin Road. In his operation order Lieutenant Colonel Goring-Jones gave instructions that the battalion would advance in two lines. The first line commanded by Captain Turner had D Company on the left and C Company on the right. The second line commanded by Captain Bowers had B Company on the left with A Company on the right. Bombing parties were detailed by Captain Bowers to work down G7, G8 and Bond Street towards Old Bond Street. Under the command of the Bombing Officer Lieutenant Kenneth Storey, they were ordered to link up with parties from 16 Brigade working along the same trenches from the other direction. The success of the attack and the subsequent holding of the position was largely due to the leadership, shown by this officer although seriously wounded, and the coolness and dash of the bombers under his command. When the bombers had established themselves and created bomb blocks they held their position throughout the day. One of their number, 7636 Private Robert Howse threw bombs all day and night until at 0900 hours on 10 August they were permitted to leave and ordered back. Private Howse, however, refused to leave the position until properly relieved, and for his work during the attack he was awarded the Distinguished Conduct Medal.

Along with the battalion machine guns the battalion were allotted a further two guns. Under the command of Lieutenant George Wiehe the guns were to follow the advance and then establish themselves in fire positions. When the attack commenced the machine-gunners and their carrying parties were well to the fore and Lieutenant Wiehe was one of the first to arrive in the captured position. He very quickly got the guns into fire positions and brought effective fire onto the retreating enemy soldiers. Throughout the battle he maintained the morale of his men with his personal coolness and cheerfulness.

In the operation order further instructions were included about special carrying parties for RE stores and additional men to assist the machine-gunners in getting their weapons forward. The front-line men of C and D Companies were each to carry four sandbags and 220 rounds of ammunition, with one shovel between two men. In the second line this was increased to 270 rounds and six sandbags per man and a shovel to every man. In an effort to assist the artillery observers when troops could advance no further, without artillery support they were to display a yellow screen. If the British barrage was hitting their own troops NCOs were to display a blue and yellow flag, BUT only with the express permission of an officer, and great care was to be taken in the use of this signal. 1/East Yorkshire Regiment was detailed to provide two 'Battle Police' posts, one at the western edge of Maple Copse and the other at the

An artist's impression of the fighting at Hooge. Now in the Regimental Museum, it used to hang in the Officers' Mess of 2/Durham LI.

RE Dump in Sanctuary Wood; their task was to prevent any stragglers leaving the battle. Any prisoners taken were to be given a small escort to Zillebeke and handed over to a detachment of the Northampton Yeomanry who would escort them back to the rear area. Advance Brigade Headquarters was located in the eastern part of Maple Copse and as part of an experiment they were allocated a portable wireless to communicate with Divisional Headquarters; however, the experiment was unsuccessful. Another experiment was the issue of steel helmets to some of those involved, but again this was unsuccessful owing to the fact that in the dark some of those wearing them were shot on by their own side because the shape was not recognised as British headgear.

So much for the planning: during the night of 8/9 August the troops moved up to the forming-up point. By 0215 hours the leading platoons were in place with a distance of 50 yards between each platoon. The wood consisted of oak, beech and ash trees with bramble and hazel undergrowth which had been partially wired and this caused a few problems, but as they got to the edge of the wood the undergrowth had been shelled away so movement was easier. At 0245 hours the barrage commenced exactly on time and then at 0305 hours the battalion closed up as close as they could to the barrage. Ten minutes later the battalion advanced and the line Crater–Stables–Menin Road was reached.

The early events of the battle were recorded by an unnamed private in a letter held by the Regimental Archives:

> At half past two we were led into a wood and got orders to lie down, and then hell opened. Our artillery opened fire and they replied; it was simply awful, but we lay there waiting for the order to charge. It came and we lost all control of our senses and went like mad, fighting hand to hand bayoneting the hounds. I did not like to kill, but it was sport like so I did it and wanted more. We got in to the first line and went straight on to the fourth and past it and then dug ourselves in under hells flames.

By 0355 hours Captain Turner sent in a report that he was digging in on the objective, but he was not in touch with 16 Brigade on the left and he had occupied the crater, The unnamed private continued:

> There were nine of us digging in the trench. I turned my back for one second and when I looked again – what a sight! I will remember it till I die. Every man in the trench blown to atoms – arms, legs and heads staring you in the face. You will hardly credit what I did under the circumstances. I sat down and lit a Woodbine for the simple reason I was not in my right senses. I stuck there by myself for sixteen hours and all the time a heavy bombardment of our trenches. When night came on I got out and walked back.

At 0400 hours ten prisoners had been delivered to Battalion Headquarters from the front line. The next message received was an hour later when a runner arrived, requesting reinforcements; ten minutes later a company of

Ruined houses at Hooge taken before their total destruction.

1/East Yorkshire Regiment was ordered forward to reinforce those fighting at the front. Half an hour later two companies of the Queen's Westminster Rifles ordered up by Headquarters 18 Brigade arrived, however, they were not utilised and were placed in the trenches vacated by 2/Durham LI when they went over the top; here they remained throughout the rest of the day. The next report to come in was at 0600 hours, when Battalion Headquarters learned that all the officers of the second line except Captain Turner and Second Lieutenant Sherriff had either been killed or wounded. A few minutes later another runner came in from Second Lieutenant William Davison of C Company, who advised that A and B Companies had been unable to make a support trench in the rear and that the trench between the stables and the Menin Road was obliterated; at the same time another message came in from Lieutenant John Cartwright that D Company were now in touch with 16 Brigade. At some stage Captain Walter Godsal had gone forward into

The view over the line after the recapture of Hooge; Bellewarde Lake can be seen behind the trees in the top right.

Second Lieutenant John Cartwright we killed in action defending the flank Hooge on 9 August 1915; he has no kno grave and is commemorated on Menin Gate Memor at Ypres.

Captain Ralph Leg killed in action at Hooge.

Private John McLaughlin from Greenside, Ryton Tyne fell at Hooge 9 August 1915.

the front line to assess the situation and assist the surviving officers. At 0730 hours on the instruction of Brigade Headquarters the Commanding Officer sent three messages to the Captain to remove men from the line to save casualties. Whatever way they were sent, by wire or by runner, these messages never reached him. However, on his own initiative Captain Walter Godsal started sending men back. Another message telling him to put a working party on trench S2 also failed to reach him.

Communications seem to have gone quiet for a few hours and the next recorded message was at 1200 hours when Captain Godsal reported that at 1020 hours the front line was a continuous front trench in touch on both flanks, the runner having taken over an hour to make his way back to Battalion Headquarters. Among the men employed as runners that day was 10396 Private Harry Hirst, who three times carried messages back from the crater and although wounded he returned with a reply. On his last journey he carried a wounded officer out on his back, showing great coolness and bravery throughout the day.

The other cause for concern was that men of the assaulting battalions Durham, Sherwood Foresters and East Yorks were mixed up, but there was no sign of a counter-attack. Captain Godsal next sent a message in saying that he had organised the front line in three companies under the following officers, on the left Lieutenant Thomas Layng and Lieutenant Frederick G. Sherriff attached from the York and Lancaster Regiment.

In the centre Lieutenant Gerald Sopwith and Lieutenant Leonard Briggs were in command. Both of these gallant officers were awarded the Military Cross for their actions during the night. Lieutenant Sopwith had been blown up and flung several yards by a large shell and although wounded in the shoulder and leg, he refused to leave the line. At a critical moment when some men had started to fall back, owing to a misunderstanding, he left the line and under heavy fire rallied them and brought them back into the firing line. Lieutenant Briggs had several times been buried by debris and each time extracted himself or was pulled out by his men, At the very critical moment and under extremely heavy fire; he too rallied the men and led them back; he remained perfectly cool and set a fine example to all those around him. These two officers were assisted by 8346 Sergeant Charles Gibbens who, when at around 1500 hours some men left the line near the stables under extremely heavy shellfire, left the trenches and rallied the men and brought them back into the line. His gallantry brought him the award of the Distinguished Conduct Medal. At the same time Company Sergeant Major Charles Kent, DCM, was winning a bar to his medal when he crossed a considerable open space under heavy fire in order to bring some men back into the line.

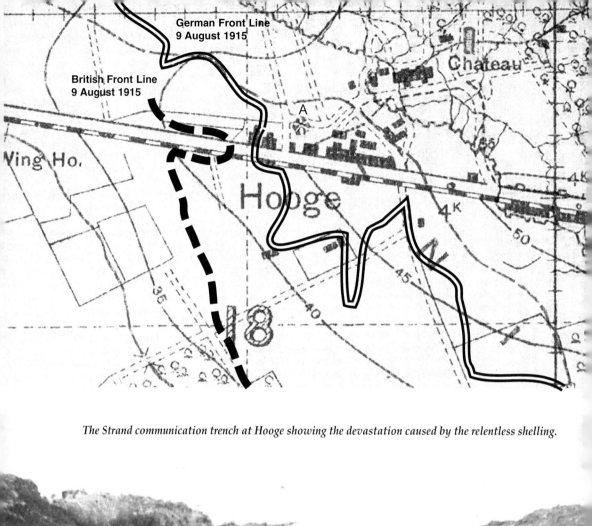

German Front Line
9 August 1915

British Front Line
9 August 1915

Chateau

A

Ving Ho.

Hooge

4 K

50

4 K

35

45

40

18

The Strand communication trench at Hooge showing the devastation caused by the relentless shelling.

The interior of the crater at Hooge, at the top left the built-up sandbag trenches can be seen.

On the right Lieutenant William R. Davison and Lieutenant John Cartwright were responsible. On this flank the bombers were too in great evidence 7958 Lance Corporal Oliver Manley assisted to hold the extreme right of the position under heavy fire. He worked hard throughout the action distributing bombs among the men. He also spent time showing untrained men how to prime and throw grenades, not only British grenades, but those of the enemy that could be found abandoned in the trenches.

As the reports came in the Battalion Medical Officer reported that 125 men had so far passed through the battalion aid post and had been evacuated. The messages then dried up until 1419 hours when a message came in from the Officer Commanding 2/Sherwood Foresters saying that a gap, of some 200 yards, had opened between his left and the right of 2/Durham LI and that he would hold G6 as his former trench no longer existed. At the same time Lieutenant Layng requested artillery support, stating that the Germans were massing in Bellewarde Wood. Shortly afterwards another report came in from Lieutenant Briggs confirming the enemy massing on the right and stating that the position seemed critical. With the situation unclear Lieutenant Colonel Goring-Jones handed over command to Major Tyrwhitt of the Queen's Westminster Rifles; then collecting all the remaining Durhams, he proceeded up G2 towards the front line. When he arrived at the front line he could see no sign of a counter-attack, so he duly returned to Battalion Headquarters.

The position remained much the same throughout the rest of the day until at 2030 hours two officers, patrols were sent up to try to locate men in the front line. At the same time a duplicate message was sent up ordering the line to withdraw. Some time shortly afterwards Lieutenant Davison and about eighty men of the right company arrived back at Headquarters followed later by another party of forty men, who reported from the ridge between the Crater and the Menin Road. Later that night those remnants of 2/Durham LI that had made it back, marched to billets in Ypres. About 0930 hours the following morning Lieutenants Sopwith, Briggs, Wiehe and Sherriff of the left and centre companies along with some forty other ranks, who had not received the order to retire, were brought back from the Crater. But that wasn't all the survivors. Still in a position on the extreme right of the front line was 3/8702 Lance Corporal John G. Smith; by midday he had gathered around twenty-four men and under heavy fire was holding on, although all other men had been withdrawn from the vicinity. He sent a message back for more bombs, ammunition and above all reinforcements, but a message was sent back for him to retire and at 1930 hours he led his party back and eventually rejoined the battalion.

The unnamed private recorded the move back to Ypres, although he does exaggerate the age of the Commanding Officer:

> When we were all formed up the survivors answered their names. The old commanding officer, who is nearly seventy years of age, and a trump, was crying. I tell you we got anything we wanted. I got a gill of rum and went to sleep. When I woke up we were marched back to rest, where we are now. It was well earned.

Another report of the action was published in the *Consett & Stanley Gazette* in one of the letters from the unnamed private from Blackhill, who wrote,

> After our artillery had peppered them the signal was given to cease fire and then we, who were standing in the trenches waiting the order to charge could almost feel the silence that followed. The order came then off we went, when we got to the first line of trenches we found that the Germans were surprised, they had evidently not expected us coming so soon as some were reading. Those that did not surrender got 'short shrift'. I know a few that will not sing 'Gott strafe England' again. It was hot work holding the captured trenches and it was during this time that

Second Lieutenant Robert Gregg was killed in action on ? August 1915.

Captain Arthur Bo? another whose nam? was added to the R? Honour at Hooge, h? served in South Afr? with 1/Durham LI.

4/9213 Private Jo? Weaver, a Castlef? man, was among ? dead at Hooge.

112

I got a small hole in my head which put me to sleep for about twenty minutes. When I came to myself again I found that I hadn't lost much blood so I thought I would hold on for a bit longer. Shortly after one of those 'Jack Johnsons' burst beside me and buried me. I scrambled out of this and got buried again. This time I was under for about ten minutes and in getting out I strained my back and was obliged to be led away. On the road back to the dressing station I had the misfortune to be partly buried again. These Jack Johnsons do shift the earth when they explode. The treatment I received at the Field Hospital was beyond praise and the sisters were angels. Everything that could be done for the wounded was done in such a kind manner sufficient to make my stay in the hospital be remembered for all time. When the time comes for me to go back to the trenches I shall go with a good heart as there is a lot to be done yet.

It wasn't long before congratulations were received from on high: the Commander of Second Army, General Sir H. Plumer KCB accompanied by Major General W. N. Congreve VC, commanding 6th Division, visited the battalion and expressed his thanks for the gallantry shown in the action at Hooge. Later the Corps Commander, Lieutenant General Sir J. Kier, KCB, arrived and also addressed the battalion, again thanking them for the work done. Last but not least the Officer Commanding 18 Infantry Brigade, Lieutenant Colonel F. W. Towsey, West Yorkshire Regiment came to visit the Durham battalion and he too added his thanks for a job well done.

The battalion had lost a total of 498 all ranks, divided up as follows:

	Killed	Wounded	Missing
Officers	7	8	0
Other Ranks	56	327	100

Total 498

Of course, many of those reported missing were indeed dead but some turned up in the Casualty Clearing Stations behind the line, whilst some of those reported wounded later succumbed to those wounds and died, some many miles from the battlefield at home in England.

Lieutenant Miles Coverdale was wounded during the battle and evacuated to England.

In the meantime the Commanding Officer, knowing the battalion's exploits would raise morale wrote to the Commanding Officer of the Regimental Depot, Durham Light Infantry, at Fenham Barracks in Newcastle. The CO of the Depot, Lieutenant Colonel F. G. Kenyon Slaney, had the letter published in the Depot Part I Orders:

From a letter dated 16th August 1915 from Lieut. Colonel M. D. Goring-Jones, OC, 2nd Battalion DLI, BEF, France.

As you probably know we have been heavily engaged. The Battalion was selected to carry out the assault on the 9th instant and right well they did it. We have lost heavily in officers and men, but the Regiment has made a name for itself and everybody connected with it ought to be proud of it. The Army Commander came here personally to congratulate and thank the Regiment on parade.

F. Thompson, Lieut

A/Adjutant,

War Depot, Durham Light Infantry

Lieutenant Colonel Goring-Jones was also writing to the Dowager Marchioness of Londonderry, who along with Lord Durham, Colonel and Mrs Kenyon Slaney and Lady Anne Lambton, had provided four wheeled stretchers for the battalion. These had arrived in time to be used by the battalion stretcher-bearers to move casualties during the fighting at Hooge. The CO wrote:

9688 Corporal Frank Brown from Bedlingto Northumberland, lan with the original battalion in Septemb 1914; he was killed at Hooge.

Dear Lady Londonderry,

The wheeled stretchers have arrived and been taken into use. Will you please accept our grateful thanks? They are exactly what we wanted, and will save many a poor lad unnecessary pain. You will probably have heard that the regiment has been heavily engaged. You will be glad to know that the battalion did very well indeed and was thanked for its services by the Army Commander in person.

Congratulations to the Division as a whole were sent in a Special Divisional Routine Order forwarded to all units of the 6th Division.

SPECIAL ROUTINE ORDER
By
MAJ-GEN W. N. CONGREVE, V.C., C. B., M. V. G.,
Commanding 6th Division

GENERAL INFORMATION

The G.O.C. has today seen Sir John French who expressed his satisfaction with the conduct of all ranks in the late attack on HOOGE (which he considers to have been one of the best conducted of the smaller operations of the Campaign) and desired that his appreciation of the work done should be conveyed to everyone in the Division. The G.O.C. desires to convey his personal thanks to all for their efforts, which have led to such a satisfactory result.

R. S. May, Lieut. Colonel

A.A. & Q.M.G., 6th Division

At the same time Major General Congreve was penning a letter to the Earl of Durham to let him know how the men of the County behaved in battle. Other generals in other battles would have cause to do the same about other battalions of the regiment, but the 2nd Battalion were regulars and to them fell the honour of the first letter.

Brigadier General Congreve VC comma 18 Infantry Brigade.

Headquarters, VI Division, 12 August 1915

Dear Lord Durham,

You may like to hear how well the 2nd Battalion of your County Regiment has done. On 9 August my Division attacked Hooge. Your Regiment was one of the attacking line. They took the hill with little loss, and accounted for all the Germans on it. They then entrenched the position and wired it, and occupied the trenches. This was all done by 8 am. From that hour on, the Germans poured heavy shells all over them, and, I am sorry to say, caused them nearly 500 casualties. Not a man came away until the Battalion was relieved about midnight, and even then, three officers and 40 men stayed on because they had not been relieved all that night and well into the next day, and a non-commissioned officer and 36 men stayed another 24 hours longer.

Most of the time they were exposed to heavy shellfire, the demoralising effect of which can only be estimated by those who have seen it. I saw the Battalion after it had come back. The men were as cheery and proud of themselves as possible, and ready to meet any number of Germans for whom they had conceived a great contempt. I have told them that I am writing to report their fine conduct to you. From first to last they did splendidly.

Believe me,

Yours sincerely,

W. N. Congreve

It was now that the news of the battle reached County Durham: across the county the local press reported news of those killed and wounded; they relied on letters released by friends and relatives to tell the stories of what had happened to local men.

At 21 Bower Street, in West Hartlepool, Mrs Brown received a letter from her husband 5806 Corporal Charles Brown, who wrote:

I have been wounded in the hip and thigh by shrapnel, we carried all the trenches we wanted and you can bet the Durhams were in the first line. My God! It was cruel! It is the first time I have bayoneted a man. You can hardly believe what a relief it is to be out of the sound of the cannon's roar after having ten months of it.

In a letter to his mother who lived at 66 Dent Street, Hartlepool, Private G. W. Raine, one of her five sons in uniform told her:

The Durhams had led the attack and we let the Germans know that we were all there. The prisoners we brought in were thoroughly demoralised and begged for mercy. We only bothered with the wounded Germans. Those who weren't wounded had to fight for it. We were sent to do a job and we did it with a vengeance. My chum was badly wounded – hit through the stomach. I could not get to him to give him any assistance and I believe he died of his wounds. In the same attack I was buried twice by two 'Jack Johnsons' blown about ten yards by another and had my hair parted by a bullet which smashed my cap and just cut the skin on the right side of the

head. Otherwise I am all right. The poor fellow carrying the stretcher with
me was killed – shot through the brain.

The relatives of another Hartlepool soldier, 10338 Private Fred Martin, had
this letter published. Fred had been among the first to be wounded when
the battalion arrived in France and when he had recovered he went
straight back up the line, only to be gassed a week or so later. Having
recovered from the gas he again went back, but once again being
wounded, he wrote:

*I am still all right except for a slight wound on top of the head. We have
just been through one of the fiercest engagements of the war. We were picked
out to make an attack at a certain place, which was the most important
position in the whole line and we were told it must be taken at all costs. We
took the position after doing a great deal of destruction on the way over. It
was simply marvellous to see our chaps wiping Germans off the earth. They
didn't stop at anything but went right on with their bayonets fixed, sticking
them right and left. You cannot imagine the sight – it was too awful for
words. We lost a good few of our men, but the numbers were nothing
compared to theirs. We simply had to walk over their dead to get to our
destination. After we had got there we dug ourselves in we were subjected
to a very heavy bombardment lasting the whole day. It did awful
destruction among our men, but we stuck it till night time and then our
relief took the position over. When we came marching along to our billets
we were cheered by different regiments who had been awaiting the result of
the battle. It made the lumps come up in ones throat to think of the small
number of us who had come out all right.*

The postman was also delivering letters from wounded men to the
colliery villages further inland from the coast. Friends of an unnamed
private who wrote to them at Thornley Colliery had his letter about the
Hooge fight published in The *Durham Chronicle*:

*Just a few lines about the scrap, to begin with, when we were marching
up the road to take our position we halted at a certain part of the road to
wait until it was dark. The enemy must have got wind of us, for they at once
started to shell the road and we lost 45 men killed and wounded.*

*Our position was situated in a big wood which goes by the name of
Sanctuary Wood. Before we made the attack, which was to have come off on
the 9th our killed and wounded had mounted up to 90. Well our regiment
led the attack and as everyone knows had the heaviest end of the stick. We
moved out of the wood about two o-clock in the morning and waited for our
artillery. At a quarter to three our guns kicked off and kept it up for half an
hour. The bombardment was short and sweet and by this time the Germans
were getting warm. Between their guns and ours it made you think that
hell, with all its imps, was let loose.*

Well we took the position with one mad rush that nothing could stop.

> *But the enemy's guns soon found us out, and although under a heavy fire from guns of all sorts and sizes, our boys held the ground until they were relieved. We lost six officers killed and six wounded. The total casualties in 2/Durham LI alone would reach over 500.*

At the home of Mr J. Cuthbert in Bath Lane, Stockton, the news arrived that Mrs Cuthbert's brother, 4/9338 Private William Nugent, had been killed in action at Hooge. One of his friends wrote with the news:

> *I have got the gospel truth from a friend who saw him pass away. I have his cap badge which I shall bring with me if I return home safely. I came in possession of it when making inquiries about him. I came in touch with a Spennymoor man who said, 'Why I knew Billy! He was my mate. We chucked together all along. Here is his badge.' 'I had not got one and had to go on duty and he lent me his when I asked him.'*
>
> *When I asked him to describe poor Billy's fate, he said, 'On the morning of the attack Billy and I were together, after a bit of bombardment we charged and took their first line of trenches. We halted for a breather and afterwards got the order to advance and just as we were making ready "Jack Johnson" shells came over. One struck the parapet where Billy was, and he and six other poor fellows were buried alive. No assistance could be given as you may know for two of these shells can plough a whole field up. So you can guess the rest.' This is the truth, God rest their souls.*

But in Sunderland the parents of 11335 Private Edward Bullock were to receive some good news. Shortly after the fighting had died down they

Looking towards the German lines.

received the dreaded telegram telling them that their gallant son had been killed in action on 9 August. One Saturday morning at the end of the month the postman delivered a letter written on 26 August by the presumably dead soldier. In the letter he stated he had recovered from his injuries and had rejoined the regiment. He had heard that he had been reported killed and that all his letters and belongings had been sent home to Sunderland but he was glad to tell them he was all right. He had been struck by a shell, but his injuries were not too severe and he had been able to crawl to the dressing station. By some unexplained mistake his presence in the dressing station had been overlooked.

Another man that went over with the battalion and survived was 4/9005 Private Henry Kirk, who although wounded had been evacuated to the Red Cross Hospital in Southend. Private Kirk had seen service in India with the Gordon Highlanders and when his time expired he returned to Durham, where his father resided at the Lodge in Redhills, Roman Catholic Cemetery. He gained employment at Bearpark Colliery and when war broke out he immediately enlisted in 4/Durham LI; as an ex-regular soldier he was quickly on a draft to France and he was one of the reinforcements that joined the battalion in early November 1914. The start of his letter home tells exactly the same story of the march up, the wait on the road and the barrage which caused casualties, but then he goes on:

> The bombers had to advance, followed by the rest of the regiment ten minutes afterwards. After we had advanced about 400 yards I was hit on the head. It was a very bad blow, but I think I must have been hit by a piece of hard clay. It stunned me for a few minutes and then I went on again, expecting every few minutes to meet the German bomb–throwers but we turned left sooner than we should have done, so we had to get out of the trench into the open. But it was a stroke of luck we went the wrong way. We caught about 200 Germans in a big hole where a mine had been blown up. They were all bombers. We had very few bombers with us but that didn't matter; we soon started throwing bombs into the hole, and we made skin and hair fly. I was mad because I had been hit on the head and I felt as if I could jump down on top of them. I did go real mad at the finish. God knows where I got to. The last thing I remember was a lot of Germans with their hand tips above their heads wanting to surrender. I must have wandered about for about an hour and a half when I got hit on the back of the hand; and that brought me back to my senses. When I looked round I was all alone, except for dead men both British and German and the shells were falling about all over. I got into a hole until the bleeding stopped, and then I set off for the hospital. The sights I met on the road back were terrible…what became of the rest of the bomb throwers I can't tell. I expect most of them got knocked out, because bomb throwing is a very dangerous game.

Some of those wounded managed to survive until they reached the hospitals on the coast. Here they received what attention could be given to them. Those that were going to survive were operated on and when stabilised were evacuated by hospital ship back to England. But many were too badly wounded to move, some lingered on the edge of death for many days before they finally gave up the fight. The huge cemeteries around the French ports show how many wounded men survived long enough to be buried many miles from the battlefield. The reader has read extracts of several letters from Charles Alderson to his sister Mrs Pettinger. He was among those wounded at Hooge and it took several days to transport the badly wounded NCO from the battalion aid post via the Field Dressing Station and the Casualty Clearing Station in Belgium down to the 13th General Hospital based in the French port of Boulogne. When he was admitted his ward sister, Sister D. Welch wrote to Mrs Pettinger and said 'He was seriously ill but was very bright and sent kind messages to all his friends.' The next post brought a postcard with the news that the condition was worse and then on Sunday 22 August the sad news came that he had passed away.

Sister Welch, who was a Nursing Sister serving with the Anglo-French Red Cross, wrote a letter that stated:

> Corporal Alderson passed away at one pm, he suffered very little pain and was brave to the last and was most grateful for all that we did for him. I don't think I need tell you that everything possible was done for him. But he had little chance from the start as he was suffering from a shell wound to the leg.

Born in Consett and brought up in Durham, Charles Alderson had been apprenticed to Messers Ruddock and Fletcher, Upholsterers in Durham City, however adventure called and before he reached manhood he answered the bugle's call and enlisted in the Durham Light Infantry. He served for one year in Ireland and seven in India and his time expired in February 1914, when he returned to Durham. As has been seen by his letters from the front, when war broke out he rejoined the colours and went out with the battalion. Popular with his comrades because of his skill as a pianist, he was thirty-three years of age and unmarried.

The battalion rested in a hutted camp at Poperinghe and whilst resting here a number of drafts arrived. On 11 August two drafts of thirty-eight and sixteen other ranks; on 17 August, fifty-two other ranks joined, among them 4/9557 Private Arthur Clark from Langley Park, one of four brothers serving in the regiment, three of whom would not see the end of the war. A week later on 25 August Captain Charles O. Greenwell arrived with 203 other ranks. These drafts came mainly from 3/ and 4/Durham Light Infantry in almost equal numbers. Also a number of officers joined at this time. On 11 August Lieutenant Reginald A. Hargreaves reported and then on 19 August Lieutenant Joseph Tindle who was commissioned from the

Seated on the right 4/9557 Private Arthur Clark arrived in France on 24 August 1915 and was posted to 2/Durham LI. His two brothers, George on the left and William in the centre, were serving with 8/Durham LI; George was killed in 1916 and William in 1918.

ranks of 2/Northumberland Fusiliers. Then on 22 August the following arrived: Captain Alfred E. Irvine, Lieutenant Noel V. Williams, Lieutenant Harry Cross, Second Lieutenants, William W. Inglis, Reginald D. Ellis, Charles H.Thompson, Herbert M. Saunders, William E. Harris, George K. Raine. Last but not least Captain Gosnall S. Legard arrived from 3/Durham LI at South Shields; well known in Durham City where he had lived for many years, he had been educated at Bow Preparatory School and then Durham School before going on to Dulwich. Just as he was about to embark he received the sad news that his brother Captain Ralph Legard had fallen at Hooge.

The Germans shelled the battalion and on 22 August the Regimental Aid Post came under fire; four men were wounded and the battalion Medical Officer, Captain James Armstrong, an Irishman from Dundalk was killed. Also on the same day 4/7026 Private Thomas Joyce, another Irishman who was born in Galway, but at the time of his enlistment was resident in Jarrow. They were buried close together in the Hop Store Cemetery.

On the day before he died, Thomas Joyce had received notification that he had been recommended for gallant conduct at Hooge. In a letter written to his wife he had described Hooge as the worst battle he had ever been in and told her how he had come to be recommended for an award. For three days he and Lieutenant Davison had been cut off without food and water. They had observed a German officer putting down a communication wire in order to signal the Germans to come on. Private Joyce, a crack shot, killed the enemy officer and then at his fourth attempt managed to cut the wire, thus preventing its use. Sadly, probably owing to the fact he was killed, no award for gallantry was ever made. It is hardly

...32 Private John G.
...Donald from
...'eshead, who had
...y arrived in France
...24 August, died of
...unds on 8 September
...5 and is buried in
... Store Cemetery.

...tenant Thomas
...ng Indian Army
...ched to 2/Durham
...as ordered back to
...UK on 2 September
...and then rejoined
...ndian Army.

surprising but other men were also told they were to receive awards. The *Durham Chronicle* records that 9029 Private James Sproates of High Tenter Street in Bishop Auckland was told he was to receive the Distinguished Conduct Medal, for locating two heavy German guns, which the British Artillery were able to put out of action once the location was known. He was a reservist who had been recalled in 1914; employed as a wireman by the GPO he was soon transferred to the Royal Engineers Signal Service. The award of the DCM was eventually reduced to a Mention in Despatches. Likewise the same paper reported that 11130 Corporal John Hunter, a regular soldier from Pelton Fell, was to gain the same award for his work at Hooge. He had gone out with the battalion in September the previous year and had been at the front ever since. Wounded in the right forearm he was expected home on sick leave, but he too never received the promised award, but was also given a Mention in Despatches.

On the evening of 25 August the battalion moved back into reserve positions; battalion Headquarters and Captain Irvine's Company moved into positions at the Canal Bank. Two companies were sent to Brielen and Lieutenant Martin's Company to a farm nearby. They remained in these positions until the end of the month. Only one man was killed during this tour, a 32-year-old Hartlepool man from 4/Durham LI, 4/9543 Private Frank Carroll, who was laid to rest in Dunhallow Advanced Dressing Station Cemetery. A number of men were detached from the battalion: five were sent to 177 Tunnelling Company, another five went to Headquarters Platoon SECOND ARMY and four others were sent to the 6th Divisional Band. Also a number of NCOs had attended courses at the Machine Gun and Bombing Schools. Each platoon in the battalion now formed a bombing squad, which was organised as follows: two riflemen called 'bayonet men', two 'throwers' and two 'carriers', the latter four are armed with knobkerries, normally the section commander is one of the throwers. For the first time in August 1915 the battalion War Diary has attached a Field Return. This return sent to the Adjutant General's Department at the Base records all casuals, i.e. men moving by themselves, which were joining or leaving the battalion.

On the night 1/2 September the battalion moved forward to Potijze; Captain Greenwell took one company to positions south of the Verlorenhoek Road, whilst Captain Irvine's Company took over the sector to the north of the road including a position known as Stink House. Captain Legard took up positions on the left with his company. In reserve was Lieutenant Martin's Company. Casualties were fairly light: only two killed and twenty-two wounded before they moved back to the billets in Poperinghe. On the night of 15 September they moved once again into the canal bank dugouts, where over the next few

121

days one man every day was killed by shellfire with still more wounded. After several days in these support positions the battalion took over trenches from 8/ and 9/King's Royal Rifle Corps, south of the Verlorenhoek Road with the left on Crump Farm, near Potijze. These positions were held until the night 27/28 September. During the last two weeks Lieutenant Charles Henry Green who had joined the battalion in 1912 and Lieutenant George K. Raine were wounded and among the men forty-eight were wounded and fourteen had been killed. On the last day of the month they went back to the Canal Bank positions with C Company in the X Line and D Company in Potijze Defences.

2/Durham LI had now been in France for a year and in that time there had been many casualties; the battalion War Diary gives the following figures:

	Officers	Other Ranks
Killed	22	308
Wounded	30	1021
Missing	1	226
Total	53	1555

Throughout October the same pattern followed; between 1 and 4 October they held the line in the Wieltje sector. From 5 to 10 October they were in reserve at Poperinghe, where they undertook training and lectures. Between 11 and 23 October they were back in the front line in the Potijze Sector; during this tour Lieutenant Harold Pybus was wounded in the thigh and twenty other ranks were also wounded, with nine men killed in action mostly by German shellfire. On 23 October three companies A, B and D went back to the reserve positions on the Canal Bank, whilst C Company remained in the Potijze Defences. In the reserve positions working parties were found for construction work. These parties were sent to Ypres to collect bricks from ruined houses. They were then carried back to the reserve line where they were laid in brick paths, to make movement through the muddy fields easier. On 28 October when he was in charge of one of these working parties, Second Lieutenant Reginald Hargreaves was wounded by shellfire. During the month three small parties of reinforcements arrived; forty-two on 7 October, nine on 27 October and fifty-six on 28 October. It was at this time that 7876 Private Wilf Crabtree was writing home to his wife at 3 Cornwallis Street in South Shields:

> If anyone wants to see what trench warfare is like and cannot get out here, it is an easy matter to see it in England. Dig a hole five feet deep and two feet wide and fill it half full of water. Then sit in it for ten days and let some one try to hit you with stones.

Describing his experiences in the trenches in France he added:

> On Friday morning I was making a cup of tea for breakfast and just

when I got it ready a sniper let blaze and upset it all over me. Well! You should have heard me lay the law down, but it all goes with the soldiering. The place where I am now is nothing but ruins. All the villages, including the churches have been knocked down by the Germans and it is awful to march through them. I don't know what the once happy and contented people will think when the war is over and they go back to look for their homes which have been destroyed and now lie in heaps of rubbish. It makes one feel like fighting when one sees such things as these. There would not be much trouble getting men to join the Army if they could only see a little bit out here. It makes one have no mercy for the enemy.

In a conclusion to the letter he said he was willing to bet a bottle of 'Johnnie Walker' it would be over by November. He would have lost the bet; he had the month right but was wrong by three more years.

One of those that fell that month was 8872 Sergeant Thomas Gilpin who was a resident of Shadforth near Durham, although he was born and bred in Oakenshaw. Having served his time with the colours, when war broke out he was employed at Sherburn Hill Colliery. Being on the reserve he immediately rejoined and had been out with the battalion since September 1914. Shortly after the Battle of Hooge he had spent four days' leave at home in Shadforth. On the Sunday evening after the news of his death, in St Cuthbert's Church in the village a short memorial service was held before evensong and special prayers were said and hymns sung by the choir. Another Shadforth man had been home at this time on a short weekend pass from hospital. 7821 Private John Brooks, who before the war was a stoneman at Thornley Colliery, had been wounded in the left forearm at Hooge, but before he had been wounded he had had the satisfaction of shooting a German sniper, before he was hit himself by crossfire from another German sniper. Private Brooks described the battle as 'Hell with the lid off.' Another letter was delivered to the village of Witton Gilbert to the west of Durham, this time to the parents of Gilbert Robson; he had been reported wounded but now it was confirmed that he had in fact been killed in action.

Having moved back to billets in huts located in a wood the battalion was supposed to undertake some training; however, the rain was so bad that the training was cancelled, but that didn't mean the men could rest. They were put to work draining the ground and building paths around the camp. Also a number of fatigue parties had to be found and a party was sent to Poperinghe station to unload coal; this job lasted for four days, whilst others had to guard the coal and another party was deployed to guard newly-constructed dugouts and others to guard the water supply. Not all the men of the battalion had left the line though, for the men of the battalion machine-gun section had remained behind, manning the reserve line trenches in the Potijze Defences. The period of rest came to an end on 5 November and the battalion struggled back to the front line south of

When out of the line the men made themselves as comfortable as possible in French barns, if they could.

124

Crump Farm. They deployed two companies in the front line and two in support. But this period was a continual struggle for the men. The weather was appalling and the continual rain brought the parapets down in both the front and reserve lines. During the day sections of the line were impassable owing to the thick slimy mud and the only way to move was over the top at night. For a number of days the right front company was cut off, except by wire. The communication trenches were continually blocked and again communication was only maintained over the top at night as the trenches were waist deep in mud and water.

In order that no strain was placed on any one company the front line was relieved every two or three nights. Luckily though the enemy were quiet, and no attacks and only a few bombardments took place; this left the battalion free to concentrate its energy on revetting and draining the trenches. Each night large working parties came up from the battalions in reserve, to assist with the task. To the credit of the men of 2/Durham LI only six men reported sick with trench foot during this tour. Although casualties were considered light, only a few men being killed and wounded, the news of two deaths soon reached Consett. The *Durham Chronicle* carried the news of the death of 11621 Private Henry McKie, a resident of Park Road, in this way. 'With an NCO he was leaving his dugout to get his dinner when a small shell landed between them. McKie was killed outright and the NCO died of his wounds.' The NCO involved must have been 9549 Company Sergeant Major Robert Jackson, who came from Ebberston, near Scarborough. On the night 15/16 November the battalion marched to the west of Ypres and boarded the light railway which carried them back to billets in Poperinghe. Only three days were spent here in which they were fully employed cleaning up, and refitting. They then moved to the Houterque area and the companies were distributed about the local farms.

Having cleaned up the battalion was inspected by General Sir Herbert Plumer, KCB, the Commander of SECOND ARMY, who expressed himself satisfied with the turn-out and bearing of the battalion. Shortly afterwards the new Commander 6th Division, General C, Ross DSO, inspected the battalion in billets. It was now that the Brigade Machine Gun Section was formed, and Second Lieutenant Reginald Ellis was appointed to command the section. Eventually along with the other battalion sections they formed the basis of 18th Company, Machine Gun Corps and from there the 6th Battalion, Machine Gun Corps, with whom some original men of 2/Durham LI would be killed later in the war.

On 26 November Second Lieutenant T. B. Barker assumed the duties of Battalion Adjutant. No reinforcements in other ranks were reported as joining during November but four officers: Second Lieutenant Thomas G. Schofield, Second Lieutenant John Watt, Lieutenant Frederick L. Newstead and Lieutenant James Jones. The last named had just been commissioned from the rank of Company Sergeant Major in the battalion. He had originally enlisted as a Band Boy in the battalion in 1896 and from that day it was his home. He rose very quickly through the ranks and for a number of years was the battalion Colour Sergeant Musketry Instructor and shortly before war broke out, he was appointed Company Sergeant Major. He was to die in the last few weeks of the war as a Lieutenant Colonel commanding the 17/Lancashire Fusiliers and by a strange coincidence was buried at Hooge Crater, where many men of the battalion are buried in unknown graves. At the end of the month new appointments were made with Lieutenant James Jones taking over B Company, and Lieutenant Joseph Tindle taking over D Company.

So November passed into December with the battalion still out of the line. But the staff didn't let them rest. On 4 December they were formed up enmasse and inspected by the Brigade Commander, Brigadier General Robert Bridgford, CMG, DSO; originally in 1889 he had been commissioned into the Manchester Regiment, but in 1905 he had transferred to the King's Shropshire Light Infantry. After the inspection he spoke to the battalion officers and congratulated them on the turn-out of the battalion, in particular the work of the NCOs which accounted for the smartness and turn-out of the men without exception. He also added that he was proud to have such a battalion in his brigade and he complimented the battalion on the way it upheld the traditions of the regiment both in and out of the trenches. The next day the battalion marched back towards the line and three companies took over a hutted camp in wood A30. The other company, B, went further forward and took over dugouts in the Yser Canal Bank near Bridge 4. On 15 December once again the Commanding Officer, Lieutenant Colonel Goring-Jones, was called away to command the Brigade and Major Irvine took over command. The same day the battalion took over the front line, taking over trenches X1–X3 and A3–A5

*480 Private
...inald Avery from
...nley, County
...ham, was killed in
...on on 20 December
...5.*

near Crump Farm about a mile and a half east of Ypres, and here for the first time their flank was protected by 14/Durham LI. The next day Second Lieutenant George Martin left the battalion on transfer to the Royal Flying Corps.

It was now that the enemy launched a heavy gas and artillery barrage on most of the salient, with St Jean, Ypres and the Canal Bank coming in for special treatment. The casualties, whilst not heavy, were not insignificant. Three officers, Second Lieutenants Foster, Schofield and Willis were evacuated wounded and Second Lieutenant William Harris died from the effect of the gas. Among the men eight were killed, twenty-one wounded and nine gassed. Lieutenant James Jones was detached from the battalion at this time and he took up the appointment as Officer Commanding the 6th Divisional NCO School of Instruction. On 20 December the battalion left the front line and took over trenches on the Yser Canal Bank with Battalion Headquarters and D Company being quartered in Ypres Prison. On Christmas Eve the battalion took over the front line from 1/West Yorkshire Regiment with 14/Durham LI on the left and 11/Border on the right. Battalion Headquarters were in Potijze Wood and were heavily shelled. Casualties among the men were six killed and eleven wounded. Also the Acting Adjutant, Second Lieutenant T. B. Barker was wounded; a few weeks later The *Durham Chronicle* carried the news that his parents had been informed that their son was lying in hospital in France severely wounded in the head. When he was once more fit in 1917 he was transferred to the Salonika Front.

But danger just didn't face those at the front: the following was reported in The *Durham Chronicle* about one of those whose time had expired whilst at the front:

Soldier in a gas hood, these were the latest protection against gas shells. Possibly taken at the battalion Transport lines.

The cold and damp conditions are clearly seen as these men cook a meal.

After passing safely through the dangers of the war in France, his actions including The Battle of Hooge, William Pigg, a time served soldier of 2/Durham LI, who resides at 25 Burns Street, Jarrow, has just had an experience which he describes as equally nerve trying as life in the trenches. After being imprisoned in the Bensham seam of Hebburn Pit for over seventeen hours he was liberated on Saturday.

When war broke out, Pigg who was a reservist rejoined 2/Durham LI and after receiving his discharge, returned to his employment as a miner at Hebburn Colliery in October.

On Friday night while he was in the Bensham Seam, there was a fall of stone covering an area of thirty feet. Pigg went immediately to inform a miner named Appleton who was further in, of the fall and Appleton hurriedly left the workings.

As Pigg was about to follow, a second fall occurred, and this effectually blocked his way to freedom. For seventeen hours he was a prisoner and all the time he was under the impression that Appleton was buried beneath the second fall. A fear which happily was unfounded. Finding himself plenty of timber at hand, Pigg protected himself; and for five hours he waited without hearing any sound from the outer world. His anxiety was

Men of 2/Durham LI in a reserve trench 1915.

relieved at the end of this time by hearing a rescue party at work and for twelve hours the work of cutting a way through the fall proceeded, with the happy result that Pigg was ultimately 'brought to bank'. As he said 'None the worse', On the whole he felt safe and comfortable in the area which he had timbered, but at one time he felt a shortage of air.

Pigg who is married said afterwards that his feelings in the mine were much the same as those he experienced in the trenches, 'certainly they were no worse'.

This small article that appeared in the newspaper slightly misleads the reader for William Pigg was not a reservist that rejoined, but a member of 3 (Reserve) Battalion of the Durham Light Infantry who was numbered 3/9316. He spent the first few months of the war in England and didn't join 2/Durham LI in France until 26 January 1915. In September 1915 just after the Battle of Hooge, the period he had signed on for expired and he was sent home to be discharged under King's Regulations 1914 para 392 xxi. That is 'time expired' still, as the article points out; Pigg had swapped one dangerous place for another just as dangerous.

It was about this time that a party of the battalion was going out to take up position in a listening post. As they moved out into No Man's Land they were met with heavy rifle fire and grenades from close range. The suddenness of this attack caused confusion in the party, but 3/10823 Private James McGall at once crawled forward and threw bombs into the listening post, which had been occupied by the enemy. The bombs thrown by the gallant soldier dispersed the enemy, and they rapidly retired, leaving the listening post in Durham hands. For his part in the action he received the Distinguished Conduct Medal.

On 29 December the battalion moved back once more to billets in Poperinghe with battalion Headquarters in Rue de Barance.

Chapter Four

1916, January–June, Holding the Salient

Although the battalion remained in billets over the New Year period of 1915–1916 the battalion War Diary doesn't record any celebrations or special meals for the men. They remained in rest until 1845 hours on 4 January 1916 when the battalion entrained at Poperinghe station and were transported up to the line. They took over the right subsector from 1/West Yorkshire Regiment and deployed the various companies in the front, support and X Lines, with Battalion Headquarters deployed in Potijze Wood. During this tour three replacement subalterns arrived: Second Lieutenants Henry D. Smith, Lionel E. Markham and William L. P. Griffith-Jones reported for duty at Battalion Headquarters and were allotted to D, B and C Companies respectively. The next day the area around Potijze and the battalion positions were heavily shelled and Second Lieutenant John A. G. Brewis

was wounded. During the day the Commanding Officer, Lieutenant Colonel Goring-Jones arrived back from Brigade Head-quarters and resumed command of the battalion. On 6 January the German gunners again shelled the trenches around Potijze and over the next few days they caused a steady trickle of casualties 5048 Private Arthur Gibson from Sunderland was killed on 7 January and the following day there were another three fatalities 8485, Private James Diston, a Gateshead man and another Sunderland chap, 4/8918 Private

In a village behind the line two men of the battalion pose with a young French girl. The man standing on the right wears the ribbons of the Queen's and King's South Africa Medals.

131

This unidentified group from the battalion collection in the regimental archives is clearly taken well behind the line.

James Smith, by birth a Welshman who came from Pontypridd, but had enlisted in Durham and 9744 Private Parry Roberts were added to the Battalion Roll of Honour. Also among the wounded was Captain Gosnall Legard who was evacuated to a hospital on the coast. On 9 January, 1/West Yorkshire Regiment arrived and relieved 2/Durham LI who moved back and three companies occupied dugouts in Canal Switch, whilst A Company and Battalion Headquarters were allotted positions in Ypres Prison. Between 0930 and 1100 hours on 11 January the Canal Switch dugouts were treated to a barrage of gas shells by the enemy artillery, which caused a number of casualties and six men had to be evacuated owing to the effects of the gas. The battalion went back into the line and relieved 1/West Yorkshire Regiment in the same trenches and during the day three men were killed in action, probably by enemy shelling 6763 Corporal George Bloomfield, a Londoner, had been with 1/Durham LI since before the Boer War and had served through that conflict; he had only arrived in France on 9 December 1915, having been sent back to the Regimental Depot from India. The second man was from the Special Reserve, 4/9491 Private Albert Bolland, who had arrived with the same draft in December. Neither of them has a known grave and they are commemorated on the Menin Gate Memorial at Ypres. The third soldier to die that day, 3/9371 Private John McDonell hailed from Jarrow and had been out in France since 5 January 1915 after the shelling he was buried behind the lines in Potijze burial ground.

An unidentified soldier of the battalion, possibly the CO's groom, holds a horse named Mariposa.

For the second time the battalion lost a much

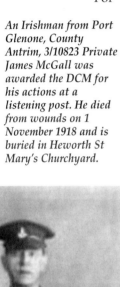

An Irishman from Port Glenone, County Antrim, 3/10823 Private James McGall was awarded the DCM for his actions at a listening post. He died from wounds on 1 November 1918 and is buried in Heworth St Mary's Churchyard.

respected Commanding Officer Lieutenant Colonel Michael D. Goring-Jones was promoted to the rank of Brigadier General and appointed to the command of 146 Infantry Brigade in the 49th (West Riding) Division. The loss of such a greatly esteemed Commanding Officer was much felt by all ranks of the battalion. He was commissioned into the Durham Light Infantry on 13 January 1886 and had left 1/Durham LI in India on promotion the previous January to take command of 2/Durham LI. Command of the battalion now passed to Major Alfred Ernest Irvine, an Irishman born in Londonderry; commissioned into 4/Durham LI in 1895 he transferred to the regular battalion in March 1897. The same day Second Lieutenant Joseph Wright, from South Shields, who had been commissioned into the Special Reserve on 15 August 1914, arrived from the base and was posted to A Company. The other change in officers at this time was that the Battalion Medical Officer, Lieutenant G. Smith RAMC was placed under arrest and was replaced by Lieutenant M. Remers RAMC. On the 14th of the month the whole of the area Potijze-St Jean came under heavy artillery fire and although casualties were light the damage to the British lines was considerable.

A week later the battalion War Diary records that on 26 January the court martial of Lieutenant G. Smith RAMC took place in Poperinghe and because Major Irvine had to attend as the defendant's Commanding Officer, this meant that the OC B Company, Captain Henry Smith had to assume command of the battalion for the day.

It was around this time that the news came through that the Battalion Transport Sergeant Major Joseph Watson was awarded the Distinguished Conduct Medal for:

Conspicuous gallantry and energy throughout the campaign. He always exhibited great courage under fire and by his coolness and resource in charge of the transport and issuing rations has set a fine example of devotion to duty.

The following day the whole area came under an intense barrage from the enemy gunners as soon as the Durhams called for fire support from the Royal Field Artillery supporting them, the enemy guns fell silent. Now the front fell quiet and on 30 January the weather changed; a dense Flanders fog fell over the battlefield and this allowed the forward companies to carry out some much-needed repairs and construct new positions in exposed places during the hours of daylight. All through the day there was very little firing by either side and at 1900 hours the battalion was relieved by 1/West Yorkshire Regiment and moved back into the reserve positions; A, B and Companies in the Canal Switch, with Battalion Headquarters on the Canal Bank and D Company in Ypres prison and the Menin Gate. On the last day of the month, Second Lieutenant C. R. Cook, 1/King's Shropshire Light Infantry, was attached to the battalion and was posted to B Company. Word was received that Captain G. S. Legard had been evacuated back to England on board the hospital ship HMHS *St Denis* and accordingly he was struck off the battalion strength. The companies changed round at this time; D Company moved to the ramparts in Ypres and B Company moved into the prison. On 5 February they marched back up to the line and relieved 1/West Yorkshire Regiment. B and C Companies went into the front line south of Crump Farm and Battalion Headquarters took up residence in Potijze Wood with A and D in the support line, the relief being completed without casualties. The night passed fairly quietly and although the enemy snipers were active there was no shelling. This changed the next morning and the gunners of both sides were hard at work. Both the front line and support line received their fair share of the enemy shells. There were however, a few casualties; four wounded and 3/10735 Private Luke Farrer of Sunderland was killed. On 7 February the 24th Division who were lying next to the 6th Division organised a heavy barrage on the German trenches at Oskar Farm and Railway Wood; this brought a swift retaliation from the German Artillery, however, most of it fell on 2/Durham LI trenches, but caused few casualties. Another spot that came in for heavy shellfire from the enemy was Potijze Crossroads. This pattern was followed for the next few days and nights. At night there was no shelling, just a bit of sniper activity but during the day various spots came under heavy artillery fire; on 8 February, Hussar Farm was shelled, the next day the Battalion Headquarters in Potijze Wood was hit but no major damage was done. Then at 1500 hours two enemy guns to the north zeroed in on the X line; this enfilade fire destroyed some fire-bays and a telephone cable to trench A3 was broken. When wires were cut in this way, the signallers of the battalion had to go out under fire and repair the line, sometimes in several places, just in case an enemy attack should take place. Later that evening at 2100 hours, Battalion Headquarters came under fire again but once more little or no damage occurred.

After a quiet night the next day, 10 February brought a heavy barrage down on a number of the locations previously mentioned, and then later in the day all the trenches held by 2/Durham LI came under fire with three bays being blown in and a number of men being wounded and two Privates Robert Corkin from South Shields and George Nicholson from Gateshead, being killed in action. Then at midnight 1/West Yorkshire Regiment arrived and took over the line, the relief being carried out without enemy hindrance. 2/Durham LI then marched back to the Asylum in Ypres and boarded a train that took them back to rest billets in Poperinghe. Having arrived in the rear area a comprehensive training programme was published, and the companies began training. This started on Friday 11 February with an inspection by Company Commanders, followed by baths for the whole battalion. Apart from the Signallers, Lewis Gunners, Grenadiers and Buglers, who paraded under their own instructors, the rest of the battalion was employed as follows. From 0900 until 1200 hours on Saturday each company took part in

physical training followed by squad drill with arms, then musketry and bayonet instruction and saluting. At 1130 the newly-arrived draft was inspected by the Commanding Officer, then after lunch, in the afternoon the Company Commanders completed their inspection. During the day Poperinghe was shelled and around 1700 hours, enemy aircraft dropped around a dozen bombs. A signal came in from Headquarters 6th Division 'Stand by to move', which was followed at 1815 by 'Troops may fall out'.

On Sunday after church parade the Commanding Officer inspected all the billets, and once again the town came under fire from the enemy artillery. During the day, Second Lieutenant John George Huggall reported for duty. Having served as a trooper in the Hussars, he had been commissioned into 17/Durham LI on 10 April 1915; after reporting in to the battalion he was posted to A Company. After breakfast on Monday 14 February there was an inspection of all ranks in marching order followed by more saluting and rifle drill, then in the afternoon the men were at the disposal of the Company Commanders.

tenant John Barkas
evacuated sick on
bruary 1916.

The only men that were not free were those aspiring to be Buglers, as there was an examination for appointment. This would consist of each man having to sound several or more calls on the bugle, the regimental call followed by whatever was ordered, reveille, 'Charlie Charlie get out of bed', or officers mess call, 'The officers wives get puddens and pies.' Those that passed the examination were then allowed to wear the bugle arm badge denoting their trade. That evening the same 'stand to' signal was received from division and all the preparations were made before the 'stand down' was received. On Tuesday morning the same routine took place as the day before and then in the afternoon everyone was cleaning up ready to hand over.

In the afternoon of 15 February the battalion marched to the station in Poperinghe and boarded a train which took them to the Asylum in Ypres. They relieved 1/West Yorkshire Regiment in the front line 100 yards south of Crump Farm to The Gully. 2/Durham LI deployed D and A Companies in the front line and C and B in the reserve line. To the south of the battalion there was intense shelling between 2100 and 2200 hours but the battalion front was quiet, then the weather turned; the wind became very strong and there was heavy rain. The following day there was a gale force wind and the enemy sent over a number of shells which blew in the parapet in one sector. That night the enemy sent over around twenty shells, among them some gas shells; these were aimed at the reserve line and Battalion Headquarters in Potijze Wood and The Dump, but no damage or casualties were reported. It was now that Lieutenant John Barkas reported to Battalion Headquarters and was posted to B Company and the news arrived that Major Irvine was promoted to Lieutenant Colonel, whilst he was commanding the battalion.

3/10735 Private Luke Farrar was killed in action on 6 February 1916; a Sunderland m he has no known gra and is commemorate on the Menin Gate Memorial at Ypres.

On 17 February the day passed quietly with just a little sniper activity until just after 1100 hours when the Potijze Defences were shelled but little damage occurred. That evening, an enemy working party were heard hard at work about 50 yards south of Oskar Farm; the battalion Lewis guns were quickly brought to bear and after a few bursts of fire the enemy party were dispersed. During the day Lieutenant Charles H. Green returned to the battalion and was posted to D Company replacing Captain Joseph Tindle, who was posted to 6 Infantry Base Depot to train new drafts. Another officer returning that day was Second Lieutenant John Brewis who had been slightly wounded the previous month, and now he took over as the Battalion Lewis Gun Officer. In the evening a number of balloons were seen travelling from behind the British lines towards the German lines, these were fired at and one was brought down. It was found to have French newspapers attached and was sent off to Headquarters 18 Brigade for further examination.

5682 Corporal Paul Kraft had been with battalion since 189? rose to the rank of Company Sergeant Major and remaine the army at the end the war.

The following day saw an increase in the amount of sniper and machine-gun fire aimed at the battalion. Although there was rain it didn't stop the German gunners, who fired a considerable amount of shells onto the Hooge sector, after which they turned their attention on to the sector held by 2/Durham LI. During this heavy shellfire Second Lieutenant John Hugall was wounded and shellshocked and had to be evacuated to the Field Ambulance. At some stage during the day Second Lieutenant Arnold Steel arrived at Battalion Headquarters and was posted to A Company. He had originally enlisted in one of the

University and Public Schools Battalions of the Royal Fusiliers and had been granted a commission into 19/Durham LI; he was then transferred to 21/Durham LI which was followed by a posting to 23/Durham LI. It was from this last unit that he was sent out to the front and joined 2/Durham LI in Flanders.

On 19 February, at about 1630 hours, the battalion positions came under fire from a new gun; this had a low trajectory and an unusual burst, around twenty shells landed from the direction of Oskar Farm. The gun was thought to be a railway-mounted weapon which was known as 'Silent Sue', which did considerable damage to the British trenches. In return the British heavy artillery fired around forty shells and the forward observers reported seeing enemy soldiers being blown high in the air. During the night the battalion Lewis guns, which were providing cover for patrols in No Man's Land, opened fire and scattered an enemy working party that made too much noise and gave away their position. Also during the night the wind changed direction and by 0600 hours there was a 'Gas Alert' but by 1000 hours the wind had dropped and there was a stand down from the alert. As the day progressed enemy machine-gun and sniper fire increased along with artillery fire. There was also a lot of activity from the enemy air force. In the early evening 1/West Yorkshire Regiment commenced the relief of 2/Durham LI, the latter moving back to billets in Ypres. Here, Battalion Headquarters, A and B Companies were located in the Canal Bank, D Company in the Ramparts and C Company went to the Ypres Prison. Again that night another 'Gas Alert' was ordered.

They only spent two days out of the line, during which time the weather had turned to snow, when they were ordered back to relieve the West Yorkshire Regiment. B Company took over the front line in Jermyn Street, about 50 yards south of Crump Farm; they held this as far as the junction A4/A3 where C Company continued the line to a position known as The Gully. Here D Company held the position as far as X3. A Company remained in the reserve line. Overnight there was a hoar-frost and the landscape turned white. Although there was only a little sporadic shelling, one man from A Company, 22263 Private William Kennedy from Gateshead, was killed in action. About the same time two other casualties occurred in D Company 11563 Private Thomas McDonald received a gunshot wound to the abdomen and 23261 Private Gilbert Butterfield got a bullet in the right leg. Both these men were quickly evacuated to a Casualty Clearing Station behind the line. The remains of Private Kennedy would have been buried close behind the line. However they were later lost, probably owing to artillery fire, and he is commemorated on the Ypres, Menin Gate Memorial.

Overnight two inches of snow fell and the front fell quiet; there was a little small-arms fire, but during the day the British Artillery opened fire on a German working party in No Man's Land, with the enemy firing at

Potijze in reply and they also launched a bomb attack against Hooge, but by 1730 hours the front was quiet again. During the night patrols were active in between the lines but nothing of note occurred. The next few days were relatively quiet with some shelling but no damage occurred. On 1 March four new officers arrived: Second Lieutenants William A. Smith, Frank D. Morris, Alfred L. Butcher and Charles William Heppleston were posted to A, C, D and B Companies respectively. In the early hours of 2 March 1/West Yorkshire Regiment came up and relieved 2/Durham LI, who proceeded to march back to billets in Poperinghe. Whilst the battalion was billeted in the village, on 3 March they came under enemy artillery fire and one billet was hit by a shell which killed six men. One of these was 27459 George Hesp, who although resident at 11 Burdon Street, Heseldon, was employed as a miner at Thornley Colliery. He had only enlisted the previous July and had not long been at the front, according to the short piece in the *Durham Chronicle*. The enemy repeated the shelling the next day, but caused little damage and no casualties. Second Lieutenant Robert J. Meikle reported for duty on 5 March and was posted to D Company, and then on the following day a draft of fifty-five NCOs and men arrived from the Infantry Base Depot; they were distributed among those companies that needed the most men to bring them back up to strength. The rest didn't last too long and on the night of 7/8 March the battalion marched back up the line and once again relieved 1/West Yorkshire Regiment in the trenches at Potijze; two companies were deployed in the line, in trenches A4 and A3, and two in support in X3 and X1. As soon as the relief was completed patrols were sent out into No Man's Land. No information was gathered and it was a quiet night. They now began preparations for a 'strafe' on the enemy line and so as to avoid any artillery retaliation, D Company sent half of its men back to the Prison in Ypres and the other half to Battalion Headquarters. Likewise C Company retired to the Ramparts at Ypres. When the enemy opened fire they succeeded in destroying nine dugouts in A4 and A3. 4/10465 Private Albert Larssen, a resident of Fencehouses, was killed and seven men were wounded 20698 Private Thomas Bowman later in the day died from his wounds. The next day the brigade on the right of 2/Durham LI carried out a bombing raid, which brought some retaliation from the German gunners, but fortunately no damage to 2/Durham LI. Once again patrols were sent out during the hours of darkness; on arrival back in the British lines, they reported that the enemy was strengthening the wire in front of his trenches.

On 11 March there was a heavy bombardment by the enemy on the Bellewarde Lake area and whizz-bangs hit X1 trench, blowing in two dugouts but without causing any casualties. Overnight the enemy snipers kept up a desultory fire and patrols from the battalion had two separate

Sergeant C. W. Hepplestone, seen here in a 1911 photograph 1/Durham LI taken in India, was sent back England and commissioned into 2/Durham LI and joi the battalion in Fran on 2 March 1916.

138

fights in No Man's Land with German patrols. When the patrols arrived safely back in the British lines they reported that the enemy were bailing water out of their front line into No Man's Land, and their line being higher, the water was running down towards the British front line. It was now that a party of NCOs and men under the command of Captain Charles H. Green moved to the wood at A30, to prepare for a special task. In the late hours of 12 March, 1/West Yorkshire Regiment completed the relief of 2/Durham LI who were clear of the line by 0500 hours on 13 March. Two companies, A and D, proceeded to the Canal Bank dugouts, the other two, B and C, went into the Dry Switch.

Captain Charles Green and his party reported to the Canal Bank; they were accompanied by Captain Smith, Royal Naval Reserve, with a party carrying Bangalore torpedoes.

The party was split up into three groups:
1. the Scouts
2. the torpedo party
3. the raiding party

The raiding party was further broken down into bayonetmen, grenadiers and prisoner escorts, the whole lot under the command of Second Lieutenant William L. P. Griffith Jones.

Artillery support was to come from 49/Battery Royal Field Artillery and they provided a Forward Observation Officer in the British Front line with orders to bring down a barrage if the situation required one.

The following officers, NCOs and men took part in the raid.

Officer in command:
      Captain Charles H.Green

Officer in command of raiding party:
      Second Lieutenant William L. P. Griffith Jones

LEFT RAIDING PARTY

9075	Sergeant	Lowe	NCO i/c
10824	Privates	Gibbons Bomber	
25419		Devlin	Prisoner escort
11626		Bowes	Prisoner escort
22625		Furn	Bayonet man
26134		Swain	Bayonet man
8915		Graham Bomber	

RIGHT RAIDING PARTY

9054	Sergeant	Tighe	NCO i/c
10143	Privates	Wilson	Bomber
9081		Darrell	Bomber
23015		Patton	Bayonet man
9744		Hamilton	Bayonet man
15966		Burdess	Prisoner escort
9628		Donnighan	Prisoner escort

OFFICERS' ESCORT
12066 Private Fletcher
9203   Stephenson

RESERVES
20750 Sergeant   Wardle
11179 Private   Lowther
8626   Ward
8487   Barrett
8899   Renwick
8808   Canavan
8471   Crawford
7286   Robinson
6447   Hamilton
10070   Turnbull

BLOCKING PARTY
11007 Sergeant   Mason
12021 Corporal   Parker
22528 Private Kettle
8651   Ward

TIME FUSE MEN
9578 Private   Colbeck
11756   Thornton

TORPEDO PARTY
Officer in command: Captain C. A. Smith RNR
9992 Private Roper
11207   Allen
27173   Dew
8277   Peacock

LADDER MEN
9785 Private Kennedy
25327   Hind
8405   Johnson
27318   McCabe

WAITING MAN
6871 Sergeant Wood

Extra details
9044 Private Layton   King's Shropshire Light Infantry

SCOUT

9023	Private	Brooman	West Yorkshire Regiment
?	Private	Wright	West Yorkshire Regiment

DRESS AND EQUIPMENT

Each man wore fatigue dress, without cap which was replaced by a cap comforter. All faces were blackened. Rifles and bayonets were carried and every man had two Mills Number 5 grenades in his pocket. NCOs carried revolvers and knobkerries, as did every man in the party.

The objective was for two parties, one from 11/Essex Regiment under the command of Lieutenant Bartlett and one from 2/Durham LI under Captain Green, to enter the German trenches and secure a prisoner. The parties were to enter the German lines at different points. The wire in front of the Essex battalion had been previously cut by the British artillery, whilst in the Durham LI sector cutting the wire would be carried out by Captain Smith RNR and his torpedo men. The explosion of the torpedo, timed for 0330 hours, was the signal for both parties to attack.

At about 0240 hours both parties left the British front line and shortly after this the Essex Regiment were in position waiting for the signal; they waited but owing to unforeseen circumstances no signal came. At around 0345 hours, a German patrol of six men coming towards them was spotted by the party from the Essex Regiment. The Germans must have spotted the raiders for they suddenly lay down. After a while they got up and made a dash for their own trench, so Lieutenant Bartlett gave the order to fire. One German was killed outright and one badly wounded. Lieutenant Bartlett and two men went forward and brought in the wounded enemy soldier and at the same time cut one of the shoulder straps off the dead man. The Germans in their trench now opened fire and the Essex party were forced to retire back to their own lines; on the way back in four of their party were wounded.

With the element of surprise lost and a prisoner and identification secured the party from 2/Durham LI were ordered to retire back to the British lines. The torpedoes had been placed under the wire, so Privates Layton and Brooman fired them and made a large gap in the German wire.

The members of the Durham raiding party were heartily disappointed in what they saw as a failure and they obtained permission to try again. The next night they made their preparations and at 2300 hours the first party left for the line, followed one hour later by the remainder. At 0100 hours the leading scouts went out into No Man's Land, they were followed by Captain Smith and his men who quietly laid the torpedoes under the German wire. With the charge laid and the raiding party in position all was reported ready. Just before the time set for firing the torpedoes, heavy rifle fire broke out from the German front line and a number of the raiding party began to fall back on the reserves. The party was steadied and formed up again by Captain Green and with the assistance of Privates Layton and Brooman they were led back across No Man's Land to the German trenches. The first man to enter the enemy line [according to the War Diary] was Second Lieutenant Griffith Jones, who shot and wounded the sentry and then accompanied by Privates Fletcher and Stephenson worked down the trench bombing dugouts as they went. From the loud cries and screams it was estimated a good number of the enemy had been wounded.

The trench was 8 to 10 feet deep and was well constructed with a wooden floor and brushwood hurdles and in places expanded metal had been used. Further along the trench 3/9023 Private John Brooman of the West Yorkshire Regiment had entered the trench and was bombing the enemy; he was, however, wounded by a bomb. The other scout, 9044 Private William Layton, King's Shropshire Light Infantry, [according to his Distinguished Conduct Medal citation] had been the first man into the trench and he accounted for a number of enemy soldiers. By now they had been in the trench a few minutes and Captain Green and Sergeant Lowe managed to capture a German soldier. With great difficulty and much against the man's will, for he started to shout and scream, they got him out of the trench and dragged him off into No Man's Land; here Captain Green gagged the man. The raiders now ran into a problem for they could not find the gap in the wire, so they decided to drag him through the belt of German barbed wire. By now all the raiding party had left the German trench and were making their way back towards the British line. The Germans recovered quickly and probably thinking their man was dead, started throwing bombs and firing into No Man's Land. Unfortunately one of the bombs hit the prisoner and blew him to bits and wounded Sergeant Tighe. They were forced to leave his remains hanging on the wire. But by 0430 hours all the raiders were back in the British line with only two men slightly wounded.

The raid had been greatly assisted by 1/West Yorkshire Regiment whose Lewis Gunners had kept up a covering fire, which muffled the sound as the torpedoes were placed in position. The Divisional Artillery had played their part too and had laid an effective box barrage on the German communication trenches, thus preventing a swift counter attack.

Praise quickly came down from XIV Corps Headquarters:

The Corps Commander has read your further report on the enterprise carried out by 2/Durham LI with the greatest interest, and has forwarded it to SECOND ARMY.

He directs me to inform you that it only confirms his previously expressed opinion of the gallantry and efficiency shown by the battalion concerned in carrying out the raid.

e Earl of Cavan
mmanding XIV
rps sent his
gratulations for a
well done.

Brigadier General
General Staff XIV Corps.

The Corps Commander, Lieutenant General The Earl of Cavan took the opportunity to congratulate the Brigade Commander, Brigadier R. J. Bridgford, personally and inform him that the gallantry awards had been confirmed:

Dear Bridgford,
I am delighted that your gallant fellows all got the rewards asked for. The sailors being delayed for approval by the admiralty. I have to be away tomorrow so will not ask for another parade but I hope you will convey my sincere congratulations to Colonel Irvine and his battalion.
Yours truly
Cavan

The rewards asked for were the award of the Military Cross to Captain Green and Lieutenant Griffith Jones and Distinguished Conduct Medals for Sergeants Lowe and Tighe as well as Privates Layton and Brooman of the Brigade Scouts. Which medal went to Captain Smith is uncertain.

Sent home to recover from his wounds, the sequel to Sergeant Tighe's story appeared in the *Durham Chronicle*, on 14 July, when medals were presented to Sergeant Tighe and CSM Hunter under the heading,

716 CSM Robert
nter DCM received
medal at Seaham
rbour on 14 July
6, but the award
s for his continual
d work throughout
time in France.

Durhams gallantry

Three members of the 4/Durham Light Infantry were decorated at Seaham Harbour on Saturday 8 July. Brigadier General English presented Distinguished Conduct Medals to Sergeant Major R Hunter and Sergeant T Tighe.

Presenting the first medal, General English said that CSM Hunter, who had enlisted in 1902, was awarded a card of honour by the GOC 6th Division, for distinguished conduct at Hooge in August 1915, and then a second card for distinguished conduct at Ypres, during a gas attack at Ypres on 12 December of the same year. Subsequently he was awarded a Distinguished Conduct Medal for good work and gallant conduct.

Presenting the award to Sergeant Tighe the Brigadier General stated the Sergeant had received a card for his gallant conduct on 14 May and was subsequently awarded the Distinguished Conduct Medal for gallantry during a raid. The Citation was then read out. Having presented the gallantry awards, the Brigadier General then presented the Long Service Good Conduct Medal to Bugler T Cook.

On 16 March three men were slightly wounded when the enemy shelled the battalion positions, then that night the battalion, less B Company, marched to Poperinghe, where they spent a quiet night before proceeding to Camp K the following day. They were joined at Camp K by B Company at 0630 hours the next day. From here Captain

Green was evacuated to the Field Ambulance and he was replaced as OC, D Company by Captain Bertie Baty, a Houghton le Spring man originally commissioned into 19/Durham LI, the Bantam Battalion, he had spent some time with 21 (Reserve) Battalion, prior to joining 2/Durham LI in France. In this camp, under the control of the Battalion Padre, there was an opportunity for the battalion to open a canteen and recreation room, which was greatly appreciated by the men. The C of E Padre, Captain Reed was a busy man, not only running the canteen but also holding services for those who wished to attend. Those of the Roman Catholic faith went to Mass in the local village church in St Jean and the Non-Conformists had a service with the Methodist Padre. On 20 March the GOC 6th Division, Major General C. Ross, came and addressed the members of the raiding party. Later that day the CO Lieutenant Colonel Irvine inspected the battalion in marching order, afterwards expressing his pleasure in a good turn-out. At 2030 hours on 21 March, a draft of twenty-one NCOs and men arrived, but as 2/Durham LI was well up to strength, the next morning they were passed on to 14/Durham LI.

27763 Private John Gibson from Leamsid. near Durham City, w wounded and evacuated back to England where he die. from his wounds 23 March 1916. He is buried in Rainton St Mary's Churchyard, County Durham

It must have seemed to the men of 2/Durham LI that every commander wanted to congratulate them; the only trouble was they had to parade in marching order to be inspected each time. On 22 March, during a shower of rain, the GOC 18 Infantry Brigade inspected the battalion; also present was the GOC XIV Corps, The Earl of Cavan, who addressed the assembled men. For the next two days the Field General Court Martial took place of a number of men, but no further details are known. The companies meanwhile were carrying out a programme of training in the mornings and went to the baths in the afternoon.

Preparations were made for a move to the Calais area; D Company, which was to act as baggage loading party proceeded to Hopoutre sidings on the Abeele Road and commenced loading the battalion baggage and

A battalion parades for the first time in the new steel helmets; one or two, particularly the officer look a bit self-conscious.

transport onto the train. On 26 March at 1100 hours 2/Durham LI marched out of Camp K and marched to the sidings and entrained and at 1300 hours left for Calais, where they arrived at 1730 hours. After detraining the battalion marched to the north of Calais, to a spot on the Dunkerque Road known as Camp C, where they arrived at 1930 hours. The next day parades took place in the morning and then at 1500 hours a lucky third of the battalion were paraded and marched into Calais; they were dismissed in the Place de'Richelieu and given the afternoon off. At 2000 hours they fell in again and were marched back to camp in heavy rain. Over the next few days training and route marches took place.

On 29 March, a Brigade route march took place over a circular route of seven miles. During the day Second Lieutenant Robert Chatt reported back to the battalion and was posted to C Company. Again around one-third of the battalion were allowed a half-day in Calais, but on the following day no one was allowed into Calais as the training programme was followed to the letter. On the last day of the month the passes to Calais were reinstated and the final third of the men were given their chance to visit the town. As March passed into April the training continued and sports were held on the sands along the Dunkerque Road. Church services were again held by the various padres attached to the battalion, but once again the Roman Catholics had to attend Mass in the village church as 18 Brigade had no RC Padre.

18 Brigade now began moving back towards the line. The whole brigade in column of route moved together, the order of march being: Brigade Headquarters, Brigade Signals, 1/West Yorkshire Regiment, 11/Essex Regiment, 18 Brigade Machine Gun Company, 2/Durham LI, 14/Durham LI, 19/Field Company Royal Engineers, 17/Field Ambulance RAMC. Formed up with the head of the column at the bridge over the river in the village of Marcke, the route followed south along the Canal de Marcke to Halte and then via Nortkerque and on to Zoutkerque, where they billeted for the night.

The march continued until they reached the area of Wormhoudt where the 6th Division was assembling. Shortly after arrival the Brigade Commander sent a letter to all Battalion Commanders:

The GOC wishes to bring to the notice of all units in the brigade, the smart appearance of the Brigade on arrival at Wormhoudt on conclusion of the march from Calais. This being the first march the Brigade has undertaken since last May.

Especially the appearance of the troops when passing the Army Corps Commander yesterday morning was all that could be desired. The Corps Commander expressed himself in very complimentary terms on the subject.

The march discipline of the transport was very good and horses and mules looked well and have all arrived fit and sound which is creditable to those concerned.

All Battalion Commanders have every reason to be thoroughly satisfied with the appearance of their Battalions and the improvement in all details daily has been most notable and creditable to their resourcefulness. Congratulations.

Various sporting competitions were organised, the men were able to take a bath and a Divisional Horse Show took place over two days at Esquebec. The battalion entered seven of the classes, doing well in the 'Pack Animal' class, but the best effort was by Captain Charles Green who took third place in the jumping on his horse 'Fermoy'. Over the next few days the companies continued training and the officers attended a lecture on artillery, in Wormhout, given by Brigadier General Gardiner Humphries CB, DSO, the Commander, Royal Artillery, 6th Division.

On 15 April the battalion moved by route march back to Camp K in Poperinghe. After the battalion had settled in, the CO and Company Commanders boarded a motor bus of the Army Service Corps and were taken up to the Pilkem Sector to reconnoitre the trenches.

Here we have three regulars from 1/Durham LI drafted to 2/Durham LI in 1916. Seated on the right is 6866 Private Frederick Gardner from Leamington in Warwickshire, he would be killed in action on 21 March 1918.

43136 Private John H. Pattison arrived in 2/Durham LI after serving with 6/Durham LI. He got right through to the end

Meanwhile the battalion remained in Camp K for the next two days. Then at 1920 hours on 17 April the battalion entrained on the light railway and were carried up as far as the Asylum in Ypres, where they went into Brigade reserve in the Canal Bank. One company, under the command of Captain Green, relieved the 6/Oxfordshire and Buckinghamshire LI at Pelissier Farm. The next night at 2100 hours the battalion commenced taking over the front line. The relief was complete by midnight. 19 April was quiet until 1700 hours, when suddenly a terrific bombardment opened up on the right of B Company and along the lines of 8/Bedfordshire Regiment who were holding the line to the right. This barrage lasted until 2000 hours and under cover of it the Germans tried to get into the British lines. They managed to take some of the line held by 8/Bedfordshire Regiment, but despite the barrage and the enemy attack 2/Durham LI, though taking casualties, hung on to their line. When the roll was taken afterwards it was found that eight men were killed outright and another ten were missing believed killed. Captain Green was evacuated with shellshock and thirty-one NCOs and men were sent down to the Field Ambulance wounded; two of this latter group eventually died from their wounds.

The next day A Company took over in the front line from B Company and later that day there was a general shelling of the front line, with the enemy trench mortars particularly active. Once again the battalion suffered losses with four men killed and eight wounded. On 21 April the heavy shelling continued. A position known as 'Dawson's City' near St Julien was shelled intermittently and the left front company in trenches E24 and E25 were heavily trench-mortared; the trenches practically ceased to exist as formed defensive positions. By the afternoon communication with the front line had been cut and only the right reserve company was in touch with Battalion Headquarters. At 2200 hours 16 Infantry Brigade launched a counter-attack and retook the trenches lost on 19 April. During the shelling on 21 April, Lieutenant Joseph Wright, from South Shields, was posted as missing believed killed; commissioned into the Special Reserve on 15 August 1914, he had been out in France since January and had only just been promoted to Lieutenant the previous month. Second Lieutenant Harry N. Heyward was wounded and among the men six were killed and forty wounded.

These casualties and the fact that the battalion had held on to its position brought praise from the Brigade Commander, Brigadier General Robert Bridgford, CMG, DSO; originally he had been commissioned into the Manchester Regiment in 1899 but later he transferred to the King's Shropshire Light Infantry. He had been evacuated to the 7th Stationary Hospital in Boulogne from where he wrote:

> 26/4/1916
>
> My Dear Irvine,
>
> I must write to congratulate you and your Battalion on the way they stuck to their trenches on the 19th. They had a very severe hammering and I am afraid your trenches must have been nearly laid flat. You were a great help to us that evening and you and your Battalion were the right men in the right place, although a very unpleasant place.
>
> I am getting on very well it takes a little time for bones to mend of course, but ribs mend quicker than anything else.
>
> I am sorry to hear of all your casualties. I hope they will make you up again quickly. Many congratulations on your excellent work.
>
> Yours very sincerely
>
> R J Bridgford

The defence of the position brought the reward of a Distinguished Service Order to the Commanding Officer, Lieutenant Colonel Alfred E. Irvine, the citation recording the example he set to his men:

During a critical period and continuous bombardment by the enemy lasting three days he was up with his front companies each night directing and organising the defences. His energy and cheerfulness and splendid example were invaluable.

On 22 April 11/Essex Regiment relieved 2/Durham LI, the relief being complete by 0300 hours on 23 April. The Durhams moved to Elverdinghe where two companies were billeted at Pelissier Farm and two in the Chateau; twice during the morning both positions came under shellfire. There was one direct hit on the Chateau and the farm was set on fire and some masonry was brought down. During this shelling three men were wounded. The next two days were quiet and working parties were sent up the line. A bath house was set up at the Chateau where both A and C Companies and the Battalion Headquarters were able to get a bath. Owing to the farm being burnt out, two platoons of B Company were moved from Pelissier Farm to some huts near Elverdinghe Chateau. The digging and carrying parties continued over the next few nights and on 26 April the huts near the Chateau and Elverdinghe village came under enemy shellfire. That night at 1900 hours a message arrived from Brigade for the battalion to 'Stand to'. The alert lasted until 2245 hours when a second message arrived to 'Stand down'.

The next night the battalion moved back up the line and took over from 11/Essex Regiment, in the trenches west of the Ypres–Langemarck Road, the relief being completed by 2200 hours. The next day Battalion Headquarters, on the Canal Bank, was shelled and there was a direct hit on the orderly room.

Another message that arrived from Brigade Headquarters at this time concerned the Brigade Commander, Brigadier General Bridgford, who was not getting better as quickly as he thought he would. In a short note the Brigade Major Captain T. G. Grenville Gavin, Rifle Brigade, passed on the Brigadier's compliments:

29 April 1916

Dear Colonel

I have today received a letter from General Bridgford from No 7 General Hospital, Boulogne and in it he asks me to tell you how truly sorry he is to be leaving 18 Brigade and how deeply grateful he is to you and all your officers for all the help and support you have always given him. He feels this parting

Lieutenant Robert Benton was on leave in England when war broke out and was attached to 2/Durham LI. Evacuated sick, he eventually rejoined his own Regiment the 53rd Sikhs and was killed in action on 7 June 1916; he is buried in the Amara War Cemetery in Iraq.

from many good friends in the Brigade very much. Officers, NCOs and men have all worked so well and responded so splendidly to any call he has made upon them.

He wishes the Brigade the very best of luck and is proud to have ever had the honour of commanding it.

Yours ever

T Grenville Gavin

Command of 18 Brigade now passed to Brigadier General William Kerr McClintock, late Royal Berkshire Regiment.

On 30 April the heavy guns of the British Corps Artillery put an effective barrage on the enemy trenches opposite the battalion. This barrage was very accurate and knocked in the German parapet in at least five places; however, it brought immediate retaliation from the German gunners who fired a barrage that lasted for more than two hours.

1 May was a quiet day to start with but later the enemy sent some shells over which hit the trenches E25 and E26 on the battalion's left flank, then at 1630 hours they put about twenty whizz-bangs onto the Dawson City sector. Also during the day a draft of forty-three other ranks joined the battalion in the trenches. The enemy repeated the shelling the next day and retaliation was called for from the British Artillery. The reply was quite effective and damaged the enemy trenches. Overhead a dogfight was taking place between two aeroplanes and A Company reported that the German machine was hit and came down in the direction of Potijze, but they were unable to say whether it was inside the British or German lines. That night 11/Essex Regiment came up and took over the front line and 2/Durham LI moved back to the Canal Bank with A and B Companies on the East Bank and Battalion HQ, C and D Companies on the West Bank. During the day the Commanding Officer inspected the new draft and Second Lieutenant John Caswell joined for duty from 4/Durham LI at Seaham Harbour. Later in the afternoon the positions on the east of the canal bank were shelled and some of B Company's dugouts were destroyed and two men were evacuated wounded.

There was a lot of aerial activity over the battalion position over the next two days. On the morning of 5 May a German machine flew low over the front and dropped a white light, whereupon the German artillery opened fire on the West Canal Bank, but fortunately there was little damage done, although two men were wounded. Later Captain James Jones returned from hospital and a draft of twenty-six other ranks came up to the line and was split between the various companies. On 7 May while the Battalion Transport Section was delivering rations and stores at Marengo House, the German Artillery opened fire and although there were no casualties to the drivers, two horses were killed. That night the battalion relieved 11/Essex Regiment, B and D Companies went up to the front line and A and C Companies moved to Elverdinghe Chateau. Battalion Headquarters went to the dugouts on the East Canal Bank. Another officer replacement arrived the next day, Second Lieutenant Stanley Dalziel originally a private numbered 12781 in the East Yorkshire Regiment before being commissioned in the Durham LI, he reported to Battalion Headquarters and was posted to C Company.

9 May was a very quiet day but at dusk one of the observation posts spotted an enemy carrying party. They appeared to be carrying knife-rests up to the front line. Likewise C Company was ordered out to carry stores and rations from Elverdinghe Chateau up to the British front line and another group were told off for some digging work.

Back in the battalion rear area the Quartermaster, Lieutenant Shea and his Transport and Quartermasters, staff were seeing action of a slightly different nature. News of this came in the form of a report from the Assistant Provost Marshal, 6th Division, to the GOC, 6th Division, which then made its way down the chain of command to Battalion Headquarters:

A.P.M. 6th Division

I desire to take the earliest opportunity of drawing your notice to the action taken today by Lieutenant and Quartermaster Shea, 2/Durham LI, and Sergeants Turton and Anslow of the same battalion.

A deserter who had previously been apprehended by Lieutenant Shea and had escaped from the 3rd Division was reported to be living in a house near G10.B3.7 armed with rifles and revolvers. This officer together with the two NCOs and two men, whose names I regret I have not, advanced to the house and although armed behaved if I may say so in a brave and cool manner. The deserter had managed to escape but was caught shortly afterwards by Lieutenant Shea and his men who drove the surrounding fields. The deserter when apprehended by Lieutenant Shea was armed. May I also add my personal thanks through you to Lieutenant Shea, the NCOs and men of 2/Durham LI who so ably apprehended the deserter without his inflicting any damage on anybody else present.

Signed Clanwilliam, Captain

Sergeant Turton, second left, and men of the Transport Section. Sergeant Turton, a Byers Green policeman, born at Thornley, County Durham, was awarded the Military Medal and promoted to Company Sergeant Major. He was posted Missing in Action and later presumed dead on 21 March 1918.

The Assistant Provost Marshal, A. V. M. The Earl of Clanwilliam was originally commissioned in the Reserve of Officers for the

Horse Guards; when his report reached Headquarters 6th Division, it was read with pleasure by Major General Ross, who ordered his AA&QMG, Lieutenant Colonel W. R. Walsh to write to Headquarters 18 Brigade.

To 18 Brigade,

The Major General Commanding has read the attached report with much pleasure. He desires that you will express to Lieutenant and Quartermaster Shea, Sergeants Turton and Anslow and the two men of 2/Durham LI his high appreciation of the courage and sense of duty displayed by them on this occasion. Will you kindly forward me the names of the two men in question.

13/5/1916 Signed W. R. Walsh Lieutenant Colonel AA & QMG 6th Division.'

When the report reached Headquarters 18 Brigade the following was added,

To 2/Durham LI

I am very pleased to forward the foregoing from the Major General Commanding expressing his high appreciation of the courage and sense of duty of Lieutenant and Quartermaster Shea and Sergeants Turton and Anslow and the two men of 2/Durham LI.

Please forward the names of the two men.

Signed W K McClintock Brigadier General

Commanding 18 Brigade

The Commanding Officer, Lieutenant Colonel A. E. Irvine, forwarded the names of the two men, 12033 Private E Simpson and 8399 Private R Smith, to Brigade Headquarters.

The two sergeants had been out with the battalion since September 1914. 8555 Sergeant Peter Anslow a Gateshead man, would end the war as a Company Sergeant Major with the award of the Meritorious Service Medal shortly after the armistice he was commissioned and served with 1/Durham LI in the Army of the Rhine. The other, 8915 Sergeant Joseph Turton, who as we have already seen was a policeman at Byers Green, would win the Military Medal and was promoted to Company Sergeant Major before being killed in action on 21 March 1918.

The number of Private Robert Smith had been sent in wrongly, for it should have read 4/8399, a special reservist from Sunderland; having arrived in France in November 1914, he would survive the war and be transferred to class Z Reserve in 1918. Unfortunately nothing further has been traced about Private Simpson.

On 10 May the battalion front was quiet but there was some artillery fire on the battalion on the right. That night on the left battalion front, it was suspected that the enemy unit opposite was being relieved; therefore the British Artillery put a barrage on the German trenches for two hours between 2130 and 2330 hours. This brought swift retaliation from the enemy gunners who shelled the roads and tracks near the East Canal Bank. There were no casualties amongst 2/Durham LI; however the Commanding Officer was evacuated to the Field Ambulance.

The same night Captain Frederick Newstead rejoined from hospital. The same pattern followed the next day, a quiet morning and then the enemy opened up with howitzers, shelling the area between Marocco Farm and Pond Farm; this lasted until late afternoon but fortunately there was only one man wounded. From the support position at Elverdinghe, A Company was sent up to provide digging and carrying parties and to assist with the reconstruction of the damaged trenches. On 12 May there was only one fifteen-minute period of shelling when the Germans shelled from 'The Mile' to 'Lancashire Farm' with shrapnel. When the shelling had ceased the rest of the day passed quietly until that night the battalion was relieved by 11/Essex Regiment. The Durhams marched down to the light railway and were carried back to Camp G. On the way out they came under shellfire and two men were wounded. The usual cleaning up and kit inspections took place and on 14 May the battalion was allotted the baths in Poperinghe, A and C companies in the morning and B and D in the afternoon, and that evening in the camp there was a service for those of the Church of England faith and the Commanding Officer returned to the battalion from the Field Ambulance. The Companies paraded under their own Commanders for the next two days and carried out training. But each day the German Air Force visited the camp dropping bombs as they went; however, their aim was poor and no damage or casualties occurred.

It was about this time that a soldier of the battalion, and a habitual absentee, decided that he would go absent yet again. 4/9170 Private George Hunter had arrived in France on 24 August 1915 and in less than a year already been absent no less than ten times; indeed on one occasion he had even managed to cross the Channel and return to England.

On the night of 17 May the battalion, less B Company, boarded the light railway and were transported up to Ypres Asylum and from there they marched up to the Canal Bank and from there to the front line trenches. B Company in the meanwhile marched up from Camp G to Elverdinghe Chateau. During the day a message was received from the Army Commander, congratulating the Commanding Officer on his newly gazetted DSO. In the early hours the enemy machine-gunners kept up an active fire on the line held by both the front-line companies. Casualties were light over the next few days: four wounded and only one man killed, 8843 Private John Burdis who had been out with the battalion from the very start. Later one of those wounded, 22655 Private Albert Furn, who hailed from Lillingstone Dayrell a village in Buckinghamshire, died from his wounds; he had survived long enough to reach a hospital on the coast at Wimereux, but sadly succumbed to his wounds.

On 19 May the enemy mortared the front line and it was described as a 'lively' night as the mortaring continued. Second Lieutenant Thomas Veitch arrived at Battalion Headquarters and on reporting his arrival was posted to D Company. During the night the enemy machine-gunners kept up a desultory fire and their trench mortars dropped a number of bombs on the line. These caused the death of 3/11961 Private Thomas Newby from Gateshead, and another man was wounded. Second Lieutenant John Caswell was sent down to the Field Ambulance. During the night a working party was out repairing a gap in the wire and they came under fire from the German trench mortars and their machine guns were active throughout the night. On 22 May Second Lieutenant Frank Morris went down to the Field Ambulance and that afternoon the enemy shelled the dugouts on the Canal Bank but caused no casualties. A party of about twenty Germans were spotted working and the battalion Lewis guns opened up on them, causing an estimated seven casualties. At 0100 hours a group of around thirty Germans was seen to be advancing towards the battalion positions. The front line 'stood to' and threw bombs at the Germans, then rifle and Lewis gun fire was brought to bear on them and they eventually dispersed and retired to their own lines. Later a German aeroplane flew low over the Canal Bank and dropped two bombs. After dark a patrol went out to examine some trenches that had been evacuated by another unit. The patrol found that they were full of water and it was probably for this reason that the Germans had not occupied them. At some stage during the day 10564 Sergeant Thomas Meginnis, a Jarrow man, was killed in action. When things had settled down a new draft of some thirty other ranks came up and joined the battalion and was sent straight into the line to join their allotted companies. During the night of 24 May the enemy mortared the left front company and 3/9452 Private John Steel, another Jarrow man, but resident at High Pittington near Durham, was killed. At the same time the German howitzers fired a number of shells at Marocco Farm, then by 0040 hours the battalion was relieved by 1/West Yorkshire Regiment.

They moved back to the support dugouts on the Canal Bank, and deployed HQ, C and D Companies on the West Bank and A and B Companies on the East Bank. Here they came under enemy shellfire and B Company suffered a direct hit on one of their dugouts; later a working party also came under fire and in total there were nineteen casualties. Second Lieutenant John S. Palmer joined the battalion and was posted to C Company and Second Lieutenant Laurence Hartshorn went to the Field Ambulance. The next four days were very quiet, the only points of note being that the CO had gone to England on leave and a German plane was shot down near Ellian Farm.

On 29 May Second Lieutenant W. Griffith Jones returned from hospital; there was only a little shelling on a few different parts of the battalion front, which resulted in one man being wounded. In the afternoon of 31 May the British Corps Heavy Artillery and the 6th Divisional Artillery, along with some French Artillery units began to shell the enemy front line, this was reasonably successful and knocked the enemy trenches in. However, the downside was that the Germans retaliated with whizzbangs against the British front and support lines held by 2/Durham LI, with the result that four men, Privates 9089 Wilson Bell and 11964 George Shaw from Hartlepool, 12363 Samuel Dent from Durham and 10798 Tom Stockton from Thornaby were all killed and eleven others wounded. Later that day Second Lieutenant Laurence Hartshorn returned to the battalion from hospital.

At the beginning of June there were some changes in the disposition of the companies, which resulted in A Company becoming the left-hand company of the British Army in Flanders and they manned a joint Liaison Post with the French. On 3 June 1/West Yorkshire Regiment conducted a well-planned raid to retake a position known as 'The Old British Trench'; to assist in this operation 2/Durham LI provided a working party, whose objective was to bridge a gap on the left of the recaptured position. There were a number of casualties: Second Lieutenant Charles Thompson, from Bromley, Kent was killed in action and Second Lieutenant Laurence Hartshorn was wounded. Of the wounded other ranks, 11661 Private Christopher Parkinson, from Carrville near Durham City, died of his wounds and today is buried in Lissjenthoek Military Cemetery. His brother received a letter which was printed in the *Durham Chronicle*:

News of the death from wounds of Private C Parkinson, Carrville 2/Durham LI, in France has been received by his brother, Mr E Parkinson, Gilesgate Moor, who has received the following letter:

No 3 Canadian CCS June 8

My Dear Mr Parkinson I promised your brother, C Parkinson of 2nd D.L.I. that I would write to you. You will have already learned of his death. He was brought to our hospital but all we could do was to make him comfortable and he passed to his well earned rest on June 4. We have had his body laid away in our cemetery on the CENSORED road and a cross will mark his grave. He was such a fine, brave fellow, and while you mourn you will remember him with pride.

Yours very sincerely

W L Archer Captain Chaplain, Church of England.

William Lawrence Archer was a Canadian Padre from London, Ontario; he had enlisted in October 1915 and had been at the CCS for a number of months.

Another fatality occurred the following day and was also reported in the *Durham Chronicle*. Said to be the first fatality of a Meadowfield resident, the death of 8798 Corporal Joseph Hunter, on 4 June 1916, of the Machine Gun Section 2/Durham LI was reported in this way:

Hunter joined the army at the outbreak of war and had been about twelve months in France. For three months at the beginning of this year he was in hospital with trench fever. In a letter to Mrs Hunter his friend, Corporal G T Brown, states that, 'the Germans dropped a large shell in the trench and Corporal Hunter was killed instantly. He was a good soldier and died like a Britisher at his post'. Corporal Hunter was twenty seven years of age and worked at Browney Colliery prior to the war. He took an interest in football. He leaves a widow and two children.

However for some reason the unit details were incorrect, for although he had been serving with 2/Durham LI, Corporal Hunter had transferred to the Machine Gun Corps and at the time of his death was serving with 17 Brigade Machine Gun Company. Although still part of 6th Division he would have been some distance from the action involving 2/Durham LI.

On the night of 4 June, B Company continued digging a trench to the recaptured trench and a covering patrol came across a German patrol, on which they opened fire and managed to force them back, having one man wounded in the brief fight. Over the next two days the enemy concentrated his fire on the battalion left flank and the point where it joined with the French. Whizzbangs, machine guns and snipers were very active, very probably trying to open a gap between the allied forces. This type of firing continued over the next few days: on 7 June, nineteen other ranks were wounded and on 8 June, when howitzers joined in, four men were killed. One spot that received particular attention was Talana Farm.

The CO now returned from leave and a draft of twenty-one other ranks arrived from the Base Depot. On 11 June there was a little shelling during the day and then that night 14/Durham LI came up and relieved 2/Durham LI. The relief was complete by midnight and the battalion marched back to the light railway. They were transported back to camps in the rear, HQ, A and D Companies to Camp G and B and C Companies to Camp P. They were all in by 0235 hours without any casualties en route. The following morning the Commanding Officer inspected the new draft and C and D Companies were sent to the new divisional baths, followed in the afternoon by A Company. On 14 June the GOC 6th Division, Major General Ross CB, DSO, inspected and then addressed the battalion and the same day Lieutenant W. E. Harker left the battalion on transfer to the Royal Flying Corps. That night at 2300 hours a new daylight saving system was taken into use.

The next day at 1330 hours the whole battalion paraded outside P Camp and marched to Houtkerque, where they were billeted in the village. The march continued the next day to Wormhoudt and again billeted, but that night a German aeroplane came over and dropped bombs on the village. The next day a draft of nineteen men arrived and then at 1415 hours the march was resumed, this time to Volckerinckhove. Here the battalion had a whole day's rest, Second Lieutenant Walter H.

Frith was promoted Temporary Captain to command A Company and two new officers, Second Lieutenants James Crawford and Frederick Vickery arrived from 16/Durham LI.

Volckerinckhove, was the site of a training area, where they could practise entrenching. Each day from 0900 hours until 1200 hours and then in the afternoon from 1400 hours until 1700 hours the battalion were employed digging on the training area. In the evenings the 6th Divisional Band played in the town square to the off duty men.

By now 4/9170 Private George Hunter had been apprehended and then arrested by the Military Police. After enquiries were made into why he was in Calais and what and where his actual unit was, he was charged and found guilty and sentenced to trial by Court Martial. The Court Martial of 4/9170 Private George Hunter took place on 22 June 1916 when the prosecution read out the list of times he had absented himself from the front and that he had also been convicted for a self-inflicted wound. In his defence George Hunter stated that he had suffered from a 'wandering mind'. It didn't take the court long to find him guilty and sentence him to death. However, the Commanding Officer noted on the proceedings of the court martial, that he thought Private Hunter was suffering from a mental defect and should be seen by a doctor. The documents were then sent up through the chain of command and eventually the sentence was confirmed.

On 23 June another thirty men arrived and were allotted to their new companies. The next day Lieutenant James Jones returned from the SECOND ARMY School and reassumed command of A Company, Temporary Captain W. H. Frith having to revert to Second Lieutenant. The battalion having constructed positions now trained in attacking them by platoons. Apart from Divine Service on the Sunday the period from 24–28 June was spent training for the attack: they progressed to Company and then Battalion attack. However, on 28 June heavy rain cancelled the morning training, but on the afternoon they were practising a Brigade attack. This continued the next day and on 30 June it had progressed to a Brigade night attack. The battalion was in position by 0215 hours and the attack commenced at 0300 hours. All was complete by 0530 hours and the men were on their way back to billets.

What was all this attacking training for? As the 18 Brigade were taking part in this training, away to the south the men of the FOURTH ARMY and to a lesser extent the THIRD ARMY were about to start the Battle of the Somme. 6th Division were not needed just yet, but as we shall read later it wouldn't be long before they were called for.

Chapter Five

1916 July–December, South to the Somme

On the morning of 1 July 1916 2/Durham LI marched away from Volckerinckhove bound for Winnerzeele. In the early afternoon the battalion halted at Arneke and the battalion cooks served a hot meal, after which they continued trudging along the pave towards their billets for the night in Winnerzeele. Here they were rejoined by Second Lieutenant John Caswell on his return from hospital. On the following morning the march continued to Camp N, which was situated on the Poperinghe–Proven road.

That day the battalion was, however, short of a number of men, for a firing party had been formed and taken to where 4/9170 Private George Hunter was waiting to be executed. On 2 July, most likely at dawn, the sentence of death by firing squad was duly carried out. Afterwards the firing party would have returned to the battalion.

On the afternoon of 3 July, Lieutenant General the Earl of Cavan, Commander XIV Corps, inspected the battalion and afterwards addressed the assembled men. Then came the time for some hard work: 200 men were sent to the Royal Engineers for railway construction work on a new light railway and that night a further 100 men were sent to work for the Corps Signals; this work involved laying and burying signal cable. On 4 July the rain was bad enough to stop the cable-burying work but not enough to stop the railway construction. The 20th (Light) Division had set up a bath unit in Poperinghe and 2/Durham LI managed to get fifty men per company a bath during the day, no doubt due to the scrounging ability of the Battalion Quartermaster.

The fatigues continued until 8 July; the day before on 7 July orders had been received for a possible move at twenty-four hours, notice. Hence all kits and blankets were packed and sent to the Poperinghe railhead. Later a message came in that the planned move was unlikely to take place and the Companies paraded under their own arrangements. The Divisional Gas Officer visited the battalion and gave lectures to the officers and NCOs and then inspected all the battalion gas helmets. During the day Second Lieutenant Harry Johnson reported from 17/Durham LI and was posted to A Company. The working party for the Corps Signals continued overnight. As the impending move had been cancelled, the work for the RE Railway Company and the Corps Signals continued daily until 12 July; those not employed on the working parties were training. It was during this training that a tragic accident occurred. Whilst one company was training on the bombing range there was a bomb explosion which resulted in the death of Second Lieutenant William Griffith Jones: born and brought up in Aberystwyth, the 26 year-old officer had, when war broke out, returned to England from the Straits Settlement, where he was an assistant manager on a rubber plantation. Also killed in the incident was 3/12055 Private John Wile who hailed from Hetton-le-Hole in County Durham; he had only been at the front since the previous December. Injured in the incident were Second Lieutenant John Caswell and four men. The next day the funerals of the two dead men took place in Poperinghe New Military Cemetery and then in the afternoon the battalion held a sports day, in which all the competitions were strongly contested. It was now time for the battalion to go back into the line and at 1200 hours on 14 July, 1/Buffs arrived to take over the camp.

At 2000 hours having handed over the camp, they marched out to the railhead and boarded a train for the Asylum in Ypres. Having arrived without mishap, they marched up to the Canal Bank and relieved 11/Rifle Brigade. They spent the night in these reserve trenches and the following afternoon the advance parties were sent up to the front line to begin the relief of 10/Rifle Brigade at Wieltje. Once darkness fell C and D Companies went up and occupied the front line, whilst A and B Companies took up residence in the support line. The relief was complete by 0050 hours. During the day Second Lieutenant Robert Chatt was evacuated to the Field Ambulance. After a quiet day, that night the enemy opened up with a minenwerfer; after this had fired a number of rounds, the British howitzers were brought to bear on it and it was quickly silenced. Second Lieutenant George Garland returned from hospital and along with him another four junior officers, Second Lieutenants Alexander Dunn, Arthur Cave, W. B. Judd and Claude Barrington, reported their arrival at Battalion Headquarters. On the afternoon of 17 July the 20th Divisional Artillery bombarded the enemy trenches in front of the battalion, cutting the wire in front of B Company. This brought retaliatory fire from the German gunners, who concentrated their fire on Battalion Headquarters in St Jean. They managed to hit the headquarters twice but caused no damage; sadly, however, 25286 Private John Swalwell from Medomsley, County Durham was killed in action. Apart from some activity by the German Air Force there wasn't much happening on 19 July and then that night 14/Durham LI came up and relieved the battalion, who moved back to billets at the south end of the Yser Canal. From these reserve positions working parties were sent out to assist in carrying stores and supplies up to the front line. One party of 150 men was still away from the battalion when it was relieved by 2/Sherwood Foresters. The handover was complete by 2320 hours on 22 July and the battalion, less the working party, were conveyed to Camp C, by train, where they arrived at 0030 hours. The working party eventually rejoined the battalion at 0430 hours. The last few days of July were spent cleaning up, refitting and bathing. Once the cleaning up was done the Companies paraded under their own arrangements and began training. There were a few working parties, mainly burying cable for the Corps Signal Company. On 27 July Second Lieutenant Robert Chatt returned from hospital. There was a battalion route march on 28 July, under the command of Second Lieutenant Charles Gibbens, while all the other officers went on a Divisional Instruction day. Then on 30 July they marched to the point where the light railway crossed the Poperinghe–Crombeke road and here they entrained for Wormhoudt. Early on the morning of 31 July, at 0730 hours, the battalion paraded and had another route march and then had the rest of the day off, owing to it being a particularly hot day.

The training continued on the following day, but owing to the heat, at lunch-time there was a 'stand down'. While the men were training, the senior officers reported to Brigade Headquarters, where at 1430 hours all Battalion Commanders were interviewed by General Sir Herbert Plumer, GCMG, KCB, commanding SECOND ARMY.

To the south on 1 July the British and French had opened the Somme Offensive; whilst on the right flank of the British attack, alongside the French, there was minor success, generally along the whole of the British front the day had been a disaster. As July wore on the British repeatedly attacked and suffered accordingly; worn-out divisions were replaced with fresh troops, or as fresh as could be expected in the case of the 6th Division who were now under orders to move south. In the early morning on 2 August, A Company and the Transport Section paraded in the main square at Wormhoudt. Platoon Sergeants would have called the roll of their respective platoons and when all the men were accounted for, a report would have been made to the Company Sergeant Major, who in turn informed the Company Second in Command or Officer Commanding, that all were present. Then when all was ready at 0645 hours they proceeded by route march to the railhead at Esquelbecq station. The remaining three companies paraded in turn in the town square at Wormhoudt and followed on at 0810 hours. At Esquelbecq the battalion entrained on the notorious cattle trucks of the French National Railways, with their sign, '8 Chevaux, 40 Hommes'. This train carried the battalion as far as Doullens, where they detrained and set off by march route for billets in Amplier. Left behind were two officers and 100 men who were tasked with unloading all of the 6th Divisional transport and when finished they rejoined the battalion later that night. Early on the morning of 3 August the battalion went for a route march and then owing to the hot weather they were allowed to have a bathing parade. Also during the day Second Lieutenants W. B. Judd and C. M. J. Barrington reported sick and were sent to the nearest Field Ambulance for treatment.

The following day, the Commanding Officer, Adjutant, the Company Commanders and the Sniping Officer were carried by motor bus up to the village of Mesnil and were given a tour of the front-line trenches in the sector north of the River Ancre, which they would soon take over. During this trip Second Lieutenant John Palmer was slightly wounded but remained at duty. The battalion in the meantime had paraded in the square at Amplier and then proceeded by march route to Acheux. More route-marching came their way the next day when the companies were put at the disposal of the Company Commanders. This was followed on the next day by a church service in the morning and then after lunch they paraded ready to go into the trenches. The sector to be taken over was the right sector of the divisional front, which was north of the village of Hamel, on the northern bank of the River Ancre. At 1300 hours the battalion began its trek towards the line to commence the relief of 8/Loyal North Lancashire Regiment of the 25th Division.

By 2300 hours the relief had been completed without mishap, A Company had taken over the right front section of the line and B Company held the left section. C Company was in support in the village of Hamel and D Company was further back in reserve positions in the village of Mesnil. The German sentries must have been alert and heard the relief taking place, for within fifteen minutes A Company had come under barrage from enemy minenwerfers. Whilst in the reserve positions D Company were forced to don their respirators as the German Artillery dropped around fifty lachrymatory shells on their positions. The next day was fairly quiet but around 1630 hours the enemy shelled Battalion Headquarters where one man was wounded. That night the right-hand sector of the front line in Gordon Trench came under fire and sadly Captain Frederick Newstead, aged twenty-four, from Blyth in Northumberland was killed. In the early hours of the following morning enemy field gunners opened fire on Burrell Avenue and then at 0400 hours the support positions in Hamel Village received a short five-minute barrage during which one man was wounded and 27449 Private Owen Murray was killed. Nineteen years of age, he came from Raglan Street, South Shields. These last two fatalities lie next to each other in Martinsart British Cemetery.

The shelling continued on 9 August. In the early evening Battalion Headquarters received their share of the German iron rations and later, at 2315 hours the front

Captain Frederick L. Newstead from Blyth in Northumberland was educated at Durham School and the Durham University College of Medicine at Newcastle. He was killed in action on 6 August 1916 and is buried in Martinsart British Cemetery.

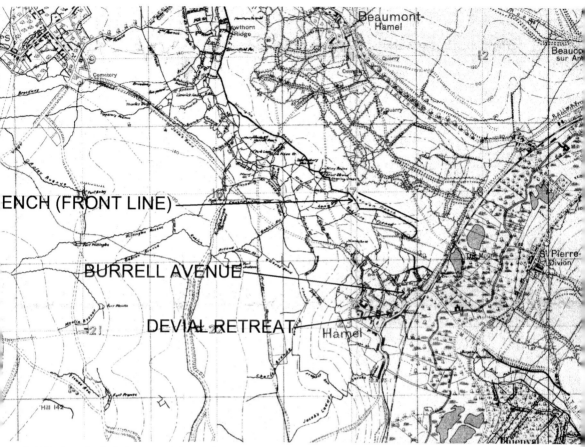

ENCH (FRONT LINE)

BURRELL AVENUE

DEVIAL RETREAT

2nd Durham Light Infantry positions taken up on arrival on the Somme Front, August 1916.

and support lines were shelled; fortunately there were no fatalities and only five men were wounded. A pattern was starting to build in the enemy shelling, again on 10 August in the early hours Devial Retreat was heavily attacked with whizzbangs. In reply the British fired lachrymatory shells from the area of the Watteau Road. This brought immediate retaliation from the German Artillery who put a box barrage around the Battalion Headquarters of 2/Durham LI and the trenches occupied near Burrell Avenue. This barrage resulted in the deaths of three men of the battalion: 9733 Private Samuel Hardy, who came from Leamside, near Durham 19/1028 Private William Allen, an 18-year-old Bantam from Hebburn Colliery, and 4/7857 Private John Mannion, a 34-year-old married man from Jarrow. The first two are buried in the small cemetery at Hamel and the latter is buried a few rows from Captain Newstead in the cemetery at Martinsart.

For the next two days the same pattern continued: in the early hours of 11 August the enemy once again shelled Battalion Headquarters and once again they concentrated on Roberts Trench which lay immediately behind Gordon Trench, the front line. However, the rest of the day was recorded in the War Diary as 'A quiet day'. Then at 0015 hours on 12 August the front right company came under enemy artillery fire; this gradually died out but at 0200 hours the front line position, 'Gordon Trench' came under a heavy bombardment when the Germans sent over many shrapnel shells until 0215 hours. Then at 0945 hours the front line stood to: 'Here they come' the cry would have run down the front-line trench, as the Germans launched an attack against a position known as 'Mill Post'. Rapid fire rang out from the rifles and Lewis guns of the Durhams, and eventually the enemy fell back leaving a wounded corporal behind. The stretcher-bearers went out: he was a wounded soldier, his uniform didn't matter, and he was brought in to safety, however, shortly after being carried to safety he died. The Battalion War Diary also records that, 'A German officer was wounded', however, it doesn't say if he was captured or not. As the attack petered out later that afternoon 11/Essex Regiment came up and took over the line from the Durhams, trudged back to billets in Beaussart.

During the early stages of the Somme battles German prisoners are brought in.

The battalion rested in Beaussart on 13 August, from where Second Lieutenant Hubert V. Stockton was sent away to the Field Ambulance. The next day on 14 August the battalion moved off to bivouacs in Mailly-Maillet Wood. Once settled the routine task of working parties came the battalion's way. Although some men were allowed to go to the Divisional Baths, the Royal Engineers were always short of carrying parties, so no sooner than the battalion was settled than working parties were on their way to the front. The following day the Companies practised attacking under company arrangements and further working parties were provided. On 16 August all training was cancelled on account of the number of men that were working for the Royal Engineers and also for 18 Brigade Headquarters.

Also that day the Commanding Officer, Lieutenant Colonel Arthur Irvine DSO, was summoned to 18 Brigade Headquarters, where he took over temporary command of the brigade, the command of the battalion passing to Major Henry Taylor. The next day training was again cancelled and a large party of over 300 men went up into the line and proceeded to dig a trench to the south of Roberts Trench. Whilst employed on this task the party came under heavy shellfire from the German Artillery and minenwerfers, so much so that the Royal Engineer officer in charge ordered the withdrawal of the working party. The shelling caused a number of casualties; fourteen men were wounded and 4/10201 Lance Corporal Bertie Alderson from Spennymoor was killed, whilst one poor unnamed soul wandered away and was posted as missing, however, the entry in the Battalion War Diary is amended with the words 'since returned'.

The working parties continued over the next three days; the only event of note was the return of the Commanding Officer on 19 August. He arrived just in time to join the battalion as it went back into the line, taking over same sector from 11/Essex Regiment. This time C and D Companies held the front line, B Company were in support in Hamel and A Company in reserve in Mesnil; the relief was completed and everyone was in position by midnight on 20 August. During the night the German minenwerfers were busy shelling the battalion front and later in the day they turned their attention on Battalion Headquarters. But no casualties occurred. The front line, Gordon Trench, came under attack at 2300 hours. The sentries in the front line were on the alert and they located a German working party repairing the wire opposite Gordon Trench. Quietly a Lewis gun was brought to bear and at 0230 hours the gun team opened up on the Germans and very quickly dispersed them. The enemy artillery replied and five men, 19824 Private John Reed, 22252 Private Edward Bell, 10226 Corporal Arthur Dodds, 12305 Lance Corporal Albert Botham and 3/9174 Private Thomas Bentham were wounded. The last named, a 25-year-old Jarrow man, who had been out at the front since October 1914 died of his wounds at the Field Ambulance based in the village of Couin, about 8 miles behind the line. Another man evacuated with shellshock that day was Second Lieutenant Robert Chatt originally a sergeant in the battalion he had been commissioned into the Connaught Rangers, but was posted back to the battalion.

On 23 August it was the turn of the left company to receive the enemy's attention. Around midday they shelled the left front line quite heavily and 30038 Private Harry Parkinson was wounded. The reserve company in Mesnil didn't escape the shelling and they suffered a two-hour-long barrage between 2000 and 2200 hours on the night of 24 August. The next day passed fairly quietly and the men must have been quite pleased to see the officers of 1/6/Cheshire Regiment going round the trenches, a sure sign that relief was imminent. However, during the morning the Germans shelled Gordon Trench and 4/10159, Private Ernest Whitehead was wounded in the buttock and 27318 Private Michael McCabe, who came from West Hartlepool, was killed. Then at 1300 hours 1/6/Cheshire Regiment arrived and commenced to take over the front line, support and reserve positions. When the handover was complete 2/Durham LI moved off and proceeded to march to a bivouac camp just north of Acheux where they spent the night. Whilst here, Second Lieutenant Robert Chatt returned from the Field Ambulance. The next day they continued moving towards the rear area and the day's march took them to Amplier. After bivouacking overnight they continued on the next day to Longuevillette. Here Lieutenant Colonel Hanway Robert Cumming arrived and took over command from Lieutenant Colonel Irvine. Colonel Cumming had last served with the regiment in 1902; commissioned from the militia in 1889 he had risen to Captain by the time the Boer War broke out. In that conflict he had served on the staff as a Railway Transport Officer. This had been followed between 1902 and 1914 with many staff appointments. His appointment to the command of the battalion was to assist him on his promotion to Brigadier General, for without a field command he couldn't rise to the next rank. The following morning the battalion rose early and after a hasty breakfast they fell in on parade at 0820 hours and set off for the training area near the village of Vignacourt.

Once settled in their new home the first thing to do was to get the men cleaned up and refitted. Parades and inspections were held under company arrangements, equipment and uniforms were cleaned and any items that were worn out or useless were exchanged for serviceable items where possible. Second Lieutenant Lawrence Alec Hartshorn arrived from Number One Officer Cadet Battalion and was posted to B Company. Now training had started in earnest, particular attention was paid to training to attack prepared enemy positions, and as August passed into September the Battalion War Diary recorded the following details as to the trench strength, which was given as officers twenty, other ranks 713. Employed

German prisoners are brought in across the Somme battlefield.

elsewhere but on battalion strength, were two officers and ninety-eight men. During August there had been one officer and seven other ranks killed and thirty-nine other ranks wounded. Another drain on the battalion strength was the fact that men with specialist civilian occupations were still being sent back to England to work in the heavy industries that supported the war effort. Two men, whose civilian occupation was given as marine engineer, were sent away from 2/Durham LI in August for this reason; 3/10181 Private John Hawthorn who had been at the front since December 1914 and 3/10106 Private David Stewart who had been in Flanders since July 1915. On 27 October 1916 the London Gazette carried the news that John Hawthorn had been awarded the Military Medal.

1 September began for the battalion with an address by the Assistant Instructor of Physical Training and Bayonet Fighting. This was followed by more training for attacking enemy positions, with doubtless many dummies being bayoneted by Durham steel as the men were fired up by the instructors. The next phase of training, Brigade operations, began the

next day but that afternoon the battalion was allotted the use of the Divisional baths between 1300 hours and 1500 hours. Four new subalterns arrived at Battalion Headquarters during the day and were allotted to companies as follows: Second Lieutenant Cuthbert Green went to A Company, Second Lieutenant Henry Barclay and Second Lieutenant Henry Carss both went to B Company and Second Lieutenant Hugh Chamberlin was told to report to C Company. Over the next three days the Brigade Training continued and all ranks could easily tell that very soon they would be back in the thick of things on the Somme front. Sergeant Major Joseph Watson DCM returned to the battalion on 5 September and took up the post of battalion Regimental Sergeant Major. The time had come to start back for the line and the first day's march along the cobbled French roads took the battalion to Coisy where they spent the night. This was followed by another day of marching which took them to Sailly-le-Sec.

The next day was a partial rest day and attack training was carried out but no further marching. Two new officers, Lieutenant Joscelyn Edward Percy and Second Lieutenant Leonard Birtles arrived with a draft of fifty other ranks. Lieutenant Percy joined B Company and Birtles with all of the other ranks reported to A Company. When the battalion went off to training the draft stayed behind and was inspected by the Commanding Officer. The final training was carried out on the night of 10 September; that night a whole Brigade night operation was practised and this was followed next day by a move to the Sandpit area near Mealte. The next day took them closer to the front when a march took them up to the area of the Citadel south of Fricourt. Here another small draft of sixteen men arrived. The officers were taken forward to reconnoitre the trenches the battalion was to occupy south of Trones Wood. The Commanding Officer, however, didn't go forward with the rest of the party, remaining behind he inspected the new draft. Next day word arrived that the CO was to be attached to 18 Brigade Headquarters and that Major Alfred Irvine would resume temporary command of the battalion. Another officer on the move was Captain Henry Taylor who took over the command of 6/Royal Irish Regiment.

The other two brigades of the Division, along with the Guards and 56th Divisions had been heavily involved in trying to take a German position known as the Quadrilateral. Whilst the other two brigades would try a converging attack from the north, west and south, 18 Brigade would be brought up from the rear through the Guards Division. 11/Essex Regiment formed up north-west of Leuze Wood, whilst 2/Durham LI moved two companies into a position known as the Triangle. The mission of the Durhams was to bomb down Straight Trench which would lead them right into the Quadrilateral. At midday the battalion moved up from Trones Wood and through the Guards to a position known as

Second Lieutenant Robert J. Meikle had joined the battalion on 6 March and was killed in action on 15 September 1916; he is buried in the Guards Cemetery at Lesboeufs, France.

Guillemont–Wedgewood trench and then from there to the Triangle. The assault was timed to start at 1930 hours but both battalions were new to the ground and had scarcely got into position before it was time to start the attack. The Corps heavy artillery provided a barrage to cover the advance but most of the shells exploded harmlessly behind the enemy position. Promptly at the allotted time both units advanced; 11/Essex Regiment came under heavy enemy machine-gun fire from the Germans in the Bouleaux Wood and was forced to withdraw. 2/Durham LI fought their way down Straight Trench and managed to take about 500 yards of it before they were held up. Nothing further could be done in the dark and it wasn't until next morning that a further advance was made. However there was an enemy strongpoint with a heavy machine gun in it that held up the attack. Casualties had been rather heavy on the night of 15 September: Captain Bertie Baty and Second Lieutenant Robert Meikle were killed and Captain Edward Hughes and Second Lieutenants Laurence Hartshorn, Alfred Watson, John Dudley and James Crawford were wounded. During the morning attack the following day Second Lieutenant Leonard Birtles was killed and Captain George Garland and Second Lieutenant Hugh Chamberlin wounded.

Later in the day Captain Edward Hughes died from his wounds.

The attack against Straight Trench by the 2nd Durham Light Infantry.

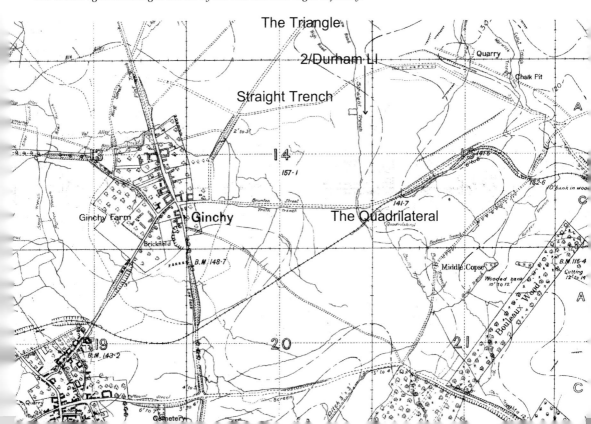

Among the men thirty had been killed, ninety-nine wounded and thirty-four were missing. That night a battalion of the West Yorkshire Regiment relieved 2/Durham LI, who moved back to Trones Wood into bivouacs. They then moved forward into a support position in Guillemont named Wedgwood Trench, and whilst 2/Durham LI were in this position the rest of 18 Brigade including 14/Durham LI attacked and captured the Quadrilateral. Between 0100 and 0200 hours on 19 September 8/Bedfordshire Regiment came up and relieved 2/Durham LI who moved back to a valley south of Montauban, where they bivouacked until 0900 hours, when they marched back to Meaulte. Here they began refitting and cleaning up yet again; officers and NCOs going round the men checking equipment, did the men have everything, replacing what had been lost where possible. In many cases equipment was recovered from the dead lying unburied on the battlefield, or brought in by salvage and burial parties and put back into use.

During the day Second Lieutenant Samuel Fox Jarrett arrived with a draft of forty men from the base depot. When war broke out Samuel Jarrett was working as a postal clerk in Canada: having already served four years between 1909 and 1913 in 6/Durham LI as a lieutenant prior to emigrating, he immediately volunteered for the Canadian Expeditionary Force and found himself serving as a private in the 11th Battalion of the CEF; he was very soon promoted to the rank of sergeant. When more officers were required for the Imperial Army he was an obvious choice for a commission, which he received in October 1915. Having refitted and absorbed the draft, at 2200 hours the battalion made its way back to Trones Wood and then at 0700 hours moved on to Ginchy where they relieved 2/Coldstream Guards in the trenches to the north-east of Ginchy. All throughout 22 September they suffered from heavy enemy shelling and next day they were employed in digging an assembly and jumping-off trench. At 0245 hours on 24 September 14/Durham LI came up and took over the task from 2/Durham LI who moved back once again to Trones Wood. They were not there long and scarcely had time to rest before at 2300 hours they moved straight back and took over from 14/Durham LI again and moved straight into the assembly trenches that they had been digging the previous day. The day was fine and sunny with some haze.

During the night the Germans had shelled the assembly trenches but there was only some sporadic shelling during the morning, which resulted in Second Lieutenant Stanley Dalziel being evacuated with shellshock. There was now to be an attack along the whole front of XIV Corps; at 0135 hours the 5th, 6th and Guards Divisions resumed the attack with the objective of taking the sunken road west of Les Boeufs. In 6th Division this was to be done

11007 Sergeant William Mason from Shildon, Co Durham, was awarded t Military Medal in Octo 1916; posted to 19/Durh LI in 1917 he was awar the DCM in 1919.

by two battalions of 18 Brigade, 11/Essex Regiment on the right and 2/Durham LI who had on their left 1/Buffs (East Kent Regiment) of 16 Brigade. At precisely 1235 hours the British creeping barrage crashed down 200 yards in front of the British line. In the assembly trenches the officers blew their whistles and the leading waves set off for the German trenches. Staying as close as they could to the barrage, the battalion went forward and entered the sunken road; after a brief but bloody action with the bomb and the bayonet, they succeeded in capturing some 200 unwounded German soldiers along with three officers, three machine guns and a great deal of artillery ammunition.

Almost immediately they began the business of consolidation; a new trench had to be dug to the east of the old position. Thankfully casualties were light, the prisoners were sent away under escort to the Divisional cage and soon every available man was at work with pick, shovel and sandbag. Later two companies were withdrawn to the old front line, a precaution against enemy artillery, which kept up its fire during the day and the night. This move was made in case there was any counter-attack by the Germans. During the day Second Lieutenant Robert Chatt was evacuated again suffering from shellshock, he was replaced by Second Lieutenant Charles Heppleston who was rejoining from hospital. For the next two days the battalion worked strengthening and improving the new trench; any serviceable equipment was salvaged and sent back down the line to be refurbished and reissued when needed. A party of men was sent back to the area of the Quadrilateral to search for the bodies of those who had been reported missing in the previous attack. Those that were found had their webbing removed and were given a hasty burial. The location of the graves was noted and passed on to the Graves registration unit. At 0200 hours one company of 1/Sherwood Foresters and one company of 9/Norfolk Regiment arrived and relieved 2/Durham LI who moved back to bivouacs in map square A.2.c between Montauban and Pommiers. After resting as best they could they set off at 1300 hours on 29 September for Meaulte where they were billeted overnight. The next day the battalion only had a short march of around 5 miles from Meaulte to Mericourt l'Abbe. So at the end of September the casualty list was far bigger than the previous month with three officers killed and nine wounded and in the ranks thirty-eight were dead, 190 wounded and nineteen missing. Although the strength in officers was the same, the trench strength was well down in men as only 545 men were available. The partial casualty list attached to the Battalion War Diary for the month shows that one man was evacuated with self-inflicted wounds, the obvious strain of the front line being too much for him.

On 1 October the whole of 18 Infantry Brigade assembled at Treux and a Divine Service was held. 2/Durham LI then marched back to Mericourt l'Abbe where they were addressed by the Brigade Commander, Brigadier

General R. J. Bridgford. There was the usual period of refitting and then training commenced; replacement specialists had to be trained to bring the battalion back up to strength in Lewis gunners, signallers and rifle grenadiers. There was also an NCO course started to train those men with the potential to take over as Non Commissioned Officers. Those not involved in this training were involved in physical training, foot drill and arms drill. The men of the new drafts were also given instruction in bayonet fighting. Then on 4 October the Deputy Director of Medical Services visited the battalion and inspected all the old men in the battalion. Just as with the horses a number of men would be 'cast' as unfit for front-line duty and sent down to the base, most likely to be transferred to the Labour Corps. During this period of training Second Lieutenant L. D. Haggie, from Sheraton Hall, Castle Eden, previously a private in the Grenadier Guards, reported for duty and along with him Second Lieutenant Joseph Tindle rejoined from hospital in England. On 5 October a small draft of twenty-eight other ranks came up from the base depot. Having spent 6 October at the disposal of the Company Commanders, at 1000 hours the next morning the bugles sounded 'Fall In' and very soon they were tramping along the French roads, away from the peaceful village of Mericourt l'Abbe towards the Citadel and the front line once again. On reaching the area of the Citadel the battalion bivouacked for the night. Under command of Captain Jones the Battalion Echelon, that is the Quartermasters, stores and the Transport Platoon as well as the first reinforcements and any men left out of battle set up a camp near Montauban from where rations and stores would be taken nightly up to the men at the front. At 0845 hours those going up the line fell in and marched off to a field adjoining Trones Wood where they lay up and rested until dusk and then went up and took over a portion of the line. Or rather they slipped and slithered up the muddy tracks; the weather had turned much for the worse and everywhere was now waterlogged and the trenches flooded.

They were only in position there until the following day and were quickly back in the reserve position at Trones Wood, but in those few short hours Second Lieutenant Samuel Jarrett and five other ranks were wounded. They rested in the reserve positions throughout the day, but at 1600 hours a German barrage fell on the camp. This caused a number of casualties: Second Lieutenant Harry Heyward was killed and Second Lieutenant Stanley Dalziel who was conducting a draft to 14/Durham LI from the base depot at Etaples and was visiting the battalion was wounded along with sixteen other ranks. On 11 October they returned to the trenches and occupied Needle Trench in Brigade Reserve; here a draft of twenty-six men arrived and during the shelling on the next day three other ranks were wounded.

Major Henry J. Taylor le̸f the battalion on 10 Octo̸ 1916 and assumed comm̸ of a service battalion of ̸ Royal Irish Regiment.

*nd Lieutenant Harry
clay from Ryton on Tyne,
nty Durham, who was
21 years of age, was
d in action on 15
ober 1916. He is buried in
court British Cemetery.*

The next move was made on 13 October when they took over the front fine which was named Rainbow Trench. In this position another draft of eleven men arrived, then during the day 4/8606 Corporal Thomas Whitcombe from Sunderland was killed and three other men were wounded. Throughout the next day they remained in Rainbow Trench where the Battalion Medical Officer, Captain B. Wallace RAMC was wounded, as were Second Lieutenants Alfred Butcher and John Palmer and sadly 33131 Private Walter Kelly from Whickham, County Durham, was killed. By now the conditions on the Somme front were so bad that mere survival was a trial to most men. The weather at this time was dull and misty and during the day there were showers with a few clear spells. At 0515 hours the battalion took part in the attack on the enemy-held Cloudy and Mild Trenches, and although 1/Sherwood Foresters captured and held some gun pits and 11/Essex bombed up the Beaulencourt Road, only to be forced back, 2/Durham LI had little or nothing to show for their part in the action, except a heavy casualty list. Second Lieutenant Hugh Chamberlin and eighteen men had been killed, Second Lieutenants Thomas Veitch, Alexander Dunn, James Crawford, Charles Heppleston and L. Haggie were wounded along with ninety-three other ranks and Second Lieutenants Cuthbert Green and Henry Barclay and thirty-one men were missing. The majority of the missing were indeed dead and their names are mainly inscribed on the Thiepval Memorial to the Missing, like that of Second Lieutenant Cuthbert Green, whilst the body of 21-year-old Second Lieutenant Henry Barclay was found later and he was reburied in Bancourt British Cemetery. The wounded were evacuated as soon as possible to the Regimental Aid Post, the stretcher-bearers doing

18 Brigade attack on Mild and Cloudy trenches 15 October 1916.

1 Mild Trench
2 Cloudy Trench
3 11/Essex Regiment
4 2/Durham LI
5 1/Sherwood Foresters

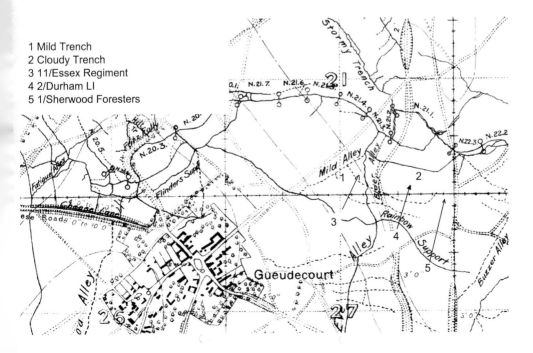

outstanding work in the conditions on the battlefield. Also admitted to hospital was Captain Evans Smith who had only just returned to the battalion two days earlier.

After the attack was over the survivors returned to the British front line and from there moved back to Needle Trench, where Major Edward V. Manger arrived and took over the duties of Second in Command.

At 1800 hours on 16 October the battalion was relieved and moved out of the line and back to a bivouac camp near Montauban. The next day the A and B Echelons rejoined the battalion and the day was spent cleaning up and refitting once more. Improvements were made to the camp where possible, in an effort to keep warm and dry. Then on the next day, after another night under canvas the Brigade Commander visited the battalion and addressed the assembled men. It was here that Second Lieutenant Alfred Russell Watson rejoined the battalion from the base; originally a sergeant numbered 6363 in the Corps of Hussars and used to working with horses he was the ideal man for the job of Transport Officer and he was quickly picked by the Brigadier for the post of Brigade Headquarters Transport Officer; this allowed Lieutenant Herbert Saunders who was temporarily attached to Brigade to return to the battalion and resume his duties as Battalion Transport Officer. Then at 1000 hours on 19 October they left Montauban and marched back down the line to the Citadel where the day was spent with more cleaning up and company parades; during the day two men reported back from the base and rejoined their companies. The night was spent here under canvas and at noon the next day they marched once more back to the billets in Mericourt l'Abbe. The Battalion Transport Section left the battalion here and proceeded by road

German gun emplacement destroyed by shell fire; Somme October 1916.

to the next location, but the tired and footsore light infantrymen were in for a treat; once more they were to ride in the luxurious cattle trucks of the French Railways. At 1700 hours on 22 October the battalion entrained in Mericourt and were carried to Oisemont, a village some 12 miles south of Abbeville. Here they arrived at 0100 hours and detrained, then they proceeded on foot to the village of Forceville where they were in billets. The following afternoon they were rejoined by the Transport Platoon.

There was a programme of normal training carried out over the next four days, specialists were trained, and all the usual drill, range work, bombing and bayonet work was carried out and there was a bathing parade and here a large draft of 141 men arrived and was distributed amongst the companies. But the higher command wouldn't let them rest long or get too comfortable and on the morning of 27 October at 0700 hours they marched from Forceville to Longpre where they arrived at 1330 hours and were accommodated in rest billets; on this march the Transport followed the battalion. Then at 1130 hours the next morning they were back on the train and were transported to Chocques where they detrained and marched to billets in Marles-les-Mines.

Over the next three days they remained here training as usual and a small draft of eighteen men arrived along with the following junior officers: Lieutenant Percy Black, a Preston man originally commissioned into 17/Durham LI, Lieutenant A. C. Lynch, Second Lieutenant Hugh James who had enlisted in the Artist Rifles prior to obtaining his commission and Second Lieutenant Frank Morris from 16/Durham LI joined the battalion for duty. On the last day of the month they took part in a Brigade route march and that day Major E. V. Manger left the battalion to command 11/Essex Regiment. Although the drafts had on the whole been relatively small they had kept the battalion up to strength with eighteen officers and 606 men available for the trenches, with two officers and ninety-three men regimentally employed. But the monthly casualty list had been higher than of late with three officers killed or missing and nine wounded and among the men eighteen were definitely dead, thirty-three missing mostly dead, and 148 were wounded.

The whole of the first week of November was spent in Marles-les-Mines training and refitting, there was a change of command at company level with Lieutenant A. C. Lynch taking over command of B Company and Second Lieutenant F. D. Morris taking the same post in D Company. Captain Neville Linzee RAMC arrived and relieved Lieutenant W. T. Warwick RAMC as the battalion Medical Officer and the last named returned to his post in 18/Field Ambulance RAMC. On Saturday, 4 October, the Brigade Commander inspected the whole Battalion in Marching Order, which is with weapons, webbing, small pack and large pack. The general expressed himself well pleased with the excellent turn-out and singled out the Battalion Quartermaster, Lieutenant and QM, J. P.

L. Shea DCM for special mention for the good condition of the men's clothing, boots and equipment. But like all inspections there was a sting in the tail, as some unnamed junior officer had failed to check his platoon's water bottles. So the Commanding Officer received a letter headed NOTES ON TODAY'S INSPECTION from the Brigade Major shortly after the parade which, whilst not a major rebuke, would have taken the shine off the Brigadier's praise. It reads as follows:

To

O.C., 2nd D.L.I.

NOTES ON TODAY'S INSPECTION

With reference to today's Inspection:

Platoon Commanders must ensure that the men's water bottles are always full. They must remember that while in reserve the Battalion is always liable to be called on to turn out quickly, perhaps during the night. If the men's bottles are not full, this would either mean delay while they were filled, or else men would have to go with them empty.

Company Commanders must take more care with the wire cutters in their charge. They must be issued to careful men who should be responsible for them. They should be inspected at each rifle inspection.

In all other respects the Brigadier considers the general turnout, smart appearance and soldierly bearing of the men were excellent, and well up to the high standard always maintained by the Battalion. He considers great credit is due to your Quartermaster for the excellent state and serviceable quality of all clothing, boots, etc.

Bde. Major

4/11/16

18th Infantry Bde.

The training was greatly hampered by the very poor, wet weather and during this period behind the line they were issued with the new box respirator. This meant that they would have spent some time learning how it was fitted, and to test they worked correctly and give the men confidence in them, on 8 October the battalion went through a room filled with gas. Second Lieutenant Harry Johnson was temporarily attached to Headquarters, 16 Brigade where he was to be instructed in the duties of a Staff Captain. In the next few days the Commanding Officer and the Adjutant went up the line to look at possible positions where the battalion may go into the line. On 5 October they visited First Corps, rear area and then the next day they visited Ninth Corps, rear area. The next phase of the training started with a Brigade attack on an enemy trench and the Bombing Officer and the Battalion Bombing NCOs were given a display of new bombing tactics for trench clearing by the bombers of 1/West Yorkshire Regiment. On 11 November the DAQMG, FIRST ARMY, Major General Percy Hobbs late Army Service Corps, who had originally been commissioned into the Royal Marines

Second Lieutenant J. Watt rejoined the ba... in December 1916.

in 1883 and transferred to the ASC in 1889, involved in Supply and Transport there wouldn't be a lot he didn't know about a horse or wagon, visited the battalion and inspected the Battalion Transport. The same day a party of thirty 'casuals' rejoined the battalion. These were men returning from hospitals, courses and detached duty and the army at that time referred to them as 'casuals', that is, they were not a formed body of troops.

On the Sunday there was the usual battalion parade for divine service and two officers reported for duty. Second Lieutenant William Thurgood had been commissioned into the Indian Army and the other man was almost returning home; Second Lieutenant Moss Cohen had come out with the battalion in September 1914 as a private rising to the rank of sergeant and as recently as the previous month the *London Gazette* had carried the news that he had been awarded the Military Medal. Now there was to be a return to work and a party of four officers and 100 other ranks went up the line to Mazingarbe and Maroc to take over the task of digging large dugouts in the 24th Division area from 9/Suffolk Regiment.

Meanwhile at Battalion Headquarters two more subalterns arrived, Second Lieutenants Robert James Appleby and James Archibald Peacock; the last named had served as a private in the Royal Fusiliers prior to being commissioned. At 0800 hours on 14 November the rest of the battalion paraded and moved out of Marles-les-Mines and marched up to Mazingarbe. A Company under Captain Jones went on to Maroc and took over the digging work from 9/Suffolk. The battalion was accommodated in a variety of places, huts, cellars and dugouts, but they were soon as comfortable as was possible. The transport accompanied the battalion for some of the way and broke off and set up the echelon in Noeux-les-Mines, from where nightly they carried rations and stores up to the battalion, whose headquarters was set up in Mazingarbe. The next week was spent on this digging work and no casualties were noted, but the main event that happened was that Lieutenant Colonel Cumming left the battalion on promotion to Brigadier, to command 91 Infantry Brigade. Also transferred were the Colonel's two servants, 1564 Private S Stewart West Yorkshire Regiment attached and 18/133 Private Palister who had originally enlisted into 18/Durham LI.

Major Alfred Irvine, who had effectively commanded the battalion throughout the Colonel's time with the battalion, was now authorised to wear the badges of rank of Lieutenant Colonel pending the announcement of his promotion in the *London Gazette*. It was also noted that at this time Lieutenant Colonel A. E. Irvine was employed at 18 Brigade Headquarters, Commanding the Brigade.

The digging work continued until the end of the month; on 29 November 18 Brigade went back into the line but the Durhams were left behind to continue the digging. Having been out of the line for a whole month the only casualties recorded are 25940 Sergeant Neil O'Donnell, who had transferred into the Durhams after serving at the front with the 15/Hussars since August 1914, and 41360 Private George Robinson and 27463 Private W. Morrison who were all injured in a bombing accident whilst on a course at the Brigade Bombing School.

As December came in, the battalion for the next two weeks continued the digging work for the 24th Division; there was little reported in the War Diary at this time, and a few 'casuals' rejoined as did Major Edward Manger who had given up the command of 11/Essex Regiment. Now was the time that all ranks had been dreading, the battalion returned to the trenches on 18 December and moved into the line where they relieved 14/Durham LI in the Cambrin sector of the front line. 2/Durham LI placed B and C Companies in the front line, D Company in support and A Company were in reserve. Here Lieutenant Robert Purvis joined the battalion and took charge of A Company. Two days later another three officers, Second Lieutenants Edward Fawcett, John Watt and Miles Hutchinson reported for duty. Then on 19 December 3/12214 Private John Lewins from Haswell was killed and 4/10454 Corporal Robert Dawson, a resident of Boldon Colliery, was wounded and sadly died the next day. Then on 23 December they were relieved by

Lieutenant Colonel Alfre[...] Irvine left the battalion [...] August 1917 on promotio[...] Brigadier.

11/Essex Regiment and moved slightly back into support positions with Battalion Headquarters and B and C Companies in billets in Annequin village; the other two companies were in a trench system known as the 'Village Line'. There is no mention of a special meal for the men over Christmas and on Boxing Day 1916 they were hard at work carrying stores and ammunition into the line, whilst another party was employed improving the trenches. On the night of 27/28 December the German Artillery heavily shelled Annequin with gas shells; the men wore their new box respirators and no casualties occurred. On the night of 28 December the battalion relieved 11/Essex Regiment in the same trenches of the Cambrin Sector; this time A and D Companies were in the front line and B and C Companies in support. Then after two days they swapped round, so that all were getting a fair share of the front line. During a period of shelling 45413 Private William Hall from Wigston, Leicestershire was killed, the last casualty of 1916.

So 1916 came to a close, the battalion had been brought back up to strength and on paper it had thirty-one officers and 865 other ranks, but the actual trench strength was twenty-two officers and 625 other ranks

Chapter Six

1917 January–June, Trench Raiding on the Loos Front

O n New Year's Day 1917 11/Essex Regiment took over the line from 2/Durham LI and they moved back to billets in Annequin, with two companies manning the Village Line. Nothing much was noted over the next three days, except that Captain James Jones was sent back to England on a senior officer's course. There must have been some enemy shelling, however, for 4/8408 Private Edward Gregson, a 22-year-old married man from Bloomfield Street, Monkwearmouth, who had been out at the front since August 1915, was killed on 3 January. The same day at a POW camp in Germany, 5642 Private Robert Scott, who had served with the Burmah Mounted Infantry Company in South Africa and had

An early shot of the damage at Loos; by the time 2/Durham LI arrived it was much flatter.

been with the battalion for seventeen years passed away. After the war his remains were reinterred in Cologne Southern Cemetery. On 5 January they went back and took over the same trenches in the Cambrin Sector from 11/Essex Regiment, whilst in the trenches on this tour two Gateshead men were killed. 28206 Private Thomas Crummey and 30534 Private William Inness were buried side by side in Cambrin Churchyard Extension.

On 9 January the same relief occurred once again as 11/Essex Regiment took over and 2/Durham LI went back to Annequin, where they became the Divisional Reserve. Here they were joined by Second Lieutenants Reginald Hargreaves and Thomas Pollard who had,been commissioned into 4/Durham LI,and along with them came eight other ranks. For the next three days the battalion provided working parties for the front line. The Commanding Officer, Lieutenant Colonel Irvine was relieved of the command of the brigade when Brigadier Bridgford returned from leave, but Lieutenant Colonel Irvine fell ill and was evacuated to hospital and when fit again was given sick leave to England, so command of the battalion fell to Major Edward Manger. The same relief took place on 13 January and three largely uneventful days were spent in the line, relieved again on 17 January, as they moved back the battalion came under enemy fire and 27754 Private Timothy Whelan from Middlesbrough was killed. He too was laid to rest in Cambrin Churchyard Extension. Whilst in reserve at this time Captains Herbert McCullagh and Ernest Gilpin reported to Battalion Headquarters and were appointed to command D and A Companies respectively. Over the next few days the battalion was finding working parties for the front line

43132 Private Thomas Meadows out of the line finds time to have his photograph taken in a French village; note the little puppy in his left hand.

and nothing much was happening, but on 21 January another group of officers arrived at the battalion; on that day Captain E. R. Sherriff, Captain Hugh C. Boxer, Captain Louis G. Hoare and Second Lieutenant David M. Rees joined for duty. At the same time Lieutenant Percy Black rejoined from hospital. During the next tour in the trenches on 23 January two West Yorkshire men who had originally enlisted as Bantams into 23/Durham LI the Reserve Bantam Battalion, 23/368 Private Harry Armitage from Holmfirth and 23/356 Private Frederick Circus, a 33-year-old married man from Barnoldswick, were killed in action. The same reliefs took place twice more before the end of the month which found 2/Durham LI in the line with Major Manger in command.

February followed the same pattern. On 2 February they were relieved

23/368 Private Harry Armitage; a rejected Bantam who found his way back to the line and was killed in action on 23 January 1917.

by 11/Essex once more and moved back to Annequin; here they were joined by a small draft of sixteen men on 4 February. But that day the High Command had plans for some of the men of 2/Durham LI, and consequently Second Lieutenant Pollard and forty other ranks were sent to Chocques where they began training for a raid on the enemy trenches. The next time the battalion was due to go into the line on 6 February, instead of taking over the left subsector from 11/Essex Regiment, they went into the right subsector and relieved 1/West Yorkshire Regiment. Three quiet days were spent in the line and on 10 February 1/West Yorkshire Regiment came back and relieved 2/Durham LI.

The raid that was planned took place that night. The main aim of the raid was to bring back a live prisoner from the enemy's trenches behind and to the north of a point known as Mad Point Sap:

RAID ORDERS

By

Major E. V. Manger, Commanding 2nd Bn. The Durham Light Infantry

Ref. Special Trench Map ?'500

10.2.17

On the night of the 10th of February at 7 p.m. (ZERO) enemy lines will be raided behind and to the North of MAD POINT SAP, with the objectives of securing an identification, capturing a machine gun, and inflicting casualties on the enemy.

The raid will be carried out by three parties under the direction of Capt McCullagh

    a) 'C' Company contingent – 2/Lieutenant. Pollard and 11

      OR.

    b) 'D' Company contingent – Lieutenant. Percy, 14 OR and two Stokes gunners.

    c) 'A' Company contingent – 2/Lieutenant. Appleby, 10 OR and one Stokes gunner.

Covering party – Sergeant O'Donnell and 10 Battalion Snipers.
Three stretchers will accompany 2/Lieut. Pollard's party. Four wire cutters with each of parties a), b) and c).

23/356 Private Frederick T. Circus from West Yorkshire, a Bantam who found his way back to the line and was killed in action on 23 January 1917.

    3. Point of entry in enemy's lines will be A.28, e.80.29.

    'C' Company covering party will remain at point of entry.

'D' Company will bomb south as far as machine-gun emplacement.

'A' Company will bomb north, destroying dugouts with mobile charges until zero plus 13 mins. At which time parties 'A' and 'D' Companies will leave the trench covered by 'C' Company and the covering party.

The Raiding Party will be in position opposite BOYAU1 2 at 6.30 p.m. and file out through the gaps already prepared. 'C' Company in front, 'D' Company right rear, 'A' Company left rear, just in front of our own wire.

    4. The requisite material will be issued at the West Yorks H.Q. at 6pm

5. The signal for retirement will be repeated blasts on whistle.

6. An electric light will be flashed on a biscuit tin on our own parados as a guide to the returning raiders.

Prisoners will be escorted to our own lines and brought to H.Q.

Salvage from enemy dead will be collected. The Medical Officer will arrange for a First Aid post to be established in a dug out at the top of BOYAU.

The signalling officer will arrange the telephone at head of BOYAU 2 to Battalion H.Q.

7. Returning Raiders to report themselves at the Rly. Line Bn. H.Q.

Table of barrages will be communicated to Commanders.

O.C. 2nd D.L.I. H.Q. will be at RAILWAY KEEP.

(Sgd).   E. V. Manger,
Major Commanding 2nd Bn. DLI

The raid was described as very successful; although all three officers and ten of the men were wounded they managed to bring a live prisoner back with them. Lieutenant Joscelyn Percy received the Military Cross for:

Conspicuous gallantry and devotion to duty, he led his men with great determination and himself killed two of the enemy. Later although severely wounded he remained in the enemy trenches until the last man of his party had withdrawn.

The same award went to Second Lieutenant Thomas Pollard, whose

Sector behind and north of Mad Point raided by the 2nd Durham Light Infantry 10 February 1917.

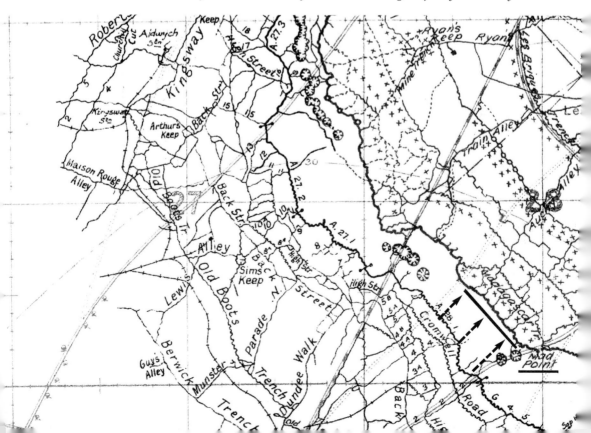

citation reads:

> For conspicuous gallantry and devotion to duty, when in command of a raiding party. He led his men with great determination and himself killed three of the enemy. Later although severely wounded he continued to conduct the operations eventually bringing his party back without the loss of a man.

Also rewarded with Military Medals were 25940 Sergeant Neil O'Donnell, 17895 Lance Sergeant Fred Jackson and 11116 Lance Corporal Charles Philips.

The Brigade Commander was very pleased with the battalion's efforts and the report below was forwarded to Headquarters 6th Division.

> REPORT ON MAD POINT SAP RAID
> The raid carried out on MAD POINT SAP at 8.0 p.m. February 10th by a party, 38 strong, of the 2/DLI exceeded expectations as a large working party were caught by the Barrage at Zero hour; the raiders having to pass over several German dead before entering the trench, seven being counted lying out in front of the trench this morning.
> As the Raiders entered the trench, the enemy, who had taken cover in their dug-outs during the bombardment, were caught coming out and killed. Stokes bombs were thrown down the entrances of the dug-outs as the men were beginning to emerge from them. In addition parties fled across the open towards the support line most of whom were killed by our bombers. The remainder ran into our barrage, which had lifted to the support line and were seen to fall. Nine were shot while taking refuge in shell holes.
> Lieutenant Pollard, who unfortunately was wounded, killed three himself. Over thirty enemy were seen lying dead in the trench, some from the effects of our barrage.
> It was evidently a large working party that was caught as they had no arms or equipment. The Raiders were to bring back one Boche, which was done.
> The suspected Machine Gun could not be found, but a Machine Gun was very active about 80 yards to the left. The enemy trench at this point was very bad, which possibly accounted for the large working party. The wire was completely destroyed by our barrage and offered no obstacle.
> Our casualties were three officers and ten Other Ranks Wounded, six of whom were so slight that they are already back to duty. All raiders returned.
> Brigadier-General
> Commanding 18 Infantry Brigade 11/2/17.

On 11 February, Colonel M. E. O'Donoghne of the 4th Training Reserve Battalion was attached to the battalion for six days so that he could study how things were being done in France and take the lessons back to the training unit in England. Also that day they received a visit from Brigadier

General Frederick P. English DSO Commander of Number 1 section of the Tyne Garrison, he had been commissioned into the Royal Dublin Fusiliers in 1879 and had served throughout the South African War and in Aden in 1905, he had commanded a column and been awarded his DSO. With 3/Durham LI based in his garrison area he would have been keen to meet with the officers of the battalion. The next day the battalion marched out of Annequin, heading to Garbecque near Lillers for Divisional rest; that night they halted at Bethune and continued on their way the next day.

On arrival it was the normal round of cleaning up, bathing and refitting and repairing equipment and then the training started. The training last two days and then on 17 February they took part in a Brigade route march. When they arrived back at the end of the day Second Lieutenant Thomas Bussell had arrived from 4/Durham LI via the base depot on the French coast, bringing with him nine other ranks. Over the next week various forms of training continued, on 19 February they represented 18 Brigade in a demonstration attack in front of the GOC 6th Division and the next day there was a special class for officers and NCOs who received instruction in bayonet fighting. It was at this time that the complement of Lewis guns in a battalion was increased to sixteen, meaning that every platoon was able to have a Lewis gun section. On 25 February the battalion moved by road from Garbecque to Locon near Bethune; the remainder of 18 Brigade stayed in the Busnes area. Here they were joined by Second Lieutenant Robert Adie and a draft of forty-five men. This was the officer's second time out at the front, having been wounded at Delville Wood the previous summer when he was serving with 10/Durham LI.

1 March saw them marching from Locon to Bethune where they spent the night and then the next day marched back to Mazingarbe, where they went into billets and became the Divisional reserve. However, they were not allowed to stay there long for next day they went up to the right subsector and relieved 10/York & Lancaster Regiment and part of 4/Middlesex Regiment in the front line. They held these trenches for four days, during which they came under enemy shellfire which resulted in the death of 43155 Corporal Robert Bamlet, a 19-year-old, Haughton le Skerne man, who was buried in Philosophe British Cemetery in Mazingarbe.

After being relieved by 1/West Yorkshire Regiment, they moved back to Mazingarbe where the time was spent digging a facsimile of the German trenches, on which 11/Essex Regiment were to train for a raid on the enemy. On 10 March, Second Lieutenant Hubert McBain reported for duty. He was the son of Sergeant Major Hugh McBain and had been brought up in the battalion moving with his father through the postings in India, Ireland and Colchester. Originally posted to 19/Durham LI, his father had written to Major General De Lisle, late

Second Lieutenant Hubert McBain: his father pulled string: have him posted to 2/Durham LI, his di is extensively quote and a number of th. photographs come f his deposit in the regimental archives

Durham LI, and asked if he could pull a few strings and get his son posted to 2/Durham LI. In his diary Hubert McBain recorded his journey up to join the battalion:

Once again I go back to Etaples where I stay for two days and then entrain for the Northern Area to join the 2nd Battalion who are near Bethune with the 6th Division. I reach Neux-les-Mines, the railhead, where I found a 2nd Battalion cart into which I put my kit and proceed six miles to the battalion transport lines at Labourse – the battalion itself is in the next village of Mazingarbe. The Quarter Master, Shea gives me a hearty welcome and asks how all the McBains are, having known us in the early days. I then go on later on 11 March to Mazingarbe and report to Colonel Irvine who also remembers the family and is very kind to me and always has been. I am posted to B Company and meet most of the officers in the battalion. We go up for a tour of the trenches on 13 March, we left at 0700 hours and had a five mile march but did not complete the relief until 1900 hours, on account of the state of the trenches due to the thaw setting in, the mud being very thick.

Again they were back in the right subsector and here they were heavily shelled by enemy trench mortars, Hubert McBain's platoon losing a number of men as well as the Platoon Sergeant:

Three officers have to share out twenty four hours of duty in the Front line, in my Platoon I lost twelve men killed or wounded by a heavy trench mortar, it was a ghastly sight as I crawled up to see what had happened. The trench mortar & shellfire during our whole time in the trenches was abnormally heavy and never a day passed without at least a few casualties along the line. I was transferred to D Company a week after our arrival in the trenches, with Black as OC, – He was a waster and neither men nor officers had any respect for him.

This in and out of the trenches carried on until the end of the month, by which time the battalion was back in Mazingarbe cleaning up yet again. The drafts that were arriving were not very regular and were very small, only four men arriving on 31 March, but they were enough to maintain the battalion at full strength.

As April began Second Lieutenant John Stuart Chalmers reported to Battalion Headquarters; commissioned into 4/Durham LI in December 1915, he had previously served as a corporal in the Natal Light Horse before being selected for a commission and on joining 2/Durham LI he was posted to D Company. The next day Second Lieutenant Richard Appleton, who came from Bensham in Gateshead, joined and he too was posted to D Company. The first four days of the month were spent in reserve at Mazingarbe. Training Lewis Gunners was given priority as well as musketry and bombing. On 4 April they once again took over the right subsector of the brigade front. The Assistant Director of Medical Services had carried out an inspection of the men of the battalion and thirteen old and unfit men were sent down to the base. As they left the front-line area there would be few of them that were sad to be leaving. On the night of 8/9 April the battalion carried out another raid on the enemy line opposite. The detailed instructions left little to chance:

SECRET – RAID INSTRUCTIONS
By
Lt Col. A.E. Irvine, D.S.O. Commanding 2nd Bn, The Durham Light Inf.

On night of 8/9 April 1917 at ZERO enemy's' line will be raided at H.31.d.9.81/2. to H.31.d.2.61/2. With the object of securing an identification, capturing a Machine Gun and destroying MG emplacement and dug outs. The raiders will only go as far as the enemy's front line.

The raid will be carried out by three parties under the direction of Capt McCullagh:-

B Coy Contingent – Second Lieutenant Moir and twelve other ranks.

D Coy Contingent – Second Lieutenant Rees and twelve other ranks.

C Coy Contingent – Sergeant Connon and twelve other ranks.

Covering party – Sergt Jackson, 10 Snipers and two Lewis guns with half teams.

1 Stokes Gunner with 3 shells will be attached to parties (a), (b) and (c).

Two wire cutters with each party (a), (b) and (c) and also a mobile charge.

Point of entry – H.31.d.2.81/2 – H.31.d.2.61/2. C Company Contingent under Sgt Connon will remain at point of entry and destroy Dug out situated 20 yards down C.T.

D. Coy. Contingent will enter at H.31.d.2.61/2. and destroy Dug out situated about 20 yards down C.T.

Both these parties will establish temporary blocks down C.T. and main trench and both parties will be provided with a mobile charge,

B. Coy, Contingent party a, will enter at H.31.d.9.7. capture MG at H.31.d.2.7. and destroy emplacement by placing mobile charge on leaving trench.

Parties will remain in trench 15 mins returning at ZERO + 19.

Signal for retiring will be whistle blasts at ZERO + 19 signals to be given by Second Lieutenant Moir's party.

Covering party will cover the retirement of the raiders and then return.

Raiding party will be in position at head of Boyau 46 at Zero minus 30 minutes and file out through gaps already prepared in the following order:-

C.Coy   *Left*
B.Coy   *Centre*
D.Coy   *Right*

And lie down in front of our wire as follows:

C.Coy   B.Coy   D.Coy

Signal for advance will be the 18 Pdr Barrage. As soon as barrage commences parties will advance in three columns (the left directing) and jump into trench as soon as barrage lifts.

Covering party (d) will by Zero minus 10 lay out lines on both flanks (men at 20 pace intervals) to within 50 yards of enemy's trenches.

O.C. snipers will arrange for 2 guides to lead the raid. These men will have previously reconnoitred the gap.

6   Prisoners will be escorted to our lines and brought to Battalion HQ, Identifications will be collected from any killed.

7   The Medical Officer will arrange for a First Aid Post to be established at Right Front Coy HQ.

8   Signalling Officer will arrange for a telephone to be at the head of Boyau 46.

9   Returning raiders will report themselves to an officer detailed by OC Right Front Coy. At Right Front Coy HQ.

10   Copy of Tables of Barrages will be communicated later.

11 OC Machine Gun Coy will arrange for flank barrages along CT from H.31.b.4.1 and H.31.d.2,31/2 and generally behind the raided area.

12 The Medium and LTMB will kindly deal with the enemy's line between 14 Bis and N edge of Bois Rase.

13 On completion of raid the raiders will be accommodated at Battalion HQ.

14 Watches will be synchronised at Zero minus 2 hours.

15 Zero Hour will be notified later.

STOKES MORTARS

Zero to Zero plus 3 – The Stokes Mortars will barrage as both flanks as shown on sketch 1,

Zero plus 3 – The two left (N) Stokes will cease fire and open again at Zero plus 4 on point shown on sketch 2,

The two right (s) Stokes Mortars will continue firing until Zero plus 20 when they and the two left Stokes will gradually slacken off.

18 Pdr Barrage and 4.5 Hows

As shown on sketches 1 and 2.

60 Pdrs   - Counter battery work beginning at Zero.

2nd Bn The Durham Light Infantry

Additional instructions in connection with the raid which will be carried out on the night 8/9th April

DRESS: Jerkins will be worn if desired. Boots and puttees.

Steel helmets coated in mud. Rifles and bayonets – bayonets coated with mud. Hands and faces blackened with charcoal.

SAA.   50 rounds 10 of which will be in the magazine before leaving remainder in pockets or a bandolier if preferred.

GRENADES   6 per man carried in aprons. They will be supplied in Dug out at 9 pm.

KNOBKERRIES

To be carried by NCOs.

REVOLVERS AND WHISTLES

To be carried by Officers and Sergeants

Revolvers will be issued at HQ tomorrow afternoon.

FIELD DRESSING

Each person to have a Field Dressing.

P H HELMET   To be worn, securely fastened in the Gas Alert position.

SPUN YARN

Each man to be provided with a piece 5 yards long for securing prisoners, Spun Yarn will be issued later on.

WIRE CUTTERS Wire cutters on rifles

ESCORT FOR PRISONERS

B Coy will detail 1 NCO and four men to be in readiness at the point of return to our trenches to escort prisoners to Bn HQ.

CONFERENCE

The Commanding Officer will see all officers and Sergeants taking part at Bn HQ at 1400 hours tomorrow.

PLACE OF ASSEMBLY

Parties will assemble at Dug Out immediately N of junction of Railway Alley and Reserve Line at 2100 hours 8th instant, in marching order and all articles of equipment not required will be left there. The men will return to the same dug out.

Tonight the men of C Coy taking part in the raid will remain in close support by Coy HQ.

Raiders will not be employed on carrying or fatigues tonight or tomorrow.

Coy Commanders will make a careful inspection of all the articles to be used in the raid.

Every precaution is to be taken in case of a counter raid by the enemy.

MOBILE CHARGES

1 man from each party will attend HQ at 14:00 tomorrow to be instructed in their use.

PERSONAL EFFECTS

Each person taking part in the raid will leave behind all personal letters etc. Cap and collar badges.

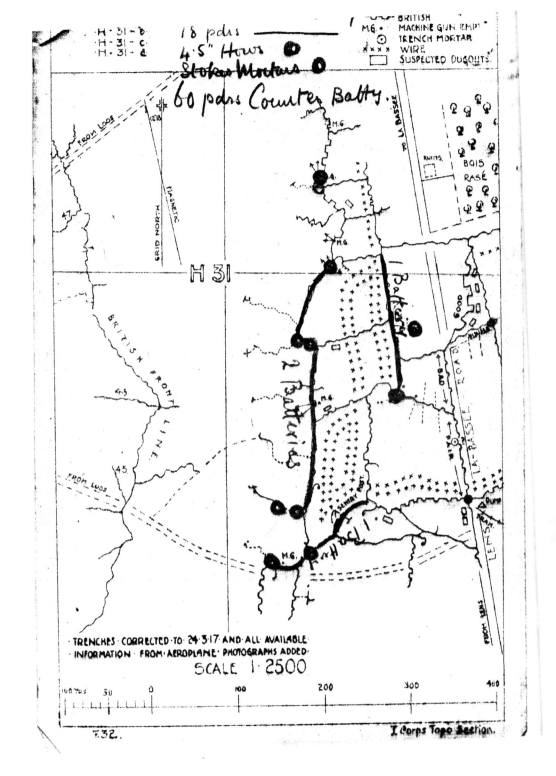

18 pdrs ————
4·5" Hows ⊙
Stokes Mortars ⊙
60 pdrs Counter Batty.

BRITISH
M.G.   MACHINE GUN EMP?
⊙   TRENCH MORTAR
x x x   WIRE
☐   SUSPECTED DUGOUTS.

H·31·b
H·31·c
H·31·d

Reg.No.	Rank & Name	REMARKS.
	Captain Mc.Cullagh H.R.	Superintending.
	2/Lieut.Moir R.B.O.	i/c Party (a)
	2/Lieut.Rees D.M.	i/c Party (b)
10138.	Sergt. Connon S.	i/c Party (c)
11895.	Sergt. Jackson F.O.	i/c Party (d) Covering.
	Party (a) 'B' Coy.	
10218.	Sergt.Hodgson J.	
~~11538.~~	~~Corpl.Graham J.~~ *8588 Cpl. J.M. Harding.*	
~~53807.~~	~~L/Cpl.Wooff R.J.~~	Waiting man.
22/41.	Pte.Hodgson W.	
9866.	: Madden J.	
14139.	: Malpass J.	
35874.	: Peart A.	
26637.	& Blackburn J.	
930.	: Robson P.	
18352.	: Wright J.T.	
26778.	: Faulkner W.	Volunteers.
43112.	: Brydon W.J.	----:----
9013	**Party (b) 'D' Coy.** *Parkes*	
11116.	L/Cpl.Phillips C. *Cpr. Alderson*	Volunteer.
8876.	Pte.Theasby J. *12217 Pte. Cudd*	----:----
8333.	: Temple G.	----:----
~~888.~~	~~: Neary~~ G.H. *26850 Reidling*	
~~37701.~~	~~: Rutter H.~~ *27102 - Shinn*	
43132.	: Meadows T.	
~~31766.~~	~~: Childs R.~~	
~~23277.~~	~~: Thompson R.~~	
1433.	: Roberts W.	
38903.	: Warburton H.	
36733.	: Watson J.	
~~37710.~~	~~: Thorley G.A.~~	~~Waiting man.~~
	Party (c) 'C' Coy.	
~~10138.~~	~~Sergt.Cawte J.H.~~	Waiting.
11338.	Corpl.Bullock J.	
38995.	L/Cpl.Taylor R.	
8095.	Pte.Agnew P.	
38499.	: Anderson E.H.	
32760.	: Walker C.	
43137.	: Raine A.	
36344.	: Tindall W.	
21963.	: Murray J.	
43153.	: Wardle J.	
16724.	: Mc.Donald R.	
42509.	: Bell J.	
8277.	: Peacook J.	
	Party (d)(Covering) - Snipers.	
43144.	Pte.Smith J.	
12444.	: Mc.Manus E.	
32175.	: Scott H.	
9578.	: Colbeck W.	Guide.
11704.	: Welsh E.	--:--
12205.	: Jennings A.	
27277.	: Barrett H.	
9416.	: Race J.	
10392.	: Kane H.	Guide.
43146.	: Smith S.	

J Gindle Lt. & Adj

7/4/17.   2nd.Battalion The Durham Light Infantry.

188

REPORT ON RAID

By The 2nd Bn The Durham Light Infantry

The raid carried out on the enemy front line between H.31.d.2.81/2 – H.31.d.2.61/2. on the night 8/9 April 1917 at 0200 hours was held up at the German wire under close rifle and Machine Gun fire, and rifle grenades.

The timing and preliminary arrangements were thoroughly understood by all ranks and worked perfectly, the raiders arriving at the enemy wire before the barrage lifted. Every man thoroughly understood the work to be done. The raiders report that the enemy sent up an S.O.S. signal consisting of Golden rain followed by pink rockets before they reached the German entanglement. His barrage, which was heavy, opened almost at once.

The three raiding columns led by guides who had reconnoitred the wire before moonrise and reported gaps quite satisfactory to allow raiding party into the trench, missed the gaps and came under fire from the Machine Gun, which was one of the objectives. At the same time another Machine Gun opened fire on their right flank from the North, and a bombardment of rifle grenades was opened from the enemy front trench.

The artillery barrage is reported as perfect and I can only assume that the barrage lifted while the raiders were struggling in the wire. Second Lieutenant Rees who was in charge of the right party reports 'Barrage excellent but did not prevent snipers manning parapet or Machine Gun firing,' Our bombers endeavoured to bomb the gun team but failed. At this stage most of our casualties were caused by rifle grenades. Officers, NCOs and men made repeated efforts to get through the wire, losing heavily, until all three parties were compelled to abandon the attempt and lie down in front of the wire. At this stage Second Lieutenant Moir was killed while trying to force a way for his party.

Second Lieutenant Rees told the men to return to our lines. This officer and Sergeant Connon, who commanded the left party remained until the men were under way. They were both wounded on rising and took shelter in a shell hole, and saw a party of fifteen Germans leave the front trench and remove the body of one of our dead from the wire. Second Lieutenant Rees and Sergeant Connon then crawled back to our lines. It is not likely that the enemy obtained any identification as all letters, badges and identity discs had been collected. Second Lieutenant Moir was wearing a uniform with the regimental buttons of the HLI.

Our Officers, NCOs and men were impressed by the gallantry of the enemy machine gunners and the coolness of his snipers under our barrage.

The repulse of the enterprise was, in my opinion, due to:-

The guides missing their way.

Artillery registering on objectives on the day of the raid.

All signalling communication was broken by enemy barrage 1 miute after raiders left our front line.

The Artillery support throughout was excellent. No shells burst short.

Some men of the right party state they passed a derelict trench after getting through the enemy wire and that they bombed a dug out. I am satisfied no men entered the German front line, which was strongly held by troops, who appeared to be well prepared and on the alert. It is possible these men entered a small enemy sap mistaking it for his front line and bombed a small dug out in it. Certainly none of the objectives were reached.

Total casualties in the raid were:-

Killed	*Second Lieutenant Moir and*	*1 OR*
Wounded	*Second Lieutenant Rees and*	*15 OR*
Missing believed Killed		*6 OR*

Total casualties from enemy retaliation on our front line system

Killed	*1 OR*
Wounded	*19 OR*

E. V. Manger Major Commanding 2nd Bn Durham Light Infantry 9/4/17

Having regained the British front line and made a report to Major Manger, 21- year-old Second Lieutenant David Rees was evacuated to Number 1 Casualty Clearing Station at Chocques; here he received what medical treatment they could give him but three days later he succumbed to his wounds and was buried in the cemetery that had grown alongside the Clearing Station. Although born in Llanhilleth, Newport, Monmouthshire, he had been brought up in Bishop Auckland, County Durham where his father was a church minister. On his way back to the British lines 3/0138 Sergeant Stanley Connon showed great initiative in withdrawing the raiding party from the German wire; after Second Lieutenant Robert Moir was killed and Second Lieutenant David Rees mortally wounded and although badly wounded in the head himself, on his way back he assisted in bringing in a man who he found lying in No Man's Land with a broken leg. Of his party of twelve men, three were killed and five wounded. For his gallantry under fire he received the award of the French Croix de Guerre. It was unusual, for not that many awards are made for unsuccessful actions. The next day a few words of praise were received from Divisional and Brigade Headquarters.

18 Infantry Brigade   6th Division No GO/2/48/3

The Divisional Commander wishes to express his appreciation of the gallantry displayed by the raiders of the 2nd DLI on the night of 8/9th April, of which the Battalion has every right to be proud.

He wishes them better luck next time.

10th April 1917

(Sgd) M Beevor Major General Staff (2) OC 2nd DLI

The Brigadier concurs with the Divisional Commander's remarks.

10/4/17   (Sgd) H E Pickling Capt

Bde Major 18 Inf Bde

On 10 April they moved back into support in the Village line, but A Company remained in Gun Trench in support of 1/West Yorkshire Regiment; that day the news came in that Second Lieutenant Walter Judd was transferred to the Royal Flying Corps. Whilst in support Second Lieutenant Frederick Pickering and eighteen other ranks arrived from the base depot. On 15 April C Company under the command of Second Lieutenant Frank Morris took over from A Company and then the next day the battalion took over the front line again. The Commanding Officer, Lieutenant Colonel Alfred Irvine was called away to command the brigade once more and command of the battalion fell to Major Edward Manger again. Midway through the tour of the trenches Captain Herbert McCullagh was sent to 8/Bedfordshire Regiment in 16 Infantry Brigade where he took up the duties of Second in Command. They came under constant shelling and every day there was a steady trickle of men killed. On 18 April three men, on 20 April two more men were killed. The enemy were also mixing gas shells in with the high explosive and one of the casualties was Second Lieutenant Hubert McBain, who managed to get a letter away to his family from the Regimental Aid Post, telling of the shelling and the casualties that were caused by it:

20/Apr/17

I have again been in the trenches doing just the usual trench warfare there is nothing to tell you about. I am still with D Company there are a few officers including Lieutenant Black, who is in charge of the company, Revell, Chapman and myself. Fritz has been shelling rather badly the last few days, he evidently expects that we are going to push him off his bit of the front. I have lost five of my platoon killed and three or four are sick and wounded. I am myself out of action for a bit, slightly gassed by a shell when I was patrolling last night with my runner. My runner got it much worse than I did on account of not getting his respirator on quick enough; he had to be sent down the line. I am thankful to say I am getting quite alright again though I was a bit scared at the time. I am now at the Regimental Aid Post for two and a half hours and hope to join my platoon again as soon as the doctor gives me permission. My servant is here as well and is looking after me and I am in the Doctor's room. It is rather hard to write as we are getting shelled a bit. I will write again as soon as I can. Hubert.

On 21 April, Second Lieutenant Robert Adie, who had only been with the battalion just over six weeks, 37710 Private George Thorley from Bradford, 38499 Private Edward Anderson and 4/5914 Private John Burkett, both Sunderland men, were killed in action. Whilst the next day 32709 Private James Keith of High Spen died from his wounds and 20319 Private George Dunn who was born in Thornley and 22096 Private John Gascoine from Winlaton were both killed in action.

Hubert McBain wrote again to his parents when the battalion was relieved:

22/4/1917

I am now back at duty none the worse for my little gas episode. My runner who was with me and was not quite so quick with his respirator has subsequently gone down the line! Rowell, my servant has been looking after me like an old brick – my platoon appreciated the cigarettes Miss Edith sent me. I had some Woodbines sent by her a few days ago so I sent them to my Platoon Sergeant to give out and when I went myself the day after and saw them on parade, one man asked permission to step out of the ranks and thank me on behalf of the men for the cigarettes. So I explained that a very kind lady in England had provided them so they are going to have a round robin to thank her.

That day no less than six subalterns reported for duty from the base: Second Lieutenants Robert Chatt, Arthur Turner, William Wright, Harold Scott, Norman Brown and Kelsick Alexander, along with thirteen other ranks. Second Lieutenant Neville Pearson arrived the following day from 17/Durham LI. Having reported to the battalion for the second time, Second Lieutenant Robert Chatt was posted straight to 18 Light Trench Mortar Battery. The last week of the month was spent in Brigade Reserve in the Village line where they were relieved by 11/Essex Regiment and moved back to Divisional reserve at Mazingarbe on 28 April. At this time Captain H. C. Boxer left the battalion on posting to 14/Durham LI. With the heavy casualty lists of April the battalion was now under strength, with only twenty-eight officers and 483 other ranks available for the trenches out of an actual strength of forty-two officers and 706 other ranks.

On 1 May the battalion became responsible for the defences of the town of Loos. A Company, under the command of Captain Ernest Gilpin, was detached and proceeded to the town and became the town garrison; Captain E. R. Sherriff, became the Commandant and Lieutenant J. S. Chalmers, the Adjutant of the Town. There was now a change in the pattern of relief and when the battalion next went into the line they relieved 14/Durham LI in the left subsector with Battalion Headquarters located in Gun Trench. The Battalion Echelon and the Transport Section moved from Labourse to Les Brebis which made the task of resupply a little easier. Second Lieutenant Henry Carss took over the duties of Brigade Bombing Officer and moved to 18 Brigade Headquarters. The battalion Signals Platoon were brought up to date with the issue of two of the new 'OL' daylight signalling equipment.

That day the enemy must have shelled the battalion positions for 8032 Sergeant William Miller, who had been out with the battalion since 9 September 1914 was killed, as was 4/8333 Private George Temple who had been in France since August 1915, arriving with the draft that brought the battalion back up to strength after the Battle of Hooge.

C Company now went into the front line replacing D Company who marched out and went to Loos where they took over the garrison duties

from A Company, who in turn went into the reserve line. Lieutenant George Garland reported back to the battalion and along with him came Second Lieutenant John Huggall from 17/Durham LI; he had served as a trooper in the Lincolnshire Yeomanry prior to obtaining a commission in the Durham LI. On 10 May they were relieved, including the company in the Loos defences, by 1 West Yorkshire Regiment, and moved into brigade at Les Brebis. The following day nineteen other ranks arrived at the transport lines from the base depot. They were back in the line on 15 May relieving 14/Durham LI in the right subsector. Battalion Headquarters was located in Tosh Alley, A Company in the right front and B Company on the left with C in the left rear and D in the right rear. At 0345 hours the Germans raided the front line between Boyau 46 and Boyau 47. They must have been in very quickly, for after the action it was found that four men were missing presumably taken prisoner by the enemy raiding party and they had left a wounded man lying in the trench. As soon as they were aware of the raid the battalion bombers immediately counter-attacked and drove the enemy out of the British lines. Second Lieutenant Hubert McBain recorded the event in his diary:

The trenches are only 100 yards apart here and patrolling and wiring are very precarious duties. I had the great good fortune towards the end of May, while visiting the sentry groups in the trenches to just miss a German raiding party who had got into our trenches. They eventually attacked a post at Boyau 46 and captured four of our men. I should have been on my way to the post but the Company Commander refused to let me have an orderly to accompany me, so I went round the support trench to visit them, in the meanwhile the Germans had got in the front and had attacked North.

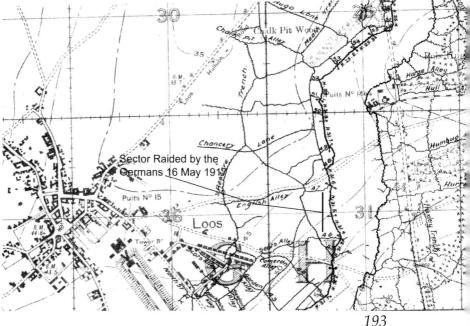

193

The following night the battalion tried to return the favour but as in the previous attempt they were held up on the enemy wire and one man was reported wounded and missing. Then in a tit for tat action the following night the enemy tried to raid between The Hump and Cameron Crater; however, the sentries were alert and the fire step was quickly manned, the enemy being driven off by Lewis gun and rifle fire. That night a patrol went out and brought in the bodies of two dead German soldiers. Identification taken from the bodies showed them to be men of the 153rd Regiment; this unit was recruited in Thuringia and had its home depot in Altenburg. The 153rd Regiment formed part of the 8th German Division which was regarded as a first class formation although it had suffered heavily from artillery fire during the raids carried out by the British on this front. There now took place an inter-company relief; C Company took over the left front and B Company the right front with D Company in the left rear and A Company in the right rear reserve.

The next couple of days passed quietly. However, on the night of 21 May 1/West Yorkshire Regiment carried out a raid opposite The Hump and Cameron Crater; they jumped off through the sector held by 2/Durham LI and in the counter-barrage Second Lieutenant John Hugall was wounded. One job that came the battalion's way was the digging of a new sap out into No Man's Land between Boyau 46 and Boyau 47. They were then relieved and moved back first into Brigade reserve and then on 25 May they marched to Hesdigneul where they became the Divisional reserve. Here they bathed and cleaned up and then started the usual round of training. At 1730 hours on 28 May, Major General C. Ross, CB, DSO, addressed the officers, warrant officers and NCOs of the battalion. The next afternoon a battalion sports day was held and that evening a concert was given on the village green by 'The Very Lights' I Corps Entertainment Troupe. On 30 May the battalion football team played a combined I Corps Schools team, however, as no result is given it is presumed that the result went against 2/Durham LI.

On 1 June the battalion carried out a route march in the morning and then in the afternoon the Commanding Officer held a parade in marching order and that day Second Lieutenant George Fillingham reported to Headquarters and was posted to D Company. Probably in place of Hubert McBain, who, having been sent on a Bombing Course was now the Battalion Bombing Officer and had moved from D Company to Battalion Headquarters, he wrote to his parents:

> We are in a different lot of trenches this tour but not far from where we were last. This bit of the line we are in now is where the Germans were two months ago it is exceedingly interesting.

On 3 June they relieved 14/Durham LI in the left subsector between Boyau 51 and Boyau 63 by 0145 hours 2/Durham LI were in control of the sector with A Company in the right front and B Company in the left front

trenches. The reserve line was held by D Company, whilst C Company took over at the Loos garrison from a company of 14/Durham LI. The next morning the enemy artillery was described as 'fairly active', but this led to the deaths of 28038 Private Richard Comerford from Birtley and 25567 Private Joseph McEvoy a Middlesbrough man, along with two men wounded, one who was able to remain at duty. That night Loos received a heavy barrage between 22:00 and midnight, but without loss to the company which was garrisoning the village. The next morning it was the turn of an area just behind the front line, known as the 'Chalk Pit', to get the full attention of the German gunners and that night the British replied with a bombardment of the enemy line opposite Boyau 63. The artillery activity was repeated by both sides and again that night Loos was the target of a barrage of high explosive shells mixed with gas shells. During the day Second Lieutenant Joseph Davison reported from 4/Durham LI and was posted to B Company. At 0015 hours on 7 June the battalion attempted a raid on the enemy trenches opposite Boyau 46. However, this was to be another failure; as soon as the British barrage opened on the German line, the Feldgrau in the German front line fired their SOS signal and within seconds a very heavy concentrated barrage came down on No Man's Land where the raiders of 2/Durham LI were forming up. Those that got through the counter-barrage reached the German wire where they were further held up by an enemy machine gun and could not get into the enemy front line. The order to retire came and those that could returned to the British lines. The whole of the operation was conducted with great coolness, which reflected credit on all involved in the raiding party. It was sad that the casualties were so heavy for such a small operation – six killed, fifteen wounded, of whom two would die from their wounds, and three wounded slightly who remained at duty. Also one man was reported missing. Those that were killed in action lie side by side in Plot II, Row Q, Graves 1-7 in Philosophe Military Cemetery in Mazingarbe. It would appear that the missing man was 38632 Private George Lambert of Gateshead, who is buried in the same cemetery but in Plot I, Row R, Grave 10. One of the wounded survived long enough to reach the Casualty Clearing Station at Chocques, where he lies in the cemetery that grew beside the Casualty Clearing Station. 19/1433 Private William Roberts, a Norfolk man who made his way to Durham to join a battalion of men the same size as himself, had originally, as his number shows, enlisted into the 19th (Bantam) Battalion of the Durham LI. Wounded on the Somme in 1916, before he could return to his battalion, the Bantams had been disbanded, and many sent to the Labour Corps. Like many of those small men who had joined to fight, not dig and carry, he found his way to a fighting battalion, in his case 2/Durham LI, where he died bravely during a trench raid:

REPORT ON RAID CARRIED OUT BY 2/DURHAM LI NIGHT
6/7 JUNE 1917

The raid was carried out as planned under the command of Major E. V. Manger and was as is stated in the Operation Order carried out in four parties under the command of Second Lieutenant Cave, Second Lieutenant Pickering and two NCOs. At 2315 hours an old telephone cable was laid from North of Scots Alley to the German sap head by a patrol who found the Sap head unoccupied, and was found very useful as a guide to the gap in the wire.

The raiders were unlucky in suffering seven casualties from an aerial dart as they were filing up Scots Alley and this weapon was very active throughout the operation. Our barrage opened punctually and simultaneously the enemy sent up his SOS and his barrage fell at once, mostly on our front line and Scots Alley. It was accurate and intense.

The Raiders got well away with our barrage and arrived in front of the gap about 45 seconds before the barrage lifted. The enemy were prepared for, and apparently expected a raid at the point selected. His trench was strongly held and a Machine gun and rapid fire opened on the raiders as they were crossing No Man's Land.

The party lay down within ten yards of the enemy wire. It was decided that an attempt to rush the trench would prove unsuccessful with the reduced numbers and the accurate Machine gun fire on the gap in the wire.

Second Lieutenant Cave ordered the party to withdraw. This was done in good order in small groups covered by the rifle fire of the remainder. All casualties were brought in from No Man's Land. A white tape which was run out as the raiders advanced was found most useful in guiding the party back to our lines. A searchlight also came into play at G.32.d.80.80. to give direction to the retirement.

The dash of the men was excellent in every way and though the raid was a failure it was a gallant attempt. All arrangements went without a hitch.

11 June 1917   (Sgnd) H Beevor Major General Staff

During the day, Lieutenant William Foster reported in from the base; originally commissioned into 17/Durham LI, he had already been out at the front with 8/Durham LI and was now returning for the second time and he was posted to D Company, who unfortunately for the new officer were just relieving B Company in the front line. Likewise C Company was taking over from A Company. B Company then moved back to the reserve line and A Company became the Loos garrison. The next day the artillery duel continued but little damage was caused to the British line.

Two new officers reported: Second Lieutenant B. R. J. Simpson was posted to B Company and Second Lieutenant Thomas Harrison, who had already seen service at the front as a sergeant with the Durham LI and the York and Lancaster Regiment, was posted to C Company. On the night of

Second Lieutena␣ Thomas Harriso␣ joined the batta␣ on 8 June 1917.

196

38669 Lance Corporal John W. Wrathmall, taken shortly before his death on 16 June 1917.

9 June the battalion sent several patrols out into No Man's Land. They evidently bumped into some enemy patrols, for one man, 37588 Private John Pescod, was killed and several others wounded; they did, however, bring in the body of the man reported missing on 7 June, as previously explained probably that of Private Lambert.

The next night enemy working parties were active and these were successfully dispersed by trench mortar and Lewis gun fire. The next few days were quite quiet with only one or two wounded, before on 12 June the battalion was relieved by 1/West Yorkshire Regiment. 2/Durham LI moving to Le Brebis became the Brigade reserve, where two days were spent cleaning up and some training was carried out. The main event was a Commanding Officer's kit inspection and then on the morning of 15 June the Commanding Officer inspected the battalion in marching order; after all, the 2nd was a Regular Battalion and certainly in the Durham Light Infantry the standards would be maintained where at all possible. Then that afternoon the battalion moved to Maroc and took over the line between Boyau 46 and Boyau 52.

The men were allowed to rest during the day and then that night the whole battalion was sent up to dig out the front line between Boyau 46 and Boyau 52; here four men were wounded but only one, 38669 Lance Corporal John Wrathmall, a Sunderland man serving in 13 Platoon of D Company, was killed in action. The next day was the same pattern: all day they rested and then at night went in to dig. That night there were several casualties, among them, 4/9557 Sergeant Arthur Clark from

The Battlefield Cross erected over the grave of 38669 Lance Corporal John W. Wrathmall in Philosophe British Cemetery, Mazingarbe.

Langley Park in County Durham who had been out at the front since August 1915. One of four brothers at the front with the Durham LI, two of whom were already dead, he was killed in action. In the grave next to him lies the other man killed that night, 32748 Private Robert Dargue from Bearpark.

On 18 June after spending the day cleaning up and bathing the battalion relieved 1/7/Sherwood Foresters in the trenches south-east of Loos; Battalion Headquarters was located at Harts Crater, with A and B Companies in the front line, C Company in support and D Company in reserve. An unexpected return during the day was the arrival of Second Lieutenant John Hugall who was discharged from hospital in England and returned to duty and was posted to C Company. In the early hours of 19 June the Germans sent over a lot of gas shells and several men were evacuated gassed and some wounded. Over the next six days the enemy was actively shelling the trenches held by the battalion.

Each day a number of men were killed and wounded; among the wounded on 21 June was Second Lieutenant Hugh James and the next day Second Lieutenant Joseph Davison was wounded too, evacuated to Number 7 Casualty Clearing Station in Nouex-les-Mines he survived until the following day before his life ran out. The Germans were now using projectiles referred to in the War Diary as 'Aerial Darts', and both the front companies received their share of these. On 23 June there was an inter-company relief; C Company took over the right front and D Company the left, while A Company went into support and B Company were the reserve. Also that day 11769 Private Joseph Clark from Easington Colliery was killed and Second Lieutenant John Hugall was evacuated to the Field Ambulance.

The enemy bombardments continued on and off with the British Artillery replying in kind over the next few days, with the normal

4/9557 Sergeant Arthur Clark, killed in action on ? June 1917, the third of four brothers to fall.

The crosses erected over the graves of Sergeant Clark and Private Dargue, in Philosophe British Cemetery, Mazingarbe.

trickle of wounded and killed. They were particularly badly hit on 26 June when Second Lieutenants Arthur Turner and Laurence T. Scollick were both killed. The first named had served as a Lance Sergeant in the Coldstream Guards and then was commissioned into the Westminster Dragoons before transferring to the Durham Light Infantry. The latter had spent only four days with the battalion and they hadn't even reported his arrival in the War Diary. Also killed at the same time was 26001 Private Albert Baker from Mudford, in Somerset, he had previously served in 15/Hussars before being transferred; the other man killed that day was 43108 Private Nicholas Buchanan who hailed from Thornaby-on-Tees. Lieutenant Percy Black was wounded the next day and then on 28 June, 2/Durham LI and 11/Essex Regiment carried out a raid on the enemy trenches. With so many of these enterprises failing owing to things like uncut wire, guides getting lost, alert enemy sentries and such, this time there was little left to chance and the raid instructions which were issued as Operation Order Number 47 were quite detailed:

SECRET

OPERATIONAL ORDER NO. 47

Reference – Trench Map 1/10,000 LOOS Ed. 8. B. LENS Ed. 8. A.

RAID 1.

A Raid will be carried out in conjunction with a DEMONSTRATION raid to be carried out by 11th Essex Regt. Immediately on our immediately on our left (North) from N.1. A.78.95to H.31.C90.13 If wind is favourable at Zero, No.4 Special Coy. R.E. will release smoke from about BOYAU 47. 16 Infantry Brigade will co-operate by making a Smoke Barrage opposite PUITS 14 BIS.

OBJECT 2.

To take prisoners, secure identifications, and kill as many Germans as possible.

AREA TO BE RAIDED 3.

The area raided will be N.1.A.85.55 and N.1A.78.95(about 200 yards of front). The raiders will only penetrate the front line.

COMPOSITION AND STRENGTH 4.

The attack will be carried out by 2 Officers and 84 ORs as follows:

No. 1 Party	*C.Coy. Contingent*		
	1 Sgt. 2 Cpls. and 18 Ptes. =		*21*
No. 2 Party	*A. Coy. Contingent*		
	1 Sgt. 2 Cpls and 18 Ptes. =		*21*
No. 3 Party	*B. Coy. Contingent*		
	1 Sgt. 2 Cpls and 18 Ptes. =		*21*
No. 4 Party-	*D. Coy. Contingent*		
	1 Sgt. 2 Cpls and 18 Ptes. =		*21*

Officer Commanding Raid – A/Capt. E. Fawcett
Company Commanders 2nd Lieut.G.S. Fillingham
Officer in charge of Nos. 1 and 2 Parties – Lieut. R.A. Hargreaves.
Officer in charge of Nos. 3 and 4 Parties – 2/Lieut. D.A.G. Johnson

Each party will go forward in 2 waves, of half sections in each wave, as follows:

B.	R.	B.	R.	B.	R.	B.	R.
R.G.	R.	R.G.	R.	R.G.	R.	R.G.	R.
	'D'		'B'		'A'		'C'

Each Coy. Contingent will consist of 1 Section –
> *Bombers and Rifle Grenadiers:1 Section – Bayonet men*
> *Distance between waves – 25 paces.*
> *Raiders will be in position along our front line in NOVEL ALLEY at*
> *Zero minus 15 mins. In the Following order:*
>> *Right to left, 'C' Coy. 'A' Coy. 'B' Coy. 'D' Coy.*

*At Zero they will advance getting as close to the barrage as possible and jump
into the trench immediately the barrage lifts at Zero plus 3.*
The signal for the advance will be the commencement of the 18 Pdr.
Barrage.Raiders will remain in the hostile trench until Zero plus 50.
The signal for the withdrawal will be blasts on Rams Horns.

*PRISONERS 5.   Prisoners will be brought to Battalion H.Q.The RSM will
arrange for a Guard to take them over to Battalion HQ and subsequently
conduct them to Brigade HQ.*

*MEDICAL ARRANGEMENTS 6.   The Medical Officer will arrange a First
Aid Post in the close support line about N.1.A.20.50. O.C. D Coy will be
responsible that the necessary Facilities are given.*

*REPORTING ON RETURN 7. Returning Raiders will report themselves to an
officer detailed by O.C. 'A' Coy. At DUG-OUT in BUG TRENCH now
occupied by 'D' Coy.*
*ASSEMBLY 8. Raiders will be assembled previous to the Raid and subsequently
accommodated in large Dug-out in BUG TRENCH Coy will make the
necessary arrangements.*

*INFORMATION 9. O.C. Raid will arrange for information to be sent down to
Battalion H.Q. Code for use is attached.*

*SIGNALLING ARRANGEMENTS 10. The Signalling Officer will arrange for
a telephone at Close Support Line (N.1.A.20.60).*
*ARRANGEMENTS OF COY COMMDRS 11. O.C. Coys. Holding the line
between NETLEY TRENCHand the Railway will bring rifle fire and Lewis gun*

fire to bear on the hostile front line during the raid.

L.T.Ms. 12.   *O.C. L.T.M. Battery will barrage the Strong Point at junction of NASH ALLEY and NETLEY TRENCH (N.1.a97.38) and enemy line at H.31.d.14.92 from Zero to Zero plus 36.*

MGs   13.   *O.C.18th Machine Gun Coy. will keep the following Trenches under fire from Zero to Zero plus 45:*
HYTHE ALLEY HURRAH ALLEY
NUNS ALLEY HUXLEY TRENCH
HURDLE TRENCH

SMOKE BARRAGE 14. *If the wind is favourable at Zero hour, 'C' Coy. will put up a smoke barrage in front of NOVEL ALLEY from N.1.c.70.80 to junction with Railway.*

BURNING OIL 15.*'B' Special Coy, R. E. will project burning oil on to the Strong Point in N.1.b. 57.85 from about M.6.d. 40.90.*

DRESS AND EQUIPMENT 16.
No officer or man will have any article by which he can be identified. Shrapnel proof helmets will be worn. All ranks will carry 50 Rds. S.A.A. – 10 of which will be in the magazine before leaving. Bayonets will be fixed. Every man will carry two bombs. Bombers will carry 10 bombs. Bombers will carry Revolvers, whistles, and Rams Horns to be carried by Officers. Sergts. will also carry Rams Horns And whistles. Wire cutters on rifles. All ranks will carry First Aid dressings Box Respirators only will be worn. All officers will carry compasses.

HOUR of ZERO 17.
        Zero hour will be notified later.

ARTILLERY PROGRAMME 18.
        Table of Artillery Barrage and Map is attached.

SYNCHRONISING OF WATCHES 19.
        Watches will be synchronised at 4am and 4pm.on. the 28th.

BLOCKING RIGHT FLANK 20.
        Lieut. R. A. Hargreaves will arrange for 'C' Coy. contingent to erect a block in NASH ALLEY on the right flank (south) to prevent enemy working from that flank.
        A. E. Irvine, Lieut. Colonel. Commanding 2nd Bn. DLI 25/6/17
Copy No. 1 – HQ Copy   .
Copy No. 2 – Mess

Copy No. 3 – 'A' Company
Copy No. 4 – 'B' Company
Copy No. 5 – 'C' Company
Copy No. 6 – 'D' Company
Copy No. 7 – OC Raid
Copy No. 8 – 18th Brigade
Copy No. 9 – 11th Essex
Copy No. 10 – War Diary

At 1910 hours the raiders went over the top in the area south-east of Cameron Crater. Once again the enemy SOS signals went up and his barrage fell on the British front line; however, this time they managed to get into the German trenches where they inflicted a number of casualties on the German defenders, before they made a successful withdrawal to the British lines.

The next morning the following signal was received at the Battalion Headquarters:

6th Div. No. GO/2/85 (6)

To OC, 2nd DLI

The following message has been received from the Divisional Commander, and is forwarded for communication to all ranks:

In view of all the circumstances, the Divisional Commander considers that the Raid carried out yesterday by the 2nd D.L.I. and 11th Essex Regt. was a very fine achievement. He wishes his appreciation and congratulations conveyed to those Battalions and to all concerned in the Raid.

(Sgd). E. Morrison, Captain. A/Bde. Major 18th Infantry Brigade 30/6/17

Praise also came down from the I Corps Headquarters, where the Corps Commander Lieutenant General A. E. A. Holland CB, MVO, DSO, said:

This is a very fine performance, and reflects great credit on the two battalions engaged, for in addition to fighting their way into the trenches they had previously carried out their role of drawing the enemy's fire, thus making their own task more difficult. The efficiency of rifle fire is well exemplified.

Four Military Medals were awarded to members of the raiding party and fortunately and unusually the citations have survived in the battalion War Diary. 46037 Private Walter Pennell was recommended for a Distinguished Conduct Medal:

For Conspicuous Bravery and Devotion to Duty on 28 June 1917 during a raid on the enemy's trenches S.E. of Loos.

Pte Pennell accompanied the raiders in his capacity of stretcher-bearer and was indefatigable in dressing and tending the wounded and conveying them back to our trenches. He himself was wounded early by a bullet

Showing signs of exhaustion, British troops after an attack on the German terenches.

passing through both buttocks, despite this he continued his work. After all
the raiders had returned he several times went out and brought in wounded.
It was chiefly due to his example that no wounded were left. All officers and
NCOs speak in the most glowing terms of his bravery.

However, the award was reduced to that of the Military Medal. The
second award went to the other stretcher-bearer, 34527 Private Harold
Allison, his citation for the award of The Military Medal reads much the
same as the first:

For Conspicuous Bravery and Devotion to Duty on 28 June 1917
during a raid on the enemy's trenches S.E. of Loos.

Pte Allison was one of the two stretcher-bearers who accompanied the
raiders. He assisted Pte Pennell in dressing and tending the wounded.
After all the raiders had returned he again assisted Pte Pennell in searching

for wounded under heavy shellfire. All Officers and NCOs speak in glowing terms of his bravery.

The next recipient, 4/9448 Private Thomas Gibbons, got his medal for his part in the fighting where his actions were very prominent:

For Conspicuous Bravery and Devotion to Duty on 28 June 1917 during a raid on the enemy's trenches S.E. of Loos.

This man has been especially brought to notice by Officers and NCOs for his gallant conduct. When in the German trenches he repeatedly got on top of the parapet and bombed Germans. He accounted for at least six Germans. He came back several times for a fresh supply of bombs and continued bombing the Germans. He set a splendid example to the other men.

34793 Private Arthur Webb, the fourth man to receive a gallantry award was one of the first into the enemy line; his citation reads as follows:

For Conspicuous Bravery and Devotion to Duty on 28 June 1917 during a raid on the enemy's trenches S.E. of Loos.

This man was in the first rush of bombers and showed the section a fine example. He was knocked down by a shell, which killed the man beside him and, although dazed, he continued to throw bombs. Seeing the Germans coming over the top he at once began to use his rifle and accounted for several Germans.

By 2130 hours the firing had largely died down and that night 1/West Yorkshire Regiment came up and relieved the battalion. Their first stop was overnight in Brigade Reserve at Les Brebis and then the following morning they marched on to Hesdigneul and became the Divisional reserve. The casualties from the raid were Lieutenant Reginald Hargreaves and three men killed, twenty-four men wounded and seven missing, that were in fact dead. As June came to an end the battalion was involved in cleaning up and they began the normal training routine when out of the line.

Chapter Seven

1917, July–December,
With the Tanks at Cambrai

As the battalion arrived in Hesdigneul on the night of 30 June, Second Lieutenant Hubert McBain managed to get a letter away to his parents:

The great thing I am thankful for is that I am out of it for a few days. I had to join a company up in the line in the latter half of the tour as it had four out of five of its officers knocked out. So Hutchinson and I had to reinforce. Both James and Black are slightly wounded and have gone down the line. We did a daylight raid just a few hours before we were relieved, which was quite successful. Davy Johnston was one of three officers to go over and one of two to come back. We did not bring any Boshe back but killed a great many and blew in a dugout. I was able to see the boys going over and the barrage start.

The next morning the whole battalion paraded for Divine Service and in the afternoon they cleaned up and had a bathing parade. The next few days were spent training and being inspected; having sent his congratulations in the form of a signal, on 3 July, the I Corps Commander, Lieutenant General A. E. A. Holland CB, MVO, DSO, visited the battalion personally and on parade thanked them for the gallantry displayed. To brighten up the training some inter-company competitions were organised, the first was an inter-company football tournament. In the first round, D Company beat C Company and B Company beat A Company. The next entry in the battalion War Diary states that Second Lieutenant D. Johnston had been admitted to the Field Ambulance; it neglects to mention that he was being evacuated with a broken leg, received in his company's football match. The next day, in the morning a shooting competition took place and then in the early afternoon a rapid-loading and bayonet-fighting competition took place. The day's finale was the B Company versus D Company final of the football, which resulted in a draw and it was agreed to play again the following day.

The following morning the battalion took part in an exercise with an aeroplane, establishing contact with ground troops. Then in the afternoon the football match was replayed, this time B Company won the game. On 8 July they marched back towards the front line and became the brigade reserve in Les Brebis. Here Second

Lieutenant George Hicks was evacuated sick on 10 July 1917.

No.13 Platoon, D Company, commanded by Hubert McBain, taken in late 1917.

Lieutenant Richard Appleton reported sick and was taken away to the Field Ambulance. On the night of 9 July they moved up into the line and relieved 14/Durham LI in the left subsector of the Brigade front. The front had been extended and now ran from Railway Alley to Cameron Crater, so now they had to hold the line with three companies actually in the line, D Company on the right, B Company in the centre and A Company on the left, with C Company in reserve, whilst Battalion Headquarters was located at Tosh Keep on the northern edge of Loos.

The next day the Germans sent over a few shells onto the battalion trenches and three men were wounded. During the day two officers reported for duty, Captain William Griffith Jones was posted to D Company. Originally commissioned into 18/Durham LI, he had been posted to 21 (Reserve) Battalion before joining the battalion. The other Captain, George Hicks, was joining the battalion for a second time and was posted to B Company; he had been out in 1914 and then served with 2/KOYLI in 1915 and 12/Durham LI in1916. Along with them came a draft of forty other ranks from the Infantry Base Depot.

The next day was very quiet and it wasn't until evening that some shells fell on the trenches around Boyau 46; this resulted in Captain George Hicks being evacuated to the Field Ambulance. The next place that came to the attention of the enemy gunners was Scots Alley, where two men were killed. The first, a 23-year-old, 45993 Private Matthew Baird was born in Seaham, but was resident in Hebburn, when he enlisted into the Third Battalion of the Tyneside Scottish in 1914; wounded on the Somme in 1916 he had been transferred to the Durham LI on his return to France at the beginning of the year. The other man killed that day was 7121 Private William Hedley, who was thirty-seven years old, originally from South Shields but at the time of his death resident in Durham; he had seen a fair bit of service with the regiment, having served in South Africa during the Boer War and then in India with 1/Durham LI. As a regular reservist he had been called up in August 1914 and had come out to the battalion with the first batch of reinforcements, on 24 September, 1914.

Over the next three days the enemy fired a large number of aerial darts and trench mortars at Scots Alley, but fortunately only a few men were wounded. The next relief came in the form of 10/Canadian Infantry Battalion who relieved the battalion on the night of 15 July. 2/Durham LI then moved back once more to Les Brebis; on the way out of the trenches one man was wounded. The next morning was spent cleaning up and bathing and then that afternoon they were transported by motor lorry to billets in Cambligneul. Here a draft of sixty-six other ranks arrived and the usual training and cleaning took place, new specialists, Signallers, Lewis gunners and Bombers had to be trained and the new draft inspected and allotted to companies. Three new officers joined at this time, Second Lieutenant William Davis originally a private with 5/London Field Ambulance RAMC was posted to A Company and Second Lieutenant

Francis Sullivan went to B Company. The third subaltern, Second Lieutenant James Eccles, who reported to D Company, had originally arrived in France as a private with 1/7/Durham LI in April 1915; having reached the rank of sergeant he was commissioned into the regiment the previous May.

Over the next week the training continued and there was a number of inspections and sporting events. On 22 July the Sergeants' Mess played the Officers' Mess at football, which resulted in a win for the NCOs. Three days later they met again but this time a rugby match took place, the result was a win for the officers. Two more officers reported to Battalion Headquarters and were posted as follows, Second Lieutenant William Henderson to B Company and Second Lieutenant James Black, who had seen service as a private with the Newcastle Commercial Battalion of the Northumberland Fusiliers, was posted to D Company. On 28 July there was another rugby match, this time the officers of 2/Durham LI met the officers of 1/West Yorkshire

19/808 Private R. Pearson, another of the Bantams that made his way back to the front and found himself serving with 2/Durham LI.

207

Out of the line the battalion band give a concert in a French village on the left is Sergeant Bugler Hart; note the wearing of Stretcher Bearer armbands by some of the men.

Regiment. The battalion War Diary records that this was a victory, by a narrow margin, for the West Yorkshire men. However, it was mentioned to his parents in a letter by Hubert McBain:

> We had a very good game of rugger with the West Yorks this afternoon, they beat us hollow. We are going to their regimental sports tomorrow and I am running in the marathon race in the afternoon. It is now 10 pm and I am writing this in our mess on a rather grimy table cloth with two candles burning and bottles and glasses and cards, being the debris the other members and guests have left before retiring.

> I had a very unpleasant duty of putting a full corporal of seventeen years service under arrest for being drunk and insulting a woman about half an hour ago. His name is Lowe and he was my Platoon sergeant when I first joined, he had his stripes taken from him a few months ago and had got two of them back. Now I am afraid he will be a Private again. Drink is the Devil in solution without a doubt.

The only Sergeant Lowe traced in the battalion is 9075 Sergeant

93152 Corporal Albert Hawcroft originally served as 14/304 in the Barnsley Pals and was transferred to the Durham LI.

James Lowe who came from Chester-le-Street and was awarded the DCM in April 1916; he would be killed in action in February 1918 as a private. His War and Victory Medal Roll sheet in WO329 at the National Archives only shows the rank of corporal.

The month ended with another Brigade Contact scheme with aeroplanes; little did they know it, but this training was the beginning of the preparations for the coming planned offensive that would take place at Cambrai at the end of the year.

The weather changed at the beginning of August and although this was a great setback to the troops fighting further north at Ypres, the only effect on the battalion was that it interfered with the training programme. The third of the month saw a large ceremonial parade at which I Corps Commander, Lieutenant General A. E. A. Holland CB, MVO, DSO, late Royal Artillery, presented medal ribbons to those who had recently been awarded them. The same day Major Edward Manger left the battalion on promotion to Temporary Lieutenant Colonel to take command of the 2/9/King's Liverpool Regiment TF which was serving in the 57th (2nd West Lancashire) Division. The Commanding Officer, Lieutenant Colonel A. E. Irvine DSO, was awarded the Officier de l'Ordre de Leopold, a Belgian decoration. This was presented to him at a church service and parade, to commemorate the start of the fourth year of the war, which was held at FIRST ARMY Headquarters at Ranchicourt, by the Army Commander, General Sir Henry Horne KCB. The battalion sent a detachment of 150 men to this event. The training continued and the battalion took part in Brigade-sized operations.

Lieutenant Colonel Herbert McCullagh assumed command of the battalion on 7 August 1917; he commanded until 16 March 1918.

Major Herbert McCullagh rejoined the battalion at this time and was appointed Second in Command. Although they carried on training, the battalion made a route march of about 40 miles north to a new area at Allouagne. On 14 August, there was a Divisional gymkhana organised in which the Battalion Transport won two events. Another officer reported to Battalion Headquarters at this time; Lieutenant Laurence Hartshorn, who had left the battalion when he was wounded in September 1916, rejoined from hospital in England. The news now came in that Lieutenant Colonel Alfred E. Irvine had been promoted to Brigadier General and had been given command of 112 Brigade serving in 37th Division. Command of 2/Durham LI now passed to Major McCullagh. Three more officers joined on 16 August; Second Lieutenant Howard St George had served as a private numbered 5558 in the Royal Fusiliers, possibly one of the University and Public Schools Battalions, he was posted to C Company. Second Lieutenant Wilfred Rice who had been commissioned into 3/Durham LI in 1915 was posted to B Company and last but not least,

Second Lieutenant Walter Allen joined A Company. He had enlisted in 1901 into 2/Border Regiment where he became a Bandsman. He saw service in India and Burma before being discharged in 1913. When the present war broke out he enlisted in 18/Durham LI where he became a Company Sergeant Major. Posted as an instructor to Number 10 Officer Cadet Battalion he became the Regimental Sergeant Major prior to joining Number 21 Officer Cadet Battalion on a commissioning course. Another event that took place at this time was the 6th Divisional Rifle Meeting to which the battalion sent eighty-eight of the best shots. Although they won no individual trophies they took the 6th Divisional Trophy for the best team. They were on the move again on 21 August when they moved by march route to Cambligneul, enroute they halted at Hermin where the battalion cooks had dinners ready for them on the mobile cookers.

On arrival at Cambligneul they were joined by Second Lieutenant James Lunn; reported in on posting from 3/Durham LI, he was sent to join D Company. Once settled in the billets the men were taken for a route march wearing gas respirators. Another officer that joined here was Second Lieutenant Thomas Walton who went to C Company. The battalion was now on its way back towards the line and their next route march took them to Bracquemont near Noeux-les-Mines and then on the following day they found themselves back in Les Brebis; here Captain Ernest Gilpin rejoined from hospital. The next day the whole battalion went through a gas chamber to make sure their respirators

A corporal and a private of the battalion in a French village in 1917.

were working properly and to give the men confidence in them. Then that night they went up the line and relieved 1/Canadian Mounted Rifles in the old German front and support lines.

Hubert McBain had been on leave in England while the battalion was out training; he rejoined them at this time and recorded his impressions in his diary:

I find the battalion back in the trenches near Lens on my return to the Transport lines at Les Brebis. During our absence the Canadians had taken

Hill 70 which overlooked Loos on one side and Lens on the other. The trenches ran through the suburbs of Lens with our Company HQ in a quarry and some brick stacks in front which are held alternately by us and the Bosche, whoever gets out there quickest at nightfall. The Germans tried to raid us many times without success; evidently they wanted an identity as to what troops were in front of them.

On 26 August Captain Gerald Sopwith rejoined the battalion as Second in Command; it was just over two years since he had been evacuated from Hooge. The next couple of days were quiet with little shelling and the battalion was employed supplying working parties during which there was a number of men wounded. On 30 August 2/Durham LI were due to take over the left subsector from 14/Durham LI, when just before the commencement of the relief, the Germans tried to raid the latter battalion. Immediately the SOS rockets went up from the British front line and the British Artillery opened up on No Man's Land and the German trenches. Owing to this shelling and the German counter-barrage, the relief was somewhat delayed and wasn't completed until 0330 hours on 31 August. The battalion was deployed with A Company in the left front line and C Company on its right, with B Company in left support and D Company as right support. Again at 0345 hours SOS rockets went up from the British lines and again the British Artillery came down on No Man's Land, with some German shells falling on the battalion positions. This resulted in the wounding of two men and caused the death of 3/10075 Corporal Henry Sherry from West Hartlepool who had been at the front since May 1915.

38402 Private George Wm. Watson, killed in action 25/8/17 he is buried in Maroc British Cemetery, Grenay.

The battalion was well under strength now and the monthly return for August shows that its trench strength was twenty officers and 433 other ranks. At the Transport lines were two officers and eighty-one men.

They did, however, have rather a lot of personnel on detached duty; there were six men sick, twenty-four on leave and forty-six on various courses.

The following units had one or more men attached from the battalion:

Army HQ, Corps HQ, Corps Troupe, Corps Laundry, Divisional HQ, Brigade HQ, Brigade Grenade School, Brigade Keeps, RE Workshop, Brigade Storeman, officers servants with officers' at 2/9/Kings, 19/DLI, 18 Infantry Brigade Pioneers, 12 Company RE and there was several reported as being AWOL.

September began with the enemy shelling the

Officers of 2/Durham LI, Noeux-les-Mines, France, August 1917. Back row: Lieutenants A.D. Black, H. Pickering, Spencer, Watt, Davis, and Harrison, Captain Fillingham. Second row: Lieutenants Walton, St. George, F. Pickering, Haylett, McBain, and Saunders, H.C. Boyce [United States Army], Captain A.D. Cave. Front row: Captain Shea, Major Sopwith, Lieutenant Colonel McCullagh, Captain Dryden, Captain Griffith, Captain Jones. Seated on ground: Lieutenants Hutchinson, B.R.J. Simpson, and Osborne.

battalion trenches during the night, which led to two men being evacuated wounded; the enemy fired the same bombardment the next night but unfortunately there were four men wounded and four killed. The dead were 31521 Private Charles Forster from Gateshead, 205089 Private Cuthbert Forster who was born in Hexham but was living at Sacriston, 205103 Private Charles Gardner, who came from West Hartlepool and the last killed, originally enlisted into 3/Durham LI, 3/10111 Private Thomas O'Niell, was a Stockton man, who had arrived with the draft that joined the battalion after the Battle of Hooge. There was a fifth man killed later in the day when 205133 Private Matthew Thompson from Sunderland died. Then at 0300 hours on 4 September, the British Artillery fired a heavy barrage onto the German front line which had the desired effect and the

German Artillery fell silent for the rest of the day. That night 9/Norfolk Regiment came up and took over the line from 2/Durham LI. As the battalion was making its way out of the line to their billets in Les Brebis, the German Artillery fired a terrific bombardment of gas shells in the area immediately to the south of Loos Crassier in square G.36.c; this lasted from midnight until 0130 hours and held the battalion up on its way to the billets. When they arrived in Les Brebis they rested until 1530 hours and then marched to Houchin where they went into a tented camp. Here the normal period of cleaning up and training started. It was now the news arrived that Major McCullagh had been promoted to Lieutenant Colonel and confirmed in command of the battalion and at the same time Captain Sopwith was promoted to Acting Major.

Another event that occurred at this time was that the Battalion Entertainment Troupe, 'The Pineapples', gave a concert at Divisional Headquarters. Mainly drawn from 2/Durham LI, the troupe had the addition of four men from other units, two Royal Engineers, one from the West Yorkshire Regiment and one mans unit is unidentified. The battalion now began moving back towards the front and took over in Brigade

'The Pineapples' the 2/Durham Light Infantry Concert Party, taken at Noeux les Mines, France, September 1917. Second row: Captain Arthur Cave, Lieutenant George Fillingham, Second Lieutenant Basil Simpson, and Captain Eric Dryden.

Reserve; Battalion Headquarters and B Company were located in Les Brebis, D Company held the Village line north of the Lens-Philosophe road, A Company were in Loos and C Company were in Mouse Trench. From these positions they provided working parties that went out into No Man's Land and wired the brigade front. This work was carried out for three nights until on 18 September 2/Durham LI relieved 14/Durham LI in the left subsection of the brigade front. The battalion was placed D Company in the right front trenches and B Company in the left front trenches. Behind them in support was C Company on the right and A Company on the left.

The first night in the line they sent parties out to continue the wiring. However, they were spotted by an alert German sentry, who called for artillery support and a barrage fell that greatly impeded the work at hand; fortunately though, there was only one man wounded. On the night of 21 September the Germans attempted to raid the battalion in Noggin Trench on the right of 2/Durham LI and at the same time opened up a heavy barrage on the Durhams' front-line companies. Then early the next morning a high-velocity gun started firing on the right support company;

Lieutenant H. McBain and No. 13 Platoon Lewis Gun Team, Le Brebis, France, 1917.
Back row: Lance Corporal Coyne, Private Hinton, Private Baker, Corporal Marriot, Private Rud.
Front row: Private Reay, Lieutenant McBain, Privates Currie, Hirst.
27610 Lance Corporal James Coyne entered France on 10/8/15 and ended the war as a Sergeant, 43123
Private James Hinton survived the war, 4/8824 Corporal Thomas Marriott entered France on 23/3/15.

two men, 23645 Private John Good and 205174 Private James Naylor, were killed and another eleven men wounded. That night Territorials of 1/6/Sherwood Foresters relieved the battalion and they were sent to different locations, Battalion Headquarters was again in Les Brebis along with C Company, A Company went to Mouse Trench, B Company to Martyrs' Alley and D Company were billeted in Loos Brewery. C Company were not allowed to stay long in Les Brebis and the next day they were sent up to the Village line–south of Railway Alley and from here they sent working parties up to the front line.

During the day Second Lieutenant Edward Tuffs, from Middlesbrough, reported to the Battalion Headquarters; he had enlisted into the Army Cyclist Corps and by the time he landed in France, on 31 August 1915, he had been promoted to Company Sergeant Major. However, he was not long on the continent for he was quickly selected for a commission and sent back to an Officer Cadet Battalion and commissioned into the Durham Light Infantry on 4 January 1916. He brought with him a much-needed draft of 100 men.

That day also word came from the 33rd Casualty Clearing Station that 8530 Private John Paul from Middlesbrough had died from his wounds. He had arrived in France on 5 January 1915 and had been wounded at Hooge that August; his name appears in the list of those men of 2/Durham LI wounded at Hooge, that was published in the *Durham Chronicle*, after the battle. After recovering from his wounds he was transferred to the Northumberland Fusiliers where he was renumbered 30669. It would appear that he was not happy with the transfer and deserted, and under his own steam rejoined 2/Durham LI in France.

There now comes what can only be described as a lack of communication between the Northumberland Fusiliers Record Office and the Durham Light Infantry Record Office, for Private Paul has two medal roll sheets in WO329 at the National Archives. The sheet for the Durham Light Infantry shows correctly that he is deceased, while that of the Northumberland Fusiliers shows that he is a deserter and is regarded as 'Still Serving'.

The next three nights they sent working parties up the line and then on the night of 27 September, they relieved 14/Durham LI in the right subsector of the brigade front. Here the Commanding Officer placed A Company in the left front trenches and C Company in the right front trenches with B Company in support and D Company in reserve. The trenches here needed a lot of work and the battalion started to repair and improve them. B Company was singled out for praise for the quality and amount of work they did. The next day brought more shelling and four men were wounded, then on the last day of the month the German Air Force started flying low over the British lines, either carrying out reconnaissance missions or spotting for the German gunners. As the month closed, the monthly report showed that the trench strength had risen by three officers and fifty-five men to thirty officers and 488 other ranks. So September passed into October.

There was now a period of inter-battalion reliefs between 14/Durham LI and 2/Durham LI. On the first of the month 14/Durham LI replaced 2/Durham LI who after being relieved moved into support, B and D Companies were placed in Catapult Trench with C Company in Nash Alley and A Company in the reserve line. For the next three nights the usual working parties were supplied, carrying stores, rations and ammunition into the line.

On 5 October 2/Durham LI relieved 14/Durham LI once again and B Company went into the left front trench and D Company into the right front trench. A Company were placed in Cobb Trench and C Company went into Catapult Trench. Over the next three days the German Artillery was active and each day one man was wounded, then on 8 October there was very heavy rain and the trenches started collapsing, despite working hard to keep them clear; Cosy Trench became impassable owing to mud slides and enemy trench mortars knocking it in.

There can be few in the battalion who were not glad to see the arrival of the men of 9/Suffolk Regiment on the night of 9 October. After being relieved 2/Durham LI went back to the billets in Les Brebis. The next morning they had a bathing parade and then that afternoon they marched to Noeux-les-Mines. Here they began training and officers and NCOs were taken over a piece of ground with German trenches laid out in tape on the ground. They then practised attacking these trenches over a few days.

On 15 October they had the use of a rifle range and the battalion was put through a course of musketry. Following this training they went back into Brigade Reserve and took over from 14/Durham LI with the companies disposed as follows: D Company in Loos Brewery, A Company in Mouse Trench, B and C Companies in Martyrs' Alley and Battalion Headquarters in Black Watch Alley. From these positions, nightly working parties went up to the line for carrying and digging work. At this time Captain Eric Dryden was attached to 18 Brigade Headquarters where he took over the duties of Brigade Major and Lieutenant Edward Tuffs took over as Battalion Adjutant. Then on 19 October Major Sopwith took over command of 14/Durham LI and rejoined his own battalion the next day as 2/Durham LI relieved 14/Durham LI in the front line.

During the relief, two men were wounded. The enemy gunners sent over some gas shells which landed near Battalion Headquarters. During the day on 21 October there was some form of accident, most likely from a grenade explosion or similar incident and four men were accidentally wounded. That night a three-man patrol under the command of 17752 Lance Sergeant Henry Race a Bishop Auckland man, went out into No

Man's Land, what their mission was is not stated in the War Diary, but they were all reported missing the next day. They must have run into a larger German patrol or walked into an ambush. There must have been some sort of fight or struggle in the pitch black and Henry Race was killed; the others presumably were taken prisoner and turned up at the end of the war, for Henry Race has no known grave and is commemorated on the Arras Memorial to the Missing.

On the night of 22 October they were relieved by 6/Linconshire Regiment and once again moved to the billets in Les Brebis. The next day they marched to Noeux-les-Mines where they entrained and were carried to Lillers and from there they marched to St Hilaire where they were in GHQ Reserve.

After spending 24 October cleaning up, they then started training. The word came through that the Quartermaster J. P. Shea DCM had been promoted to Captain and that 10595 Private J. Greenlaw from New Washington had been awarded the Military Medal. On 29 October they marched from St Hilaire to billets at Dieval, and on the next day continued on to Gouy-en-Ternois. The training carried on as normal and on 30 October Captain Dryden left Brigade Headquarters and went to FIRST ARMY Headquarters. Captain Gilpin meanwhile became Town Major of Houchin.

When the Germans had withdrawn to the Hindenburg Line in the spring of 1917, there had been a proposal to attack in the area of Cambrai, but at the time the British had still been involved at Arras and as the year progressed their attention was held in Belgium, firstly at Messines and then in the series of battles that generally became known as Third Ypres or the Battle of Passchendaele. As early as May 1917, Headquarters III Corps had been asked by FOURTH ARMY to submit a plan to attack the Germans between the St Quentin Canal and the Canal du Nord. This plan was eventually submitted and GHQ ordered that some preliminary preparations should begin. There were some changes along the British front and part of the sector held by FOURTH ARMY was taken over by THIRD ARMY, which was commanded by General the Hon. Sir Julian Byng, whose army would now have to fight the coming battle. Meanwhile at GHQ, the Commander of the Tank Corps, Brigadier General H. J. Elles and his General Staff Officer, Lieutenant Colonel J. F. C. Fuller were proposing operations for the use of tanks on ground where the machines could operate and not get bogged down as they were in Flanders. Various plans were proposed but one that caught attention was a scheme for a raid on a large scale, with tank support, with the objective of destroying as many guns as possible in the area of Banteux–Crevecoeur–Ribecourt. This plan was put to General Byng by the Commander of III Tank Brigade, Colonel J. Hardress, in August and Byng was willing to include some sort of tank action in his coming offensive.

At the same time in IV Corps, the Commander Royal Artillery of 9th (Scottish) Division, Brigadier General H. H. Tudor was thinking about other ways that they could surprise the defenders. He came up with the plan that the guns should register by survey methods instead of the usual method of aeroplanes registering the fall of shot and reporting back to the battery by radio. The second part of his plan was that tanks would go forward and crush the enemy barbed wire, thus creating a path for the advancing infantry and there would be no need for the guns to fire until the actual zero hour. The plan was discussed at IV Corps Headquarters, and then passed on to THIRD ARMY Headquarters, where General Byng realised that if surprise was possible then there might be more advantages if a quick advance was achieved. So it came to pass that a plan was approved and the final plan had four objectives:

1) To break the enemy's defensive position by a coup de main with the help of tanks.

2) To pass cavalry through the break.

3) To seize Cambrai, Bourlon Wood and the crossings of the Sensee River, cutting off the German front-line troops between the river and the Canal du Nord.

4) To exploit the success by advancing north-eastward and rolling up the German line from the south.

For the coming battle General Byng's THIRD ARMY had under command the following:

VII Corps, 24th and 55th (West Lancashire) Divisions.

III Corps, 6th, 12th (Eastern), 20th (Light) and 29th Divisions.

IV Corps 36th (Ulster), 51st (Highland), 56th (1st London) and 62nd (2nd West Riding) Divisions.

XVII Corps, 4th, 15th (Scottish) and 61st (2nd South Midland) Divisions.

V Corps, which was in reserve with the Guards, 40th and 59th (2nd North Midland) Divisions.

Also available was the Cavalry Corps 1st, 2nd, 4th and 5th Cavalry Divisions and of course I, II and III Tank Brigades.

For their part in the attack III Corps intended to use from right to left 12th , 20th and 6th Divisions, the latter was to advance with tank assistance and take the Premy Chapel spur west of Marcoing.

So this was the reason for 2/Durham LI training with tanks behind the line west of Arras. All formations that were to take part in the battle were carrying out this training. However, in each formation tactics and methods differed. In some the infantry followed the tanks closely in single file, in others the infantry held back from the tanks by as much as 50 yards and notably the 51st (Highland) Division, developed its own method of attack, the troops were not to follow the tanks, in section files but were to advance in extended line, in two ranks. In all other formations when the troops

Tanks being taken forward in preparation for the coming battle at Cambrai.

entered the enemy trench they were to turn left to roll up the enemy flank. In the 51st Division they would turn right.

6th Division were allotted B and H Battalions from II Tank Brigade for their part in the operation. The Divisional plan was for 16 Brigade with its right flank on the main Peronne railway track and the 71st Brigade to deliver the assault, and 18 Brigade would follow on and take the Premy Chapel Ridge.

On 1 November there was an inter-company football competition in which A Company defeated D Company and C Company beat B Company. In America they had recruited a number of divisions which would in time arrive on the Western Front; what they lacked was instructors with battle experience. Certain officers and NCOs were selected to go to the United States as instructors; in 2/Durham LI, chosen for the posts were Lieutenant Robert Chatt and Corporal Murphy, who left the battalion for England, en route for America, on 2 November. That afternoon A Company beat C Company to win the football tournament. On 5 November they were joined by First Lieutenant Boyle, United States Army Medical Service, who joined as the Battalion Medical Officer. Two days later the whole battalion went to visit H Battalion Tank Corps for instruction in cooperating with tanks. But that afternoon the Commanding Officer was forced to report sick and was evacuated to the Casualty

Clearing Station, command of the battalion falling to Major Sopwith. This training with tanks was new to the battalion and it was obvious to most of the soldiers that some big attack was planned. Second Lieutenant Hubert McBain made these notes in his diary of that time:

> Unexpectedly on October 2nd after over a month at Lens, we were relieved by the 11th Division from Ypres and went out to reserve at St Hilaire, behind Bethune. From where we expected to go North for the heavy fighting around Ypres, but instead we marched south for five days and came to rest at Gouy-en-Ternois near St Pol. Here we get into training with Tanks ready for the Cambrai offensive. We are shown maps and sand models of the whole of the proposed Cambrai attack.

The training continued and on 12 November word was received that Lieutenant George Fillingham had been promoted to Captain but was to remain on the battalion strength as an additional Captain. On 15 November all was ready, the training complete and it was time to move forward into the battle zone. This began with a route march to Bouquemaison where the battalion entrained and were carried in the familiar cattle trucks to Peronne, where they detrained and marched to Haut Allaines. Here Hugh Boxer, who had left the battalion as a Captain in the previous April, rejoined with the rank of Major and took over command of the battalion. The next day saw them again on foot marching towards the front, and that night they billeted in Equancourt. The next march made on 17 November took them to a camp in Dessart Wood, specially constructed to house and hide the infantry that was moving up to the front. Here they rested and completed checking equipment and making sure all was ready.

This was also recorded in Hugh McBain's diary, although the training period he remembers is longer than that recorded in the War Diary:

> When we have completed five weeks training we leave by train for Peronne, a large town then razed to the ground. Then on by march route through Etricourt then on to Manancourt and finally into Dessart Wood near Fins which is to be our hiding place before the attack. Here we put on the final touches, issue ammunition, field dressings, bombs, etc and as with the other eleven divisions are in our jumping off positions at 06:00 on 20 November.

At 1930 hours on 19 November the battalion left Dessart Wood and marched up to Dunraven assembly trench south of Beaucamp where they arrived at 0130 hours. The battalion was to advance in artillery formation by platoons, with D Company on the right front and C Company on the left front. A Company were right support and B Company left support. At 0610 hours on 20 November it was still dark and as the leading tanks went forward the sound of their engines was muffled by British aircraft flying low over the German lines. Ten minutes later they were followed by the leading waves of infantry. As dawn broke over the tanks and infantry the

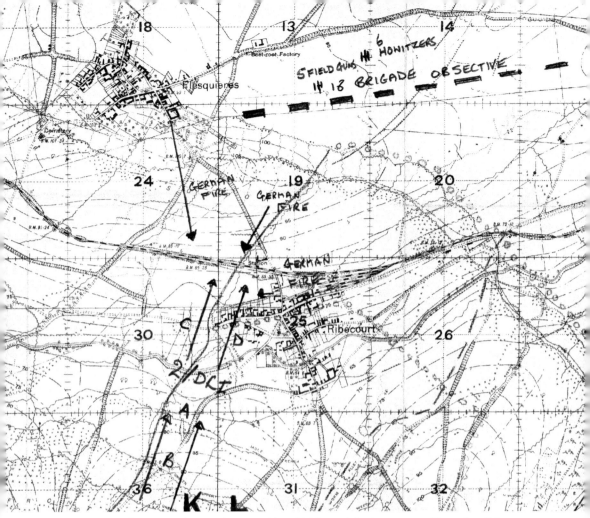

2nd Durham Light Infantry attack towards Premy Chapel Ridge and the German guns November 1917.

British barrage opened and a thousand guns produced a deafening roar as they poured their shells into the German positions. The Germans were totally surprised, some stout-hearted men manned their positions but in most cases they either surrendered or fled.

At 0820 hours 2/Durham LI began to move forward; leaving Dunraven Trench they passed through Beaucamp and using Argyle Road as its right boundary passed quickly on to Beaucamp Trench, where they arrived at around 0915 hours. Here they waited until at 1015 hours they moved forward to Unseen Trench, which was reached by 1045 hours. At this time they came under enemy fire from some 77mm guns, which were firing shrapnel but fortunately caused no casualties. Then at 1145 hours, they moved off towards their final objective, the RED LINE. They had now adopted a section artillery formation, so as to spread out and lessen the

Infantrymen kneeling waiting for the order to advance.

casualties. They had also moved from a two companies in support formation to A Company in support and B Company following in reserve. The battalion seems to have seen little of the tanks as most of H Battalion was operating around Marcoing and had then moved on to Nine Wood to secure the eastern edge of the Premy Chapel Ridge.

As they advanced 2/Durham LI passed through the western edge of Ribecourt village and when they climbed the Flesquires Ridge beyond the village, they came under enemy machine-gun and rifle fire. This fire came from three directions, from Flesquires and from the area of map squares L.25.a and L.19.c, but largely the shooting was poor and inaccurate and caused no casualties at this stage. By now the front two companies had reached Kaiser Support Trench; A Company in support had taken up position in Kaiser Trench and B Company was some way back in reserve at the Sunken Road at L.19.b.5.2. D Company now pushed on and reached the objective with little problem and scarcely any opposition, except from the machine-gun fire from Flesquires, which was holding up the 51st Division on the left. When C Company tried to advance they were met by heavy fire from five field guns which forced them back into Kaiser Support Trench. Here the Company Commander, Captain Edward Fawcett, made his plans. He split his company into three; the Lewis guns

would remain where they were, giving covering and supporting fire. The rest were split into two groups, one under Captain Fawcett and the other under Captain George Fillingham. They worked their way round to the right of the guns and when they arrived at a suitable position they charged the guns, with fixed bayonets. A number of the gunners quickly surrendered and were made prisoner, those that did not either fled or were killed. Behind and to the right of the battery position was another gun position with six howitzers in it. The crews of these guns, on seeing what had just happened to their comrades and possibly panicked by the fleeing survivors of the field gun crews, took to their heels too and ran off leaving the guns to the Durhams, giving them a total haul of eleven guns and eighteen prisoners. The companies then had to begin consolidating the position and started digging in, when they noticed that at about 1,000 yards distance some enemy batteries were limbering up intending to make

Infantry in open formation ready to advance.

The advance begins, shells explode in the distance as the leading waves keep close to the barrage.

Captain Fillingham was awarded the Military Cross for his part in the capture of the German guns on Premy Chapel Ridge.

their escape; these were engaged by rifle and Lewis gun fire.

The battalion now formed an outpost line along their portion of the Premy Chapel Ridge; on the right flank they were in touch with 1/West Yorkshire Regiment and on the left they found men of 1/6/Gordon Highlanders of 152 Brigade. In the rear Battalion Headquarters had moved forward and established itself in Ribecourt village with B Company in reserve. The whole day had gone really well for the battalion and they had got through with only four privates and two NCOs killed. One of the dead, 11542 Private Albert Capp from Leeds, was an original 1st Battalion man and he had arrived at 2/Durham LI with a draft from India in June 1915.

Second Lieutenant James Peacock, the Battalion Signals Officer, and some of his signallers had laid a line to Brigade Headquarters and had been in a forward trench and watched the battalion advance in artillery formation:

> They looked and were magnificent; the influence of the pre war Regular battalion was still very strong. After the action, Captain Fillingham, who had charged the guns earlier that day was very upset over the death of one of the pre war Regulars, Private Capp. He gave instructions that the wood for the cross over his grave had to be twice as thick as normal.

For the next two days they carried on consolidating the positions taken, on 22 November B Company relieved C Company and A Company relieved D Company. Another two nights passed quietly and on the night of 25/26 November they moved forward to the outpost line at Cantaing where they took over from 2/Grenadier Guards. B Company went into the right front line and A Company took over the left front line, with D Company in right

Hyacinth of H Battalion ditched. H Battalion of the Tank Corps was supporting 6th Division of which 2/Durham LI were part.

On a ridge in the distance small figures can be seen on the skyline above some recently captured trenches.

support and C Company in left support. For three days they were in these positions and things were generally very quiet.

The Germans were spending this time regrouping; they brought up reinforcements and then on 29 November they shelled the village very heavily throughout the day. Indeed they had been planning to counter-attack for a number of days, and on 30 November at 0530 they started a bombardment of the 55th Division, mixing gas shells and high explosive. During this barrage many machine guns and Lewis guns with their crews were blown to smithereens. In the barrage that fell on 2/Durham LI, 19-year-old Second Lieutenant Geoffrey Addington, who had only been with the battalion since 12 November, was killed.

As the main action didn't affect 2/Durham LI until the next day and to cut a long story short, Gouzeaucourt fell to the enemy and the leading German troops were able to push on to the west of that village. Around about 1,000 yards west of the village they came upon the Transport sections of three battalions of 18 Brigade, namely 1/West Yorkshire Regiment, 11/Essex Regiment and 2/Durham LI. Having been alerted to the enemy advance by the large numbers of men from various units falling back through their position, the three Battalion Quartermasters acted very quickly and all transport was loaded with the stores and equipment and sent off in good order towards the rear. All surplus men were retained and formed into fighting units; any men left over, Transport men, cooks, tailors, shoemakers, and store men dug in quickly and formed a fighting line. Unsupported on either flank they hung on, but the Germans did not push their advantage. They had a few men wounded and the Adjutant of 1/West Yorkshire Regiment, Captain W. Paul, who had played a major part in the defence, fell badly wounded. Command now fell on Captain J. P. L. Shea, MC, DCM the hero of Vaal krans, he took over and commanded the defence until relief in the form of troops from the Guards Brigade arrived. In order to hand over correctly and show the incoming commander the position, Captain Shea exposed himself and fell mortally wounded. As he lay on the stretcher just before he died he talked of 'The regiment' to the man who lay on the next stretcher. One of those wounded early in the action was 9171 Private Ernest Cardwell, one of the regular soldiers who had landed with the battalion in September 1914. A Yorkshire man, from Halifax, he was evacuated to Ytres where he was admitted to either Number 21 or Number 48 Casualty Clearing Station, where he died from his wounds.

9547 Private Fred Sawyer was transferred to the Labour Corps in late 1917 and was renumbered 611357.

The view from the battalion position across the French landscape after they had dug in.

At 1345 hours on 1 December the enemy poured out of La Folie Wood and launched an attack on the main battalion position at Cantaing and on the ridge to the south of that position. The SOS signal was sent up and a timely barrage of shrapnel, as well as machine-gun, Lewis gun and rifle fire drove the Germans back to their starting position and they did not come again. That night the battalion was relieved by 11/Essex Regiment and moved back to the reserve position in Kaiser Trench. Here Lieutenant Colonel McCullagh rejoined the battalion and Major Boxer returned to 14/Durham LI. The next night they moved forward onto Premy Chapel Ridge and began consolidating and improving the trenches there, generally improving the state of the defences.

On 6 December the enemy advanced from Cantaing but swerved away from the front held by the battalion. Some went to the left towards Flesquires and others to the right towards Nine Wood. The battalion front held and the enemy left them alone except for sending over gas shells. These caused some casualties and one who had to be evacuated gassed was First Lieutenant Boyle USAMS, the battalion doctor. He was temporarily replaced by Captain Evans RAMC from one of the Divisional Field Ambulances. On the night of 10 December they were

Second Lieutenant Frederick A. Pickering who was wounded during the German-counter attack on 30 November 1917.

relieved by 8/North Staffordshire Regiment and moved back to the Hindenburg Support Line, Unseen and Valley Trenches. Then the following night 9/Welsh Regiment took over these positions and 2/Durham LI moved by foot to a camp at Etricourt. One night was spent in this camp and then the next day they were given a rare treat. Motor buses of the Army Service Corps arrived and carried them well away from the battle zone and took them to a hutted camp at Blairville. Here they cleaned up and a parade was held where the ribbon of the Military Medal was presented to 3/10098 Lance Sergeant Henry Broxon, who was a resident of Shepperdson Street, Murton Colliery and also to 49914 Private

Andrew McGarvie, a Glaswegian serving in the Durham LI. On 15 December Second Lieutenant Wilfred Fryer joined the battalion, but the time for rest was cut short and the next morning they were transported to Mory and from there they marched up to the line and relieved 4/Royal Fusiliers and 12/West Yorkshire Regiment in the Bullecourt sector. The battalion had to place three Companies, A, B and C in the line, and D in support. The Germans were not very active and apart from some sporadic shelling around 1500 hours each day there was little to report, that is until the relief was due, when a few of the enemy tried to bomb a trench block held by A Company. However they were driven off by a Lewis gunner and left two men dead behind them. This period was recalled in Hubert McBain's diary as follows:

We are the last Division to be relieved [after the Cambrai battle] and on the night 11/12 December we get back to rest billets after a very heavy march and are very well looked after by Watson the new Quartermaster, Shea having been killed in the counter attack, sufficient hot food and drink is provided for officers and men, who are in dire need of rest and nourishment. The morning of the 13th we travel in buses for Divisional rest to Blairville, but after two days in huts with snow eight inches deep on the ground we are again sent to the trenches at Bullecourt, to take over from 3rd Division, who have been attacked and badly handled by the Huns. I am in the front line again with my platoon, holding a block in the trenches where the Germans have broken through. Fortunately casualties are few, but the weather is bitterly cold and we are all tired after Cambrai. The dead are lying about in great numbers after the last attack, but the frost keeps the smell away.

On 20 December the battalion was relieved by 8/Bedfordshire Regiment

Captain & Quarter Master J. P. L. Shea MC, DCM, He won his DCM at Vaalkrans during the Boer War; as he lay dying on the stretcher on 1 December 1917, his last words were about the regiment.

and moved by march route to the huts in Mory; here they received the news that Captains Fawcett and Fillingham had been awarded the Military Cross for the capture of the German guns on Premy Chapel Ridge the previous month. The next day the buses arrived and took them back to Blairville. They remained here having a proper rest; presumably the men were given a special Christmas dinner, but if they were it isn't mentioned in the War Diary. On 27 December the battalion moved on foot to Berles ou Bois and continued to rest. Hubert McBain continued the story in his diary in this way:

We are relieved and embuss at Ervillers – on the main road between Arras and Bapaume, for rest billets at Berles ou Bois, where we have an excellent time. The village is practically in ruins and we live in the rooms that haven't been razed to the ground and the inhabitants of which there are few left are very good to us. We are inspected by the Brigade Commander, who is pleased with the turnout. We also have a good concert party performing under the able management of Fillingham. Here I get my second lot of leave and set off for England via Boulogne.

So ended 1917; the early months of 1918 would prove even more trying.

Chapter Eight

1918, January–June, On the Back Foot, The Kaiser's Battle

Regimental Sergeant Major Joseph Watson MC, DCM, was promoted to Lieutenant and QM to fill the vacancy left by the death of Captain Shea.

O n New Year's Day, 1918, the battalion was still in billets in Berles-au-Bois; here the news came in of the gallantry awards published in the King's New Year's Honours List printed in the London Gazette. The late Quartermaster, Captain J. P. L. Shea MC, DCM received a Bar to his Military Cross, 6402 Regimental Sergeant Major Joseph Watson, who had been promoted to Lieutenant and Quartermaster in place of Shea, received a Military Cross, and 8425 Sergeant Alfred Squires was Mentioned in Dispatches on 21 December. Lieutenant E. Dryden who was employed at FIRST ARMY Headquarters as a General Staff Officer Grade 3, was promoted to Acting Captain for the period of his attachment. For the next sixteen days the battalion War Diary simply states 'Battalion in rest'; however, some training must have been carried out and of course the normal period of refitting and training new drafts, although again, the arrival of any new reinforcements is not mentioned. It does mention that two parades were held; one, a full brigade parade, on 8 January for the presentation of Medal Ribbons and a second on 11 January, when the Brigade Commander inspected the battalion. So it was on 18 January 1918 that they began making their way back towards the firing line; that day they marched to Courcelles, where they billeted for the night and the next day's march took them on to the village of Le Bucquiere. Here they rested for a full day until they moved into one of the new hutted camps, O'Shea Camp, where battalions in reserve were posted whilst they supplied working parties for those in the line. Four days were spent here until on 28 January, they moved forward and took over the right subsector of the 18 Brigade front near Beaumetz-les-Cambrai, with A and B Companies in the line and C and D Companies in support. At the

Lieutenant Colonel David Brereton seen here when he was a Captain in 1910; he was promoted to command the battalion after Lieutenant Colonel Irvine left.

beginning of February RSM Joseph Watson was confirmed in his new rank and position of Lieutenant and Quartermaster of the battalion. After four days in the line they were relieved by 11/Essex Regiment and moved back to Brigade reserve in a hutted camp at Beugny. It was here that Major David L. Brereton rejoined the battalion and took over command from Lieutenant Colonel McCullagh. It was now that there was trouble with reinforcements from England.

A Cabinet committee had met in London to discuss the reinforcement of the BEF and the manpower shortages that would be met in 1918. It was suggested that the BEF would need 615,000 men to keep it up to strength in 1918, but the Ministry of National Service estimated that there would only be 100,000 men available. Various ways of overcoming the shortages were suggested but the main two that were accepted were: 1) reduce the wastage in manpower, and 2) make more men available for front-line service. There was a proposal that the number of infantry battalions in a division should be cut from twelve to nine and that the Divisional Pioneer Battalion would be reduced from four companies to three. Then on 10 January 1918 the War Office issued the orders for the reorganisation of the BEF, but these orders were not simple, for no Regular or First Line Territorial Battalion or Yeomanry Regiment was to be disbanded, only Second Line Territorial and Service (Kitchener) Battalions would be disbanded. In the Regular 6th Division that went overseas in 1914 this would have had no effect, but on 11 October 1915, 17 Brigade had been exchanged with 71 Brigade of 24th Division. At the same time, 14/Durham LI had joined 18 Brigade from 64 Brigade of 21st Division in exchange for 1/East Yorkshire Regiment. So now with two battalions of one regiment in the Brigade it was obvious that the junior service battalion would have to be disbanded. Therefore on 1 February 1918 14/Durham LI ceased to exist; the men were dispersed among the other battalions of the regiment in France. The War Diary of 2/Durham LI records that, Lieutenant William Eltringham and Lieutenant John Briggs were cross-posted from 14/Durham LI to 2/Durham LI, but no numbers of other ranks being transferred are supplied. Then on 6 February the War Diary records that four officers from the similarly disbanded 10/Durham LI joined the battalion; Lieutenant Frank Richards, Second Lieutenant Geoffrey Cates and Second Lieutenant Gordon Hislop were posted to A Company, whilst the last one, Lieutenant Joseph Dennison,was posted to C Company. For the next three days they were in Brigade Reserve. It was during this spell in the rear area that they had, once again, to perform the

An unidentified Warrant Officer stands in the middle of the road, part of the battalion collection in the regimental archives.

unpleasant task of forming a firing squad. 11606 Private Wilfred Clarke had been found guilty of desertion and had been sentenced to death. Some months previously the battalion had been warned that they were moving back into the line. When the roll was called prior to moving off, Private Clarke was found to be absent. It was about two months later that he was apprehended by the Military Police in Calais. The dice were loaded against Clarke from the start, for he had previously been absent without leave at least twice and had what can only be described as a 'bad character' reference from his officers. It was hardly surprising that the verdict at his court martial was 'Guilty'. On the morning of 9 February 1918 the sentence was duly carried out and today his remains lie in Bancourt British Cemetery.

The following day on 10 February the news came in that 9649 Sergeant S. W. Raine and 10737 Private G. A. Griffin had been awarded the Belgian Croix de Guerre. Then on 12 February 2/Durham LI took over a longer front from 11/Lancashire Fusiliers. The length of the front taken over needed three companies in the line; thus D Company was holding the right sector, A Company held the centre and C Company was on the left, with B Company in support; also that day Second Lieutenant Robert Haylett, late 7279 Company Sergeant Major 2/Durham LI, joined for duty. Nightly over the next three days the battalion sent out patrols into No Man's Land, they were looking for enemy

201360 Private Alfred Watt having been evacuated from 20/Durham LI; when he was fit again he was put on a draft to 2/Durham LI.

activity, but the Germans were very quiet and no signs of them were found. On 17 February, 11 Essex Regiment came up and took over the front line. 2/Durham LI moved back to the support line and took over duties from 1/West Yorkshire Regiment. From this position, each night they sent working parties up to work on the front-line system. On 20 February two new Second Lieutenants arrived: Christopher Poxon had already seen service at the front as a Lance Sergeant with 16/King's Royal Rifle Corps, where he had won the Military Medal; this battalion had been raised from members of the Church Lads Brigade, and he was posted to B Company. The second man, Second Lieutenant Neil Mackinnon, who was posted to D Company, had served with the Royal Fusiliers. The battalion remained in the support trenches until 23 February when they were relieved by 11/Essex Regiment and moved into Brigade Reserve at Beugnatre. The usual refitting took place and training began. This period was recalled in Hubert McBain's diary:

On my return to France I find the battalion have moved south and are in very quiet trenches astride the Bapaume–Cambrai Road with the Transport at Beugny. We proceed into Divisional reserve at Bahagnies.

Colonel Brereton having come out from England to take charge of the battalion, Colonel McCullagh proceeded to Ypres to take over the 19th Battalion. Gilpin takes over the duties of Adjutant from Cave. While at Bahagnies we find working parties night and day – the whole front being a hive of industry digging and wiring in preparation for the German attack that is expected in a short time.

Whilst the battalion was located at Beugnatre another subaltern reported to Battalion Headquarters; Second Lieutenant George Brown, a Territorial officer, from Liverpool, who had been commissioned into 5/Durham LI and had been in France since the previous November, was posted to B Company.

On 1 March 2/Durham LI left Beugnatre and marched up to the front line in the Morchies Sector, where they relieved 1/West Yorkshire Regiment. The line was held with D, B and C Companies in the front line and A Company was in support. The next three days were very quiet indeed and with the rumours of a German attack it became imperative that a prisoner be captured. This was so that any useful information and identification of the unit opposite could be gained. To this end a raid by 2/Durham LI was planned for the night of 4 March. Under the command of Captain H. F. Pickering, Second Lieutenants Wilfred Rice and Geoffrey Cates and thirty-seven men left the battalion trenches at 1940 hours.

205129 Private Thomas Drakard joined the battalion with a draft from the 35th Infantry Base Depot in June 1917; he was wounded during the attack on Premy Chapel Ridge and rejoined the battalion when he was fit again. He was promoted Lance Corporal and was wounded in the buttocks in November 1918.

They were heading for an enemy post, known to the British as 'The Nest'. The night was very dark and as quietly as possible they made their way over No Man's Land towards the enemy position. However, when they got there the enemy were not in occupation. Hoping that someone may come along, the raiding party lay down in ambush and waited. They waited for almost four hours, but still no German soldiers visited the position. By 0030 hours the raiding party had returned to the British trenches; they had suffered no casualties but had failed to take a prisoner. On 5 March, Brigade Headquarters decided that the front line would be held by two battalions, so 1/West Yorkshire Regiment moved up and took over from C Company on the left flank. C Company then moved into reserve alongside A Company. On 8 March the companies changed over and A Company and C Company took over the front line. They held this position until 13 March when once again they were relieved and moved back to Beugnatre Camp, where they became Brigade Reserve. B Company and two platoons of D Company remained near Morchies where they were employed constructing a new Brigade Headquarters. On 17 March C Company and the two remaining platoons of D Company left the camp at Beugnatre and marched to Morchies, where they relieved the party working on the new headquarters. The latter party rejoined the main battalion party in the huts at Beugnatre. On 19 March the battalion left the camp and marched back to the front line, where they took over from

11/Essex Regiment in the left subsection of the line held by 18 Brigade; this was the Morchies sector. The battalion placed B Company in the right front sector and D Company in the left front; behind B Company, A Company held the right reserve trench and in the left reserve the men of C Company held the position. The Brigade was holding the right of the Divisional Front with 51st (Highland) Division on the right and 71 Brigade on the left.

The Germans had long been plotting an attack against the British and French in the hope that with a number of strong blows they could win the war. As early as 11 November 1917, General Ludendorff summoned the Chiefs of Staff of the Group of Armies commanded by Crown Prince Rupprecht of Bavaria and the German Crown Prince Wilhelm, to a conference in Mons to discuss plans for 1918. The collapse of the Russian Army allowed the Germans to move around forty divisions from the Eastern Front to the Western Front, thus giving them a numerical superiority, which would allow them to strike a decisive blow in the west and possibly win the war. A number of proposals were put forward at this first conference, but they did not make any final decisions and the staff officers separated to study the problems of any offensives in the west.

By 15 December it was clear that Russia was out of the war and that the number of divisions available could be increased, along with a certain amount of heavy artillery. Troops were given three weeks; training in offensive operations and the best divisions were taken out of the line and put through an intensive training course. Men over the age of thirty-five were sent to the divisions left in the east and men under that age were brought from those divisions to replace the older men. Ammunition and shells were stockpiled and plans prepared. Another conference was held on 27 December 1917 where a number of operations were proposed: 'George', an offensive near Armentières, possibly combined with 'George II', an offensive near Ypres, 'Mars', an offensive in the Arras area and 'Michael', an offensive on both sides of St Quentin. Other attacks planned included 'Archangel', an attack by Seventh Army south of the Oise, 'Hector' and 'Achilles' east of Reims and 'Roland' on the old Champagne battlefield along with 'Castor' and 'Pollux', two attacks on either side of Verdun.

Preliminary orders were issued on 24 January 1918 and again on 8 February; it was decided that the 'George' offensives were too dependent on the weather, if there was a wet spring the Valley of the Lys would be difficult to cross until possibly May. With the British in possession of Vimy Ridge the 'Mars' attack was regarded as difficult. 'Hector', 'Achilles' and 'Roland' were kept on hold, whilst 'Castor' and 'Pollux' were abandoned. The main attack would be 'Michael' which was divided into three sub-attacks, 'Michael 1' to be carried out by the left wing of Seventeenth Army, in the direction of Bapaume. 'Michael 2' was the responsibility of Second

Army, advancing in the direction of Peronne and 'Michael 3' required the Eighteenth Army to attack towards Ham, whilst on the French front diversions and demonstrations would delay the French from sending support to the British.

After several days the right wing of Seventeenth Army would start the 'Mars' offensive, when the artillery had been regrouped and moved to the new sector. Whilst the German High Command was making these plans the British helped them by taking over and extending the British right southwards to the Oise.

At around 1700 hours on 20 March a ground mist started to rise along the length of the front of FIFTH and THIRD ARMIES. This mist rose and gradually got thicker and thicker, until by 2100 hours it was described as a ground fog. Along the front British patrols were out in No Man's Land which they found empty of enemy soldiers. They did, however, find many gaps cut in the German wire and when they approached these gaps they were found to be strongly defended. The few raids that took place were in the main unsuccessful, and any prisoners that were taken were anxious to be sent to the rear as quickly as possible; a good indication that something was about to happen. In the early hours of 21 March, German Engineers left their front line and quietly moved into No Man's Land and started cutting the wire where additional or improved gaps were needed. On the front held by 2/Durham LI they had been warned of a possible attack and throughout the night several patrols led by officers went out; at 0500 hours the battalion 'stood to'. Just as they were taking up their positions the German bombardment opened and a heavy barrage of gas shells fell on the battalion positions, especially the support line. B and D Companies in the front line had each placed one platoon in the support line, Jackal Support and Leopard Support. A Company and C Company were manning their positions in Autumn Reserve and Winter Reserve. The Commanding Officer, Lieutenant Colonel David Brereton, was in telephone contact with the front-line companies until at 0700 hours the OC B Company reported that the shelling was getting worse. Almost at once the line went dead and all communication with the front-line companies was lost and shortly after that, the wires to both Brigade Headquarters and the 1/West Yorkshire Regiment on the right, were cut. With the communications cut the CO sent two runners, Privates Matthews and Turnbull, to try to find out what was happening in front. The two men set off down Leech Avenue and went through a heavy bombardment and managed to visit both Company Commanders. The news that they brought back to the Battalion Headquarters was not good. Both front-line companies, although they were holding on had had very heavy casualties.

The men in the front-line companies were, as was to be expected by 1918, a mixture of the men that made up the British Army at this time. One

18/1549 Private Arthur Rowell from Darlington; batman Second Lieutenant Hubert McBain, he was mentioned in McBain's letters to h[...] parents, Arthur was killed in action on 2[...] March 1918

or two regulars, old India and South Africa veterans, Special Reservists from 3 and 4/Durham LI, some of whom had been out since 1914, Territorial's who had been out since 1915 and Derby men and conscripts. In B Company one of the fire bays was manned by one of these mixed groups which now formed VI Platoon. One was a Special Reservist from 4/Durham LI, 4/9901 Private David McCulloch from Thornaby-on-Tees. One a Territorial from 1/5/Durham LI, 204786 Private Thomas Hammond from Darlington, along with a conscript 36673 Private Percy Wright from

Birstall near Leeds, and Derby scheme enlistment 250671 Lance Corporal Charles Dance, a house painter from London who had somehow found himself transferred from 24/King's Royal Rifle Corps to the Durham Light Infantry. Drafted from the 5/Reserve Battalion to France he found himself sent up to 18/Durham LI and then sent to 2/Durham LI.

250671 Lance Corporal Charles Dance; seen here wearing his King's Royal Rifle Corps cap badge, he died on the fire step in the front line on 21 March 1918.

The four men held their position until at around 0930 hours when they came under heavy shellfire, a piece of shrapnel hit Charles Dance and knocked him unconscious and he died within a few minutes. The other three held on as long as they could; the estimated time varies, Private Thomas Hammond reckoned about one and a half hours, whilst Percy Wright estimated three hours. The position was eventually surrounded and over run and the three survivors were taken prisoner. After their release made statements to the Red Cross about what happened to Lance Corporal Dance. Private David McCulloch stated, 'I saw him hit by shrapnel March 21st at Morchies, we were captured then. He was an artist and came from London.' Private Thomas Hammond said 'I saw Dance killed on the fire step with a piece of shrapnel at Morchies, I was standing by him – 21 March – 9.30 am. We lost the trench and I was captured $1^{1}/2$ hours later. He was a London man, moustache; thin; married.' Some time after the first two had made their statements Private Percy Wright turned up and added this, 'We were at Morchies on 21st March and I was in the same post as Dance. I saw him killed by shrapnel which hit him in the back. He died within a few minutes – unconscious. The post was captured three hours after and the body was left.'

Meanwhile back at the battalion command post lack of communication was becoming a problem, so Privates Matthews and Turnbull were sent out again, but this time they were taken prisoner and did not return. With the amount of gas about, the men in the reserve trenches had to keep their respirators on for a long time and it wasn't until around 0900 hours that they were able to take them off safely. Conspicuous in the defence was 4/9893 Corporal Patrick McGlone, an Irishman from Toomebridge, County Antrim, who manned his

78829 Private Francis Boam from Nottinghamshire was killed in action 21 March 1918.

Lewis gun and held up the advancing enemy until he was almost surrounded and forced to withdraw.

The CO now got a message away to Brigade by the use of a pigeon, in which he was able to give some idea of what was going on and the heavy casualties that the battalion had already taken. Shortly after this the shelling died away and it became obvious that the enemy had taken the front and support lines and were now beginning to attack the reserve line. They started bombing up Leech Avenue and a counter-attack was organised. This was led by Second Lieutenant Hubert McBain wrote of the incident in his diary:

> At 0500 hours on 21 March the Germans start a bombardment of great strength on our front support and reserve lines, – by 0700 hours all communication with the front line has ceased with the buried cables being knocked out of action. I report to the Adjutant in the HQ dugout and am told to stand by and await orders. The last message from the front line is at 0820 hours, 'The Germans are now attacking'. By this time the bombardment had lifted and we can see the hill side in front of us covered with advancing Germans. By 10:00 we can see the Germans going through on both flanks, but our front line has held so well we in the reserve line have not been attacked. At 10:20 the Germans advance towards our reserve line in extended order but are mown down by our rifle and Lewis gun fire and after two or three attempts give up. At 1045 hours a bombing party of Germans work down the communication trench and attack our battalion headquarters which causes a momentary panic. But we soon counter attack with bombs and soon kill or wound them all and establish a block in the communication trench and fire rifle grenades with good effect at the next

Morchies Sector. Approximate positions of 2nd Durham Light Infantry 21 March 1918.

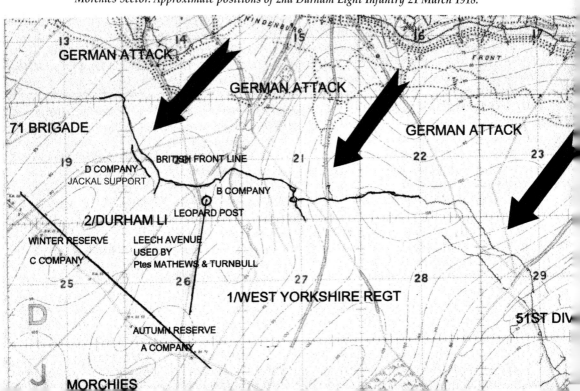

party of Germans who are thinking of attacking up the trench, but fortunately they do not.

This party under Hubert McBain managed to capture four German heavy machine guns with a number of boxes of ammunition and these were turned on their former owners. Another man who was counter-attacking about this time was 300173 Sergeant Robert Castling, from Annfield Plain, County Durham. He had gone out to France with 8/Durham LI in April 1915 and after fighting at Ypres and on the Somme he spent some time with 7/Durham LI, before he was posted to 2/Durham LI. Forced out of his position by an overwhelming enemy attack, he reorganised his section and then led them in a very courageous and determined counter-attack which drove the enemy back.

The panic at Battalion Headquarters mentioned by Hubert McBain occurred when the Germans who had bombed their way up Leech Avenue got into the reserve line. One German soldier, possibly an officer, was actually killed in the act of throwing a bomb down the steps of the Battalion Headquarters dugout. On the body of one of the dead German officers a map was found and this was quickly sent off to Divisional Headquarters. Although the artillery bombardment had died away, the Germans kept up a heavy machine-gun fire on the reserve line. A wounded man was spotted lying out in front of the trench and the Adjutant, Captain Ernest Gilpin assisted by Corporal Robson went out to get him, in spite of the heavy fire. When they were about 80 yards from the trench, Captain Gilpin was hit in the head and killed instantly, whilst Corporal Robson was wounded in the thigh. Corporal Wade and Lance Corporal Dairs then made an attempt to bring them in. However, owing to the heavy fire they had to give up. The Germans could be seen advancing towards Lagnicourt; their guns could be seen being moved up and mounted German officers could be seen in the distance, and there was a chance that the battalion left flank could be turned. A message to this effect was sent, by runner, to the CO of 1/West Yorkshire Regiment on the right. However, the runner returned with the news that the same was happening on the right of the Yorkshire battalion. At 1500 hours Colonel Brereton received a message that he was to retire and he began making the arrangements. Then at 1600 hours a message arrived from the CO of 1/West Yorkshire Regiment that they would be falling back into the section held by 2/Durham LI because they were almost surrounded. At almost the same time the block in Leech Avenue was forced in but the men manning it fell back fighting. The shelling increased again and the men of 2/Durham LI were falling fast, but the wire in front of the reserve line was still intact and the enemy were repulsed by rifle and Lewis gun fire. This was achieved by a party of men sent out into shellholes in front of the position, from where they could engage the enemy. Predominant in this group was 45188 Private John Muir from Milngarvie. The men with him were killed one by one, and he was eventually all alone, but he remained at his post and killed many of the enemy as they tried to outflank him. Eventually just before he was surrounded he was forced to retire and made it back to the main party.

A company of 11/Essex came up in support and in view of the planned retirement Colonel Brereton deployed them behind the battalion so that they could give covering fire as the surviving Durhams fell back. At 16:30 Lieutenant Colonel Alfred Boyall DSO, 1/West Yorkshire Regiment and Major Guy Stockdale MC, West Yorkshire Regiment, Commanding 11/Essex Regiment, along with the survivors of their battalions, arrived at the headquarters of 2/Durham LI, and arrangements were made for them to cover the right flank. A conference took place, the Commanding Officers decided that it would be impossible to retire in daylight and that the only thing they could do was to hang on until nightfall and then attempt to get back. The enemy were easily stopped coming over the open from the front, but they were moving quickly round the flanks and a series of blocks were made in Autumn Reserve and Winter Reserve in order to check them. By 1850 all the bombs had been used and the position appeared hopeless; it was decided that the only thing they could do was to fight it out as dusk wasn't

Lieutenant James A. Black originally a private in 16/Northumberland Fusiliers was killed in action on 21 March 1918; he is buried in Vaulx Hill Cemetery.

No. 45188. Pte J. C. Muir

2ⁿᵈ Bⁿ Durham Light Infantry

Your Gallant Conduct in the Field

on 22ⁿᵈ March 1918

in holding up the enemy from a shell-hole in the open when all your comrades had been killed has been reported to me, and I have had much pleasure in reading the record of your gallantry.

S. G. Cromwood

Brigadier-General.
Commanding
18th Infantry Brigade.

In the Field.

April 5 1918.

18 Brigade Card of Honour presented to 45188 Private J.C. M...

expected for another hour. At about 1915 hours the mist started to rise again and gradually got thicker. It became obvious that this was the opportunity that they needed and the order was quickly passed that every man must make his own way back to the Corps line. The order was given just in time, for as the Durhams and West Yorkshire men left at one end the Germans got in the other. It was estimated that around 300 men left the reserve line and that out of that number about 250 reached the Corps line. As they left the Germans opened up with heavy machine-guns and a number of men were killed; there was no chance to rescue any wounded and those that fell had to be left behind. Most who made it did so via the copse in front of Morchies. A number of officers that had been in the reserve line and were known to have left for the Corps line failed to turn up: Major Sopwith, Captain Fawcett, Lieutenants Osborne and Tuffs and Second Lieutenants Davis, Jebb, and McBain. Also missing were Lieutenant Colonel Alfred Boyall DSO, of 1/West Yorkshire Regiment and Major Guy Stockdale MC, West Yorkshire Regiment, Commanding 11/Essex Regiment. The latter was killed, but Colonel Boyall was a prisoner of war. Nothing further was seen of C Company's Company Sergeant Major who had been out with the battalion since September 1914; 8915 CSM Joseph Turton MM, who had been evident in the defence, but afterwards was posted missing believed killed. A Company's Sergeant Major, 7073 CSM Edward Paddon, another of the original regulars, was recommended for a gallantry award by the Commanding Officer, written on 17 November 1919: with these words, 'CSM Paddon was with A Company in the Corps Line He was of the greatest assistance to his company commander and I can personally testify to the fine example he set to his men.' Alas, no gallantry award has been traced.

458 Private Samuel ~llett from Ryton on ~ne, killed in action ~ 21 March 1918.

Not one man had tried to leave the battalion position until ordered to do so, indeed of the two front-line companies only two officers, who had been wounded very early on and one man who had accompanied them to the Regimental Aid Post, got back. At the Aid Post the Battalion MO, Captain Joseph Muir RAMC, went to and fro during the day between the line and his Aid Post. He was so cool and calm that he inspired all ranks with confidence; it was assumed that he remained at the Aid Post looking after the wounded and was taken prisoner when the enemy broke through.

Hubert McBain, although posted as missing was in fact wounded, and having been evacuated he continued his story in his diary:

Second Lieutenant William T. Davis was killed in action on 21 March 1918 aged 20.

We hang on till dark when Brereton sends for me, I have been in charge of the block all day and I am given orders to take a few men out and form a flank, should the Germans, who are now well in the

~vate Frederick ~dner killed in ~ion on 21 March ~.

rear of us, decide to attack us. As soon as we dash out of the trench to take up a position we come under machine gun fire, CSM Osborne and Sergeant Allen were both knocked out. As soon as I get to the ground overlooking the rear of our trench I am sniped at by a German about eighty yards away in a dip in the ground where our aid post is. I dash for a shell hole in order to take cover and I am wounded in the thigh by the same man.

While all this fighting was taking place, officers and men were returning from leave, courses and attachments to other units; these were gathered at the Battalion Transport lines by the Quartermaster, Lieutenant Joseph Watson MC, DCM. Here he gathered Captains Potts and Cave and Second Lieutenants Scott and Brown along with Second Lieutenant Dennison who was Acting Transport Officer. Eventually the Transport lines came under German shellfire and during the night 21/22 March they moved to a new location in a valley west of the Monument at H.14.d.3.0, which is just west of Favreuil. The Officer Commanding, C Company, had gathered all his wounded in a large dugout and when the retirement was made, he remained behind with them. The only officers who made it back to the Corps line were the Commanding Officer and Second Lieutenant Eccles with ninety men and Second Lieutenant Spencer who had fifty-six men with him.

Second Lieutenant H. A. Pickering was taken Prisoner of War on 21 March 1918.

The enemy followed up closely to the remnants of 18 Brigade and during 22 March there was further fighting as they fell back towards Morchies. 58 Brigade had come up behind 18 and 71 Brigades and established a line about 1,000 yards behind Morchies on which the survivors fell back. During this fighting 11513 Private John Richardson from Newcastle was killed in action; he was another of those who had landed with the battalion in September 1914. The enemy could be seen in large numbers around Morchies and the gunners of 256 Brigade Royal Field Artillery pulled their guns out of the gun pits and for four hours fired over open sights. Being close to the Divisional dump they had plenty of ammunition, indeed the men of B Battery fired 1,750 rounds per gun. Meanwhile the Battalion Echelon had moved yet again, this time to Buchanan Camp near Achiet-le-Grand. Here Second Lieutenants Gordon Hislop, Christopher Poxon and Howard St George rejoined from courses.

Second Lieutenant Miles Hutchinson taken Prisoner of on 21 March 1918

Later that night the exhausted survivors under the command of Second Lieutenant Walter Spencer rejoined what was left of the battalion. The next day word was received that the Germans were in possession of Mory and that 6th Division was to form an outpost line. Lieutenant Colonel Brereton took command of what remained of 18 Brigade and took over the centre of the Divisional Front, covering Achiet-le-Grand. Trenches were dug and were completed by about 1600 hours. They manned these hastily-dug trenches until 2300 hours when they returned to Buchanan Camp. Here Captain Walter Frith and twenty-three other ranks rejoined from the 6th Divisional Wing and Captain V. E. Lloyd RAMC was temporarily attached

to the battalion as MO. There was a reorganisation of those that were left: A Company was commanded by Second Lieutenant Hislop, B Company by Second Lieutenant Poxon, C Company was led by Second Lieutenant Scott and Captain Cave commanded D Company. On 24 March the Transport moved by road and headed for Mondicourt; they were followed by the rest of the battalion who marched as far as Puisieux-au-Mont where they entrained at around 1600 hours. The next morning those on the train arrived at Mondicourt near Doullens and detrained. They were joined by the Transport and the whole battalion entrained again at 1300 hours. The train travelled north into Belgium and eventually arrived at Peselhoek where they alighted and marched to Whitehall Camp at Elverdinghe. Here they were joined by the Reverend B. C. Hopson CF, who was attached to the battalion as its padre. The following day they marched to a hutted camp, which was known as Road Camp at Sint Jan-ter-Biezen. Here they received a special message from the Brigade Commander, Brigadier General G. S. G. Crauford:

A RECORD OF GALLANTRY
IN KEEPING WITH THE HIGHEST TRADITIONS OF THE ARMY

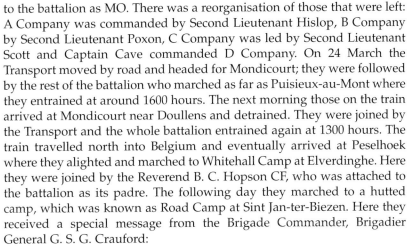

The battle which opened on the 21st March is intended by the enemy to be the opening phase of the final struggle for supremacy between the British and German Nations and their divergent National ideals.

The courage and devotion to duty displayed by the Brigade has never been surpassed in our national history and will add fresh laurels to the Regiments concerned. Our comrades who have fallen have died fighting in one of the most decisive battles of the world. Out of 1600 men of all ranks who went into action, on the morning of the 21st, 80 men came out on the morning of the 23rd, retaining their discipline to the last.

In the interval, the Reserve Line had maintained its front intact till dusk on the evening of the 21st, though the right flank was turned by noon and the left by 3 pm on that day.

On the 22nd, the remnants of the Brigade still held the Corps Line intact till 2 p.m., when fresh troops on the left gave way, and the flank of the Brigade was driven in and overwhelmed.

It is not too much to say that the fine stand of the Brigade was not only of extreme importance to the IV Corps, but it also had decisive results on the whole of the Third Army battle front.

H.Q., 18 I. B.   *Brigadier General*
27 March 1918   *Commanding 18 Infantry Brigade*

Then on 28 March they moved yet again, this time to billets in farmhouses in the Steenvoorde area. That afternoon His Majesty King George V visited the 6th Division and inspected some of the survivors of the recent battles. A few men of each battalion were drawn up in the Town Square in Steenvoorde and His Majesty went slowly along the ranks and spoke to each man there and asked about his experiences; the parade was totally unhurried and finally the King thanked them all for their services and congratulated them on their achievements.

SPECIAL ORDER OF THE DAY
His Majesty THE KING this afternoon paid a visit to the 6th Division, and talked to Officers and men who had taken part in the recent fighting. On departure, THE KING asked the Divisional Commander to let the Division know how much he appreciated their magnificent defence on 21st and 22nd inst. He wished them all luck, and was sure that he could depend on them to fight as well again.

The Divisional Commander is sure that all ranks will proudly remember the honour done to them by this special visit of His Majesty, and is confident that they will uphold in future actions the splendid reputation for fighting which they have won throughout the War, and added to in the recent Battles of CAMBRAI and BAPAUME.

(Signed)P. HUDSON
Lieut. Colonel
A. A. & Q. M. G.,
6th Division

Word reached the battalion that Second Lieutenant Hubert McBain had managed to evade capture and had been evacuated with a bullet wound in the thigh. He had ended up at the 3rd General Hospital at Le Treport on the French coast from where he wrote to his parents:

3 Gen Hosp
APO13
Sun 24 Mar
I got slightly wounded in the thigh on the day of the great attack (21st) but you must not worry about it at all. It was the best thing that could have happened to me. My wound was quite clean and the bullet has not touched the artery at all, it went in at the left side of my thigh and has come out at the front. I am afraid that most of the battalion who were in the front line in front of Queant are wiped out. We hung on to the battle line for thirteen and one half hours and at 1730 hours in the evening we found the enemy were getting round our flank so a few of us rushed out but were mostly knocked out by enemy machine gun and rifle fire, that's when I got hit by a Bosche who was only a hundred yards away. I crawled as best as I could to our next line of defence and just when I was about done in I crept into a trench which happened to contain an Advance Dressing Station where I

came to the end of my troubles. My wound was bound up and four sturdy men of the RAMC carried me to the CCS.

There was further reorganisation on 29 March when Captain Frith took over the duties of Adjutant; Second Lieutenant Hislop became Intelligence Officer and Second Lieutenant St George was appointed Lewis Gun Officer. Second Lieutenant George Brown took over command of A Company and Lieutenant Carss who had rejoined from his attachment to Brigade became Officer Commanding B Company. That day an inspection of the battalion by the GOC, SECOND ARMY, General Sir Herbert Plumer GCMG, GCVO, KCB, took place. Also the same day Captain Burke RAMC joined the battalion as a replacement for Captain Lloyd. It was now time to start rebuilding the battalion and on the last day of March two large drafts, one of 359 men and the other of 101 men, joined from the base depot.

Some time later a list of gallantry awards to the battalion for its actions on 21/22 March was published. The DSO went to Lieutenant Colonel Brereton, the MC was awarded to Second Lieutenants Spencer and McBain. 300173 Sergeant R. Castling, 9893 Corporal P. McGlone and 45188 Private J. C. Muir all received the DCM. One bar to the Military Medal and six Military Medals were also awarded.

The month of April began with some difficulty for the battalion; being in scattered billets it was difficult to get the men together and start the business of reorganisation and training. The battalion strength had now been brought up to fifteen officers and 862 other ranks. An informal Brigade sports day took place on 2 April but no results were published. The next day they proceeded by march route to Belgian Chateau just south-west of Ypres where they took over huts in Marquise Camp and the Transport moved to Dickebusch Wood. They were now in Divisional Reserve. The strength in officers was increased over the next two days when Lieutenant Robert Haylett, Second Lieutenants Francis Sullivan, Thomas Harrison and B. Simpson returned from leave and Lieutenant Charles Handcock joined for duty from the Regimental Depot in Newcastle and took over C Company. A reconnaissance party consisting of Captain Walter Potts, the Acting Second in Command, the four company commanders and the Intelligence Officer went up to the Reutel subsection of the front and had a good look at the section of the line that was to be taken over by the battalion. Captain Sidney Streatfield rejoined the battalion on 8 April and Major James Jones reported back from the Divisional Wing and assumed the position of Second in Command.

That afternoon the Brigade Commander presented Cards of Honour in recognition of gallant conduct to a number of officers and men of the battalion. In the early hours of 10 April there was an alarm at the front and the battalion stood to arms and moved to the area of Otago Camp between Ypres and Zillebeke Lake, which is described as 'Pond' in the War Diary.

Having stood by all morning, they were not needed and returned to camp at 1300 hours. That night they moved forward and took over from 1/Leicestershire Regiment of 71 Brigade in the Reutel subsector with 11/Essex Regiment on the left and 1/West Yorkshire Regiment on the right. 2/Durham LI placed A Company in the right front trenches, B Company in the left front trenches with C Company in support and D Company in reserve. The front line was very quiet but the men were warned to stay vigilant as another German attack was expected.

On 11 April no less than ten officers of the Northumberland Fusiliers reported for duty with the battalion; Lieutenants Eustace Keating, Sidney Brewin MC and H. A. Gratton were posted to A Company. Lieutenants F. C. Dagnall and Ernest Smith went to B Company, Lieutenants Herbert Allison and Welford Bolam were both sent to C Company and Lieutenants G. R. Fortune, George Martin and Harold Booth reported to D Company. During the day enemy shelling started to take its toll on the battalion again and six men were killed and three wounded.

During the next two days the British Artillery were preparing and registering counter-barrage targets. There was now some shuffling about of the battalions; 11/Essex Regiment were taken out of the line and 2/Durham LI side-stepped northwards and took over the portion of the line vacated. The battalion now had to hold a longer front; B Company stood fast and C Company moved in on their left, to become the centre company with D Company taking over and holding the trenches on their left. A Company was relieved by 1/West Yorkshire Regiment who also extended to their left, which allowed A Company to become the battalion support company. During the day Lieutenant Eustace Keating, Northumberland Fusiliers, and three men were killed; the 26-year-old officer came from South Shields and prior to the war had gained a BA at Oxford. At the same time another man was evacuated wounded.

Second Lieutenant Welford Bolam Northumberland Fusiliers Attached 2/Durham LI joined the battalion on 1 April 1918, he was awarded the Military Cross in September 1918.

On the night of 14 April further orders for another readjustment of the positions were issued, but then cancelled. Further orders were then issued for a partial withdrawal; A Company took over posts from 11/Essex Regiment in the Corps line, D Company moved to Polygon Dugouts and Battalion Headquarters, with B and C Companies moved into Westhoek Dugouts. They were replaced in their positions by men of B and C Companies of 1/West Yorkshire Regiment. All this movement was accomplished without loss and at 1400 hours on 15 April, Battalion Headquarters along with the two companies previously named moved to a bivouac camp in map square I.24.b. The next day they were moved back nearer to Ypres and commenced work on a new support line. This was later known as the Doll's House Line, in front of this was the Zillebeke Line which was manned by 11/Essex Regiment. The trenches that already

246

A destroyed railway station in France.

German prisoners and British stretcher-bearers make their way, under shellfire, along a plank road.

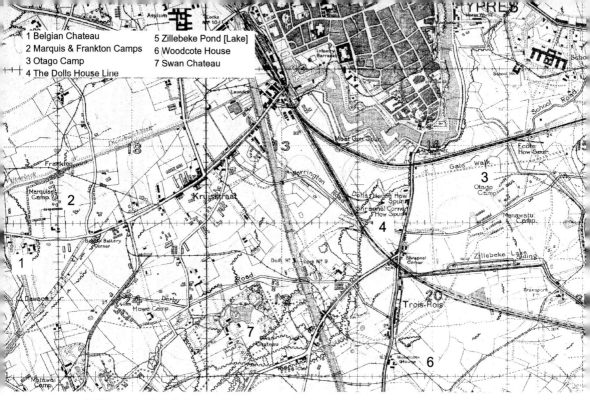

2nd Durham Light Infantry area of operations April 1918.

existed were much improved and where needed new trenches were dug.

During the night the camp they were in was shelled but the company in the part of the camp hit moved out without incurring any casualties. Their next task was to work on the 'Kruisstraat Line', which involved digging lengths of trenches along the canal bank, which ran slightly south-east from Ypres through map square I.13.c to I.19.a; during this work, Second Lieutenant Scott was sent away to hospital. With the threat of another German attack many of the camps that had sprung up around Ypres had been abandoned as some units had been moved further back; these camps were now utilised by the infantry working parties employed on digging new defence lines around Ypres. The front line was now held by a series of posts which were known as 'Corps Posts' and their defenders as the 'Advanced Force'. After spending a further day working on the 'Kruisstraat Line' on the night 19/20 April C and D Companies moved up to the Westhoek Dugouts in support of the Advanced Force, which was provided by two companies of 1/West Yorkshire Regiment who held Corps Posts 3, 4, 5 and 5a. The same day Lieutenant Allison was sent away to hospital along with one man who had been wounded. The following night the two companies of 2/Durham LI replaced the companies of the West Yorkshire Regiment in the Corps Posts. D Company manned post 3 and C Company placed a platoon in each of posts 4, 5 and 5a. The rest of the battalion moved forward and took over in the Westhoek Dugouts. 2/Durham LI was now the 18 Brigade advanced force, with 16 Brigade on the left and 110 Brigade of 37th Division on the right. During the day Captain George Fillingham rejoined the battalion and the following officers reported for duty: Lieutenants L. Silburn and W. Kish from the Army Service Corps TF and Second Lieutenants Robert Simpson and John Folliott. There was some sporadic shelling during the day and six men were wounded. At around 1500 hours the enemy were seen advancing towards the battalion posts and the SOS rockets were sent up. The British Artillery opened fire and the Germans scattered and fell back to their own positions and the attack petered out. Just to the south the Germans had started the next phase, George II, of their offensives in the west. They captured Mont Kemmel and now began to extend their attack to the north and soon had a footing on Hill 60, from where they could enfilade the trenches held by the battalion.

On the night of 21/22 April the 6th Division extended its front to the right of its present position; to this end D Company remained where they were, C Company was replaced by a company of 1/East Kent Regiment and moved back into reserve at Hooge Crater. B Company took over the three left-hand posts manned by one company of 6/West Yorkshire Regiment, and A Company took over the remaining four left-hand posts from the same battalion. So 2/Durham LI now held the front with three companies: A on the right, B in the centre and D Company was now the left-hand company. Later in the day a company from 1/Essex Regiment, who were part of 112 Brigade of 37th Division, arrived at Hooge Crater and were attached to 2/Durham LI as an extra reserve company.

During 22 April five officers reported at Battalion Headquarters for duty with the battalion: Captain John Everatt, Lieutenant William Sidgwick and Second Lieutenants James Harrison, Wolsey Lawson and Richard Ware. There was some shelling and one man, 93080 Private George Smith, a Rochdale man who had previously served in the York and Lancaster Regiment, was killed. This was followed the next day by the deaths of two more men and the wounding of three others. Whilst in the line during this tour, the battalion sent out a number of patrols each night. They tried to take a prisoner, for identification, but all attempts were unsuccessful. The enemy made no serious attempts to attack, but the enemy trench mortars were very troublesome and although at the start of the tour their artillery was fairly quiet, by the end they had increased their fire considerably.

On the night of 26/27 April all along the line there was a planned general withdrawal of the advance posts. The plan was timed to start at 2100 hours and the advanced companies were to begin leaving at 2200 hours. A platoon from each company covered the movement of their comrades and gradually fell back themselves. This was recorded in *The*

Australian Pioneers repair a plank road as an Ammunition Column moves off towards the line to resupply the guns. In the foreground two men are setting fuses on shells.

Bugle the Regimental Magazine in 1927 although the author is unidentified:

> During the whole of that day there had been excursions and alarums particularly on the 21st Division front on our right. The plan of the withdrawal was to make the Germans think we were still there. We copied his tactics and Verey light men were left here and there and at intervals pooped off with their pistols.
>
> Eventually word came that 15/Cheshire, our neighbours had got away and that we could start. Gradually each company got back platoon by platoon, leaving only a small rear party per company, to go back under the orders of Major Jones MC, the Second in Command who remained at the Crater. Battalion Headquarters had moved off at zero hour. It was difficult to tell how we felt at that time, all keenly anxious that the Germans should not spot the withdrawal, and prepared to act if they did.
>
> Everything went well, the most advanced posts had withdrawn by 0400 hours and met us at the Crater; one yet remained. Meanwhile at the Crater,

Jones was telling us about the attack of 1915 and how bitterly he felt at handing over Hooge without firing a shot.

The last party came in. As luck would have it, a shell dropped and knocked out two of them and wounded two others. Time was getting on. The stretcher bearers took away the wounded and we buried the dead quickly and quietly, Major Jones superintended. This sad job ended we set off down the Menin Road past Birr Cross Roads into reserve at our new line behind White Chateau. It was a bitter time, a hard time and every man felt angered at giving up that place for which many of the regiment had fallen. Tails were not up that night but the men were far from disheartened.

Given the passage of time it is understandable that the author should get some facts slightly wrong, The War Diary records the shell that fell on the party in Hooge Crater but gives the casualties as eight other ranks wounded, four killed and one died of wounds. The dead were 4/9155 Corporal Robert Bruce, from Hebburn Quay, and 19/1556 Private Thomas Costello, a Darlington man, who was one of the Bantams rejected by the GOC 35th Division in 1917. The others were later reinforcements; 79110 Private Reginald Payne, who came from Lewisham and 77694 Private Henry Thorneycroft, from Chatham. The man who died from his wounds was a Yorkshire man, 79215 Private Frederick Marwood, who came from Kirk Deighton near Wetherby.

Having got safely away without coming under attack the battalion made its way to Frankton Camp near Belgian Chateau, which was occupied by Battalion Headquarters. In the camp, near to the huts that they were to occupy, the men in the rifle companies started to dig or improve shelter trenches; these were so constructed that they could be used as fire trenches should the enemy break through. All surplus officers were now ordered back to the Transport lines; these had on 29 April moved to a new camp 1 mile west of Poperinghe, which while it was a safer place than the line, they were still in range of the German guns. This was soon confirmed by the men of the Transport Platoon and the Battalion Quartermaster, Lieutenant Joseph Watson MC, DCM. As they made their way forward with stores, rations and ammunition, they came under enemy shellfire and the QM and three men were wounded.

Sadly Joseph Watson died from his wounds and the battalion lost another fine and experienced Quartermaster. That night the battalion came under heavy and sustained shellfire, the signal that an attack was imminent. The barrage was a mixed one with many gas shells mixed in with the high explosive and shrapnel. Although three men were killed and eleven wounded, there were many more men evacuated suffering from the effects of the gas. So ended April 1918: the battalion was well up to strength with forty officers and 843 other ranks and they had received a large draft of eighty-eight men during the month. Since the news of the March retreat and the lists of the missing and killed had reached families in England, many anxious wives and mothers had written to battalion commanders all along the front. Mrs Dance was one of those who wrote to the Commanding Officer of 2/Durham LI, Lieutenant Colonel David Brereton. On 1 May he replied:

> *1 May 1918*
>
> *Dear Madam,*
>
> *I have to acknowledge your letter of April 25th. I regret to say that many men of the Battalion were missing on March 21st and 22nd + that No 250671 L/Cpl C Dance was amongst the number.*
>
> *It is impossible for me to say whether he was taken prisoner or not, nor is it known if he was wounded.*
>
> *Please accept my deep sympathy in your anxiety,*
>
> > *Believe me*
> >
> > *Yours Truly*
> >
> > *D Brereton Lt Col*
> >
> > *Comdg 2 Durham L Infy*

At 2100 hours on 1 May 2/Durham LI commenced the relief of 11/Essex Regiment in the Zillebeke Pond section of the Corps Outpost line, by midnight they had completed the takeover. B Company held the left front, from Warrington Road to the south-west corner of Zillebeke Pond. C Company was in the Outpost line from the south-west corner of Zillebeke Pond to the Divisional Boundary, just north of French Farm, in map square I.27.a. One platoon of C Company was in support at I.21.c.2.8. D Company was manning the new switch line from I.20.b.5.0. to I.19.d.8.7. A Company was behind them in the Dolls House Line. Their left flank was just south of the railway crossing south of the Lille Gate at Ypres and ran down to I.20.a.1.8. During the day Second Lieutenant M. Cohen was appointed Assistant Adjutant. The next three days passed quietly.

A captured German airman volunteered the information that the enemy would attack at 0400 hours on 4 May; the battalion 'stood to' but the attack did not materialise. The morning passed fairly quietly but in the early afternoon shells started falling on the Dolls House Line and Shrapnel Corner, but this gradually died out. Then at 1800 hours C Company came under enemy fire and four other ranks were wounded. The Battalion was well up to strength in officers and there had been an instruction that only a certain number would be in the line at any one time. So it was found practical that an arrangement of reliefs was set up, with each officer having a few days at the Transport lines and then going back up the line and another officer having a few days' rest.

On 6 May the battalion was relieved by 1/West Yorkshire Regiment and was this completed by midnight. 2/Durham LI then took up the positions vacated by the Yorkshire men in the Dolls House Line and Kruisstraat Line and D Company manned the Derby Road Switch near Swan Chateau. The next couple of days were spent improving the positions and then on 8 May the Germans shelled the battalion with gas between 0330 and 0430 hours and all ranks were forced to wear their respirators, however, no casualties occurred.

On 13 May 6th Division side-stepped to the south and 2/Durham LI relieved 9/Norfolk Regiment of 71 Brigade on a front from Iron Bridge to Sandbag Track; on the right the line was still held by 71 Brigade and on the left 11/Essex Regiment continued 18 Brigade's front. 2/Durham LI held the front with B Company on the right, with two platoons in close support at Bedford House. On the left A Company was responsible for the defence with one platoon in close support at Woodcote House. C Company was still in support in the Dolls House Line and in reserve was D Company in the Kruisstraat Line. Battalion Headquarters was located well back at Belgian Chateau. Over the next three days the front was reasonably quiet apart from some shelling each day, which wounded a total of four men. On 18 May they were relieved by 1/West Yorkshire Regiment and went back into Brigade reserve at Belgian Battery Corner.

From this position, on 20 May they sent out patrols in to No Man's Land searching for enemy positions and information. One of these patrols from C Company met a German patrol near 'Blauwe Poort Farm. A short sharp action took place in which at least eight of the enemy were wounded or killed and the remainder withdrew. The men from C Company came away totally unscathed. The patrols had noted a number of enemy positions and the decision was taken that the battalion would carry out a raid on some of these positions with the aim of taking a prisoner. The instructions for the raid were comprehensive and tried to cover all aspects of the raid.

Operation Order No 2
Lieutenant Colonel D. L. Brereton DSO
Commanding 2nd Battalion, the Durham Light Infantry
Ref Map: Ypres sheet 1:10,000

1 A & C Coys will carry out a raid tomorrow night with the object of procuring prisoners. Zero hour will be stated later. The raid will be preceded by an artillery bombardment.

2 Area to be raided.

From HAZELBURY FARM to pillboxes at I.27.c.45.30 thence to MIDDLESEX ROAD at point I.27.d.80.45 to BLAUWE POORT FARM.

3 Barrage.

An artillery barrage under orders of OC Left Group 6th D.A. is being arranged as follows:

i) Zero Hour for 15 minutes on following objectives:

Pillboxes at I.27.c.45.30 to BLAUWE POORT FARM.

Dugouts N & S of Railway track running through I.27.d.

ii) 2nd Phase Barrage lifts at Zero plus 15 minutes for one hour to following line: I.33.a. to LA CHAPELLE with a gap between CHESTER FARM and LA CHAPELLE thence to I.33.b.9.4.

iii) LANKHOF FARM and SPOIL BANK will be shelled from Zero till Zero plus 45 minutes.

4 Raiding Parties.

1 Right Group to consist of 5 Officers and 77 ORs under Captain R. Haylett, Comdg A Coy.

2 Left Group to consist of 5 Officers and 77 ORs under Captain C. G. Handcock MC Comdg C Coy.

5 Action of Raiding Parties.

i) The Right Group will assemble at HAZELBURY FARM at Zero minus 15 minutes and will move as near as possible to their objectives, which they will attack as soon as the barrage lifts.

This group will be divided into parties as under:-

No 1 Party, Objective, Farm at I.27.c.60.50.

Consisting of two Platoons each of 1 Officer, 1 Sergeant and 3 Sections each of 1NCO and 3 men.

First Platoon under Lieutenant J D Forsyth.

Second Platoon under Second Lieutenant H. A. V. Gratton.

No 2 Party, Objective, Pillboxes at I.27c.45.30.

Consisting of two platoons organised as No 1 party

Third Platoon under Lieutenant S. Brewin MC.

Fourth Platoon under Lieutenant L. Silburn.

No 3 Party, In support at I.26.d.62.42 consisting of Coy Commander and 25 Ors inclusive of stretcher-bearers and runners.

ii) The Left Group will assemble at I.21.d.25.55 at Zero minus 15 minutes and will move as near to their objectives as possible and will attack them as soon as the barrage lifts.

This group will be divided into parties as under:-

No 1 Party, Objective, BLAUWE POORT FARM.

Organised as Nos 1 & 2 parties in Right Group

First Platoon under Second Lieutenant J. Folliott

Second Platoon under Second Lieutenant R. F. Ware.

No 2 Party, Objective, Pillboxes in I.27.d. N of Railway.

Organised as No 1 Party.

Third Platoon under Second Lieutenant W Bolam.

Fourth Platoon under Second Lieutenant R B Y Simpson.

No 3 Party, In support at I.21.d.25.55 consisting of Coy Commander and 25 Ors inclusive of stretcher-bearers and runners.

6. Return of Raiding Parties.

Parties will complete their circle of operations rejoining our lines if possible at their Group HQ. On arrival at Group HQ parties will be sent back direct to Battalion HQ at H.26.a.50.90.

To assist in direction a fix will be lit at I.19.a.15.65 at Zero plus 30 minutes.

Prisoners will be conducted by the parties to Battalion HQ.

7. Signals.

In addition to the fire referred to in para 6, each Group Commander will be given 12 Green Very Lights, which will be used as a signal to indicate his position should any party fail to return within reasonable time.

8. Reports.

Group Commanders will report the situation on the conclusion of the raid, denoting number of casualties by.......hours, prisoners by........minutes, missing by......seconds. OC Right Group will send messages to HQ 1/West Yorkshire Regiment using Coy HQ of that Regiment. OC Left Group will send messages to HQ 11/Essex Regiment using Coy HQ of that Regiment. The Commanding Officer will be at HQ 1/Essex Regiment and the Second in Command at HQ 1/West Yorkshire Regiment. Messages to be addressed to 'PASTRY' and signed 'HAYLETT' or 'HANDCOCK'.

9. First Aid Post.

The First Aid Post will be established at the 'DOLL'S HOUSE' and relay Aid Posts at 'BEDFORD HOUSE' for right group and at 'TUNNEL JUNCTION'

10. DRESS.

SBR's, Rifles, Bayonets, 30 rounds SAA, 4 bombs to be carried by the man. Equipment will not be taken. Caps or cap comforters to be worn instead of steel helmets. Faces and hands to be blackened.

2nd Durham Light Infantry, Trench Raid 21 May 1918.

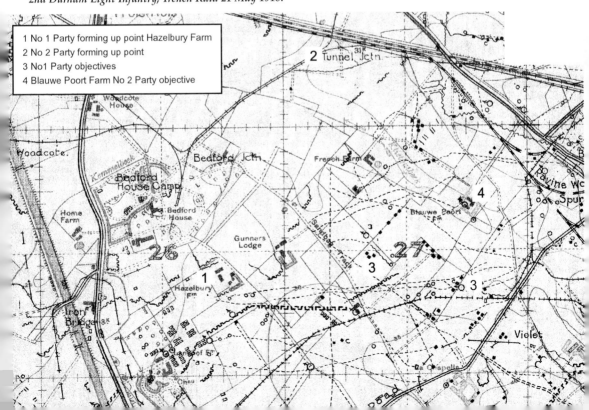

1 No 1 Party forming up point Hazelbury Farm
2 No 2 Party forming up point
3 No1 Party objectives
4 Blauwe Poort Farm No 2 Party objective

Knobkerries, electric torches and wire cutters will be distributed as considered necessary by Group Commanders.

All identifications to be removed before leaving camp.

11. Password.

The Password will be 'SUNDERLAND'. The Battalions holding the line will be notified.

20/5/18 Sgd S. R. Streatfield Captain A/Adjt   2/DLI

The raid was planned to begin at midnight on 21 May and was one of the most successful carried out by the battalion; it was organised as was laid down in the operation's order. The right group was assembled by 2330 hours in the trench at I.26.d.80.55. The wire was cut in front of the trench and a path made through it. At 2340 hours both parties moved off towards their respective objectives, while No 3 Party took up a covering position near the assembly point. As soon as the barrage lifted, No 2 Party reached its objective, which was found to be unoccupied. They then headed straight for the farm which was the objective of No 1 Party. This party had worked their way round to the south, in order that they could attack the farm from the rear. No 2 Platoon was positioned as a flank guard and No 1 Platoon joined up with No 2 Party and entered the farm. This position too was found to be unoccupied.

The officers had a quick conference and all three platoons set off in a south-easterly direction towards the large pillbox at I.27.d.25.20. When they arrived at the pillbox it was found to be strongly wired and occupied. The place was surrounded and the occupants were ordered to come out. There was no movement or reply, so one of the raiders threw a bomb through a slit; when the bomb exploded they heard cries and moaning. Lieutenant Brewin and Private Bradshaw then entered the pillbox and found six men huddled in a corner. They were made prisoner and passed out of the pillbox; as quickly as they could the two raiders gathered up papers and other articles that could lead to identification.

While they were inside, there was a German counter-attack which threw bombs at the men of the raiding party still outside, which wounded one man. This was successfully driven off and the prisoners were sent back to the British lines. The three officers and the four men that were still with them then moved off north-east, towards the railway line where they came across another post manned by the enemy. The German sentry was alert and challenged the raiders, who immediately rushed the post and captured the garrison which consisted of four men. Somewhere in the confusion one man who was known to be wounded went missing.

Meanwhile the left group was also out in the German lines. At 1135 hours the three parties of this group had formed up on the railway line at I.26.b.35.85. While they were waiting there they could hear a German working party talking and handling galvanised metal sheeting. When the barrage opened this working party was caught in the open and suffered some casualties, by which time the raiders were on their way to their objective and the covering party had got themselves into position.

As soon as the barrage lifted, No 1 Platoon rushed Blauwe Poort Farm from the south-west and No 2 Platoon from the east. It was estimated that there were about twenty Germans holding this post. In the mêlée that took place six were made prisoner, the remainder were either killed where they stood or managed to escape. The raiders themselves were attacked by a party of Germans who were either coming up to relieve the post or had heard the noise and were coming to the aid of their comrades. No 1 Platoon drove these men off with rifle fire and then the order to retire was given. They successfully withdrew and reached the British lines just as the barrage ceased.

The men of No 2 Party of the left group had by far the most unsuccessful part in the operation. The two platoons of this group worked together and went along Middlesex Road and checked several dugouts as they went, but all were found to be unoccupied. When they reached their objective, that position too was found to be unoccupied. They had moved fairly quickly and by 0035 hours the work was completed. It was then that they heard rifle fire from the direction of Blauwe Poort Farm, so they set off in that direction in the hope of cutting off any Germans retiring from there. However, the rifle fire ceased so they changed direction again in order to check some dugouts at I.27.b.80.80. On the way they came across a downed British aeroplane. The ground now became wet and boggy and full of shellholes, it was difficult to move. The men had to spread out and it was found the dugouts were strongly held and wired; the wire was hidden in the long grass, which again made movement difficult and in the centre dugout there was a heavy machine-gun. The defenders then started throwing bombs at the raiders and the officers found themselves separated from their men. Corporal Hughes gathered the men together and was just about to lead them back when he was wounded. Owing to the fact that the men were exhausted, no further attempt was made to capture the dugouts. They then withdrew and somewhere during the time in the enemy lines another two men went missing. But among the six prisoners brought in was an NCO.

All of those who took part spoke very highly of the artillery barrage which had enabled them to get up close to the objective; the bonfire lit behind the line as an aid to direction was also found to be very useful, as were the green flares to indicate the reporting point. They had taken sixteen prisoners for the loss of four wounded and three missing. These three were all reinforcements; 248056 Private Colin Thompson from Sheffield and 93139 Private George Alderson, a Barnsley man, had both served with the York and Lancaster Regiment prior to joining the Durham LI. The third man had originally joined the East Yorkshire Regiment; 93026

Private Arthur Dawson from Hull had enlisted into the 4th Hull Pals, or as it was locally known to Hull folk, 'T'Others' a reference to the fact that after raising Commercials, Tradesmen and Sportsmen's battalions, they didn't have a name for the 4th Battalion.

The Commanding Officer wrote of the raiders:

> I cannot speak too highly of the spirit and dash shown by all ranks in the raiding party, and their initiative in searching for prisoners beyond their objective. The Officers took great pains in reconnoitring the ground before the raid and displayed fine leadership during it.
>
> Meanwhile behind the line the battalion transport section was making its way up to the replenishment point, where they were to meet a carrying party that would take the night's rations into the line. As the horse-drawn wagons were making their way forward they came under shellfire; Second Lieutenant Christopher Poxon MM who was Acting Quartermaster was wounded, along with several of the drivers and a number of the horses and mules.

The next three days were very quiet and eventually 1/East Kent Regiment came up and relieved them and 2/Durham LI went back into Divisional Reserve in the Dickebusch–Goldfish Chateau–Brielen Line, where they were joined from England by Captain H. M. Saunders. The next day Lieutenant and Quartermaster John Keith, Nottinghamshire and Derbyshire Regiment, joined the battalion and took over the duties

Lieutenant Arthur Cave, died, Netley Hospital, Hampshire, 10 November 1918 and Lieutenant Moss Cohen, killed in action 24 July 1918, taken at Gosnay, France, May 1917.

of Quartermaster; at the same time Second Lieutenant William Severs arrived and was posted to B Company. At 0050 on the morning of 27 May the Germans started a particularly heavy bombardment, which was heavily laced with Yellow Cross gas shells; these were aimed especially at Company and Battalion Headquarters.

At 0300 hours the expected infantry attack started and the battalion immediately 'stood to' awaiting orders that would tell them to counter-attack. By 0600 hours the infantry attack petered out and everything quietened down; however. the shelling was kept up throughout the day. This led to the cancellation of all the scheduled working parties. During the day Second Lieutenant James Harrison and one man were killed and eight others wounded.

At 0330 hours the next morning the Divisional Artillery opened fire and put down a barrage on the enemy positions; this was followed by 11/Essex Regiment and French troops on their right launching an attack on the German lines. This was very successful and all objectives were taken. However, a gap had opened up between the Essex Regiment and the French; to put things right No 9 and No 10 Platoons of C Company were sent up with orders to fill the gap. After reporting to the Commanding Officer of 11/Essex Regiment for orders, they proceeded under heavy artillery fire until they reached the GHQ II Line at

H.30.c.40.50. They pressed on and soon they were in the GHQ I Line. This advance was made under very heavy artillery fire and the two platoons became separated. No 10 Platoon under the command of Lieutenant Welford Bolam NF was reorganised and moved to the right flank. Here they began the business of clearing the trench of enemy soldiers. The enemy fell back leaving behind the two machine guns and lots of documents. The platoon now formed four posts and started to dig in. Throughout the day they repeatedly had bomb and rifle-fire exchanges with the enemy and suffered several casualties.

A runner arrived from the OC of C Company, 11/Essex Regiment, who requested that Lieutenant Bolam report to his headquarters as soon as possible. During his absence from the platoon the Germans counter-attacked and retook their two machine guns and most of the trench that No 10 Platoon had taken. No 9 Platoon in the meantime had gone straight out over the top, under heavy sustained machine-gun fire, in order to reach their objective quickly. When they got to where they were to form a defensive flank, they dug and like moles disappeared as quickly as they could into the ground.

Here they remained until relieved by French troops at 0100 on 29 May when they made their way back and rejoined their company. At 0315 hours another bombardment started and again they 'stood to', but no attack came. Throughout the day the shelling continued but little damage was done. On 30 May working parties were sent up the line carrying the usual trench stores and rations and a number of men were wounded, some of whom later died from their wounds. At dawn on the last day of the month the French on the right attacked and retook Scottish Wood. Later in the day C Company came under fire from German heavy artillery. So May came to a close: the line had been held and they were now starting to retake some of the ground lost.

June opened with 18 Brigade in Divisional Reserve and Colonel Brereton was allowed to go to England on leave. Major Robert Turner rejoined the battalion and took over as Second in Command from Major James Jones MC. The 6th Division was relieved by 33rd Division and the battalion marched to Proven Station where they entrained at 0800 hours on 7 June and were carried to St Omer, where they detrained and marched to a tented camp at Cormette. A number of gallantry awards were announced for those who had taken part in the raid on 21 May. Between 8 and 11 June there was musketry training on the nearby ranges; this consisted of zeroing, grouping and then application practices and on the fourth day an inter-unit competition. The GOC 18 Brigade put up a silver cup for the winners of this competition, which after all the scores were counted up was won by 2/Durham LI.

On 12 June they began making their way back towards the Ypres Salient in slow stages; by 15 June they were working on another defence line known as the Poperinghe East Line. Here the next day the Brigade Commander visited the battalion and brought with him the promised silver cup which was duly presented to the shooting team. He also awarded a number of Gallantry Cards of Honour to those who had carried out brave deeds but had not been awarded a gallantry medal. It was now that an epidemic fever, similar to influenza, started to seriously affect the battalion and very soon over 220 men had been evacuated to hospital; even so the working parties continued.

On 21 June the battalion, all cleaned up and smart, fell in on parade and were inspected by General Sir Herbert Plumer GCMG, GCVO, KCB, Commanding SECOND ARMY; he was accompanied by Lieutenant General Sir Claude Jacob KCB, Commanding II Corps. The next three days were spent training and preparing to go back into the line. On 25th June they moved forward to a camp near Hagbeart where they relieved the 15th Chasseurs Alpines of the French Army. The next day they moved up into the front line near Dickebusch where they relieved the 13th Chasseurs Alpines in the left subsector of the Divisional Front. C and D Companies were in the front line, A Company in support and B Company in reserve. The last four days of June were spent quietly in the line and they reported that the German Artillery was unusually quiet during the day. During this last part of the month there had been a lot of coming and going of officers, a number of whom were posted to England to join the Royal Air Force and the Machine Gun Corps.

32138 Corporal W H. Wilson, from Hes County Durham, taken prisoner and c Germany on 11 June

The original cross erected over the grave of 32138 Corporal William H. Wilson in Niederzwehren Cemetery in Germany..

Chapter Nine

1918, July-April 1919, Advance to Victory and The Army of the Rhine

As July began the battalion remained in the front line north of Dickebusch Lake; although the days were relatively quiet, in the early hours the German Heavy Artillery shelled the battalion positions. The enemy infantry did not follow up the shelling; however, through the storm of the enemy fire and under difficult and trying conditions, an ammunition party led by 6147 Regimental Sergeant Major James Creswell arrived at a critical moment, which brought the award of the Distinguished Conduct Medal to the RSM who had served in the Durham Light Infantry since June 1887.

The same pattern occurred the next day but during the shelling one man was wounded: another incident occurred during the day when Second Lieutenant Wilfred Fryer was accidentally wounded and was sent away to the Field Ambulance. On the night 2/3 July the British Artillery bombarded the German trenches. The enemy were not taking this lying down and turned every calibre of gun, howitzer and mortar onto the

Three Buglers of 2/Durham LI 1918, right to left: 38676 Bugler Thomas Armstrong from Sunderland was awarded the Military Medal in August 1918 for his actions on 21 March 1918. Centre: J Gates from Byker and on the left 27972 Bugler Henry Dunwell from Nottinghamshire.

British lines just after midnight. After the enemy shelling died out, the rest of the day was reasonably quiet however, Lieutenant William Taylor was wounded after just one week's service with the battalion.

During the day two subalterns, Second Lieutenants Ernest Archer and Gordon Lawes, arrived at the Transport lines and were sent up to Battalion Headquarters. At 2300 hours 11/Essex regiment arrived to take over the front line and 2/Durham LI moved back and became the Divisional Reserve. The next day was spent in the usual cleaning up and there was even time for a bath. Over the next two nights they moved back towards the front line; on the night of 7 July they were supposed to put barbed wire entanglements out in No Man's Land, but owing to the amount of gas shells that had been dropped in the area where they were to work, the job was cancelled. The next night they relieved 1/West Yorkshire Regiment in the left subsector at Dickebusch. The Commanding Officer placed A and B Companies in the front line, D in support and C in reserve. The line was very quiet and apart from a little shelling which caused a few casualties, there was not much to report. On 12 July Lieutenant Colonel Brereton was posted to the Infantry Base Depot and command of 2/Durham LI passed to Major W.

38881 CPL Sidney Taylor from Byker, who was awarded Military Medal fo[r] part in the captur[e] the four German machine guns on 2[?] March 1918.

Original cross ove[r] grave of 18197 Pri[vate] Thomas B. Longth[?] from Bishop Auck[land] County Durham [who] was killed in acti[on] 14 July 1918.

Lieutenant and QM James Law joined the battalion in July 1918.

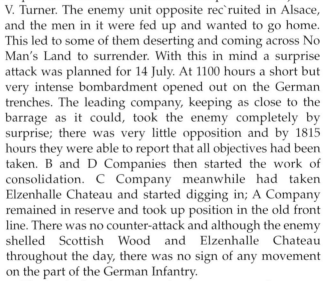

V. Turner. The enemy unit opposite rec`ruited in Alsace, and the men in it were fed up and wanted to go home. This led to some of them deserting and coming across No Man's Land to surrender. With this in mind a surprise attack was planned for 14 July. At 1100 hours a short but very intense bombardment opened out on the German trenches. The leading company, keeping as close to the barrage as it could, took the enemy completely by surprise; there was very little opposition and by 1815 hours they were able to report that all objectives had been taken. B and D Companies then started the work of consolidation. C Company meanwhile had taken Elzenhalle Chateau and started digging in; A Company remained in reserve and took up position in the old front line. There was no counter-attack and although the enemy shelled Scottish Wood and Elzenhalle Chateau throughout the day, there was no sign of any movement on the part of the German Infantry.

The haul of equipment and prisoners was a large one; ten light machine guns and one heavy machine gun were captured as well as seven officers and 338 men, for the loss of eight other ranks killed and Lieutenant H. Allison and seventy-seven men wounded. Then during the night a German limber carrying rations was driven up the road towards the newly-captured position. It was halted and in

a bit of a struggle one of the crew was killed and the other captured. The working party that was bringing up the rations and resupplying the battalion with bombs and ammunition encountered a lot of problems as they struggled up the line with their heavy loads, and it was late at night before any food arrived.

Later they were relieved by 1/King's Shropshire Light Infantry and moved back to billets in Divisional Reserve. They had been there two days when A and C Companies were shelled with high explosive mixed with gas and had to be moved to new billets away from the area affected by the gas. A new Quartermaster, Lieutenant James Law, reported to the battalion on 18 July and training was carried out under company arrangements during the day and at night they were employed on working parties. There was an alarm on the night of 21 July and the battalion was ordered to occupy battle positions, as a large-scale enemy attack was expected on the morning of 22 July. The Battalion Band returned to the Transport lines and a nucleus from the battalion was sent back to the Divisional Details camp. This nucleus would be used to rebuild the battalion in the event of major losses. The various companies took up position along the Reninghelst Road. The other two battalions of 18 Brigade, 1/West Yorkshire Regiment and 11/Essex Regiment were in a position known as the Ouderdom Line in front of 2/Durham LI, who were the Brigade Reserve. The expected attack didn't take place and on 23 July they relieved 11/Essex in the Ouderdom Line. It was now that Major James Jones left the battalion on posting to 19/Durham LI; he would eventually be killed commanding 17/Lancashire Fusiliers. In his place, Major Percy Parker, West Yorkshire Regiment took over as Second in Command, along with him three subalterns; Lieutenants E. H. F. Krause and John B. Lambdin, 1/7/West Yorkshire Regiment and Second Lieutenant Claude Maxwell. The last named, born at Ibrox in Glasgow, had enlisted in 1914 into 17/Highland Light Infantry, the Glasgow Commercial Battalion, which was raised by the Glasgow Chamber of Commerce and after service at the front was selected for a commission.

The days passed very quietly with only some sporadic shelling and on the night of 24 July they were relieved by 2/Sherwood Foresters and moved back into the line with A Company in the front line, C Company in the Dickebusch–Sherpenburg Line with D Company on their left in the same line and B Company in support.

These positions were held until 27 July when 11/Essex Regiment took over and 2/Durham LI moved back into reserve. The rest of the month was spent in this location supplying working parties which went out and placed barbed wire in front of the defended locations.

On the evening of 2 August the battalion moved up to the front line and took over trenches from the Doughboys of the 105 Infantry Battalion of the American Expeditionary Force. Here they only had one company, D, in the line; the other three, A, B and C, were located in the support trenches. They remained here for a number of days; each night working parties were sent out to assist in digging for other units. Occasionally the enemy shelled their positions and caused casualties. Preparations were made for an attack on the enemy line on the night of 8/9 August and the posts in No Man's Land were withdrawn. At midnight the barrage opened and A Company moved forward and managed to take their objective without meeting any serious resistance. At once they started consolidating the position but on the right they had lost touch with 15/Hampshire Regiment, so the right-hand post was withdrawn. In the evening, once they had regained touch with the Hampshires they took over two posts from them but they were still not in touch with the next post on the right. During the day the Germans had put down an irregular barrage that had caused the deaths of two men, 92051 Private Charles Lazenby and 91994 Lance Corporal John Reed, as well as wounding fourteen others. The next day was very quiet and they managed to re-establish touch with the battalion on the right. In the early hours of 11 August the enemy put down a heavy bombardment just behind the front line, and under its cover launched a counter-attack on the right.

The morning was very misty; communication was slow and reports were therefore slow in coming back from the outpost line. At one point the Germans were supposed to have taken one of the posts. Then at the same time word came from the rear that some German prisoners had escaped and were supposedly wandering around in 2/Durham LI rear area. Patrols were sent out, some forward to establish just what was going on and where the enemy were, and some to search for the escaped prisoners. Those not engaged in the patrols 'stood to' in their battle stations. The mist gradually cleared and on inspection all the outlying posts were found to be alright, the enemy having fallen back to his starting point. Throughout the day the German machine-gunners kept up a heavy harassing fire which led to five men being evacuated wounded.

In the early morning of 12 August the British Artillery started a heavy counter-preparation barrage on likely forming-up points in the German line and the German Artillery were very quick to reply; however, no infantry attack materialised and after the shelling died down all was quiet for the rest of the day. In the evening 2/York and Lancaster Regiment relieved 2/Durham LI, who moved back into Divisional Reserve.

The first night in the reserve position was spent in a practice of manning the battle positions, then for the next five days they were kept busy with working parties until on 19 August they commenced training. Preparations were being made for the battalion to be relieved and duly on 21 August, II Battalion, 105th US Infantry Regiment took over the positions held by 2/Durham LI. At 0130 hours the battalion entrained at Abeele and was carried to St Omer where they arrived at 0325 hours and

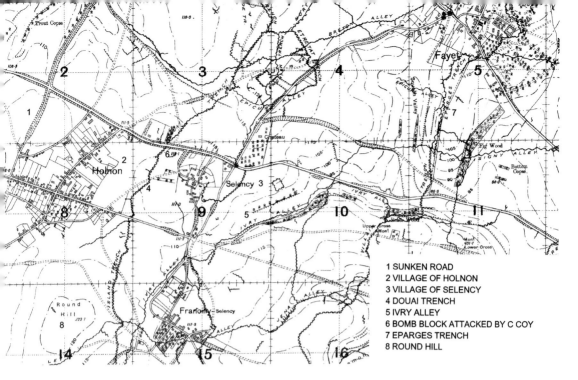

1 SUNKEN ROAD
2 VILLAGE OF HOLNON
3 VILLAGE OF SELENCY
4 DOUAI TRENCH
5 IVRY ALLEY
6 BOMB BLOCK ATTACKED BY C COY
7 EPARGES TRENCH
8 ROUND HILL

2nd Durham Light Infantry Area of operations September 1918.

trekked to billets in the area; they had the rest of the day to themselves and rested where possible. Then the next day the training started, cleaning up to start with, then parades and inspections, old and worn equipment replaced or repaired where necessary. In the evening sporting events took place, this became an inter-platoon competition. Range work followed and then Lewis gun drills and grenades on the ranges. On 29 August the battalion practised an attack and then that evening the sports competition was won by No 14 Platoon of D Company. The next stage of the training was a full Brigade attack on 30 August and the last day of the month was spent packing up ready to move back into the line.

At 1300 hours on 1 September, the battalion left Zudausques and travelled on foot to the railway station at Wizernes. At 1515 hours they started boarding a special train; loading the transport wagons, horses and mules took some time and it wasn't until 1625 hours that the train steamed out of the station headed for Mericourt sur Ancre; it travelled on through the night until it reached its destination at 0530 hours on 2 September. After leaving the train the battalion formed up in column of route and marched to Ribecourt, a few miles behind Albert. Here they went into billets and rested throughout the rest of the day. For the next eight days they practised and trained for open warfare; gone were the tactics of bombers and bayonet men, now it was flanking attacks and fire and movement. In the evenings there was entertainment from 'The Pineapples', the battalion concert party; on another night the Divisional

Concert party provided the fun. They also had a concert by the 6th Divisional Band and on the night of 7 September there was an 18 Brigade boxing competition, however, no results appear in the battalion War Diary.

The training continued until they were finally practising capturing an enemy strongpoint, at which stage they were deemed ready to go back into the line. At 1400 hours on 12 September, the men of 2/Durham LI started making their way back towards the fighting. The first night's march took them to billets in Le Hamelet, where the next morning they embussed and were carried towards St Quentin. By 15 September they were in Brigade Reserve from where Second Lieutenant W. Severs MC and Lieutenant G. R. Fortune, Indian Army, were ordered back to England. In these reserve positions they came under enemy shelling and Second Lieutenant Sidney Brewin MC was wounded; this shelling proved to be a mixture of high explosive and gas. They now started preparing for an attack; in the evening of 17 September, Lieutenant John Lambdin was detailed to take the guides up to the line and learn the route in for the companies. However, this party came under heavy shellfire and at least ten of the guides were killed. Those that were left, having found out the route into the line, returned to the battalion and under Lieutenant Lambdin's guidance led the battalion into position.

Then at 2200 hours that night, B Company led by Captain Potts attempted to take the village of Holnon. Unfortunately the village was very strongly held by infantry supported by a number of machine-guns and the attackers, who had by now run out of bombs and were low on ammunition, were very soon forced to give up the attempt. Conspicuous among the attackers was Second Lieutenant Ernest Archer; three times he led his platoon into the village and tried to establish posts in the ruins but each time they were forced back.

On the right flank of the 6th British Division, the 34eme French Division had orders to attack at the same time as the British. In the front line 2/Durham LI had as its objective the village of Selency which was about 1,000 yards east of and behind the previous day's objective of Holnon. The attack was timed to start at 0200 hours, with A and D Companies leading and B and C Companies in support; the battalion advanced with bayonets fixed, under the cover of a creeping barrage. The leading companies went straight through Holnon and although they took eight prisoners, it appeared that the rest of the garrison had withdrawn. It was now that they came under heavy machine-gun fire from the French objective of Round Hill on the right, as well as from Selency itself.

Captain Sidney R. Streatfield was wounded 18 September 1918.

This fire caused heavy casualties and by now in the two leading companies all the officers had been wounded. At the Regimental Aid Post, the Battalion Medical Officer, Captain Michael Burke MC, RAMC, eventually worked his way through those wounded he could treat and get

them away from the action. He then led the battalion stretcher-bearers back into the midst of the fighting, and under heavy machine-gun fire and shelling collected more of the battalion wounded. Searching the battlefield he found a number of wounded in an enemy trench and it was only when he was bombed out of the trench by a party of enemy soldiers that he returned to the aid post. Meanwhile on the left, the attack made by 1/Leicestershire Regiment was successful. With the attack bogged down the two support companies took up position in the sunken road west of Holnon. That night parties of German soldiers armed with machine-guns worked their way round the leading companies and almost cut them off. They were forced to fall back on the supporting companies on the western edge of Holnon.

On 18 September, B Company again tried to clear the village of Selency, this time by a flanking attack, but they were met by heavy machine-gun fire and gas shelling. Thus once again the attack failed and they fell back to their starting positions. However, two of these machine-guns and some of the crews were captured by Captain Robert Haylett, who inspired his men and kept them going until he was evacuated wounded.

During the night C Company established a line of posts east of Holnon and these were held throughout the next day, despite being heavily shelled. On the night 19/20 September C Company pushed forward and established another line of posts which conformed with the line held by 1/Leicestershire Regiment. However, on the right they could not get in touch with the French. It was a brilliant moonlit night and several attempts were made to locate the left-hand French post, but every one was driven back by machine-gun fire. Also that night B Company thoroughly searched the village of Holnon and declared it clear of the enemy. Given the number of casualties, a composite company was formed and they took up position in the sunken road. The day was now spent consolidating the position and although they were heavily shelled and a counter-attack made, it was beaten off.

The following night of 20/21 September the battalion was relieved by 2/Sherwood Foresters and moved back into billets where they were reorganised into three companies. They were only in reserve one day when they went up and relieved 2/Sherwood Foresters in the same trenches. An attack was planned with A and B Companies in the line and C Company in support; however, one platoon of C Company was detailed to attack and capture a trench block at S.9.a.5.9. By 0200 hours they were all in position and the barrage came down on Douai Trench as the assaulting companies went forward. The right company, A, had heavy casualties as they ran into three belts of barbed wire that had been left uncut by the barrage, but despite this they managed to get a footing in Douai Trench. B Company on the left also ran into uncut wire and they too suffered many casualties, among them the three officers and the majority of the survivors withdrew, apart from a small party that established a post about S.9.a.2.5 0.5.

Meanwhile, A Company was attacked by hostile bombing parties on both flanks. Very fierce fighting took place for well over an hour before the company was forced back to the jumping-off point, bringing back five prisoners with them. The support company was established in the jumping-off trench and this position was held and strengthened, despite being under heavy rifle and machine-gun fire. That night another attack was made by four companies of 1/Leicestershire Regiment and despite having heavy casualties the attack was successful. Casualties had been the heaviest the battalion had suffered since the March retreat. No less than four officers were dead, either killed in action or died of wounds, and seven were wounded. Among the men 295 were listed as casualties, of whom at least forty-six were either killed in action or died of wounds.

On 25 September the battalion rested and a number of reinforcements arrived; these men were distributed and the companies were reorganised. The next day they took over from 1/Leicestershire Regiment in the line which was now beyond the eastern side of Selency, from the crossroads in S.9.b to the crossroads in S.9.c where they were in the touch with the French on their right. In support in Douai Trench was a composite company.

The Commanding Officer made his rounds of the battalion positions and then reconnoitred Argonne Trench. The enemy were known to be in this location the previous night, but it was now found to be empty, the evidence suggesting that the occupants had left in a hurry. Accordingly the battalion took up positions in Argonne Trench and Ivry Alley. During the night of 27/28 September a patrol found that the enemy was still occupying Eparges Trench; however, at daylight a second patrol found that it had been evacuated, so a platoon from C Company moved forward and occupied a position at S.11.c.9.0. The next morning the area east of Selency was heavily shelled.

This shelling led to the wounding of Lieutenant Wosley Lawson and Second Lieutenant Gordon Hislop and two other ranks, and sadly the deaths of two other men; the first, 375343 Private Horace Elliott who was reinforcement from the East Yorkshire Regiment. The second man to die that day was 8728, Sergeant William Caddy a Staffordshire man, from Rugeley, he had landed as a private at St Nazaire with the battalion on 8 September 1914. He had enlisted in 1904 and had married an Essex girl, Minnie, whilst the battalion was stationed in Colchester. During the night the battalion was relieved by the 12th Chasseurs of the French Army and moved back to bivouacs in Leaf Wood.

The last day of the month was spent reorganising the battalion; over 100 other ranks arrived as well as the following officers: Lieutenants Tom

Shepherd who came from Ilford, Essex and William Lapham. With them were Second Lieutenants Harold Stainforth, Ernest Gillard, Lionel Harvey, Percy Stockley and James Evans all were attached from the York and Lancaster Regiment and they had all seen service at the front as NCOs in other regiments.

At the beginning of October the refitting and reorganisation continued and then the training of the reinforcements started. The remainder of the battalion was kept busy preparing for an inspection of 18 Brigade by the GOC 6th Division, which took place on 3 October. The next morning they started marching back towards the line; the battalion passed through Vraignes, then Hancourt and pushed on to Bernes and eventually they bivouacked in the front line of the Hindenburg Line. Here they continued with the training of specialists such as Lewis Gunners, Signallers and Bombers. On 6 October they received orders to move up to Magny-la-Fosse and take over billets from 71 Brigade. However, when they arrived at the village the billets were still occupied. So they halted to await orders, and bivouacked for the night. They were now in Divisional Reserve and at 0520 hours the leading troops attacked and took the next objective. That evening they moved forward but remained in reserve. Here they remained until 11 October when they moved to Brancourt where they remained for the night. During the night of 13 October they moved forward and took over the front from 2/Sherwood Foresters. In these positions A Company held the left front and C Company the right front, in touch with 11/Essex Regiment, B Company were in support and D Company in reserve. These dispositions left a gap between the two front companies and also left the enemy in possession of the high ground. Therefore a plan was made that C Company along with 11/Essex Regiment would capture this ridge. At 1630 hours the supporting bombardment opened on the German trenches and hammered these positions for fifteen minutes before creeping slowly forward into the enemy second line. C Company captured their portion of the ridge easily, but ran into their own barrage which caused a few casualties. They were also forced to move to the right away from the barrage.

During the advance they had taken a number of prisoners and sending these men back with an escort further reduced the numbers of men left. The Germans now launched a counter-attack supported by machine guns and bombers, which pushed C Company back off the ridge to a position where they formed a defensive flank. During the night of 14 October patrols from A Company were able to re-establish touch with C Company and the line was once more intact. However, the following night they were relieved by 2/Sherwood Foresters and moved back to very comfortable billets in the village of Bohain. Here they rested and refitted and took the opportunity to have a bath, but they were not there long, for that night they went straight back up into the line.

A and B Companies were in the line with D Company in support and C Company in reserve. Zero hour was at 0520 hours when the barrage opened and crept forward at a rate of 100 yards every three minutes. There was unfortunately a very thick fog and it was impossible for the men to keep direction and in touch with the platoons on either flank. The enemy counter-barrage came down but wasn't very heavy, but almost immediately both leading companies met with strong opposition and had run into belts of uncut wire. A Company had drifted to their right and the Essex Regiment on the right were moving left across the front of 2/Durham LI. Owing to the fog, the various platoons were fighting their own small battles independently of the rest of the battalion. The way forward was severely held up and B Company was much delayed whilst the barbed wire was cut and a path opened towards Bellvue Trench. But once they got into that trench they were forced to bomb along to their right as there was no sign of A Company.

Having taken the trench and mopped up and now reduced in numbers they pressed forward, but were soon held up by an enemy machine-gun position. Being to weak to go any further the company halted and started to dig in. In the meantime, having been told Bellvue Trench had been taken, D Company moved forward but one of the platoons suffered a lot of casualties from a machine-gun post that hadn't been accounted for. Just as the steam was running out of the attack, troops from the 1st Division passed through the captured positions, and still being fairly fresh were able to take the objective. 2/Durham LI had suffered a number of casualties during this action which included twenty dead, one of whom was 11029 Private Michael Varley from Bishop Auckland. One of those who had landed on 8 September 1914, he had spent some time with the West Yorkshire Regiment where he was numbered 47775, but had managed to get himself posted back to the Durhams and had eventually rejoined his old battalion; today his remains lie in Grave A.7 of Vaux-Andigny British Cemetery, however, he is identified as H. Varley.

Just in case there was a counter-attack 2/Durham LI remained in their positions, for intelligence reports indicated that the Germans had a spare

Under the shade of the dear old
  Away over land and sea,
Lies two of the best and bravest
  Who died so that we remain fr

Standing 200177 Private Robert McCreedy was killed in action on 17 October 1918; seated is his father, 19768 Private Samuel McCreedy Border Regiment who died of sickness in Salonika on 13 August 1917.

division available for counter attack purposes. The next day was spent in these positions as the 1st Division carried the battle forward into the enemy lines and captured Wassigny. As the battle progressed 2/Durham LI were withdrawn to Vaux-Andigny and from there they marched back to billets in Bohain where they rested for the day. From here they were supposed to move by bus at 1430 hours to St Souplet, but the transport was late and it wasn't until 2200 hours that they arrived in St Souplet, where they remained in billets for the night. On 21 October they moved back into the line and the next day was spent preparing for a continuation of the advance. Unfortunately at 0215 hours on 23 October the Germans put down a very heavy counter-preparation barrage; this hit all around the village of La Jonquiere where the battalion was forming up. This bombardment, a mixture of high explosive and gas shells, caused many casualties and a lot of disorganisation among the leading companies.

The objective was the high ground commanding the Sambre–Oise Canal and the attack was to be made by 2 Brigade of 1st Division on the right, 18 Brigade in the centre and 71 Brigade on the left. In 18 Brigade, 2/Durham LI were on the right and 1/West Yorkshire Regiment on the left with 11/Essex Regiment in reserve. 2/Durham LI had C Company on the right front and D Company on the left, with B Company in support and A Company in reserve. Owing to the German counter-preparation barrage it was found necessary to reinforce C Company with B Company. When the British barrage opened, almost immediately the German gunners put down a counter-barrage which caused heavy casualties in the leading companies; indeed, both Company Commanders were among those wounded. The advance was very slow and as the attacking platoons cleared the barrage they advanced in small parties up the forward slope between the St Maurier River and the Catillon–Baseux Road. Here they met some opposition but managed to take some prisoners, but were then held up by machine-gun and rifle fire from some houses on the right. One party managed to cross the road but was forced back owing to the lack of numbers and a particularly heavy machine-gun fire. On the left Captain Walter Frith noticed that on his flank two machine-gun posts, that should have been captured by 1/West Yorkshire Regiment, were still intact and were firing into the left rear of the company. Taking with him one of the platoon sergeants they worked round behind the guns and knocked them out, either killing or capturing the crews. This prompt action saved many casualties and assisted the battalion in achieving its objective.

The position on the battalion front was that B, C and D Companies consisted of some small parties of men, some under the command of officers and some under the command of NCOs, and in one or two cases led by a private showing a lot of initiative. Most parties had moved too much to their right and were too weak to deal with the machine-gun fire that was holding them up. It was now that the Commanding Officer ordered up A Company, with a view to breaking the stalemate. A Company passed to the left of the other companies, successfully overran all the opposition and captured Gibremont Farm. It was largely owing to the initiative and ability of the Commanding Officer that the battalion reached its objective; throughout the action he reorganised the companies and directed them onto the objective. During the next day the battalion reorganised and managed to get in touch with 2 Brigade on the right and with the West Yorkshire Regiment on the left. C Company, or what was left of it, was in support and D Company was in reserve. On 24 October the battalion remained in these positions but pushed forward patrols to Malmaison Farm. The patrolling continued the following day and occupied a post at Le Gard Station. The next day the enemy tried to retake this position but were beaten off.

During the fighting Second Lieutenant Claude Maxwell, in the words of the citation of the Military Cross awarded for his part in the action, 'assisted in the capture of his objective, together with forty prisoners and ten machine guns, and reorganised the remains of his company on the objective. Later he pushed on with his company successfully and carried out very good patrol work'. However, Lieutenant Maxwell was writing to his sisters: on 19 October he wrote to the younger Beatrice:

*LT George M. Garlan
was wounded for the
fourth time on 23
October 1918.*

> *I have just come out of the line after being in an attack. We gained all our objectives but my company lost very heavily. I finished up commanding the coy. It was great coming out today. Just imagine me on my horse (gee whiz) leading my company out of battle.*
>
> *Of the four officers who went over the top, two were killed and one wounded. My luck is tremendous, I'm touching wood. We advanced 2,500 yards and, with a party of men, I captured a strong point, taking 50 prisoners and ten machine-guns.*

The following day he wrote to his elder sister Janet:

> *Things were in a bit of a mix up for a while owing to very heavy fog making keeping in touch very difficult. I managed to keep a party of men together and we were pushing on after having crossed the Boche front line when we heard him firing behind us. We went back and attacked a strong point and I finished up in command of the Company and brought them out of the line at the finish yesterday. However there is not much rest these days and we go up to hold the line again tonight, The news from all over is simply wonderful these days and I can't help hoping for a speedy end to it all.*

On 28 October they were relieved by 1/Leicestershire Regiment and marched back to St Souplet where they spent the night in billets. At 1400 hours on 29 October they were relieved by troops of 32nd Division and marched to Busigny. From here Second Lieutenant Claude Maxwell again wrote to his sister Janet:

*Private John Armstr
Crawcrook, County
was transferred to t
London Regiment ar
renumbered 45310. F
killed in action 1 Oc
1918. When he enlist
May 1915 he was en
a hewer at the Emm
in Ryton on Tyne.*

272

I am having a fairly active and busy time these days but am hoping for a rest for a week or two soon. Have been in two stunts in the last fortnight and since the last one eight days ago my company has held the front line ever since. Our patrols every night getting up to the waist in streams and bog and altogether having a most delightful time. I'm writing this to you from a house that is right in the front line. There is absolutely no one between me and Boche so I hope he does not get nasty and interrupt my writing, Waiting for relief is about the most wearisome job imaginable as the minutes crawl and something invariably goes wrong with the incomers.

On the following day at 1300 hours they marched again to Fresnoy-le-Grand,; here on the last day of the month they began the business of refitting and reforming and that night 'The Pineapples' gave one of their famous performances.

November began with a programme of training; Captain Russell Licence, Essex Regiment, joined the battalion and took up the post of Adjutant and at the same time Captain Sidney Streatfield rejoined and took over command of C Company. Then on 3 November a church parade was held at which Brigadier General Crauford the Brigade Commander, read the lesson; after the service the Divisional Band played in the town square from 1130 hours until 1300 hours. The Commanding Officer went away to Fontainebleau on a course and Major Parker assumed command. The next day the battalion was placed at two hours' notice to move, ready to support the operations that were still taking place on the Corps front. The weather at the time was very bad but it didn't stop the battalion receiving orders to move, and the next day they marched out of Fresnoy-le-Grand to Busigny. Here they continued training, expecting at any moment to be summoned back into the line.

However, on 7 November the order to be ready to move at two hours' notice was cancelled. They remained in Busigny for the next few days and on 11 November the news arrived that an armistice had been signed and would take effect from 1100 hours that morning. The next few days were spent cleaning up and doing ceremonial drill. 6th Division was one of the divisions selected to join the army of occupation and so they left Busigny and marched to St Souplet. From here Lieutenant Rice and two sergeants were sent back to the Regimental Depot in order to bring the battalion Colours out from England. There now began a series of daily marches towards the German frontier; St Souplet to La Groise, then on to Marbaix and then Beugnies, followed on 20 November to Grandieu. Here they halted and rested; however, they were called upon to supply a large fatigue party for road clearing. Some training was carried out but the main occupation was ceremonial drill under the Commanding Officer, who had by now returned from his course. There was a lot of football played and the Officers XI was particularly keen and played all comers, drawing with the sergeants and the Transport Platoon but was defeated by the Battalion

Band. Another move was made to Boussu on 24 November where they remained until 2 December. Hubert McBain was on his way back to the battalion having recovered from his wounds and recorded the journey in his diary:

> On 23 November I proceed once again to France via Etaples – we proceed by train to the Divisional Reinforcement camp at Molain where all reinforcements are being held up on account of the lack of transport to get us up to our units, who are now on their way to the Rhine. I go into another village – Wasigny, and I am billeted there for a week until eventually on 7 December we get into lorries and passing through Mons and Le Cateau we get to Charleroi in the evening. It is certainly interesting to be in the old German back areas and to see how delighted the Belgians are to see all their allies once again. We entrain in Charleroi and are carried to Sovet, where on the morning of 8 December I see the battalion march past in column of route through the streets. I report to them at the first halt.

The Colour Party, Lieutenants Ware a McBain MC, CSM Bradley and Sergea, Gott DCM and Sergeant Reed MM.

The march, continued every day, and brought them a few miles closer to Germany. On 15 December as the battalion prepared to fall in the Colours were uncased but not unfurled and they set off on the last leg towards the border. At 1300 hours 2/Durham LI crossed the German frontier. Here the Colour Party, Lieutenants Ware and McBain MC, CSM Bradley, Sergeant Gott DCM and Sergeant Reed MM paused and the Colours were unfurled and the order was given for the battalion to fix bayonets. D Company provided the Escort to the Colour and with bayonets fixed, rifles at the slope and the Band and Bugles playing the Regimental March 'The Light Barque', they marched into the town of Malmedy. The population were on the whole indifferent to the occupation, but suddenly the sound of cheering rang out from the side of the road. Stood there was a ragged and bedraggled party of prisoners of war, who were trying to smarten themselves up, among them a handful of Durhams who had been taken prisoner during the German offensive the previous March. They came to attention and saluted the Colours as the battalion swung past them into the town.

Among the prisoners released from captivity was 204786 Private Thomas Hammond who on his return to England received a letter from Mrs Dance, He replied as follows:

17/12/18
17 John Street
Darlington

Dear Mrs Dance

Just a few lines in answer to your letter, which I received on Monday. I am very sorry I can't give you any better news than you have already received because I was on the next fire step to your husband when he was killed. He did not live ten minutes after he was hit but I am sorry to say I can't tell you what became of his body as we lost the trench shortly after so you will see that his body was in the hands of the Germans. Your husband was very well liked by all the Officers, NCOs and men and all miss the loss of him very much. You will be pleased to hear that your husband stuck to his post until the last. I hope you are keeping well, as I am keeping in the pink. So no more at present.

I remain yours sincerely
Thomas Hammond

Eventually the battalion arrived in the village of Lechenich some 12 miles south-east of Cologne. Here on 25 December they held a special Christmas dinner with beer and plum pudding for every man. Almost every day batches of men, mainly miners, were sent away for discharge. Training, sports and education classes took place as the battalion gradually reduced in numbers. However, as one would expect, some of the men decided to remain in the army and signed on for three or five years. This was the

Three officers of 2/Durham LI in Germany after the Armistice, in the centre is Lieutenant L. S. Briggs MC.

pattern throughout January and February 1919, until in March those men that were not eligible for discharge were transferred in batches to 9/Durham LI. The transport and equipment was handed over to 52/Leicestershire Regiment. 2/Durham LI was now earmarked for Foreign Service and was ordered back to England to reform. On 14 April they crossed the frontier into Belgium and so brought to an end this chapter in the battalion's history.

Between September 1914 and November 1918 the battalion had 1,306 other rank fatalities; this includes those that were killed in action, died of wounds, both at home and overseas and those that died as prisoners of war. This figure would increase if an accurate total of those who died of wounds after being discharged could be achieved. It is estimated that the figure for wounded could be over 5,000 but the numbers for wounded vary in accuracy, and of course many who were wounded returned to the battalion and were subsequently killed. Of the officers, no less than 308 served with the battalion; of these, seventy-five were either killed or died of wounds and 136 were wounded. The battalion gained the following battle honours during the war:

Having enlisted o 3/8/16 and taken prisoner of war in March 1918; 4517 Private John John was discharged o 2/1/19, only to di home in Fencehou on 22/6/1919.

> *Aisne, 1914, Armentières, 1914; Hooge, 1915; Flers-Courcelette, Morval, Le Transloy, Somme, 1916; Hill 70, Cambrai, 1917; and in 1918: Somme, Kemmel; Epehy, Selle, Sambre.*

Too soon, in 1940, 2/Durham Light Infantry would start adding to those Battle Honours.

Now that the time has come for you to leave the Army and go back to civil life, I wish, both personally and officially, to thank you for the service which you have given.

You take away with you the priceless knowledge that you have played a man's part in this great War for freedom and fair play. You will take away with you also your remembrances of your comrades, your pride in your Regiment, and your love for your country.

You have played the game; go on playing it, and all will be well with the great Empire which you have helped to save.

I wish you every prosperity and happiness.

S. G. Crawford
Brig. Genl.
Commanding 18th Infantry Brigade.

A. P. & S. S. Press—Second Army. (W. P. & Co.)

When they were disc each man of 18 Brig received one of these you' certificates from Brigade Commander

Honours and Gallantry Awards 2/Durham Light Infantry 1914-1919

Order of the Bath
Irvine, Alfred Ernest, Major & Bt Lt Col, T/Brig Gen CB
03/6/1919   CMG DSO

Order of St Michael & St George
Goring-Jones, Michael Derwas Lt Colonel DSO   CMG   03/6/1919
Irvine, Alfred,Ernest, Major & Bt Lt Col, T/Brig G CMG   DSO
03/6/1918
McMahon, Bernard W. L. Lt Col, T/Col   CMG   04/6/1917

Order of the British Empire
Bristow, Frank Anstie, T/Lt T/Capt   OBE   03/6/1919
Cruickshank, Jasper Wallace, Lt Colonel RAF   OBE   01/1/1919
Gales, John Russell, Captain   MBE   03/6/1918
Greenwell, Charles Okey, Major   OBE   03/6/1918
Griffith-Jones, Morgan Philip, T/Major   OBE   22/3/1919
Lavery, Andrew, Lt T/Capt   MBE   03/06/1919
Wood, John Hardy, Major   OBE   03/06/1919

Distinguished Service Order
Congreve, Charles Ralph, Lieutenant   01/12/1914
On 28 October saved the life of Captain Wallace by bringing him, when wounded, into cover under heavy fire.

Cumming, Hanway Robert, Lt Col, T/Brig Gen   04/06/1917

Goring-Jones, Michael Derwas Lt Colonel T/Brig Gen   01/01/1918

Irvine, Alfred Ernest, Major, T/Lt Col,   31/05/1916
For conspicuous gallantry and devotion to duty. During a critical period and continuous bombardment by the enemy lasting three days he was up with his front companies each night directing and organising the defences. His energy and cheerfulness and splendid example were invaluable.
Bar to Distinguished Service Order, T/Brig, Cdg 112th Inf Bde.
                               01/02/1919

For conspicuous gallantry and devotion to duty on 8 and 9 September, 1918 near Haverincourt. The plans for attack on the village necessitated the possession of a slag heap known to be held by the enemy. Pushing out patrols to locate the exact position of the enemy, he went out himself, and with his intelligence officer, made a personal reconnaissance about 200 yards in front of the outposts to the top of the slag heap and as he was not fired on ordered the patrols to push on there. The next morning he again went up to the outpost line, and reconnoitred some 250 yards beyond under constant sniping. The knowledge he gained enabled him to capture a post and light field gun, and his personal determination cleared up the situation.

Jones, James Andrew, Lt, T/Major, A/Lt Col, Cmdg 17/Lanc Fus.

15/02/1919

He commanded his battalion with conspicuous success during a most difficult operation, involving the capture of Zandvoorde on 28 September, 1918. By his behaviour under heavy machine-gun fire at close range he set a splendid example to the officers and men of his battalion at a very critical period of the attack. All ranks were unanimous in praising his coolness and courage.

McCullagh, Herbert Rochfort, Capt, T/Major, A/Lt Col, 2nd att 19th Bn

01/01/1919

Turner, Robert Villiers, Major, A/Lt Col   08/3/1919

For conspicuous gallantry and able leadership. During the operations on 23 October, 1918, near Catillon, owing to the enclosed nature of the ground the barrage was lost before the final objective overlooking the canal was reached. All further advance was carried out by means of fighting patrols. The success of the DLI in reaching positions commanding the canal was due to his personal leadership and initiative in the forward area, where he reorganised and personally directed the whole of the operations.

Military Cross

Archer, Ernest William, Second Lieutenant   8th Bn att 2nd Bn

01/2/1919

For conspicuous gallantry and devotion to duty throughout the operations at Holnon from 18th to 20th September 1918. He worked unceasingly, leading his men three times in attempts to establish posts in the village, and succeeding in doing so on the following day. He set a fine example of coolness and determination.

Bolam, Welford, Second Lieutenant, Northumberland Fusiliers att 2nd Bn

16/09/1918

For conspicuous gallantry, devotion and initiative in leading up two platoons in support of an attack. He brought up his men his men to reinforce an exposed flank during heavy shelling and machine gun fire at a very critical moment, with the greatest courage and determination. Later in the day he captured and put into use two enemy machine-guns, extending his flank to do this, till all final objectives had been gained.

Briggs, Leonard Scott Second Lieutenant   06/09/1915
For conspicuous gallantry at Hooge on 9 August 1915, both in the attack and subsequent defence of the position won. At a critical moment under very heavy fire of all descriptions he left his trench, rallied some men who were retiring owing to a misunderstanding, and led them back. He was several times buried by debris from large shells, but remained perfectly cool and set a very fine example to those around him.

Brown, Norman, Lieutenant Special Reserve att 2nd Bn   30/01/1920
For gallant and distinguished services in the field which have been brought to notice in accordance with the terms of Army Order 193 of 1919 to be dated 5 May 1919. Escaping or attempting to escape whilst a POW.

Burke, Michael Charles, MC Captain RAMC att 2nd Bn, Bar to MC
                                                          04/10/1919
In the operations in the vicinity of Holnon on 18/24 September 1918, he displayed conspicuous gallantry and devotion to duty. Having dealt with all cases at his aid post, he led out stretcher- bearers, and, under machine-gun and shellfire, collected more wounded. His search led him into an enemy-held trench, where he only desisted when bombed out. His efforts and his fine example were instrumental in saving many lives.

Ellis, Reginald Donald, 2/Lieutenant 2nd Bn att 18th Machine Gun Coy
                                                          04/06/1917
Fawcett, Edward Second Lieutenant, A/Capt   05/07/1918
For conspicuous gallantry and devotion to duty. During the advance his company came under point blank fire from a hostile field battery, which was holding up the attack on the flank. Under orders, he with great promptitude organised two parties, one of which he himself led. These parties converged and charged the guns, capturing the battery, all the gunners being either killed or captured. It was due to this officer's coolness and initiative under heavy fire that a critical situation was saved, thereby enabling the attack to proceed.

Fillingham, George Sidney, Lieutenant, A/Captain   05/07/1918
For conspicuous gallantry and devotion to duty. During the advance his company came under point blank fire from a hostile field battery which was holding up the attack on the flank. Having located and reported the exact position, he was sent forward with two parties to attack the battery. The success of the enterprise was due to his gallant reconnaissance and dashing leadership.

Frith, Walter Henry, Lieutenant, A/Captain   15/10/1918
For gallantry and fine leadership while commanding his company in the assaulting wave. During the advance perceiving that the left battalion had not cleared two enemy machine-guns , which were firing on the left rear of his

company, he worked round with a sergeant and captured them. This quick action saved heavy casualties and helped the success of the whole operation. His untiring efforts previous to the attack and his coolness under bombardment are greatly to be commended.

Garland, George Macauley Lieutenant, A/Captain   01/02/1919
For conspicuous gallantry and devotion to duty at Holnon from 18 to 20 September 1918. After many previous attempts had failed, he led his company through the village and established them in a position which was maintained under heavy shellfire. He showed a quick grasp when dealing with difficulties.

Green, Charles Henry, Lieutenant   15/04/1916
For conspicuous gallantry. He led a raid on the enemy's trenches, after forcing his way through the wire, and having accounted for several, withdrew successfully bringing in a prisoner.

Grey-Wilson, William Arthur, Captain, T/Major 2nd Bn Comdg 200th Coy
MGC   03/06/1919

Haylett, Robert, Lieutenant, A/Captain   30/07/1919
This officer led his company with great gallantry in the attack on 18 September 1918, until he was wounded. He was instrumental in the capture of seven prisoners and two machine guns. He has always displayed gallantry and devotion to duty, and inspired his men with confidence.

Jones, James Andrew, Lieutenant, T/Captain   01/01/1917

Lambdin, John Reginald, Lieutenant, West Yorkshire Regiment att 2nd Bn
                                                         04/10/1919
For marked gallantry and devotion to duty near St Quentin Wood on the night 17/18 September, 1918. He was sent to show the battalion guides the route to the assembly position. He took the party up and got shelled. Out of the sixteen guides six came back, the remainder being killed. Although himself badly shaken, he returned to the battalion and practically unaided, guided the companies into position. He then volunteered to take a message over ground swept by shellfire.

Layng, Thomas Malcolm, Lieutenant, Indian Army, att 2nd Bn
                                                         14/01/1919
Maxwell, Claude, Second Lieutenant   04/10/1919
For great gallantry and good leadership in the operations on 17 October and 23 October 1918, near Vaux Andigny. He assisted in the capture of his objective, together with forty prisoners and ten machine-guns, and reorganised the remains of his companion the objective. Later he pushed on with his company successfully and carried out very good patrol work.

McBain, Hubert, Lieutenant   16/09/1918
Morchies 21 March 1918, for conspicuous gallantry and devotion to duty. He led a counter- attack and established a block in a trench at a very critical time. He held this position for four hours and greatly assisted his battalion to remain in its position. He showed great fearlessness and devotion to duty. In the afternoon he was wounded.

Percy, Joscelyn Edward Seymour, Lieutenant,   17/04/1917
For conspicuous gallantry and devotion to duty. He led his men with great determination and himself killed two of the enemy. Later although severely wounded, he remained in the enemy trenches until the last man of his party had withdrawn.

Pollard, Thomas Barnes, Second Lieutenant,   17/04/1917
For conspicuous gallantry and devotion to duty when in command of a raiding party. He led his men with great determination and himself killed three of the enemy. Later, although severely wounded he continued to conduct the operations, eventually bringing his party back without the loss of a man.

Saunders, Herbert Mellor, Second Lieutenant, A/Captain   15/10/1918
For conspicuous gallantry and tenacity whilst commanding his company in assaulting and mopping up a strong position held by the enemy with machine-guns. He carried out the task in a very able manner, several machine-guns and many prisoners being taken, while he himself captured the officer commanding the post. He then consolidated a support position under heavy shellfire, and by his cheerfulness and coolness inspired all ranks with confidence.

Severs, William, Second Lieutenant.   15/10/1918
For great gallantry during an attack when he carried out the task allotted to him with much skill and coolness. After reaching the objective he consolidated the position and remained for forty eight hours until relieved. He had previously done very good patrol work, the correctness of which was proved in the delivery of the assaults on the points he had located.

Shea, Joseph Patrick Lambert, DCM, Lieutenant & QM, MC 01/01/1918
        Bar to MC, Captain & QM   18/07/1918
For conspicuous gallantry and devotion to duty. The enemy were seen from the Transport lines to be suddenly advancing and many men from various units were withdrawing through the lines. Having got the transport away, he led all available men of his battalion forward in support and commanded until the arrival of reinforcements. He fearlessly exposed himself in pointing out the situation to the officer commanding the relieving troops, and he was severely wounded in so doing.

Sopwith, Gerald, Lieutenant   06/09/1915

For conspicuous gallantry and devotion to duty at Hooge 9 August 1915, Although blown several yards by a large shell, wounded in the shoulder and slightly in the leg he refused to leave the firing line taking command of his company when the commander had been badly wounded and another officer killed. At a critical moment he left the trenches under heavy fire, rallied and led back some men who were retiring owing to a misunderstanding. At 0500 hours on 10 August he was again wounded and his jaw broken. He had to lie down but continued to command and encourage his men till he was relieved.

Storey, Kenneth, Second Lieutenant,   06/09/1915

For conspicuous gallantry and skill on 9 August 1915 at Hooge, when in command of bombing parties. He was seriously wounded while directing his men. The success of our attack and the subsequent holding of the position were largely due to the coolness and dash of the Battalion bomb throwers under Second Lieutenant Storey.'

Watson, Joseph, Regimental Sergeant Major, later Lieutenant & QM,
    01/01/1918
Wiehe, George Ivan, Second Lieutenant,   06/09/1915

For Conspicuous gallantry and skill in the attack on Hooge on 9 August 1915, when in charge of the battalion machine-guns. He was one of the first to reach the final position, and quickly bringing his guns into action, inflicted very heavy losses on the enemy. During the whole day and the night of 9/10 August he did excellent execution with his guns, and kept his men in good spirits by his coolness and cheerfulness.

Distinguished Conduct Medal

43103 Blair, T. Lance Corporal.   30/10/1918

For conspicuous gallantry and devotion to duty and resource in an attack while in charge of the Lewis gun section with the mopping-up platoon. He assisted in the capture of a large number of prisoners and three, machine guns. Seeing that the assaulting wave had lost half its men, he took up his two Lewis guns to the front line and directed the consolidation in the vicinity. He then returned through the barrage to report his action.

300173 Castling, R. Sergeant.   3/09/1918

For conspicuous gallantry and devotion to duty, when in command of a section. After having been driven out of his post by overwhelming odds, he reformed his section and retook it, driving the enemy well back. He showed fine courage and determination.

6147 Cresswell, J. RSM   1/01/1919

He had served for two years in the field as a CSM and during the period under review as a R.S.M. At Dickebusch, on 1 July 1918, he showed marked gallantry and succeeded in bringing up ammunition to the battalion throughout the fight under very difficult conditions and under heavy shellfire. His work has at all times been excellent.

10704 Duddy, T.S. Sergeant, A/CSM   11/03/1916

For conspicuous gallantry and consistent good work with the battalion machine-gun detachment. Since his arrival at the front he has always displayed great ability and resource in the performance of his duties.

8345, Gibbens, C, Sergeant.   15/09/1915

For conspicuous gallantry on the 9 and 10 August, 1915, at Hooge. About 3 p.m. some men started to withdraw from the vicinity of the "Stables", Sergeant Gbbens assisted by three others, succeeded in rallying them and leading them back, under considerable shellfire, to the vacated trench. Later he, in company with an Officer, ran across some exposed ground in order to head off some men who had commenced to withdraw. The action was very gallant owing to the heavy shellfire.

7051 Gott, J. Corporal   15/09/1915

For conspicuous energy and devotion to duty throughout 9 August, 1915, at Hooge. He refused to quit the portion of the trench which he was holding when a retirement was permitted on 10 August, and held on until relieved at dark.

6742 Harrington, G.W. Sergeant   10/3/1915

For conspicuous gallantry on 20 September, 1914, at Troyon., in the valley of the Aisne, in voluntarily rescuing wounded men on two occasions whilst under heavy fire. On 21 September he went out to the enemy trenches at dawn, and brought back information of great value to our Artillery.

10396 Hirst, H. Private   15/09/1915

For conspicuous gallantry on 9th August 1915, at Hooge. He was sent with messages three times from near the Crater to Battalion Headquarters under heavy fire, and although wounded, returned each time. He carried back an officer and showed the greatest bravery and coolness throughout the day.

7636 Howse, R D. Private,   15/09/1915

For conspicuous gallantry and devotion to duty on the 9th August,1915, at Hooge. He stood all day and night in a communication trench bombing the enemy, and at 9 a.m. on 10 August, when his party was permitted to withdraw, he refused to quit his post until relieved.

41571 Hunter, R. CSM.   03/06/1916
For conspicuous and consistent good work throughout. He has shown a fine courage under trying circumstances.

9496 Johnson, T O. CSM   30/01/1920
For gallant and distinguished services in the Field, which have been brought to notice in accordance with the terms of Army Order 193 of 1919, to be dated 5s May, 1919.

5558 Kent C. CSM   10/03/1915
For gallant conduct on 20 September, 1914, at Troyon, in the valley of the Aisne, when he voluntarily assisted in the rescue of a wounded officer under a heavy fire.
        Bar to DCM   15/09/1915
For conspicuous gallantry on the 9August, 1915, at Hooge, during the attack. later, about 3 p.m., some men started to withdraw from the vicinity of the 'Stables' Company Sergeant Major Kent, with three others, succeeded in rallying them and leading them back to the vacated trench under persistent shellfire. In rallying these men considerable open space had to be crossed. He remained in his position until about 9.30 a.m. on the 10 August, no orders to withdraw having been received.

9075 Lowe, J. Sergeant   15/04/1916
For conspicuous gallantry when leading a party during a raid. He cleared the enemy's trench with great determination and brought out a prisoner.

7958 Manley, O. Lance Corporal   15/09/1915
For conspicuous gallantry and initiative as a bomb thrower, on the 9 August, 1915 at Hooge. When a portion of our trench had been evacuated and the Battalion on the right had withdrawn, he assisted to hold the extreme right of our line with bombs under heavy fire. He did excellent work in collecting and distributing bombs and in showing untrained men how to use both our own and those of the enemy.

9200 Martin, G. Corporal   30/06/1915
For great zeal and devotion to duty, and for excellent work in connection with transport.

3/10923 McGall, J Private   14/01/1916
For conspicuous gallantry. Private McCall was one of a party which, when going to occupy a listening post, met with heavy rifle and grenade fire at close range. The suddenness of the attack caused confusion, but he at once crawled forward with his grenades and threw them into the listening post, whence the fire proceeded, causing the enemy to retire.

4/9893 McGlone, P. Corporal   03/09/1918

For conspicuous gallantry and devotion to duty. He held up the advancing enemy with his Lewis gun until practically surrounded, thereby rendering important service at a critical moment.

45188 Muir, J. Private   03/09/1918

For conspicuous gallantry and devotion to duty when one of a party sent out into shell holes in front during an enemy attack. All except him were killed or wounded, but he remained at his post, killing many of the enemy and greatly assisting in holding them back. He showed great courage and determination.

4/8393 Nimmo, J. Private   14/01/1916

For conspicuous gallantry. The battalion was resting in a field, when the enemy started shelling the field with shrapnel. An officer was wounded, and the men were told to scatter and obtain cover. Private Nimmo went to the assistance of the wounded officer, bandaged him in the open and then carried him, about 100 yards to cover.

11344 Peverley, W. Private   30/06/1915

For conspicuous gallantry and ability in carrying messages. Has proved himself a cool and reliable soldier.

16746, Pike, E. CSM   25/11/1916

For conspicuous gallantry in action. He rescued several men who were buried, later, he went forward under heavy fire to ascertain the situation; and obtained most valuable information. He displayed great courage and determination throughout the operations.

51132 Shakespeare, F. Sergeant.   30/10/1918

For conspicuous gallantry and devotion to duty as acting CSM. He was of great assistance in making arrangements before the attack. During the assault he controlled and steadied the man, reorganising them on reaching the objective. Later; although wounded, he remained with the company until it was relieved

8702 Smith, J. G. Lance Corporal,   15/09/1915

For conspicuous gallantry and initiative as a bomb thrower on 9th August, 1915, at Hooge. When a portion of our trench had been evacuated and the Battalion on the right withdrawn, he held the extreme right of our line with bombs under heavy fire. About mid-day on 10 August he collected about 24 men when all other troops had been withdrawn from his vicinity, and held on till 7.30 p.m., sending back for bombs and reinforcements, till more troops arrived.

4/9054 Tighe, T. Sergeant.   15/04/1916

For conspicuous gallantry during a raid. he volunteered to reconnoitre the enemy's trench, and afterwards went with the officer leading the raid. He was one of the first to enter the trench, which he boldly attacked with bombs.

25290 Tugby, J.W. Sergeant [10721 Private 2/DLI] A/WOII, MGC
03/09/1918

For conspicuous gallantry and devotion to duty in action. When his officer was wounded he took command of his section, directing their fire with great effect and covering the retirement of infantry until practically surrounded. He then skilfully withdrew. his guns, remaining behind with one to cover their retirement. On reaching a new line, he again brought his guns into action, beating off several attacks and inflicting severe casualties on the enemy. He continued in action until all his team were casualties except himself and one man, and when his last gun was knocked out he fought his way back. His courage and endurance were splendid.

Sergeant Bar to DCM   MGC   03/06/1918
gazetted before DCM

For conspicuous gallantry and devotion to duty. This non-commissioned officer has rendered consistently good service during the last six months. On one occasion, when the section officer and many of the gun detachments had become casualties under the heavy barrage of fire of the enemy. Sergeant Tugby reorganised the gun teams and brought them into action again.

8757 Warwick, J. Private   01/04/1915

For gallant conduct on 20th September, 1914, at Troyon, in the valley of the Aisne, when he voluntarily assisted in the rescue of a wounded officer under a heavy fire.

5945 Waters C. CQMS   11/03/1920

He has shown great devotion to duty. During most of the two and a half years he brought up and personally supervised the supplies of his company, frequently under shell and machine-gun fire and rifle fire.

6402 Watson, J. RSM   14/01/1916

For conspicuous gallantry and energy throughout the campaign. Sergeant Major Watson has always exhibited great courage under fire, and by his coolness and resource in charge of transport and issuing rations has given a fine example of devotion to duty.

79318 Witherwick, C. Lance Sergeant   10/01/1920

For conspicuous gallantry and devotion to duty during the operations of 19-20 September, 1918, at Holnon. He took charge of the advanced posts for 48 hours after his platoon officer had become a casualty, visiting them continually and encouraging the men under heavy shell and machine-gun fire. On three occasions the posts were shelled out, but he immediately reorganised them in their positions, setting a fine example throughout.

10628, Wootton, W. H. Lance Corporal   16/01/1915
For gallantry on 28th October in dressing an officers wounds and helping to bring him into safety under fire.

3/8995 Wray, T. Sergeant.   30/03/1916
For conspicuous good work as Chief Scout of his Brigade. One night on patrol, having found an enemy working party, he sent back for a machine-gun and, firing himself, killed several of the enemy, subsequently carrying back a wounded man of his patrol.

Military Medal

Name	Rank	Number	Date
Allen, T.	Private	78822	17/06/1919
Sheffield			
Allison, H.	Private	34527	16/08/1917
Armstrong, T.H.	Private	38676	06/08/1918
Sunderland			
Atkinson, W.	Sergeant	19238	17/06//1919
York			
Attwood, S.T.	Private	93036	17/06/1919
Harlow, Essex			
Barry, J.	Corporal	27232	09/12/1916
Bayles, J.	Private	4/9508	09/12/1916
Black,E.	RQMS	5824	10/05/1919
Broomfield.	A.L/Corporal	28271	21/10/1918
Fencehouse			
Bradshaw, R.H.	Private	73503	07/10/1918
Stockton-on-Tees			
Bridgens, F.H.	Private	93185	21/10/1918
Sheffield			
Bar to MM			17/06/1919
Brimer, W.N.	Private	19302	06/08/1918
Pelaw-on-Tyne	attd. 18 Inf. Bde HQ		
Broxon, H.	Sergeant	10098	23/02/1918
Murton			
Burkitt,, A.	Sergeant	79239	11/12/1918
Hull			
Bum, G.W.	Private	27280	09/12/1916
Clark, J.	Sergeant	10535	27/10/l916
Bar to MM			06/08/1918
Clements, E.	Private	66500	17/06/1919
Burton-on-Trent			
Cohen, M.	Sergeant	9666	27/10/1916

Cole, T.H, Chester-le-Street	Private	203344	21/10/1918
Conway, P. South Shields	Private	73535	17/06/1919
Cook, F. Clayton	Private	77433	13/03/1919
Corkin, T.	L/Corporal	30740	21/12/1976
Cumberland, F.	Sergeant.	10767	27/10/1916
Daley, J.	Private.	6411	27/10/1916
Darrell, J.M. Middlesbrough	Private	4/9081	27/10/1917
Fairbairn, T.	Corporal	8317	27/10/1916
Fawcett, R.	Private	30555	21/09/1916
Fitter, H.	Sergeant	10998	27/10/1916
Fox, A. Ilkeston	L/Corporal	25359	17/06/1919
Gibbons, E. Rowlands Gill	Private.	10824	21/10/1918
Gibbons, T.	Private	39448	16/08/1916
Gorden, W.	Private	311069	27/10/1916
Gould, A.R. Midsomer	Corporal	201071	17/06/1919
Norton Graham, J. Gateshead	Private	11538	17/06/1919
Greenlaw, J, New Washington	Private	10595	28/01/1918
Gurnett F,	Private	77451	13/03/1919
Hawthorne, J.W.	Private	3/10181	27/10/1916
Higgins, A. Newcastle	Corporal	79263	17/06/1919
Horner, J. Selby	Private	93097	17/06/1919
Howard, F. Sunderland	Sergeant	28361	21/10/1918
Hudson, H.	Private	41799	27/10/1916
Hughes, W. Gateshead	Corporal	19/1081	07/10/1918
Hunsley, F. Barton-on-Humber	Private	77255	13/03/1919
Hurdman, J.S. Sunderland	Private	38406	06/08/1918
Jackson, F.O.	L/Sergeant	17895	26/03/1917
Kane, P.	A/Corporal	11337	28/07/1917

Lilley, A.E. Hull	Private	79269	14/05/1919
Lowe, C.E. Ferryhill	Private	45595	13/03/1919
Lowerson, G. Shiney Row	Private	46748	13/03/1919
McGarva, A. Glasgow	Private	49914	23/02/1918
McGurk, J.	Private	12635	27/10/1916
McKinnon, J.	Private	9020	27/10/1916
Mason, W.C.	Sergeant	11007	27/10/1916
Miller, W. Stewarton	Private	43896	21/10/1918
Milner, S. Hull	Private	93044	21/10/1918
Moore, S. West Hartlepool	Corporal	1657	21/10/1918
Moore, W.J. Hartlepool	Sergeant	10039	13/03/1919
Moulds, E. Hull	Corporal,	79315	07/10/1918
Nattrass T. Bishop Auckland	Private	32885	17/06/1919
Noble, G.A.M.	Private	4/8328	03/06/1916
O'Brien, J.	Private.	4/9052	27/10/1916
O'Donnell, N.	Sergeant	25940	26/03/1917
O'Rourke, C.	Private	41872	27/10/1916
Parker, J.W.	Sergeant	12021	27/10/1916
Pearce H. Hull	Private	93050	21/10/1918
Pennell, W.	Private.	46031	16/08/1917
Phillips C. E..S.	L/Corporal	1116	26/05/1917
Pratt, N.	Corporal	11429	21/10/1916
Raine, S.W.	Corporal	9649	11/05/1917
Ramsey, T,W. Easington Colliery	Private	36268	06/08/1918
Ray, W. with 25/DLI	Sergeant	10053	27/10/1916
Reed, T. South Moor	Sergeant	14034	17/06/1919
Reidling C. F.	Private	26850	26/05/1917
Riley E.	Private	9713	27/10/1916
Ripley J. Darlington	Private	36543	17/06/1919

Robinson W. H. Middlesbrough	Sergeant	43521	06/08/1918
Ruffle A. W. Farnborough	Private	9727	11/02/1919
Ryder, F.	L/Corporal	9596	27/10/1916
Satterley, A.M. Durham	Sergeant	12723	13/03/1919
Shaw, C.A. Hull	Corporal	79248	13/03/1919
Shearstone H. Sheffield	Private	300823	17/06/1919
Smith, J, South Shields	Private	3/9598	21/10/1918
Speed, J. Blackhall Colliery	Private	10049	17/06/1919
Sullivan, B. Hull	Corporal	79247	21/10/1918
Sykes, A.H. Sunderland	L/Corporal	12032	21/10/1918
Taylor, S. Newcastle-on-Tyne	Private	38881	06/08/1918
Turton J. Byers Green	Sergeant	8915	21/10/1916
Walker, A. High Heaton	Corporal	49913	13/03/1919
Weatherhead, M. Pannal	Private	43981	13/03/1919
Webb, A.	Private	34793	16/08/1917
Wells, A. Ripon	Corporal	92089	13/03/1919
Wiliiamson J W. Sheffield	Private	93125	07/10/1918
Willoughby J,.J. Gateshead	Private	32988	21/10/1918
Wilson, T.E. Sheffield	Private	93194	17/06/1919
Witts, J.E. Dudley	Sergeant	10518	07/10/1918
Wood, J.A.	Sergeant	6871	27/10/1916

Meritorious Service Medal

Anslow, P. Gateshead	CSM	8555	18/01/1919
Cameron, J. R. West Hartlepool	Sgt, A /CQMS	10563	03/06/1919
Cooper, F. Peterborough	CQMS	10695	03/06/1919
Jiggins, S.E. Lichfield	Col Sgt, ORS.	10539	18/01/1919
Jones, L.	Sgt	9229	18/10/1916
Longstaffe, J. Bishop Auckland	Private	10174	03/06/1919
Parkin, W. Sunderland	L/Cpl.	11070	17/06/1918
Tucker, H. Colchester	CQMS	9976	18/01/1919
Wray, T. Hartlepool	A/CSM (DCM)	3/8995	03/06/1919

Mentioned in Despatches

Beart, C. W.	Lt T/Capt (MC)		30/05/1918	Staff Italy
			06/01/1919	Staff Italy
Black, E	QMS	5824	22/06/1915	
Bolam, O.	L/Cpl	5646	17/02/1915	
Bradford, R. B.	Lt		17/02/1915	
	Lt, T Capt (MC)		15/06/1916	Adjt 9/DLI
	Lt, T/Lt Col (MC)		04/01/1917	Comdg 9/DLI
	Lt, T/Brig Gen (VC, MC)		28/12/1917	
	Comdg 186 Brigade			
Brereton, D. L.	Major, A/Lt Col		28/12/1918	
Briggs, J. M.	Lt, A/Capt		28/12/1918	att 6th Bn MGC
Brown, B. A.	Pte, A/Sgt	32984	09/07/1919	
Cartwright, J. D.	Second Lt		01/01/1916	
Chatt,, R.	Lt		09/07/1919	att 48 LTMB
Christopher, W.	CSM	8500	09/07/1919	
Congreve, C. R.	Lt, T Capt		01/01/1916	GHQ Staff
	Capt		04/01/1917	" "
	Bt. Major		11/12/1917	" "
	Bt. Major		20/12/1918	" "
Crosthwaite, J. A.	Major		17/02/1915	"
			22/06/1915	
Cumming, H. R,	Lt Col, T/Brig Gen		15/05/1917	Staff
	Lt Col, T/Brig Gen (		03/02/1920	North Russia
Gibbens, C.	Lt, T/Major (DSO, MC, DCM)		05/06/1919	2 att 12/DLI Italy

Name	Rank	Number	Date	Notes
Godsal,. W. H.	Capt & Adjt		22/06/1915	
	Capt		01/01/1916	
	Major (MC)		21/12/1917	
	Major (MC)		20/05/1918	
Goring-Jones, M. D.	Lt Col		01/01/1916	
	Lt Col, T/Brig Gen		15/06/1916	
	T/Brig Gen (CMG)		04/01/1917	
	T/Brig Gen (CMG		11/12/1917	Staff
Greaves, J.	Sgt	45843	09/07/1919	
Greenwell, C. O.	Capt, T/Major		04/01/1917	Special Res att
			24/05/1918	
	Capt, T/Major (OBE)		09/07/1919	
Grey-Wilson, W. A.	Capt		28/11/1917	att Salonika
Hoare, L. G.	Lt, T/Capt		05/07/1919	Special Res att
Hunter, J.	L/Cpl	11130	17/02/1915	
Irrvine, A. E	Major, T/Lt Col		15/06/1916	
	Major, T/Lt Col		04/01/1917	
	Bt. Lt Col, T/Brig Gen (DSO)		11/12/1917	Staff
	Bt. Lt Col, T/Brig Gen (DSO)		20/05/1918	
Bt. Lt Col, T/Brig Gen (CMG, DSO) 5/07/1919				"
Jones, J. A.	Lt, T/Capt		15/06/1916	
Lt, T/Major, A/Lt Col (DSO, MC)			09/07/1919	2/DL93106
			09/07/1919	
Lowe, J.	Cpl	9075	22/06/1915	
McCullagh, H. R.	Capt, A/Lt Col		24/5/1918	2/DLI Cmdg 19/DLI
	Capt, T/Major, A/Lt Col		28/12/1918	2/DLI Cmdg 19/DLI
McMahon, B. W. L.	Lt Col, T/Col		27/07/1917	Sec of States list
Maughan, F. G.	Major		7/04/1915	Staff
			01/01/1916	Brigade Staff
Metcalfe, D.	Pte	10246	17/02/1915	
Northey, W.	Major, (DSO)		17/02/1915	
Norton, L. G.	Lt		22/06/1915	
Oliver, W. F. L.	Second Lieutenant		22/06/1915	
Parke, W. E.	Lieutenant		17/02/1915	2/DLI
Petfield , T.	Sgt	83200	12/01/1920	
Potts, W. D.	Capt		28/12/918	3/DLI att
Rice, W.	Lieutenant		09/07/1919	3/DLI att
Shea, J. P. L.	Lieutenant		01/01/1919	
	Pte	9029	22/06/1915	
Steel, A. K.	Second Lieutenant		04/01/1917	att MGC
Storey, K.	Second Lieutenant		01/01/1916	
Taylor, H. J.	Major, T/Lt Col,		21/12/1917	

Tucker, H.	CQMS	9976	24/05/1918	
Tuffs, E. W.	Lieutenant		30/01/1921	whilst POW
Turner, R. V.	Major, T/Lt Col (DSO)		09/07/1919	
Watson J.	CSM	6402	22/06/1915	
			01/01/1916	
	RSM (DCM)		25/05/1917	
Willis, H. G.	Second Lieutenant		15/06/1916	
Yate, R. A.	Lt, A/Capt		30/12/1918	2/DLI att 5/ York & Lancs

FOREIGN AWARDS

BELGIUM

Croix de Guerre

Blenkinsop, M.   Pte   11366   01/4/1919
Sunderland
Irvine, A. E.   Bt Lt Col, T/Brig Gen, (DSO)   11/03/1918
Raine, S. W.   Sgt   9649   12/07/1918
Bishop Auckland

Ordre de Leopold
Irvine, A. E.   Bt Lt Col, T/Brig Gen, (DSO)

FRANCE

Croix de Guerre
Nimmo, J.   Pte   4/8393   24/02/1916

Legion d'Honneur
Cumming, H. R.   Lt Col, T/Brig Gen   07/10/1918
                  Commandeur 22/11/1918 Croix d'Officier

RUSSIA

Cross of St George 4th Class
Kent, C. CSM (DCM)   5538   25/08/1915

Medal of St George 2nd Class
Harrington, G. W. Sgt   6742   25/08/1915

UNITED STATES OF AMERICA
Distinguished Service Cross
Rice, W. Lieutenant   18/08/1920   Special Res
                                                 att 2/DLI

Nominal Roll of Officers who served in the 2nd Battalion Durham Light Infantry 1914-1918 and Nominal Roll of Other Ranks who were awarded the 1914 Star

Officers Embarkation Roll
2nd Battalion The Durham Light Infantry 14 September 1914

McMahon	B W L	Lieutenant Colonel	Commanding
Crosthwaite	J A	Major	Second in Command
Northey	W	Captain	Comdg A Coy
Mander	D'A W	Major	Comdg B Coy
Blake	E A C	Major	Comdg C Coy
Robb	A K	Major	Comdg D Coy
Maughan	F G	Captain	Staff Captain 18 Inf Bde
Wood	J H	Captain	
Hare	H V	Captain	
Godsal	W H	Lieutenant	Adjutant
Taylor	H	Lieutenant	
Congreve	C R	Lieutenant	
Twist	W B	Lieutenant	
Norton	L G	Lieutenant	
Grey-Wilson	W A	Lieutenant	
Green	C H	Second Lieutenant	Att 6th Div Cyclist Coy
Parke	W E	Second Lieutenant	Machine Gun Officer
Conant	N G P	Second Lieutenant	
Beart	C W	Second Lieutenant	
Yate	VAC	Second Lieutenant	
Bradford	R B	Second Lieutenant	
Stanwell	C H	Second Lieutenant	
Marshall	R	Second Lieutenant	
Shea	J P L	Lieutenant & QM	
Smith	C E	Lieutenant	3/DLI attached
Sales	J R	Second Lieutenant	3/DLI attached
Mearins	C	Second Lieutenant	Special Reserve attached
Baker	C H	Second Lieutenant	Special Reserve attached
Bracken	G P A	Captain	RAMC attached

Nominal Roll of Officers that served with
The 2nd Battalion The Durham Light Infantry

Name	Initials	Rank on joining	Served with Bn From	To	Wounded	Killed or DoW	Remarks
Adams	Bernard	2nd Lieutenant	12/09/15	03/03/16	03/03/16		CSM East Lancashire Regt Comm 25/07/1915
Addington	Geoffery W	2nd Lieutenant	12/11/17	01/12/17		01/12/17	RIBECOURT BRIT CEM Age 19.
Aderne	E A	2nd Lieutenant	08/12/18				
Adie	Robert R	2nd Lieutenant	25/02/17	21/04/17		21/04/17	With 10th Bn June 1916 - 27/08/1916 wnd Delville Wood, PHILOSOPHE CEM MAZINGARBE Age 26.
Alexander	Kelsick E	2nd Lieutenant	22/04/17	21/03/18	21/03/18		4/DLI POW 21/3/18, Pte Wiltshire Regt 32496 to 5 O Cdt Bn wnd by hand
Allen	Walter L	2nd Lieutenant	16/08/17	27/09/17			Regular Border Regt 1903 - 1913 CSM 18/DLI to 21 O Cdt Bn Convicted b GCM for AWOL 30/11/1918, Police Constable.A/RSM 10 O Cdt Bn 11/2/1
Allison	Herbert	Lieutenant	11/04/18	14/07/18	14/07/18		Northumberland Fus Att
Anderson	A P	2nd Lieutenant	10/10/18	28/10/18	28/10/18		from a Svc Bn
Appleby	Robert J	2nd Lieutenant	13/11/16	08/02/17	08/02/17		
Appleton	Richard A	2nd Lieutenant	03/04/17	21/03/18		21/03/18	SERVED WITH 18th Bn 8/1916 - 10/4/1917 ARRAS MEM Age 20,MISSIN 21/02/1918
Archer	Ernest W	2nd Lieutenant	04/07/18	24/09/18	24/09/18		8/DLI
Armstrong	James N	Captain	24/12/14	22/08/15		22/08/15	Royal Army Medical Corps Att, HOP STORE CEM Age 26.
Badcock	Walter F E	Captain	17/11/18	14/12/18			From 1/4 Cheshire Regt, To England resuming Dental studies Pte 1/5 York
Baker	Charles H	2nd Lieutenant	08/09/14	20/10/14	20/10/14		Special Reserve attached
Bale	George W	2nd Lieutenant	02/08/18	18/09/18	18/09/18		Comm from RASC No O91760 to 3/DLI
Bamlet	Geoffery A	2nd Lieutenant	29/07/12	16/08/17			4/DLI , Adjutant 20/Durham LI 29/9/17 - 27/3/18
Barclay	Henry	2nd Lieutenant	02/09/16	15/10/16		15/10/16	BANCOURT BRIT CEM Age 21.
Barkas	John C P	Lieutenant	16/02/16	24/02/16			Evacuated Sick
Barker	T B	2nd Lieutenant	14/10/15	28/12/15	28/12/15		Pte 3421 Artist Rifles Lcpl 11/7/15, Gassed 13/12/15, Wnd head 28/12/1 Salonika 1917
Barrington	Claude M J	2nd Lieutenant	16/07/16	04/10/17			
Batty	Bertie C	Captain	12/03/16	15/09/16		15/09/16	19/DLI, 1/3/15, 21/DLI 1/8/15, 23/DLI 14/1/16, Thiepval Memorial.
Beart	Charles W	2nd Lieutenant	08/09/14	20/10/14	20/10/14		ADC 7/1915, Staff Capt 25/2/1917, Brig Maj 29/8/17
Benton	Ronald M	2nd Lieutenant	28/03/15	20/04/15		07/06/16	Evacuated sick Unattached list Indian Army Att, D Company 53rd Sikhs(F Force) KiA in Mesopotamia Buried Amara War Cemetery Iraq.
Birt	Ernest W	Captain	11/09/14	27/10/14	27/10/14		Lt Col Comdg Detention Barracks
Birtles	Leonard	2nd Lieutenant	08/09/16	16/09/16		16/09/16	THIEPVAL MEM Age 23.
Biscoe	Hugh V	Major	26/11/18	20/01/19			Indian Army Att
Black	James A	2nd Lieutenant	26/07/17	21/03/18		21/03/18	16/364 Northumberland Fus Comm 3/DLI, VAULX HILL CEM Age 22.
Black	Percy D	Lieutenant	29/10/16	31/07/17	27/06/17		Comm 17/DLI, with 4/DLI 3/11/1914 - 9/11/14 to 17/DLI
Blake	Edward A C	Major	08/09/14	20/09/14		20/09/14	Comdg C Coy, PLOEGSTEERT MEM, Age 43.
Bolam	Welford	2nd Lieutenant	11/04/18	11/06/18			16/Northumberland Fus Att
Booth MM	Harold G B	2nd Lieutenant	12/04/18	05/08/18			Northumberland Fus Att Formerly CPL K/808 22 Royal Fusiliers
Bowers	Arthur H M	Captain	26/10/14	09/08/15		09/08/15	MENIN GATE MEM
Boxer	Hugh Caldwell	Captain	21/01/17	24/04/17			Temp Major Svc Bn DLI 1917
Boyle	George P A	1st Lieutenant	15/11/17 05/11/17	06/12/17 05/12/17			United States Army Medical Service Att
Bracken		Captain	08/09/14	23/12/14			Royal Army Medical Corps Att
Bradford	Roland B	2nd Lieutenant	08/09/14	02/05/15		30/11/17	Lt Col Comdg 9/DLI VC, Brigadier Comdg 186 Bde, HERMIES BRIT CE 25.
Brereton	David L	Captain	09/12/14 01/02/18	05/08/15 13/07/18	05/08/15		Major Acting Lt Col DSO
Brewin	Sidney	Lieutenant	11/04/18	14/03/19	17/09/18		11/Northumberland Fus Att
Brewis	John A G	2nd Lieutenant	17/05/15	30/04/16	05/01/16	11/10/17	att Royal Flying Corps, ARRAS FLYING SERVICES MEM. Age 22.
Briggs	John M		02/02/18	13/03/18			3/DLI late att 14/DLI, to 6 Bn MGC
Briggs	Leonard S	2nd Lieutenant	06/02/15	16/08/15			Evacuated sick.
Bristow	Frank Anstie	2nd Lieutenant	30/04/17	19/05/17			
Brown	Frank C	2nd Lieutenant	09/12/14	13/02/19			from a Svc Bn
Brown	Frank D	Lieutenant	08/07/17	17/07/18			5/DLI
Brown	George	2nd Lieutenant	26/02/18	18/06/18			5/DLI
Brown	Norman	2nd Lieutenant	22/04/17	21/03/18			4/DLI POW 21/3/18
Burke	Michael C	Captain	30/03/18				Royal Army Medical Corps Att
Bussell	Thomas C H	2nd Lieutenant	17/02/17	18/03/17	18/03/17		4/DLI
Butcher	Alfred L	2nd Lieutenant	01/03/16	14/10/16	14/10/16		
Carmichael	Hugh H	2nd Lieutenant	22/01/18	21/03/18			POW 21/3/18
Carss	Henry	2nd Lieutenant	02/09/16				
Cartwright	John D	2nd Lieutenant	20/06/15	09/08/15		09/08/15	age 20 MENIN GATE MEMORIAL, brother KiA with 20th Bn
Caswell	John B	2nd Lieutenant	02/05/16	12/07/16	12/07/16		4/DLI accidentally wounded
Cates	Geoffrey	2nd Lieutenant	05/02/18	21/03/18		21/03/18	10/DLI ARRAS MEM, Age 24, Brother of 2LT G CATES VC.
Cave	Arthur D	2nd Lieutenant	16/07/16	26/07/18			
Chalmers	John S H	2nd Lieutenant	01/04/17	23/01/18			In the ranks Aug 1914 - June 1915
Chamberlin	Hugh F W	2nd Lieutenant	02/09/16	15/10/16	16/09/16	15/10/16	THIEPVAL MEM
Chatt	Robert	2nd Lieutenant	12/03/16 22/04/17	26/09/16 22/05/17	26/09/16		MiD, To America as an instructor November 1917
Coddington	Hubert John	Captain	21/05/19	07/07/15		07/07/15	LA BRIQUE MIL CEM No2
Cohen MM	Moss	2nd Lieutenant	04/11/16 27/04/18	12/10/17 24/09/18		24/09/18	TREFCON BRIT CEM CAULAINCOURT, Age 28.
Conant	Nigel C P	2nd Lieutenant	08/09/14	18/10/14	18/10/14		ADC to the Govenor of Victoria 1915.
Congreve	Charles R	Lieutenant	08/09/14	23/07/15			Staff Capt 22/7/1915, Brig Maj 23/10/1915. Gen Staff Off 24/2/1917 D 6 times.
Cook	Cyril R	2nd Lieutenant	31/01/16	14/09/16			Gloucestershire Regt Att
Coverdale	Miles	2nd Lieutenant	21/07/15	09/08/15	09/08/15		
Crawford	James	2nd Lieutenant	18/06/15	15/09/16 14/10/16	15/09/16 14/10/16		
Crawley	S F A	2nd Lieutenant	23/12/17 26/12/18	22/03/18			
Cross	Harry	2nd Lieutenant	22/08/15	10/11/15	10/11/15		
Crosthwaite	Joseph A	Major	08/09/14	01/07/15			2 i/c, Lt Col York & Lancaster Regiment, MiD twice.
Cruickshanks	Joseph W	Lieutenant	26/10/14	06/04/15			3/DLI To Royal Air Force.

Surname	Forename	Rank				Notes
Cumming	Hanway R	Lt Colonel	28/08/16	19/11/16		Temp Brigadier 28/11/16 - 26/5/17, Comdg MGC Trng Centre 3/8/17, DSO, Legion d' Honuer, MiD twice.
?agnall	F C	Lieutenant	11/04/18	16/05/18		Northumberland Fus Att
?alziel	Stanley	2nd Lieutenant	08/05/16		23/09/16	
			10/02/17		10/10/16	
?avis	William T H	2nd Lieutenant	18/07/17	21/03/18		21/03/18 ARRAS MEM Age 20.
?avison	Joseph J	2nd Lieutenant	06/06/17	22/06/17	22/06/17	23/06/17 4/DLI NOEUX-LES-MINES COM CEM Age 22.
?avison	William	2nd Lieutenant	21/05/16	15/09/15		Att 6th Div Cyclist Coy.
?ennison	Joseph S A	2nd Lieutenant	05/02/18	12/06/18		10/DLI
?itcham	H J	2nd Lieutenant	31/07/18	18/08/18		7/DLI
?ryden	Eric	2nd Lieutenant	09/03/16	18/10/17		Attached 18 Brigade HQ 18/10/1917
?udley	John	2nd Lieutenant	02/09/16	15/09/16	15/09/16	17/DLI
?unn	Alexander	2nd Lieutenant	16/07/16	15/10/16	15/10/16	
?ccles	James E	2nd Lieutenant	18/07/17	21/03/18		POW 21/3/18
?llis	Reginald D	2nd Lieutenant	22/08/15	28/12/15		Trf 18 Machine Gun Company
?ly	Dennis H J	2nd Lieutenant	13/10/15	16/10/15		16/DLI
?vans	James F	2nd Lieutenant	30/09/18	17/10/18	17/10/18	240499 York & Lancaster Regt COMMISSIONED 4 Y&L 28/5/1918
?vans	James	Captain	06/12/17			Royal Army Medical Corps Att
?veratt	John J	Captain	22/04/18	25/03/19		22/DLI
?awcett	Edward	2nd Lieutenant	20/12/16	21/03/18		3/DLI POW 21/3/18
?illingham	George S	2nd Lieutenant	01/06/17	27/04/18	21/03/18	
?olliott	John	2nd Lieutenant	21/04/18	19/09/18		19/09/18 TREFCON BRIT CEM CAULAINCOURT, Age 20.
?orsyth	John D	Lieutenant	14/04/18			25/Nothumberland Fus 2nd Tyneside Irish Att
?ortune	G R	Lieutenant	11/04/18	15/09/18		Northumberland Fus Att
?oster	Albert W	2nd Lieutenant	13/10/15	17/12/15	17/12/15	
?oster	William M	Lieutenant	07/06/17	12/08/17		
?ranklen-Evans	George P	2nd Lieutenant	30/08/18	18/09/18		18/09/18 4/DLI, BRIE BRIT CEM.
?ith	Walter H	2nd Lieutenant	12/09/15	27/06/16		6933 SGT 1/EAST LANCASHIRE REGT, ENT FRANCE 22/8/1914
			13/01/18			
?yer	Wilfred V	2nd Lieutenant	15/12/17	01/07/18	01/07/18	accidentally wounded
?ales	John Russell	2nd Lieutenant	08/09/14	20/09/14	20/09/14	3/DLI
?arfit	Thomas N C	2nd Lieutenant	24/01/15	30/04/15		30/04/15 HOUPLINES COM CEM EXT Age 22.
?arland	George M	2nd Lieutenant	30/06/15	09/08/15	09/08/15	
			16/07/16	08/02/17	16/09/16	Medical Board
			05/05/17	31/10/17	31/10/17	Att LTMB
			03/08/18	23/10/18	23/10/18	
?ibbens DCM	Charles	2nd Lieutenant	05/03/16	30/07/16		Att 12/DLI 1917.
?ibson	William	Captain	15/11/12	15/12/14		DLI Reserve of Officers, Evacuated sick.
?ilbertson	F J	Lieutenant	05/10/14	20/10/14	20/10/14	3/DLI TRF Tank Corps Captain
?illard	Ernest W	2nd Lieutenant	30/09/18	17/10/18	17/10/18	York & Lancaster Regt Att
?lpin	Ernest H	Captain	18/01/17	01/11/17		ADC to Govenor of Madras 1916
			20/01/18	21/03/18		21/03/18 ARRAS MEM Age 35.
?odsal	Walter H	Lieutenant	08/09/14	20/09/14	20/09/14	Adjutant, Brig Maj 28/9/15 - 28/12/16, Gen Staff Off grade 2 29/12/16.
			11/11/14	28/09/15		26/03/18 ST PIERRE CEM AMIENS, Age 34.
?rdon	R E	2nd Lieutenant	14/01/17	09/01/18		Highland LI Att
?ring Jones	Michael D	Lt Colonel	11/06/15	16/01/16		Temp Brig Comd 16/1/16 - 17/10/17
?attan	H A V	2nd Lieutenant	11/04/18	24/06/18		Northumberland Fus Att
?een	Cuthbert	2nd Lieutenant	02/09/16	15/10/16		15/10/16 THIEPVAL MEM Age 23.
?een	Charles H	2nd Lieutenant	16/09/15	23/09/15	23/09/15	Att 6th Div Cyclist Coy, rejoined Bn 16/09/1915, MC, Comdg Off Cadet Coy.
			17/02/16	15/03/16	15/03/16	
				20/04/16	20/04/16	
?een	Herbert	Lieutenant	08/07/17	17/07/18		5/DLI
?eenwell	Charles Okey	Captain	25/08/15	02/10/15		3/DLI
?egg	Robert	2nd Lieutenant	21/05/15	09/08/15		09/08/15 MENIN GATE MEMORIAL
?ey-Wilson	William A	Lieutenant	08/09/14	20/09/14	20/09/14	Trf MGC Instructor MGC Trg Centre 1915 - 1916, Major MGC 11/7/16 - 9/16 MiD MC
?ffiths-Jones	Morgan Philips	Captain	10/07/17	21/03/18		POW 21/3/18
?ffith-Jones	William L P	2nd Lieutenant	03/01/16	12/07/16		12/07/16 3/DLI accidentally killed POPERINGHE NEW MIL CEM Age 26.
?ggie	L D	2nd Lieutenant	03/10/16	15/10/16	15/10/16	
?ndcock	Charles G	Lieutenant	06/04/18	24/09/18	24/09/18	1/DLI
?re	H V	Captain	08/09/14	20/09/14		20/09/14 LA FERTE-SOUS-JOUARRE MEM, age 33.
?rgreaves	Reginald A	2nd Lieutenant	04/08/15	28/10/15	28/10/15	4/DLI
			21/04/16	24/09/16	24/09/16	
			09/01/17	28/06/17		28/06/17 LOOS MEM.
?ker	W E	Lieutenant	26/03/16	15/06/16		
?ris	William E	2nd Lieutenant	22/08/15	19/12/15		19/12/15 LIJSSENTHOEK MIL CEM Age 22
?rison	James S	2nd Lieutenant	22/04/18	27/05/15	27/05/18	28/05/18 ESQUELBCQ MIL CEM, Age 23
?rison	Thomas	2nd Lieutenant	08/06/17	26/08/18		
?ter	John G	Lieutenant	28/10/14	21/04/15		03/04/16 Capt acting Brig Maj 151 Bde, LIJSSENTHOEK MIL CEM. Age 27.
?tshorn	Laurence A	2nd Lieutenant	20/04/16	03/06/16	03/06/16	4/DLI DoW whilst att to Bde LTMB
			30/08/16	15/09/16	15/09/16	
			13/08/18	14/10/17		26/03/18 FLESQUIERES HILL BRIT CEM Age21.
?vey	Lionel J	2nd Lieutenant	30/09/18	17/10/18	17/10/18	York & Lancaster Regt Att
?lett	Robert	2nd Lieutenant	19/04/15	12/02/16		7279 CSM Durham LI Evacuated sick 02/1916
			11/02/18	18/09/18	18/09/18	
?derson	William	2nd Lieutenant	25/07/17	21/03/18		21/03/18 ARRAS MEM Age 20.
?plestone	C W	2nd Lieutenant	01/03/16	15/10/16	15/10/16	
?ward	Harry N	2nd Lieutenant	18/10/15	10/10/16		10/10/16 Posted to 15/DLI BENEFRAY WOOD BRIT CEM MONTAUBAN Age 26
?ks	George A	Lieutenant	26/10/14			4/DLI Evacuated sick
			10/07/17	10/07/17		
	John R	2nd Lieutenant	07/01/15	02/06/15		02/06/15 3/DLI, POTIJZE BURIAL GROUND CEM, Age 25.
	Robert	2nd Lieutenant	07/02/15	11/07/15	11/07/15	
?p	Gordon	2nd Lieutenant	05/02/18	29/09/18	29/09/18	In the ranks France 25/04/1915 to 9/1/1916, Feb to Mar 1916, April to Dec 1916, From 10/DLI
?re	Louis Gurney	2nd Lieutenant	21/01/17	15/04/17		3/DLI
?g	Robert M	2nd Lieutenant	19/01/08	21/03/18		POW 21/3/18
?croft	Gilbert C	2nd Lieutenant	11/06/15	09/08/15		09/08/15 MENIN GATE MEMORIAL
?ward-Krause	E	Lieutenant	24/07/18	18/09/18	18/09/18	General List

Surname	First name(s)	Rank	Date 1	Date 2	Date 3	Date 4	Notes
Howie	John L	2nd Lieutenant	05/10/18	25/03/19			from a Svc Bn
Hugall	John G	2nd Lieutenant	13/02/16	18/02/16	18/02/16		
			05/05/17	23/06/17	20/05/17		
Hughes	Edward	2nd Lieutenant	12/09/15	16/09/16	15/09/16	16/09/16	BRONFAY FARM MIL CEM BRAY SUR SOMME
Hutchinson	Miles Middleton	2nd Lieutenant	20/12/16	21/03/18	06/05/17		POW 21/3/18
Hutchinson	William R C	Captain	08/12/14	18/05/15	18/05/15		4/DLI
Inglis	William W	2nd Lieutenant	22/08/15	30/05/16			
Irvine	Alfred E	Captain	22/08/15	16/08/17			
Jackson	William C	2nd Lieutenant	27/06/18	10/08/18			6/DLI
James	Hugh W	2nd Lieutenant	29/10/16	21/06/17	21/06/17		Private Artists Rifles, Trf to Labour Corps 5/3/1918
Jarrett	Samuel F	2nd Lieutenant	30/10/15	27/11/15			
			20/09/16	12/10/16	10/10/16	12/10/16	
Jebb	Hope E	2nd Lieutenant	07/02/18	21/03/18		21/03/18	ARRAS MEM Age 19
Jeffrey	Joseph H	2nd Lieutenant	05/10/18	23/10/18		23/10/18	ST SOUPLET BRIT CEM Age 26 formerly 11428 Cpl 2/DLI
Johnson	Harry	2nd Lieutenant	09/07/16	04/05/17	04/05/17		
Johnston	David A S	2nd Lieutenant	25/05/17	05/07/17			7312 CSM Durham LI
Jones	James Andrew	2nd Lieutenant	01/10/14	20/07/15	20/07/15	14/10/18	Temp Lt Col Comdg 17/Lancashire Fus DSO MC, HOOGE CRATER
Judd	W B	2nd Lieutenant	16/07/16	11/04/17			
Keating	Eustace G L	Lieutenant	11/04/18	13/04/18		13/04/18	3/Northumberland Fus Att POLYGON WOOD CEM Age 26
Keith	John W	Lieutenant & QM	25/05/18	23/07/18			Notts & Derby Regt Att
Kent	James M	2nd Lieutenant	07/01/15	05/08/15		05/08/15	3/DLI, LIJSSENTHOEK MIL CEM Age 29.
Kish	W	Lieutenant	21/04/18				from ASC TF
Lambdin	John R	Lieutenant	24/07/18	24/09/18	24/09/18	24/09/18	1/7 West Yorks Regt Att, BRIE BRIT CEM Age 21
Lancaster	John S	2nd Lieutenant	08/10/18	17/10/18	17/10/18		3/DLI
Lapham	William G	Lieutenant	30/09/18	17/10/18	17/10/18		York & Lancaster Regt Att
Lavery	Andrew	2nd Lieutenant	26/10/14	27/10/14	27/10/14		In ranks 20 yrs 323 days. Adjutant Spec Res Bn 1916 MBE
Law	James M	Lieutenant & QM	18/07/18	01/02/19			
Lawes	Gordon W	2nd Lieutenant	04/07/18	17/09/18			
Lawson	Wosley	2nd Lieutenant	22/04/18	29/09/18	29/09/18		
Layng	Thomas W	2nd Lieutenant	14/12/14	02/09/15			Unattached list Indian Army Att Ordered ba+H270ck to UK
Legard	Gosnall S	Captain	22/08/15	08/01/16	08/01/16		3/DLI
Legard	Ralph H	Captain	26/10/14	09/08/15		09/08/15	4/DLI
Leng	William N	2nd Lieutenant	14/10/18	23/10/18	23/10/18		5/DLI
Licence	Russell E	Captain	31/10/18	19/01/19			Essex Regt Att formerly 2822,& 305459 Cpl R Warwickshire Regt
Linzee	Neville H	Captain	02/11/16				Royal Army Medical Corps Att
Lloyd	Vernon E	Captain	23/03/18	29/03/18			Royal Army Medical Corps Att
Lock	Joseph S	2nd Lieutenant	09/12/18	25/01/19			from a Svc Bn
Lunn	James J	2nd Lieutenant	21/08/17	21/03/18			POW 21/3/18, Served in the ranks in France 25/01/1915 - 12/02/19
Lynch	A C	Lieutenant	29/10/16	22/12/16			
Mackinnon	Neil O	2nd Lieutenant	19/02/18	21/03/18	21/03/18		
			21/07/18	26/07/18	26/07/18		
Maitland	Alexander S	2nd Lieutenant	14/10/15	19/01/06	19/01/16		accidentally wounded 22/10/15
Mander	D'Arcy W	Major	08/09/14	20/09/14		20/09/14	Comdg B Coy, VENDRESSE BRIT CEM, Age 51.
Manger	Edward V	Major	15/10/16	03/08/17			Lt Colonel Comdg TF Bn The King's Liverpool Regt 4/8/17 Legion d MiD. Wounded.
Maples	Stuart	2nd Lieutenant	29/05/15	18/06/15			Evacuated sick
Markham	Lionel J	2nd Lieutenant	03/01/16	16/02/16			
Marshall	L	2nd Lieutenant	15/01/19				
Marshall	Roger	2nd Lieutenant	08/09/14	20/09/14		20/09/14	LA FERTE-SOUS-JOUARRE MEM, age 23.
Martin	Douglas	2nd Lieutenant	11/04/16	21/06/18			Northumberland Fus Att
Martin	George N	2nd Lieutenant	22/08/15	16/12/15			Trf to RFC 15/12/1916
Marwood	Joshua S	2nd Lieutenant	01/11/18	13/02/19			
Masters	Charles W	Lieutenant	10/06/18	18/09/18			Northumberland Fus Att
Maughan	F G	Captain					Staff Captain 18 Inf Bde, Brig Maj 14/7/1915 - ??/10/1915, employ Office.Lt Col DSO.
Maxwell	Claude	2nd Lieutenant	24/07/18	14/03/19			
May	Richard W	2nd Lieutenant	28/03/15	09/08/15		09/08/15	MENIN GATE MEMORIAL
McBain	Hubert	2nd Lieutenant	11/03/17		20/04/2017 Gas		
			21/03/18	21/03/18			
			18/12/18				
McCullagh	Herbert Rochfort	Captain	18/01/17	18/04/17			Acting Lt Col Svc Bn Bedf Reg 3/6/17 13/6/17, Att KSLI 14/7/17 -
			07/08/17	16/03/18			Durham LI 31/8/17 DSO MiD twice.
McMahon	Bernard W L	Lt Colonel	08/09/14	05/01/15			Commanding School of Musketry 1917
McMonagle	H R C	2nd Lieutenant	03/08/18	15/11/18			Royal Irish Rifles att
Mearns	Colin	2nd Lieutenant	08/09/14	20/09/14	20/09/14		Special Reserve attached
Meikle	Robert J	2nd Lieutenant	06/03/16	15/09/16		15/09/16	4/DLI, GUARDS CEM LESBOEUFS Age23
Meldon	William W	Captain	26/10/14	12/11/14			4/DLI
Moir	Robert B O	2nd Lieutenant	14/01/17	09/04/17		09/04/17	3/Highland LI Att, LOOS MEM, Age 19.
Morris	Frank D	2nd Lieutenant	01/03/16	21/05/16	21/05/16		accidentally wounded
			29/10/16	07/05/17			
Morris	S F A	2nd Lieutenant	05/10/18	30/10/18			from a Svc Bn
Mortimer	William B	Lieutenant	26/10/14	12/01/15			4/DLI POTIJZE BURIAL GROUND CEM Age 39
			21/05/18	13/06/16		13/06/15	
Muir	Joseph C	Captain		21/03/18			Royal Army Medical Corps Att POW 21/3/18
Neal	A	2nd Lieutenant	26/10/14	20/01/15			in ranks 16 yrs 175 days, Capt Service Bn DLI Apr 1917
Newstead	Frederick L	Lieutenant	26/10/14	24/04/15			3/DLI
			28/11/15	07/08/16		07/08/16	
Northey	William	Captain	08/09/14	20/10/14	20/10/14	20/10/14	Comdg A Coy, BOULOGNE EASTERN CEM, Age 38.
Norton	Leopold G	Lieutenant	08/09/14	20/10/14		20/10/14	PLOEGSTEERT MEMORIAL Age 24.
Oliver	William F L	2nd Lieutenant	29/12/14	17/05/15			Evacuated sick.
Ord-Bell	H J	Lieutenant	15/01/19	14/03/19			3/DLI
Osborne	Derrick	2nd Lieutenant	20/09/16	21/03/18		21/03/18	3/DLI ARRAS MEM Age 21
Owen	Philip	2nd Lieutenant	06/09/17	02/10/17			
			08/10/18	30/01/19			
Palmer	John S	2nd Lieutenant	24/05/16		03/08/16		
			14/10/16	14/10/16		18/10/16	GROVE TOWN CEM MEAULTE Age 26.
Parke	Walter E	2nd Lieutenant	08/09/14	13/10/14		13/10/14	OUTTERSTEENE COM CEM EXT BAILLEUL, Age 23.

Surname	Forename	Rank					Notes
Parker	Percy C	Major	23/07/18	31/12/18			West Yorks Regt Att
Parkes	J C P	Lieutenant	06/02/16	24/02/16			
Peacock	James A	2nd Lieutenant	13/11/16	08/03/18			4/DLI
			25/10/18	23/02/19			
Pearson	Neville A	2nd Lieutenant	23/04/17	21/03/18	21/03/18		
			18/10/18	23/10/18	23/10/18		
Peart	Thomas E	2nd Lieutenant	09/04/16	23/04/17			4/DLI
			12/02/19	23/02/19			
Percy	Jocelyn E S	2nd Lieutenant	08/09/16	08/02/17	08/02/17		4/DLI
Pickering	Frederick A	2nd Lieutenant	29/07/17	30/11/17	30/11/17		POW 21/3/18
Pickering	H A	2nd Lieutenant	14/04/17	21/03/18			
Pollard	Thomas B	2nd Lieutenant	09/01/17	08/02/17	08/02/17		
Pollock	Louis	2nd Lieutenant	08/10/18	17/10/18		17/10/18	from a Svc Bn BRANCOURT-LE-GRAND MIL CEM, Age 19.
Potts	Walter D	2nd Lieutenant	20/02/15	05/08/15	05/08/15		
			22/01/18	23/09/18			Demobilised 29/01/1919
Poxon	Christopher W	2nd Lieutenant	19/02/18	21/05/18	21/05/18		10/DLI
Pratt	John H	Lieutenant	26/12/18	14/03/19			5/DLI
Purvis	Robert	2nd Lieutenant	26/10/14	15/11/14			in ranks 17 yrs 111 days, Capt Trg Res Bn 1917 To 52 & 1/Durham LI
			18/06/15	13/07/15			
			19/12/16	02/03/17			
Pybus	Harold R	Lieutenant	21/09/15	14/10/15	14/10/15		4/DLI
Raine	George K	2nd Lieutenant	23/08/15	26/09/15	26/09/15		16/DLI
Ramsay	C	Lieutenant	12/10/18	23/02/19			6/DLI
Rees	David Melvyn	2nd Lieutenant	21/01/07	09/04/17	09/04/17	12/04/17	CHOCQUES MIL CEM Age 21.
Reid	D W	2nd Lieutenant	13/04/18	18/09/18	18/09/18		Northumberland Fus Att
Reynolds	B R J	2nd Lieutenant	22/01/18	21/03/18	21/03/18		
Rice	Wilfred	Lieutenant	16/08/17	21/03/18	21/03/18		
			05/07/18	14/03/19			
Richards	Frank H	Lieutenant	05/02/18	18/09/18	18/09/18		10/DLI
Richardson	Frederick S	2nd Lieutenant	10/10/18	14/03/19	23/10/18		from a Svc Bn
Robb	Alexander K	Major	08/09/14	20/09/14		20/09/14	Comdg D Coy, VENDRESSE BRIT CEM, Age 42.
Robson	R K	2nd Lieutenant	20/05/15	09/08/15	09/08/15		
Rowlandson	Samuel M	Captain	05/12/14	13/01/15	13/01/15		3/DLI
Rushworth	Tom	Lieutenant	21/01/19	25/03/19			7/DLI
Saunders	Frederick G	2nd Lieutenant	05/10/18	23/02/19			3/DLI
Saunders	Herbert M	2nd Lieutenant	22/08/15	15/02/18			
		Captain	24/05/18	31/07/18			
Schofield	Thomas G	2nd Lieutenant	04/11/15	19/12/15	19/12/15		
Scollick	Laurence T	2nd Lieutenant	21/06/17	26/06/17		26/06/17	MAROC BRIT CEM GRENAY Age 21 L/SGT Coldstream Guards
Scott	Harold G	2nd Lieutenant	22/04/17	24/06/18			4/DLI, TRF MGC 26/6/1918
Severs	William	2nd Lieutenant	25/05/18	17/09/18			14/DLI
Shea DCM	Joseph P L	Lieutenant & QM	08/09/14	01/12/17		01/12/17	
Shepherd	T	Lieutenant	30/09/18	17/10/18			York & Lancaster Regt Att, PREMONT BRIT CEM
Sherriff	E R	Captain	21/01/17	22/05/17			3/DLI
Sherriff	Frederick G	2nd Lieutenant	01/05/15	11/09/15	11/09/15		9849 CSM 2/DLI Comm 3/York & Lancaster Regt then att 2/DLI. TRF RAF
Shield	David L	2nd Lieutenant	05/10/18	23/10/18	23/10/18		from a Svc Bn
Sidgwick	William A	Lieutenant	22/04/18	31/07/18			14/DLI
Silburn	L	Lieutenant	21/04/18	24/09/18			POW 24/9/18 from ASC TF
Simpson	B R J	2nd Lieutenant	08/06/17	18/09/18	18/09/18		
Simpson	Robert B Y	2nd Lieutenant	21/04/18	12/06/18			
Smith	Cecil E	Lieutenant	08/09/14	13/10/14	13/10/14		3/DLI
Smith	C E	Captain	05/10/18	28/03/19			2/Welch Regt att
Smith	Ernest G	2nd Lieutenant	11/04/18	05/08/18			Northumberland Fus Att
Smith	Henry D	2nd Lieutenant	03/01/16	28/02/16	28/02/16		
Smith	William A	2nd Lieutenant	01/03/16	05/03/16			
Snowball	Sydney G	2nd Lieutenant	05/10/18	14/03/19	23/10/18		from a Svc Bn
Sopwith	Gerald	2nd Lieutenant	24/01/15	09/08/15	09/08/15		
			25/08/17	21/03/18			Major Missing 21/03/1918
Spencer	Walter	2nd Lieutenant	14/05/17	06/06/18			8733 L/CPL 2/DURHAM LI
St George	Howard B	2nd Lieutenant	16/08/17	14/03/19			
Stamforth	Harold	2nd Lieutenant	30/09/18	18/10/18			York & Lancaster Regt Att
Stanuell	Charles M	2nd Lieutenant	08/09/14	20/09/14		20/09/14	LA-FERTE-SOUS-JOUARRE MEM Age 20.
Steel	Arnold K	2nd Lieutenant	18/02/16	04/03/16			19/DLI, TRF Machine Gun Corps.
Stockley MM	Percy H	2nd Lieutenant	30/09/18	18/10/18			York & Lancaster Regt Att
Stockton	Hubert V	2nd Lieutenant	22/06/18	13/08/16			
Storey	Harry H	2nd Lieutenant	01/10/14	13/10/14		13/10/14	PLOEGSEERT MEM Age 39.
Storey	Kenneth	2nd Lieutenant	15/01/18	09/08/15	09/08/15		1717 Private Artist Rifles. Captain Royal Defence Corps.
Streatfield	Sidney R	Captain	26/10/14	06/05/15			4/DLI
			08/04/18	31/12/18	18/09/18		
Sullivan	Francis J	2nd Lieutenant	18/07/17	28/05/18	28/05/18		NINE ELMS BRIT CEM Age 21.
Swabey	Alan M C	2nd Lieutenant	30/10/14	26/02/15		20/04/15	3/Somerset LI Att Posted to and KiA with 1/KOYLI , MENIN GATE MEM Age 20.
Swetenham	Edmund	Lieutenant	26/10/14	27/10/14		27/10/14	PLOEGSTEERT MEM Age 24
Taylor	Henry J	Lieutenant	08/09/14	05/05/15			Lt Col Comdg Svc Bn R Irish Regt 10/10/16 - 7/4/17,
			08/03/16	14/09/16	??/8/1917		Lt Col Comdg Svc Bn R Welch Fus 8/4/17. MiD DSO.
Taylor	William K	Lieutenant	24/06/18	01/07/18	01/07/18		7/DLI
Thompson	Charles H	2nd Lieutenant	22/08/15	03/06/16		03/06/16	ESSEX FARM CEM
Thurgood	William J	2nd Lieutenant	12/11/16	15/03/17	15/03/17		accidentally wounded
Tindle	Joseph	2nd Lieutenant	19/08/15	18/02/06			4915 CQMS 2/Northumberland Fusiliers
			03/10/16	14/05/17			
Tuffs	Edward W	2nd Lieutenant	23/09/17	21/03/18			POW 21/3/18, 5117 CSM Army Cyclist Corps. To France 31/8/15
Turner	Arthur	2nd Lieutenant	22/04/17	26/06/17		26/06/17	4/DLI, MAROC BRIT CEM GRENAY, Age 31.
Turner	Robert Villiers	Captain	26/10/14	30/01/15	30/01/15		
			21/05/15	09/08/15	09/08/15		
			04/06/18	14/10/18	14/10/18		
Twist	W B	Lieutenant	08/09/14	20/09/14	20/09/14		Adjutant, Spec Res Bn 1/5/15 - 30/5/16, Comdg Off Cadet Coy 1917.
Vane	Ralph F	Lieutenant the Hon	26/10/14	20/12/14			Evacuated sick, Capt att KOYLI
Vaughan	H R	2nd Lieutenant	01/10/14	27/10/14		27/10/14	Connaught Rangers attached

Veitch	Thomas	2nd Lieutenant	20/05/16	05/10/16	15/10/16		
Vickery	Frederick W A	2nd Lieutenant	18/06/16	15/09/16			
Walker	Russell E	Captain		??/01/16			Royal Army Medical Corps Att
Wallace	B	Captain		14/10/16			Royal Army Medical Corps Att
Walton	Thomas H	2nd Lieutenant	22/08/17	06/02/18			
Ward	Robert H	2nd Lieutenant	25/01/18	12/02/18			
Ware	Richard F	2nd Lieutenant	22/04/18				
Warwick	W T	Lieutenant		01/11/16			Royal Army Medical Corps Att
Watson	Alfred R	2nd Lieutenant	23/12/15	31/12/18	15/09/16		
Watson	Joseph St J	Lieutenant & QM	01/12/17	29/04/18	29/04/18	30/04/18	ARNEKE BRIT CEM, Age 40, SERVED 20 Years.
Watt	John Unite	2nd Lieutenant	16/11/15	12/02/16			
	Cavendish		20/12/16	30/04/17			
			29/08/17	01/03/18			
			25/10/18				
Weyman	G	2nd Lieutenant	11/01/15	12/03/15			To UK for duty.
Wiehe	George I	2nd Lieutenant	28/03/15	27/08/15			evacuated sick, Captain attached Machine Gun Corps
Williams	Frederick	2nd Lieutenant	05/10/18	08/01/19			
Williams	Noel V	2nd Lieutenant	22/08/15	27/12/15			
Willis	Henry G	2nd Lieutenant	30/10/15	22/12/15	19/12/15	22/12/15	BOULOGNE EASTERN CEM Age 26.
Wilson	Alexander	2nd Lieutenant	05/10/18	23/10/18	23/10/18		3/DLI
Wilson	Stephen M	2nd Lieutenant	17/10/18	13/02/19			6/DLI
Wood	John H	Captain	08/09/14	28/10/14	28/10/14		Half Pay 22/6/16, Born 1877
Wright	H F	2nd Lieutenant	05/10/18	12/12/18	12/10/18		
Wright	Joseph B	2nd Lieutenant	15/01/16	21/04/16		21/04/16	MENIN GATE MEMORIAL Age24.
Wright	William C	2nd Lieutenant	22/04/17	06/06/17	06/06/17		4/DLI
Yate	Victor A C	2nd Lieutenant	08/09/14	20/09/14	20/09/14		Act Major Loyal North Lancs, Adj TF Bn DLI 5/5/15 - 16/12/16.
			26/02/15	05/05/15			

Nominal Roll of Other Ranks of the 2nd Battalion Durham Light Infantry who were awarded the 1914 Star

NUMBER	RANK	NAME	INITIALS	REMARKS SERVICE IN SOUTH AFRICA AND PLACE OF BURIAL OR MEMORIAL
8809	PTE	ABBOT	Edward	ENL 18/03/1904 TRF 3/DLI DIS 21/11/1918
4/9100	PTE	ADAMS	John	TRF ARMY RESERVE CLASS W 18/05/1917
8482	PTE	ADAMS	William	TRF LABOUR CORPS 387201
9010	PTE	ADAMSON	John	TRF ROYAL ENGINEERS 251790 RAOC S/8570
9422	PTE	ADAMSON	John	TRF LABOUR CORPS 167141 SGT
4/8095	PTE	AGNEW	Peter	ENL 8/11/1910 WOUNDED AT HOOGE DIS 10/4/1918 TRF DEPOT
8697	PTE	AIREY	Thomas	ENL 04/01/1904 DIS 05/11/1915 BULLET WND HEAD TRF DEPOT
4/8031	PTE	AITCHISON	Jonathan	TRF TRAINING RESERVE BN TR5/4624 CQMS
8421	PTE	ALCOCK	Louis	KiA 21/09/1914 LA-FERTE-SOUS-JOUARRE MEM
9257	PTE	ALDERSON	Charles	DoW 20/08/1915 BOULOGNE EASTERN CEM
9630	L/CPL	ALDRIDGE	William J	PRISONER OF WAR
8624	PTE	ALEXANDER	Henry	DESERTED 23/4/1915
10169	PTE	ALGAR	James	TRF MACHINE GUN CORPS 16380 SGT
4/5780	PTE	ALLEN	James	TRF LABOUR CORPS 37719 RENUMBERED 572190
9300	L/CPL	ALLEN	R	SGT CLASS Z RES
11040	PTE	ALLEN	Richard	DISCHARGED 31/10/1917
9585	PTE	ALLEN	William F	KiA 21/09/1914 LA-FERTE-SOUS-JOUARRE MEM
10482	PTE	ALLSOPP	Thomas	WOUNDED AT HOOGE TRF LABOUR CORPS 519912
9826	PTE	ALLUM	H J	TRF WEST YORKSHIRE REGT 47460, ROYAL DEFENCE CORPS 60419
8935	PTE	ALMOND	Thomas	DISCHARGED 29/03/1917
6447	PTE	ANDERSON	John	DISCHARGED 25/11/1915 SOUTH AFRICA 1st BN QSA ORANGE FREE STATE, TRANSVAAL, TUGELA HEIGHTS, RELIEF OF LADYSMITH, LAING'S
8783	PTE	ANDERSON	T	TRF SCOTTISH RIFLES 19/10/1916 30979
8774	PTE	ANDERSON	Thomas M	TRF LABOUR CORPS 702063
9230	PTE	ANDERSON	W	DISCHARGED 05/09/1917
8555	SGT	ANSLOW	Peter	CSM, COMMISSIONED 1/DLI
7155	PTE	APPLETON	John	TRF 10/DURHAM LI, KiA 25/08/1916 SOUTH AFRICA 1st BN, QSA, ORANGE FREE STATE, TRANSVAAL1901, 1902. DELVILLE WOOD CEMETERY
11382	L/SGT	ARCHBOLD	Frederick	WOUNDED AT HOOGE SGT AWOII INITIAL T ON STAR ROLL
9210	L/CPL	ARMIN	Thomas	ENL 7/8/1905 DIS 25/11/1918 WOUNDS TRF DEPOT SGT
9492	PTE	ARMSTRONG	Ernest	DESERTED 6/2/1915
11578	PTE	ARMSTRONG	James	KiA 21/09/1914 LA-FERTE-SOUS-JOUARRE MEM
8658	PTE	ARNOTT	James	PRISONER OF WAR TRF NORTHUMBERLAND FUS 90322
10954	PTE	ASHFORD	Edgar	PRISONER OF WAR
11358	CPL	ASHMAN	Robert	TRF LABOUR CORPS 376108
8030	PTE	ASHTON	Edward	25/11/1902 DIS 22/11/1915 TRF DEPOT
8021	PTE	ASPIN	Charles	ENL 10/11/1902 DIS 2/11/1915
10942	L/SGT	ATKINSON	Frank	KiA 09/08/1915 YPRES MENIN GATE MEM
10461	PTE	AYLIN	Edgar	PRISONER OF WAR
8615	PTE	AYRES	William	TRF SOUTH LANCASHIRE REGIMENT 63064
9569	PTE	BAGE	Thomas	DISCHARGED 3/10/1917
11216	L/CPL	BAGNALL	R D	PRISONER OF WAR
7786	PTE	BAILEY	John R	CONVICTED BY FGCM OF DESERTION 10/12/1917
8324	L/CPL	BAILEY	Thomas R	KiA 28/12/1915 SGT POTIJZE BURIAL GROUND
8875	PTE	BAINBRIDGE	J William	WOUNDED AT HOOGE TRF LABOUR CORPS 376897 01/10/1917
7398	PTE	BAINBRIDGE	Joseph	KiA 27/10/1914 PLOEGSTEERT MEM
9687	PTE	BAINES	B	TRF NORTHUMBERLAND FUSILIERS 94400
10208	PTE	BAIRD	Peter	TRF LABOUR CORPS 519585
6671	L/CPL	BAKER	William	TRF 3/DLI, ENL 18/01/1899 DIS 14/01/1918 SOUTH AFRICA 1st BN, QSA TRANSVAAL, LAING'S NEK. KSA 1901, 1902
8000	PTE	BALDWIN	Edward	ENL 8/10/1902 DIS 18/05/1915 TRF DEPOT
8359	PTE	BALF	John	TRF 12/DURHAM LI KiA 17/7/1916 THIEPVAL MEM
7402	PTE	BALLS	Emmanuel	TRF MACHINE GUN CORPS 29518, A/SGT SOUTH AFRICA 1st BN, ORANGE FREE STATE, TRANSVAAL, 190
3/8795	L/CPL	BAMBOROUGH	Freddy	ENL 30/3/1908 WOUNDED AT HOOGE DIS 10/12/1918 TRF ARMY RES CLASS W
8896	PTE	BAMBOROUGH	Robert W	PRISONER OF WAR
4/8173	PTE	BAMBOROUGH	T	TRF WEST YORKSHIRE REGT 50844
7904	PTE	BAMBROUGH	Edward	KiA 09/08/1915 YPRES MENIN GATE MEM
10801	SGT	BARBER	E	PRISONER OF WAR
8608	PTE	BARBER	J	TRF NORTHUMBERLAND FUSILIERS 21106 ALIAS CORR
8853	PTE	BARKER	Robert H	KiA 21/09/1914 LA-FERTE-SOUS-JOUARRE MEM
9138	PTE	BARKER	Robert H	ATT CONV DEPOT , 2/DURHAM LI, 18/LTMB. 15/DURHAM LI. DoW 15/09/1918 TRELINCTHUN BRIT CEM
8680	PTE	BARKER	Walter	TRF 52 GRAD BN NORTHUMBERLAND FUS
3/7042	PTE	BARNARD	Edward	ENL 11/01/1900 DIS 23/04/1915,
9646	PTE	BARNES	Joseph	
8481	SGT	BARRATT	William	ENL 11/9/1903 DIS 03/04/1917 ATT 8 ENTRENCHING BN 3/DLI
8614	LCPL	BARROW	John	WOUNDED AT HOOGE
7977	PTE	BARTLETT	Thomas	C COMPANY REP MISSING LATER KiA 20/10/1914 PLOEGSTEERT MEM
10879	PTE	BARTLEY	Thomas	DIED 17/10/1914 LONGUENESSE SOUVENIR CEM ST OMER
7753	PTE	BASSINGTON	Alfred	ENL 30/01/1908 DIS 09/12/16 TRF 1/GARR BN DLI
8960	PTE	BATES	John T	ENL 19/3/1904 DIS 14/12/1917 ARMY RES CLASS W
4/8913	PTE	BATEY	John	TRF ARMY RESERVE CLASS Z 31/10/1916
10511	PTE	BATEY	John H	DISCHARGED 26/10/1917
11535	PTE	BATTYE	J E	TRF 10th 15/DURHAM LI ARMY RESERVE SECTION B
11277	LCPL	BAXTER	Frederick C	ENL 17/11/1911 DIS 10/06/1915 WOUNDS TRF 3/DURHAM LI
8043	PTE	BEAN	William	ENL 5/12/1902 DIS 14/7/1916
4/8061	PTE	BEARD	John	ENL 30/10/1910 DIS 18/04/1915 WOUNDS TRF DEPOT
7173	PTE	BEATON	Frank	TRF WEST YORKSHIRE REGT 24/9/15 47466 DISCHARGED 07/08/1917. WOUNDED AT HOOGE SOUTH AFRICA 1st BN, QSA TRANSVAAL, 1901, 190
11618	PTE	BEATTIE	George	KiA 23/10/1914 PLOEGSTEERT MEM
8988	LCPL	BEATTIE	William	PRISONER OF WAR
10068	PTE	BECKETT	E	
11472	LCPL	BEEDHAM	Frederick	PRISONER OF WAR

8583 PTE	BEIRN	Charles	KiA 16/10/1914 PLOEGSTEERT MEM
4/5959 PTE	BELL	Appollas	KiA 09/08/1915 HOOGE CRATER CEM
8000 PTE	BELL	C	
9016 PTE	BELL	Enoch T	
10765 CPL	BELL	George	SGT CLASS Z RES
9107 PTE	BELL	George	TRF 19/DURHAM LI KiA 27/10/1917 TYNE COT MEMORIAL
11478 PTE	BELL	George	TRF 14/DURHAM LI ARMY RESERVE SECTION B
8668 PTE	BELL	John	CLASS Z RES
4/8021 PTE	BELL	Ralph M	KiA 09/08/1915 YPRES MENIN GATE MEM
8788 PTE	BELL	Robert H	DISCHARGED
6955 PTE	BELL	William	TRF CLASS Z RESERVE SOUTH AFRICA 1st BN , QSA, CAPE COLONY, ORANGE FREE STATE, TRANSVAAL. KSA 1901, 1902
9255 PTE	BELLAIRS	Edward D	DoW 20/07/1915 BISHOPWEARMOUTH CEM SUNDERLAND
9180 PTE	BELLAIRS	William	KiA 20/09/14 LA-FERTE-SOUS-JOUARRE MEM
11341 PTE	BENBOW	Charles	PRISONER OF WAR
8440 PTE	BENHAM	William H	TRF KO YORKSHIRE LI 22672 A/SGT
10444 BGLR	BENNETT	Thomas	KiA 20/09/14 PLOEGSTEERT MEM
9839 PTE	BENTLEY	John	KiA 21/09/1914 LA-FERTE-SOUS-JOUARRE MEM
11499 PTE	BENTLEY	Robert	KiA 28/10/1914 PLOEGSTEERT MEM
9595 CPL	BERRY	W	STILL SERVING 30/03/1920
8449 BNDSMN	BERRY	William	STILL SERVING 30/03/1920
11339 PTE	BESTFORD	Robert	TRF ROYAL FLYING CORPS 30/01/1917 61923 SGT
6657 PTE	BESTON	James	TRF WEST YORKSHIRE REGT 14/3/1916 52775, LABOUR CORPS 420132. SOUTH AFRICA 1st BN, QSA TRANSVAAL, LAING'S NEK, KSA 1901,
11015 PTE	BIGGIN	Harry	MISSING 15/10/1916 THIEPVAL MEMORIAL
10820 SGT	BILTON	J W	PRISONER OF WAR
11261 PTE	BIRD	Walter C	DISCHARGED 01/04/1915
9244 PTE	BIZZARD	Frank D	TRF LABOUR CORPS 26/04/1917 123881
5824 RQMS	BLACK	Ernest	TRF DEPOT, ENL 25/02/1896 DIS 02/08/1917 SICKNESS
8291 PTE	BLACK	Thomas	ENL 13/10/1902 DIS 14/10/1915 TRF DEPOT
11368 PTE	BLACK	Thomas R	ENL 4/4/1912 DIS 25/4/1918
11664 PTE	BLACKBURN	W W	TRF MACHINE GUN CORPS 09/05/1916 34084
9128 PTE	BLACKIE	Henry R	ENL 30/1/1905 DIS 10/10/1918 LCPL TRF 14/DURHAM LI
8479 PTE	BLACKWELL	Joseph C	ENL 31/08/1903 DIS 08/08/1916 GSW CHEST FROM 1st GARR BN DURHAM LI
8720 PTE	BLAKESTONE	Percy B	ENL 18/1/1904 DIS 16/03/1915 GSW BACK TRF 3/DURHAM LI
11343 LCPL	BLANCHARD	George	PRISONER OF WAR
8621 SGT	BLEACKLEY	John	KiA 21/09/1914 LA-FERTE-SOUS-JOUARRE MEM
11366 PTE	BLENKINSOPP	Matthew	TRF ARMY RESERVE SECTION B
8863 PTE	BLOWER	William	ENL 22/6/1904 DIS 31/10/1916 TRF ARMY CLASS W RES
5645 LCPL	BOLAM	Owen	SGT DISCHARGED
11640 PTE	BOLLAND	W	SGT
9275 PTE	BONNER	A E	PRISONER OF WAR
9151 PTE	BOOTE	Robert	PRISONER OF WAR DIED 27/10/1918 HAMBURG CEMETERY
10413 PTE	BOOTES	Stanley E	KiA 20/09/1914 LA-FERTE-SOUS-JOUARRE MEM
9226 PTE	BOOTH	Wallis	DoW 23/10/1914 BOULOGNE EASTERN CEM
9539 PTE	BORRILL	Walter	TRF 18/DURHAM LI DISCHARGED
8401 PTE	BORTHWICK	Matthew	DISCHARGED 12/06/1915
9541 PTE	BOULTON	Frederick	TRF YORK & LANCASTER REGT 6th BN 422??, LABOUR CORPS(360 EMP COY) 219243
9030 PTE	BOWEN	Charles	DoW 14/05/1915 BOULOGNE EASTERN CEM
9682 PTE	BOWMAN	Herbert	ENL 8/10/1906 DIS 12/03/1915 TRF 3/DURHAM LI SICK
10159 PTE	BOWMAN	Marmaduke	KiA 20/10/1914 PLOEGSTEERT MEM
10210 PTE	BOWNESS	Thomas	TRF KO YORKSHIRE LI, LABOUR CORPS 391306
11726 PTE	BOYERS	Joseph	TRF LABOUR CORPS 384770
10513 PTE	BRADBURY	William	ATT 1st ARMY, 2/DURHAM LI, ATT 4th CORPS COOKERY SCH, 2/DURHAM LI
10232 CPL	BRADFORD	James	ENL 20/11/1907 DIS 20/9/1918 TRF TRAINING RESERVE 1st BN TR5/3741 WOII
8543 PTE	BRADLEY	Michael	TRF NORTHUMBERLAND FUSILIERS 24664
9134 PTE	BRANTON	Harry	ENL 9/2/1905 DIS 24/07/1916 NEURASTHENIA 3/DURHAM LI
10886 PTE	BREW	H D	PRISONER OF WAR
9786 PTE	BRIGGS	Alfred	KiA 16/09/1916 THIEPVAL MEMORIAL
7891 LCPL	BROOKS	Joseph	SGT
10057 PTE	BROPHY	M	PRISONER OF WAR
9699 PTE	BROWN	Cyril E	DESERTED 19/06/1915
9443 PTE	BROWN	E	TRF ROYAL AIR FORCE 318855 WOII
9688 PTE	BROWN	Frank	KiA 09/08/1915 CPL YPRES MENIN GATE MEM
9063 PTE	BROWN	George	TRF NORTH STAFFORDSHIRE REGT 1st GARR BN 25782, DURHAM LI 85861.
8518 PTE	BROWN	James	ATT 6th DIV BAND, 209 EMPLOYMENT COY
8830 PTE	BROWN	James	TRF 20/DURHAM LI KiA 15/9/1916 THIEPVAL MEMORIAL
8994 PTE	BROWN	Robert H	CLASS Z RES
9071 PTE	BROWN	Thomas	TRF 10/DURHAM LI, ROYAL WEST KENT REGT L/11659
8325 PTE	BROWN	Thomas B	DISCHARGED 19/01/1916
8371 PTE	BROWN	William	ENL 11/3/1903 DIS 11/03/1916 TRF DEPOT
10488 PTE	BROWN	William	WOUNDED AT HOOGE DESERTED 26/12/1915
11064 PTE	BROWN	William	WOUNDED AT HOOGE TRF SOUTH LANCASHIRE REGT 63215
11645 PTE	BUCKINGHAM	Edward H	DISCHARGED 27/05/1916
11017 PTE	BUFF	Reuben	TRF LABOUR CORPS 599778
10347 PTE	BULLOCK	Alfred	KiA 09/08/1915 YPRES MENIN GATE MEM
11335 PTE	BULLOCK	Edward	WOUNDED AT HOOGE.
10627 PTE	BUNKER	Arthur	ATT 6th DIV HQ, 13 CORPS HQ, 7 CORPS HQ, 10 CORPS HQ, 12 CORPS HQ, ARMY RES SECTION B
10161 PTE	BUNTING	Robert	AWOII DISCHARGED
7587 PTE	BURDETT	Charles F	ENL 26/08/1901 DIS 11/06/1919 KR PARA 392
8843 PTE	BURDIS	John	KiA 19/05/1916 ESSEX FARM CEM
8817 PTE	BURKE	John	TRF ROYAL ENGINEERS 14/11/1916 214471 LABOUR CORPS 118283

Number	Rank	Surname	Forename	Notes
8885	PTE	BURKE	Michael	PRISONER OF WAR
8605	PTE	BURN	Henry	KILLED BY COLLAPSE OF EARTH 02/01/1915 HOUPLINES COM CEM EXT
9261	PTE	BURNETT	J W	TRF ROYAL FLYING CORPS 10/8/1917 135443 AIR MECHANIC III CLASS
10080	PTE	BURNS	John	DISCHARGED 14/07/1915
9575	PTE	BURNS	M	DISCHARGED 06/07/1915
11587	PTE	BUTLER	Edward	PRISONER OF WAR
10485	PTE	BUTLER	George H	TRF ARMY RES SECTION B
8728	PTE	CADDY	William T	SGT KiA 29/9/1918
11049	CPL	CAIRNS	James	TRF 20/DURHAM LI DoW 08/04/1918 ETAPLES MIL CEM
9028	PTE	CAISLEY	Thomas	ENL 8/11/1904 DIS 28/04/1916 WOUNDS TRF DEPOT L/SGT
10909	SGT	CALDER	Frederick	PRISONER OF WAR
11496	PTE	CALLAGHAN	Thomas	WOUNDED AT HOOGE
8535	PTE	CAMPBELL	James	KiA 26/09/1916 THIEPVAL MEMORIAL
8749	PTE	CAMPBELL	James	ENL 26/1/1914 DIS 08/09/1916 TRF 1 GARR BN DURHAM LI
6713	PTE	CAMPBELL	John Wm	WOUNDED AT HOOGE DISCHARGED 08/03/1916
9171	PTE	CARDWELL	Ernest	DoW 01/12/1917 ROCQUIGNY-EQUANCOURT ROAD BRIT CEM
10585	SGT	CAREW	Frederick	DISCHARGED
8381	PTE	CARLON	Michael	DISCHARGED 31/03/1916
8231	PTE	CARNEY	Peter	ENL 30/08/1908, TRF NORTHUMBERLAND FUSILIERS 24591 DIS 22/01/1916
8760	PTE	CARR	William	PRISONER OF WAR
8549	PTE	CARROLL	William	TRF LABOUR CORPS 650687
10249	PTE	CARTER	Albert	PRISONER OF WAR
7940	PTE	CARTER	John W	PRISONER OF WAR
11351	PTE	CARTER	Thomas	WOUNDED AT HOOGE.
8465	PTE	CARTY	Joseph	DISCHARGED 19/06/1915
8639	LCPL	CASS	William	AWOl
9814	PTE	CAWLEY	Thomas	ENL 16/1/1907 DIS 01/03/1915 LEG AMPUTATED TRF DEPOT
8827	PTE	CAWOOD	James	WOUNDED AT HOOGE TRF LABOUR CORPS 164177, ROYAL FLYING CORPS 148552
8828	PTE	CAWOOD	William	PRISONER OF WAR 12/04/1915 DIED 25/10/1918 BERLIN SOUTH WESTERN CEMETERY
9079	PTE	CHAMBERS	Thomas	PRISONER OF WAR
8504	PTE	CHAPMAN	Thomas	CONVICTED OF DESERTION 20/12/1916
8740	PTE	CHARLESWORTH	Wilfred	ENL 21/1/1904 DIS 20/12/1914 GSW SKULL TRF 3/DURHAM LI
10410	PTE	CHARLTON	Edwd V	DISCHARGED
8364	PTE	CHARLTON	John	DoW 21/09/1914 VENDRESSE CEM, TROYON CH YARD MEM 15
8860	PTE	CHARLTON	Robert	ENL 16/6/1904 TRF DEPOT DoW 25/04/1917 AFTER DISCHARGE
11364	LCPL	CHARLTON	William	ENL 21/3/1912 DIS 01/04/1915 GSW LEFT SIDE TRF 3/DURHAM LI
11056	PTE	CHESNEY	Frank D	KiA 20/09/1914 LA-FERTE-SOUS-JOUARRE MEM
9861	PTE	CHESTERS	Charles H	SGT ENL 29/1/1907 DIS 22/3/1919
10118	LSGT	CHESTERS	George W	TRF MACHINE GUN CORPS SGT 14051
8470	PTE	CHESTERS	Richard J	TRF LABOUR CORPS 04/10/1917 117664
8511	PTE	CHRISTIE	George	ASGT
7952	PTE	CLARK	Henry	TRF MACHINE GUN CORPS 22/12/1915
9140	PTE	CLARK	T	TRF ARMY CYCLIST CORPS 1233 ALCPL CORPS OF HUSSARS 70005
8880	PTE	CLARK	George W	ENL 3/8/1904 DIS 02/09/1915 GSW RT HAND TRF 3/DURHAM LI
9532	PTE	CLARKE	Charles E	ATT GHQ 2nd ECHELON, HQ 43 INF BDE, ATT 34th DIV HQ, 13th CORPS HQ DISCHARGED
11628	PTE	CLARKE	Frederick S	KiA 09/08/1915 LCPL YPRES MENIN GATE MEM
8046	PTE	CLARKE	George	DESERTED 17/02/1915
10535	PTE	CLARKE	J	WOUNDED AT HOOGE
5671	PTE	CLARKE	Jonathan	DIED 26/03/1915 HEWORTH ST MARY'S CH YARD
11620	PTE	CLARKE	Robert	LCPL
8333	PTE	CLEGG	Edmund	DISCHARGED 04/02/1916
10475	SGT	CLEGG	James C	DISCHARGED 06/07/1915
10793	PTE	CLEGHORN	J	DESERTED STILL ABSENT DEC 1920
8491	PTE	CLIFFORD	George	ENL 20/9/1903 DIS 17/06/1917 TRF 3/DURHAM LI
11588	PTE	CLINTON	James	PRISONER OF WAR
11553	PTE	COGDON	Allan	PRISONER OF WAR TRF ROYAL ARMY SERVICE CORPS M/47286
4/5842	PTE	COGGINS	James	SENTENCED BY FGCM 10 YRS PENAL SERVITUDE
9666	PTE	COHEN	Moss	SGT COMMISSIONED 2/DURHAM LI
11737	PTE	COKER	William	PRISONER OF WAR
4/6880	PTE	COLBORN	Kirby	TRF MOTOR CYCLIST CORPS, ARMY SERVICE CORPS 22/10/1917 M/40039
6978	LCPL	COLEMAN	Ernest	TRF LABOUR CORPS 1917 401787 SGT SOUTH AFRICA 1st BN, QSA, CAPE COLONY, ORANGE FREE STATE, TRANSVAAL. KSA 1901, 1902
9241	PTE	COLLINS	James F	DoW 22/09/1914 ST NAZAIRE (TOUTES-AIDES) CEM
9115	PTE	COLLYER	ISAAC	PRISONER OF WAR
8902	PTE	COLVIN	William	ENL 10/08/1904 DIS 02/09/1915
4/6098	PTE	CONLEY	James	TRF TRAINING RESERVE 86th BN, NORTHUMBERLAND FUS 26337, KO YORKSHIRE LI 29243 R ENGINEERS 260857 RENUMBERED WR/41025
9142	PTE	CONNOLLY	T	TRF KO YORKSHIRE LI 22814
9765	SGT	CONNOLLY	Thomas	AWOl REGTAL SERGEANT MAJOR
9701	PTE	CONNOR	James	TRF KO YORKSHIRE LI 22790, DOW 27/06/1916 BOUZINCOURT COM CEM EXT
10500	PTE	CONNOR	John	TRF LABOUR CORPS 471 IRISH HOME EMP COY 316882
7324	PTE	CONNOR	Joseph	TRF ROYAL ENGINEERS 251786. SOUTH AFRICA 1st BN, ORANGE FREE STATE, TRANSVAAL, 1901, 1902
11124	PTE	CONNOR	Patrick	KiA 09/08/1915 LCPL YPRES MENIN GATE MEM
9158	PTE	CONQUEROR	Charles	TRF 15/DURHAM LI KiA 01/07/1916 GORDON DUMP CEM OVILIERES LA BOISELLE
9731	PTE	CONWAY	Christopher	WOUNDED NOV 1914
8601	PTE	COOK	Charles	ENL 11/11/1903 DIS 01/04/1915 FROM 3rd BN GSW LEFT THIGH
9665	PTE	COOK	Isaac	DESERTED 20/07/1917 TRF ROYAL ENGINEERS 361424 RENUMBERED 344874
10148	PTE	COOMBES	Christopher	REPORTED WOUNDED 24/11/1914, DISCHARGED 10/07/1915
9680	LSGT	COOMBES	William	TRF NORTHUMBERLAND FUSILIERS 24598
9199	PTE	CORNER	William	TRF NORTHUMBERLAND FUSILIERS 38550 LCPL
7995	PTE	CORNS	James	TRF KO YORKSHIRE LI 22678 DISCHARGED 08/10/1915
6739	RQMS	COUCHMAN	Charles A	TRF WEST YORKSHIRE REGIMENT 65053

11033 SGT	COULSON	Lawrence	CQMS DISCHARGED
9689 PTE	COURT	Harry	TRF 14/DURHAM LI KiA 25/09/1916 NETLEY MIL CEM
11613 PTE	COVERDALE	George	KiA 21/03/1918 VAULX HILL CEM
9007 LCPL	COWIE	Jonathan	PRISONER OF WAR
10319 PTE	COWTON	Albert	ENL 28/2/1908 DIS 19/05/1916 GSW L FOOT TRF DEPOT
8704 PTE	COYNE	John	TRF KO YORKSHIRE LI 22784
8736 PTE	CRADDOCK	John	KiA 03/05/1915 STRAND MIL CEM
10140 PTE	CRAIG	William	ENL 6/8/1907 DIS 15/12/1917 TRF 3/DURHAM LI
11594 LCPL	CRAWFORD	Andrew	TRF NORTH STAFFORDSHIRE REGT 67699
10438 SGT	CREBER	John M	PRISONER OF WAR 01/03/1915 REMAINED IN ARMY POST WAR 4435159
8634 PTE	CREIGH	William C	TRF ARMY SERVICE CORPS 12/08/1916 M/38921
7866 BNDSMN	CRITCHLEY	William H	LCPL STILL SERVING MARCH 1920
10818 BGLR	CRITCHLOW	Stanley	KiA 21/09/1914 LA-FERTE-SOUS-JOUARRE MEM
9119 PTE	CROSBY	Ernest	KiA 09/08/1915 YPRES MENIN GATE MEM
9548 PTE	CROSS	Christopher	TRF ROYAL FLYING CORPS BALLOON SECTION 24/11/1917 105728 AIR MECHANIC II CLASS
8950 PTE	CULLEN	Michael	TRF NORTHUMBERLAND FUSILIERS 2nd GARRISON BN 26244, NAME CAULKIN & CULKIN ON MRC
10767 PNR SGT	CUMBERLAND	F	TRF ROYAL FLYING CORPS 09/03/1917 65869. BN PIONEER SGT, INITIAL F ON 1914 ROLL E ON W&V
8763 PTE	CUMMINGS	Thomas	KiA 19/11/1914 PLOEGSTEERT MEM
8034 PTE	CUNNINGHAM	Frederick	
11597 PTE	CUNNINGHAM	William	TRF NORTHUMBERLAND FUSILIERS 26268. GREEN HOWARDS 3rd BN 35431
11570 PTE	CUTHBERT	Robert Wm	KiA 28/12/1914 HOUPLINES COM CEM EXT
8559 PTE	CUTTRIS	Stanley E	PRISONER OF WAR 20/10/1914
9012 PTE	DALBY	Alfred	WOUNDED AT HOOGE, TRF TRAINING RESERVE 1st BN 30/04/1917, ROYAL FLYING CORPS 130147
11560 PTE	DALEY	Thomas	TRF MACHINE GUN CORPS 27/12/1915
10415 PTE	DALY	John	KiA 09/08/1915 YPRES MENIN GATE MEM
7992 PTE	DANBY	Charles	KiA 19/11/1914, RESERVIST SERVED 7 YEARS IN INDIA PLOEGSTEERT MEM
7417 CPL	DAVIDSON	Thomas	TRF MACHINE GUN CORPS 27808 SOUTH AFRICA 1st BN, QSA TRANSVAAL, 1902
11090 CPL	DAVIS	Henry	PRISONER OF WAR ENL 29/12/1910 DIS 15/1/1919
10129 PTE	DAVIS	John	TRF ARMY RESERVE CLASS W 26/05/1917
8989 PTE	DAWSON	George	PRISONER OF WAR
8453 PTE	DAWSON	John	DISCHARGED 19/05/1915
8798 PTE	DEANS	Robert	DISCHARGED 05/08/1915
8370 PTE	DEARLOVE	Arthur	WOUNDED AT HOOGE
10633 CSGT	DEE	William A	WOII
9650 PTE	DEFTY	Lancelot	
9147 PTE	DEMPSTER	William	PRISONER OF WAR
11019 PTE	DENNIS	Thomas	TRF MACHINE GUN CORPS 08/04/1916 30713 SGT
8983 PTE	DENNISON	Thomas H	ENL 1/10/1904 WOUNDED AT HOOGE DIS 21/02/1917 ARMY RES CLASS W
8008 PTE	DEVEREUX	William	DISCHARGED 14/10/1915
8057 PTE	DEVLIN	John	PRISONER OF WAR 01/03/1915
6714 PTE	DEVONPORT	Joseph	TRF ROYAL DEFENCE CORPS 20/02/197 66163. SOUTH AFRICA 1st BN, QSA TRANSVAAL, LAING'S NEK
8051 PTE	DINGLEY	Henry	TRF LABOUR CORPS 02/09/1917 400175
8765 PTE	DISNEY	John	KiA 07/05/1915 STRAND MIL CEM
11212 PTE	DITCHBURN	Joseph W	DoW 14/10/1914 SEC-BOIS COM CEM VIEUX-BERQUIN
8365 CPL	DIXON	Frederick A	WOII
8956 PTE	DIXON	Peter	REP WND 7/10/1914 MISSING 20/10/1914 PLOEGSTEERT MEM
10278 PTE	DIXON	Robert	PRISONER OF WAR
8509 PTE	DODD	George	WOUNDED AT HOOGE, TRF KO YORKSHIRE LI 12/03/1917 48006, CHESHIRE REGT 77699, ROYAL FUSILIERS 93827
11577 PTE	DODD	Jonathan	TRF LABOUR CORPS 15/10/1917 403046, ROYAL ARMY PAY CORPS 20663
9574 PTE	DODD	Joseph	TRF WEST YORKSHIRE REGT 24/02/1917 59699, TRF BACK TO 2/DURHAM LI
7960 PTE	DODDS	James H	DoW 27/09/1914 VENDRESSE CH YARD
8345 PTE	DODSON	Arthur	SGT
10742 PTE	DODSON	Frederick	TRF IN FROM DORSETSHIRE REGT PRE WAR 8623, MISSING 02/07/1916
8529 PTE	DOLAN	Michael	TRF LABOUR CORPS 26/06/1917 213956
11027 BGLR	DONAGHUE	James	PRISONER OF WAR 01/03/1915
11407 LCPL	DONNELLY	Michael A	KiA 10/06/1915 CPL POTIJZE BURIAL GROUND
6587 PTE	DONNELLY	Patrick	TRF KO YORKSHIRE LI 22765 SOUTH AFRICA 1st BN, QSA CAPE COLONY, ORANGE FREE STATE, TRANSVAAL, LAING'S NEK, KSA
9967 PTE	DORKIN	Benjamin	ATT ENT BN ROUEN 2/DURHAM LI DISCHARGED
7983 PTE	DOUGLAS	Frank	TRF KO YORKSHIRE LI 01/06/1915 22850
8657 PTE	DOUGLAS	Thomas	TRF KO YORKSHIRE LI 01/05/1915 22682
8972 PTE	DOUGLAS	Walter C	TRF WEST RIDING REGT 31156
11574 PTE	DOUTHWAITE	David R	ENL 28/3/1913 DIS 24/03/1916 TRF 3/DURHAM LI
9658 PTE	DOWLING	William	WOUNDED AT HOOGE TRF KO YORKSHIRE LI 1st GARRISON BN 26/09/1916 28746
8583 PTE	DOWNEY	James	TRF NORTH STAFFORDSHIRE REGT 1st GARRISON BN 18/04/1916 23798
9626 PTE	DOWNEY	John N	KiA 21/09/1914 LA-FERTE-SOUS-JOUARRE MEM
10343 PTE	DOWNEY	Thomas	TRF DEPOT STAFF RENUMBERED 260527, SCOTTISH RIFLES 55143
11534 PTE	DOYLE	John W	KiA 28/10/1914 PLOEGSTEERT MEM
6974 PTE	DOYLE	Walter	TRF ARMY EDUCATION CORPS 511249, LABOUR CORPS 24659, NORTHUMBERLAND FUSILIERS 60579, LANCASHIRE FUSILIERS 98483, SO
11842 PTE	DRAY	Alfred H	DoW 05/11/1914 DIED AT SEA
11147 PTE	DRUMMOND	Frederick	DISCHARGED
9661 SGT	DRUMMOND	John P	KiA 06/04/1915 HOUPLINES COM CEM EXT
10704 CPL	DUDDY	Thomas S	SGT AWOII COMMISSIONED 11/10/1917 POSTED 20/DURHAM LI
9575 PTE	DUGGAN	Francis	WOUNDED AT HOOGE TRF MACHINE GUN CORPS 14/03/1916 27905
9627 PTE	DUNCAN	Robert	TRF NORTH STAFFORDSHIRE REGT 1ST GARRISON BN 18/04/1916 23783, LABOUR CORPS 569228
9973 PTE	DUNSTON	Thomas	TRF 3rd BN, ENLISTED 18/03/1907, DISCHARGED 12/06/1915, GSW THIGH
9240 PTE	DUTTON	Thomas	ENL 28/8/1905 TRF ARMY RESERVE CLASS P 25/05/1917
11284 CPL	DYER	Robert	TRF NORTHUMBERLAND FUSILIERS 2nd GARRISON BN 22/10/1915 26235 CSGT DLI SGT NF
10173 PTE	DYSON	Walter	KiA 13/10/1914 PLOEGSTEERT MEM
11480 PTE	EALES	Robert W	PRISONER OF WAR
8803 PTE	EARLE	John	TRF ARMY RESERVE CLASS W 24/11/1917

6714 PTE	DEVONPORT	Joseph	TRF ROYAL DEFENCE CORPS 20/02/197 66163. SOUTH AFRICA 1st BN, QSA TRANSVAAL, LAING'S NEK
8051 PTE	DINGLEY	Henry	TRF LABOUR CORPS 02/09/1917 400175
8785 PTE	DISNEY	John	KiA 07/05/1915 STRAND MIL CEM
11212 PTE	DITCHBURN	Joseph W	DoW 14/10/1914 SEC-BOIS COM CEM VIEUX-BERQUIN
8365 CPL	DIXON	Frederick A	WOII
8956 PTE	DIXON	Peter	REP WND 7/10/1914 MISSING 20/10/1914 PLOEGSTEERT MEM
10278 PTE	DIXON	Robert	PRISONER OF WAR
8509 PTE	DODD	George	WOUNDED AT HOOGE, TRF KO YORKSHIRE LI 12/03/1917 48006, CHESHIRE REGT 77699, ROYAL FUSILIERS 93827
11577 PTE	DODD	Jonathan	TRF LABOUR CORPS 15/10/1917 403046, ROYAL ARMY PAY CORPS 20663
9574 PTE	DODD	Thomas	TRF WEST YORKSHIRE REGT 24/02/1917 59699, TRF BACK TO 2/DURHAM LI
7960 PTE	DODDS	James H	DoW 27/09/1914 VENDRESSE CH YARD
8345 PTE	DODSON	Arthur	SGT
10742 PTE	DODSON	Frederick	TRF IN FROM DORSETSHIRE REGT PRE WAR 8623, MISSING 02/07/1916
8529 PTE	DOLAN	Michael	TRF LABOUR CORPS 26/06/1917 213956
11027 BGLR	DONAGHUE	James	PRISONER OF WAR 01/03/1915
11407 LCPL	DONNELLY	Michael A	KiA 10/06/1915 CPL POTIJZE BURIAL GROUND
6567 PTE	DONNELLY	Patrick	TRF KO YORKSHIRE LI 22765 SOUTH AFRICA 1st BN, QSA CAPE COLONY, ORANGE FREE STATE, TRANSVAAL, LAING'S NEK,
9967 PTE	DORKIN	Benjamin	ATT ENT BN ROUEN 2/DURHAM LI DISCHARGED
7983 PTE	DOUGLAS	Frank	TRF KO YORKSHIRE LI 01/06/1915 22850
8657 PTE	DOUGLAS	Thomas	TRF KO YORKSHIRE LI 01/05/1915 22682
8972 PTE	DOUGLAS	Walter C	TRF WEST RIDING REGT 31156
11574 PTE	DOUTHWAITE	David R	ENL 28/3/1913 DIS 24/03/1916 TRF 3/DURHAM LI
9658 PTE	DOWLING	William	WOUNDED AT HOOGE TRF KO YORKSHIRE LI 1st GARRISON BN 26/09/1916 28746
8583 PTE	DOWNEY	James	TRF NORTH STAFFORDSHIRE REGT 1st GARRISON BN 18/04/1916 23798
9626 PTE	DOWNEY	John N	KiA 21/09/1914 LA-FERTE-SOUS-JOUARRE MEM
10343 PTE	DOWNEY	Thomas	TRF DEPOT STAFF RENUMBERED 260527, SCOTTISH RIFLES 55143
11534 PTE	DOYLE	John W	KiA 28/10/1914 PLOEGSTEERT MEM
6974 PTE	DOYLE	Walter	TRF ARMY EDUCATION CORPS 511249, LABOUR CORPS 24659, NORTHUMBERLAND FUSILIERS 60579, LANCASHIRE FUSILIEI
11842 PTE	DRAY	Alfred H	DoW 05/11/1914 DIED AT SEA
11147 PTE	DRUMMOND	Frederick	DISCHARGED
9661 SGT	DRUMMOND	John P	KiA 06/04/1915 HOUPLINES COM CEM EXT
10704 CPL	DUDDY	Thomas S	SGT AWOII COMMISSIONED 11/10/1917 POSTED 20/DURHAM LI
9575 PTE	DUGGAN	Francis	WOUNDED AT HOOGE TRF MACHINE GUN CORPS 14/03/1916 27905
9627 PTE	DUNCAN	Robert	TRF NORTH STAFFORDSHIRE REGT 1ST GARRISON BN 18/04/1916 23783, LABOUR CORPS 569228
9973 PTE	DUNSTON	Thomas	TRF 3rd BN, ENLISTED 18/03/1907, DISCHARGED 12/06/1915, GSW THIGH
9240 PTE	DUTTON	Thomas	ENL 28/8/1905 TRF ARMY RESERVE CLASS P 25/05/1917
11284 CPL	DYER	Robert	TRF NORTHUMBERLAND FUSILIERS 2nd GARRISON BN 22/10/1915 26235 CSGT DLI SGT NF
10173 PTE	DYSON	Walter	KiA 13/10/1914 PLOEGSTEERT MEM
11480 PTE	EALES	Robert W	PRISONER OF WAR
8803 PTE	EARLE	John	TRF ARMY RESERVE CLASS W 24/11/1917
10305 PTE	EDGAR	Robert	DISCHARGED 23/04/1915
9231 PTE	EDWARDS	Arthur	KiA 10/06/1915 CPL POTIJZE BURIAL GROUND
8531 PTE	EGGLESTONE	George	PRISONER OF WAR 23/11/1914
8027 PTE	EGGLESTONE	Henry	ENL 18/11/1902 DIS 17/11/1915
9475 PTE	ELLWOOD	Thomas	TRF KO YORKSHIRE LI 22834
9048 PTE	EMBLETON	J W	DISCHARGED 10/12/1915
8592 PTE	ERRINGTON	Alfred	CPL
8355 PTE	EVANS	George	PRISONER OF WAR
11391 BGLR	EVANS	James	PRISONER OF WAR
8744 PTE	EWART	William	ENL 26/1/1904 DIS 27/07/1917 GSW TRF DEPOT
9037 PTE	FAIR	Joseph	LA-FERTE-SOUS-JOUARRE MEM
8683 PTE	FAIRBAIRN	James F	DOW 21/10/1914 BOULOGNE EASTERN CEM
8688 PTE	FAIRWEATHER	George	
8925 PTE	FARBRIDGE	Robert	PRISONER OF WAR REGT NUMBER 8915 ON MRC 8925 ON STAR ROLL
8719 PTE	FARLEY	Reuben	PRISONER OF WAR 01/03/1915
8656 PTE	FARRELL	Ambrose	KiA 21/09/1914 LA-FERTE-SOUS-JOUARRE MEM
10279 PTE	FARRELL	James	TRF ROYAL ENGINEERS 278 TUNNELLING COY 152962
8917 PTE	FAWELL	Edward	KiA 21/09/1914 LA-FERTE-SOUS-JOUARRE MEM
4/7542 PTE	FEATHERSTONE	Henry	DoW 29/07/1915 ETAPLES MIL CEM
11445 PTE	FEATHERSTONE	Robert	PRISONER OF WAR TRF GREEN HOWARDS 83618
8821 PTE	FELLINGHAM	Thomas	DISCHARGED 13/10/1915
9704 PTE	FENWICK	Charles W	TRF NORTHUMBERLAND FUSILIERS 1st GARRISON BN 25146 LCPL
10541 PTE	FENWICK	George	TRF 1/7th 18/DURHAM LI STILL SERVING 1920
10105 PTE	FIELDING	George W	CPL
7844 PTE	FINKLE	Thomas	TRF 10/DURHAM LI, KiA 16/09/1916 THIEPVAL MEMORIAL
10794 SGT	FISHER	John	TRF 12/DURHAM LI KiA 09/08/1916 DCM ST SEVER CEM ROUEN
10411 PTE	FISHER	Ralph	TRF LINCOLNSHIRE REGT 24/03/1917 45172, LABOUR CORPS 31805.
10998 LSGT	FITTER	Henry	REPORTED WOUNDED 24/11/1914, WOUNDED AT HOOGE
8656 PTE	FLAHERTY	Thomas	TRF ARMY RESERVE CLASS W 27/07/1916
11714 PTE	FLANNIGAN	John	KiA 25/09/1916 POTIJZE BURIAL GROUND
7883 PTE	FLATLEY	William	ENL 26/5/1902 DIS 24/4/1916 TRF DEPOT
9074 PTE	FLEETHAM	Joseph E	TRF KO YORKSHIRE LI 01/05/1915 22676, 10/MANCHESTER REGT ACPL KiA 11/12/1917 GORRE BRITISH & INDIAN CEM
8771 PTE	FLEMING	Robert	TRF WEST YORKSHIRE REGT 24/02/1917, ROYAL DEFENCE CORPS 60593, ROYAL FUSILIERS GS/132738
8772 PTE	FLOWERS	William	KiA 21/09/1914 LA-FERTE-SOUS-JOUARRE MEM
9109 PTE	FORD	Edward	PRISONER OF WAR
8762 PTE	FORD	Harry	TRF GREEN HOWARDS 1st GARRISON BN 22186
10405 SGT	FORD	James	WOII
8892 PTE	FOREMAN	Charles	PRISONER OF WAR
6717 PTE	FORREST	John W	TRF NORTHUMBERLAND FUSILIERS 07/06/1915, NYASALAND FIELD FORCE 24838. SOUTH AFRICA 1st BN , QSA, CAPE COLO
9888 PTE	FORSTER	Thomas	TRF MACHINE GUN CORPS 14/03/1916 27809

Number	Rank	Surname	Forename	Notes
8904	PTE	FORSYTH	Thomas	ENL 19/08/1904 DIS 10/10/1916 GSW HAND & THIGH TRF DEPOT
11525	PTE	FOSTER	Frederick D	KiA 27/10/1914 SERVED IN B COY PLOEGSTEERT MEM
9600	PTE	FOSTER	J H	TRF NORTHUMBERLAND FUSILIERS 29/10/1915
/113	SGT	FOSTER	Robert W	WOII STILL SERVING MARCH 1920 PTE IN SOUTH AFRICA 1st BN, QSA 1901, 1902.
6085	PTE	FOWLER	R J	DESERTED 13/02/1915
11663	PTE	FOX	James	ENL 19/11/1913 DIS 10/06/1915
8037	PTE	FRAME	John W	PRISONER OF WAR 09/03/1916
9751	PTE	FRANKLIN	R	TRF KO YORKSHIRE LI 22847 01/05/1915,
9960	PTE	FRANKLIN	William	TRF ROYAL MUNSTER FUSILIERS 9/99 01/04/1917
10548	LCPL	FRANKS	Francis	DOW 08/10/1914 CITY OF PARIS CEM BAGNEUX
8369	PTE	FRAZER	William	ENL 09/03/1903 DIS 08/03/1916 TERMINATION OF ENGAGEMENT
6829	LCPL	FREEMAN	Niels	SOUTH AFRICA 1st BN, QSA TRANSVAAL. KSA, LIJSSENTHOEK MIL CEM
9172	LCPL	FRIEND	Charles A	PRISONER OF WAR 25/11/1914
11684	PTE	FROST	John	KiA 19/12/1915, SERVED A COY YPRES MENIN GATE MEM
8671	PTE	GAFFNEY	John	ATT QM CAMP, 6th DIV SANITARY SECTION, 6th DIV FANCIES (CONCERT PARTY)
9625	PTE	GAFFNEY	Martin	TRF NORTHUMBERLAND FUSILIERS 50566
9664	PTE	GAINFORD	John	TRF ROYAL ENGINEERS 09/12/1915 79124
8943	PTE	GALBRAITH	George	CLASS Z RES
8616	PTE	GALES	Samuel	TRF LABOUR CORPS 23/06/1917 260661
8795	PTE	GALLAGHER	John T	ENL 8/3/1904 DIS 24/08/1915 TRF DEPOT SICK
7887	PTE	GALLON	George	WOUNDED AT HOOGE
9584	PTE	GALLON	Robert	DISCHARGED 31/05/1917
11314	PTE	GARBUTT	George	PRISONER OF WAR
9001	PTE	GARROD	George A	WOUNDED AT HOOGE TRF R ENGINEERS 32826 SGT
9653	PTE	GARTLAND	C	TRF NORTHUMBERLAND FUSILIERS 3rd BN 20/05/1915
11573	PTE	GATES	James J W	ATT 6th DIV WING
8457	PTE	GEE	Albert	ATT V CORPS HQ
10612	PTE	GENTRY	Horace	TRF ARMY RES SECTION B
11486	LCPL	GIBSON	Arthur G	DISCHARGED 19/06/1915
9710	PTE	GIBSON	Thomas	CLASS Z RES
10196	PTE	GIDNEY	George	CPL
6049	PTE	GILES	Charles	CPL DISCHARGED. BUGLER SOUTH AFRICA 1st BN, QSA CAPE COLONY, ORANGE FREE STATE, TRANSVAAL 1902, KSA 1901 & 1902
11657	PTE	GILES	Harry J	DISCHARGED 02/08/1916
8627	PTE	GILL	John	TRF 10/DURHAM LI DISCHARGED
8375	PTE	GILLESPIE	Thomas	PRISONER OF WAR
9031	PTE	GILMORE	Michael	ENL 16/11/1904 CONVICTED OF DESERTION 04/02/1915, DIS 06/12/1916 TRF DEPOT
8872	PTE	GILPIN	Thomas H	KiA 09/10/15 YPRES MENIN GATE MEM
8456	PTE	GINDER	William	DISCHARGED 29/03/1917
8392	PTE	GLEDHILL	John	WOUNDED AT HOOGE DISCHARGED 11/05/1916
10799	PTE	GOLDEN	John	KiA 20/10/1914 PLOEGSTEERT MEM
11463	PTE	GOODALL	William	PRISONER OF WAR
10477	PTE	GORDON	Robert	TRF ROYAL ENGINEERS 30/12/1915 31680
8659	PTE	GOULD	William	TRF LABOUR CORPS 615000
9719	PTE	GRAFTON	Michael	KiA 21/09/1914 LA-FERTE-SOUS-JOUARRE MEM
10431	PTE	GRAHAM	Charles	DoW 21/10/1914 BOULOGNE EASTERN CEM
7982	PTE	GRAHAM	John	ENL 12/09/1902 DIS 11/09/1915, TERMINATION OF ENGAGEMENT
11538	PTE	GRAHAM	John	RENUMBERED 4435530
11377	PTE	GRAHAM	Patrick	KiA 21/09/1914 LA-FERTE-SOUS-JOUARRE MEM
9239	PTE	GRAHAM	Robert	CLASS Z RES
8011	PTE	GRANT	Edward	DISCHARGED 24/10/1915
8330	PTE	GRANT	Frederick	ENL 21/1/1903 DIS 12/08/1915 GSW RT HAND
10003	LCPL	GRANT	Henry	KiA 21/09/1914 LA-FERTE-SOUS-JOUARRE MEM
10870	PTE	GRAY	James	DISCHARGED
8951	PTE	GRAY	Oswald	ENL 7/3/1904 DIS 26/11/1916 WOUNDS TRF DEPOT
9512	PTE	GRAY	Robert	TRF LABOUR CORPS 05/10/1917 370474
8689	PTE	GRIFFITHS	William	PRISONER OF WAR 1914
8971	PTE	GRIGG	John H	KiA 13/10/1914 PLOEGSTEERT MEM
11546	PTE	GROSVENOR	David	TRF ARMY RESERVE SECTION B
11545	PTE	GROSVENOR	John W	TRF ARMY RESERVE SECTION B
9181	CPL	GROVES	Edward	KiA 28/11/1914 BAILLEUL COM CEM
8582	PTE	GROVES	Walter G	LA-FERTE-SOUS-JOUARRE MEM
9041	PTE	GUNTON	Benjamin	ENL 23/11/1904 DIS 19/06/1915 GSW HAND CONNAUGHT HOSPITAL ALDERSHOT
8654	PTE	HACKWORTH	James	PRISONER OF WAR 25/11/1914
9777	SGT	HAGAN	William	TRF WEST YORKSHIRE REGT 27/01/1917 45943, ROYAL DEFENCE CORPS 68986
8433	PTE	HAGGERTY	Peter	KiA 20/10/1914 PLOEGSTEERT MEM
4/8202	PTE	HAIR	George	KiA 19/11/1914 PLOEGSTEERT MEM
4/7427	PTE	HALDON	Norman	TRF ROYAL DUBLIN FUSILIERS 01/02/1917 29692
7893	PTE	HALEY	Thomas	ENL 05/01/1914 DIS 20/11/1914 FROM 3rd BN
9130	PTE	HALL	John	PRISONER OF WAR
9201	LSGT	HALL	Thomas	KiA 19/12/1915 POTIJZE BURIAL GROUND
9513	PTE	HALL	Thomas	TRF 10th BN KiA 16/09/1916 THIEPVAL MEMORIAL
8331	PTE	HALLIDAY	Joseph	TRF NORTHUMBERLAND FUSILIERS 22/10/1915 LCPL 26304
8343	PTE	HALLIDAY	William	KiA 20/10/1914 PLOEGSTEERT MEM
8909	PTE	HALSE	John L	PRISONER OF WAR
11126	PTE	HAMER	Harry	PRISONER OF WAR
8480	PTE	HAMILTON	Alfred	CONVICTED OF DESERTION 19/04/1916
11644	PTE	HANLEY	Alfred	PRISONER OF WAR
9827	PTE	HANNAH	Neil	TRF 14th, 2/DURHAM LI
11110	PTE	HARDY	Raymond	KiA 21/09/1914 LA-FERTE-SOUS-JOUARRE MEM
8313	PTE	HARGREAVES	Frederick W	KiA 05/08/1915 HOP STORE CEM

Number	Rank	Surname	Forename	Details
9703	PTE	HARKER	John W	CONVICTED BY THE CIVIL POWER OF THEFT
9189	PTE	HARLAND	Thomas Val	PRISONER OF WAR DIED 31/10/1918
6742	PTE	HARRINGTON	George W	TRF MACHINE GUN CORPS, TANK CORPS, 95512 WOII CSM
8595	PTE	HARRIS	Edward	WOUNDED AT HOOGE TRF LABOUR CORPS 7th LABOUR BN 169485
6689	PTE	HARRIS	Herbert J	DISCHARGED 10/05/1916, SOUTH AFRICA 1st BN, QSA ORANGE FREE STATE, TRANSVAAL, LAING'S NEK, 1901 & 1902
11591	PTE	HARRISON	Nicholas	TRF LABOUR CORPS 165986
5508	CQMS	HARRISON	Percy	DISCHARGED 23/04/1917 CQMS, SGT IN SOUTH AFRICA 1st BN, QSA, CAPE COLONY, ORANGE FREE STATE, TRANSVAAL, RELIEF OF
8833	PTE	HARRISON	Walter	PRISONER OF WAR
9008	L/CPL	HARROWER	John	ENL 24/10/1904 DIS 12/6/1915 WOUNDS TRF 3/DURHAM LI
7566	BANDSM	HART	Edward	CPL
11316	PTE	HART	John	TRF NORTHUMBERLAND FUSILIERS 53739, EAST YORKS 23224.
4/8084	PTE	HART	Robert	KiA 01/11/1914 YPRES MENIN GATE MEM
8810	PTE	HATTON	Ernest	DISCHARGED 12/06/1915
11629	PTE	HATTON	G F	DISCHARGED 19/06/1915
11479	PTE	HAWKINS	John W G	ATT 6th DIV HQ TRF ARMY RESERVE SECTION B
7279	CSM	HAYLETT	Robert	COMMISSIONED
8338	PTE	HAZELGROVE	Frederick W	KiA 09/08/1915 LCPL YPRES MENIN GATE MEM
8366	PTE	HEATHCOTE	George	KiA 20/10/1914 PLOEGSTEERT MEM
11601	PTE	HENDERSON	Frederick	ENL 10/8/1913 DIS 09/01/1915 TRF DEPOT
9557	PTE	HEPPLE	Robert	ATT 18 INF BDE HQ, 112 INF BDE HQ, 2/DURHAM LI DISCHARGED
8016	PTE	HERRING	James	KiA 28/10/1914 TRUE NAME VILES PLOEGSTEERT MEM
5829	C/SGT	HESLOP	Thomas E	INSTRUCTOR OFFICER CADET BN, AWOII TRF LABOUR CORPS 569559
11281	PTE	HETHERINGTON	George	ENL 21/11/1911 DIS 26/05/1916 WOUNDS TRF DEPOT
9662	L/CPL	HETHERINGTON	Hugh	SGT TRF 13/DURHAM LI ENL 19/9/1906 DIS 21/1/1919
8460	PTE	HEWICK	Louis	KiA 21/09/1914 LA-FERTE-SOUS-JOUARRE MEM
10147	SGT	HEWITT	Sydney	TRF SCOOL OF MUSKETRY 735
8638	PTE	HICK	George	PRISONER OF WAR 20/10/1914
8413	PTE	HICKMAN	Henry	DISCHARGED
8650	PTE	HIGGINS	Harold	DISCHARGED
8362	PTE	HINES	George W	TRF MACHINE GUN CORPS 43711 CPL
10396	PTE	HIRST	Harry	WOI RSM
11689	PTE	HODGSON	J	CONNAUGHT HOSPITAL ALDERSHOT
10218	PTE	HODGSON	John W	SGT
7974	PTE	HODGSON	Samuel	KiA 13/10/1914 PLOEGSTEERT MEM
10491	PTE	HOGAN	Dennis	PRISONER OF WAR
8438	PTE	HOLLAND	John	DISCHARGED
9516	PTE	HOLMES	Thomas	SENTENCED BY FGCM TO PENAL SERVITUDE FOR LIFE (DESERTION), COMMUTED, SECTION B ARMY RESERVE
9129	PTE	HOLROYD	George	TRF 19/DURHAM LI, AWOII CSM, KiA 05/05/1917 THIEPVAL MEMORIAL
6830	CPL	HOOK	Alfred J	SGT ATTACHED 5th TRAINING BN AUSTRALIAN INFANTRY ENL 17/08/1899 DIS 20/12/1918 KR para 392 SOUTH AFRICA 1st BN , QSA, CAPE COLONY,
7787	PTE	HOPE	John	SGT
8785	PTE	HOPE	William T	CPL
8446	PTE	HORE	Hubert	DoW 01/02/1916, CONNAUGHT HOSPITAL ALDERSOT WOUNDED DEC 1914 BOULOGNE EASTERN CEM
9716	PTE	HORN	Thomas	KiA 21/09/1914 LA-FERTE-SOUS-JOUARRE MEM
8750	PTE	HORNE	Robert	WOUNDED AT HOOGE DISCHARGED 22/11/1917
10459	PTE	HORRIGAN	John	PRISONER OF WAR
11318	PTE	HORSEMAN	Arthur	KiA 09/08/1915 YPRES MENIN GATE MEM
9681	PTE	HOWAT	Frederick	INITIAL T ON STAR ROLL
9113	PTE	HOWE	George	TRF KO YORKSHIRE LI 22693 01/05/1915 DISCHARGED
7636	PTE	HOWSE	Robert D	WOUNDED AT HOOGE TRF 14/DURHAM LI DoW 26/07/1916 ST SEVER CEM ROUEN
7544	PTE	HOWSON	Joseph	TRF LABOUR CORPS 239 LAB COY 16/05/1917 CSGT
8437	ASGT	HUDSON	Arthur	TRF LABOUR CORPS 380932
7453	PTE	HUDSON	Henry	ENL 15/04/1901 DID 23/04/1919 KR PARA 392 A RES CLASS P SOUTH AFRICA 1st BN, QSA CAPE COLONY, ORANGE FREE STATE, TRANSVAAL,
8841	SGT	HUDSON	Hugh	STILL SERVING 1920
8708	PTE	HUDSON	James	TRF WEST YORKSHIRE REGT 47688, KO YORKSHIRE LI 50831, R ENGINEERS 355039 RENUMBERED WR/100505, CONVICTED OF DESERTION
9279	PTE	HUGHES	Thomas	KiA 21/09/1914 LA-FERTE-SOUS-JOUARRE MEM
9621	PTE	HULLEY	George	TRF LABOUR CORPS 700582, ENL 16/8/1906 ARMY RESERVE CLASS W 27/01/1917 DIS 4/2/1918
11130	CPL	HUNTER	John E	SGT
11500	PTE	HUNTER	Lawrence	ENL 14/11/1912 WOUNDED AT HOOGE CPL DISCHARGED 17/08/1915
8045	PTE	HUNTLEY	William	PRISONER OF WAR
9235	PTE	HUNTON	Thomas	ENL 25/8/1905 TRF 15/DURHAM LI, DISCHARGE 05/08/1917 LSGT TRF 3/DURHAM LI
8393	PTE	HURST	William	CONVICTED OF DESERTION 30/01/1917, SELF INFLICTED WOUND
7876	PTE	HURST	William L	PRISONER OF WAR TRF NORTHUMBERLAND FUSILIERS 90163
8001	PTE	HUTCHINSON	Frank	TRF KO YORKSHIRE LI 22858 DISCHARGED 08/10/1915
11021	PTE	HUTCHINSON	Herbert	KiA 28/10/1914 SERVED IN B COY PLOEGSTEERT MEM
10640	PTE	HYATT	William	TRF ARMY RES SECTION B
10668	CPL	IBBITSON	Alfred	ENL 21/12/1908 DIS 01/04/1915, GSW LEFT FOOT TRF 3/DURHAM LI
11558	PTE	IDE	Jesse	KiA 21/09/1914 LA-FERTE-SOUS-JOUARRE MEM
8310	PTE	IRVING	Matthew T	ENL 13/01/1903 DIS 12/06/1915 FROM 3rd BN FROSTBITE
10430	PTE	IRWIN	Norman	DISCHARGED 10/06/1915
10629	PTE	IVESON	Charles J G	ENL 5/12//1908 DIS 13/10/1917 IRESON ON MRC
10454	PTE	JACKSON	Hyman	SGT
9612	PTE	JACKSON	Thomas	TRF TRAINING RESERVE 86th BN 112013, LABOUR CORPS 656326
10063	PTE	JACKSON	Walter	DISCHARGED 23/04/1915
8985	PTE	JACQUES	Edwin	KiA 21/09/1914 LA-FERTE-SOUS-JOUARRE MEM
11098	BUGLER	JAGGS	Sidney	TRF 13th, 20th, 14th & 18/DURHAM LI STIL SERVING APR 1920
9013	PTE	JAMES	Edward	PRISONER OF WAR
8991	PTE	JAMES	William	PRISONER OF WAR ENL 5/10/1904 DIS 18/7/1918 ARMY RES CLASS W
7013	PTE	JAMSON	Thomas	KiA 13/10/1914 PLOEGSTEERT MEM
9559	PTE	JANE	Richard	ATT 18 INF BDE HQ, 2/DURHAM LI, DISCHARGED
9592	PTE	JEFFERY	James	PRISONER OF WAR

11428 CPL	JEFFERY	Joseph H	SGT WOUNDED AT HOOGE COMMISSIONED SECOND LIEUTENANT DURHAM LI
10539 LSGT	JIGGINS	Sidney E	ORDERLY ROOM COLOUR SERGEANT
8629 PTE	JOHNSON	George	KiA 20/0/1914 LA-FERTE-SOUS-JOUARRE MEM
11490 PTE	JOHNSON	George	PRISONER OF WAR
9111 PTE	JOHNSON	James	DISCHARGED
8578 LCPL	JOHNSON	Joseph H	WOUNDED AT HOOGE TRF ROYAL FUSILIERS 57126
8318 PTE	JOHNSON	Matthew	PRISONER OF WAR
8412 PTE	JOHNSON	Robert	TRF MACHINE GUN CORPS 159700 REENLISTED DLI 22/3/1920
9248 PTE	JOHNSON	T	TRF WEST YORKSHIRE REGT 47682
11497 PTE	JOHNSON	Thomas	WOUNDED AT HOOGE
9496 SGT	JOHNSON	Thomas O	AWOI REGIMENTAL SERGEANT MAJOR
8886 PTE	JOHNSON	W	TRF WEST YORKSHIRE REGT 46570
11660 PTE	JONES	Edward	KiA 09/08/1915 YPRES MENIN GATE MEM
9175 PTE	JONES	George	CONVICTED OF DESERTION 23/12/1915, TRF 19/DURHAM LI
5617 CSM	JONES	James	COMMISSIONED ATT CONNAUGHT RANGERS DOW 14/10/1918, LT COL COMDG 17 LANCASHIRE FUS HOOGE CRATER CEM
9229 CPL	JONES	Llewellyn	COMMISSIONED SECOND LIEUTENANT
11510 PTE	JONES	Robert	DoW 05/06/1915 LCPL BEDFORD HOUSE CEM
10502 PTE	JOPLING	William	LSGT TRF 12/DURHAM LI, 1,/6/DURHAM LI, ARMY RES SEC B
10693 PTE	JORDAN	Patrick	KiA 28/10/1914 PLOEGSTEERT MEM
7914 PTE	JORDAN	Samuel	DESERTED 03/09/1915 TRF LABOUR CORPS 682691
8517 PTE	JOYCE	Thomas	DESERTED 01/09/1918 & 04/09/1919 SERVING
10392 BUGLER	KANE	Henry	ATT 18/LTMB DISCHARGED
11337 PTE	KANE	Patrick	TRF 15/DURHAM LI KiA 01/07/1916 THIEPVAL MEMORIAL
10434 PTE	KEEBLE	Horace	KiA 29/06/1915 DUNHALLOW ADS CEM
8797 PTE	KEELER	Thomas	KiA 20/09/1914 LA-FERTE-SOUS-JOUARRE MEM
9694 PTE	KELLY	Edward	KiA 18/10/1914 TRUE NAME KNOTT FORMERLY SERVED K OWN ROYAL LANCASTER REGT PLOEGSTEERT MEM
11458 PTE	KELLY	James	DISCHARGED 03/07/1915
11551 PTE	KELLY	James	PRISONER OF WAR
9217 PTE	KELLY	John	WOUNDED AT HOOGE
8015 PTE	KELLY	Thomas	PRISONER OF WAR ENL 4/11/1902 DIS 11/6/1918 TRF DEPOT
5558 CSGT	KENT	Charles	WOUNDED AT HOOGE COMMISSIONED LIEUTENANT & QUARTERMASTER 03/03/1917
6678 PTE	KETTLEWELL	William	PRISONER OF WAR. SOUTH AFRICA 1st BN, QSATRANSVAAL, LAING'S NEK, KSA
10017 PTE	KIMPTON	Harry W	PRISONER OF WAR
11069 PTE	KING	George	TRF 9/DURHAM LI RENUMBERED 9/7500, 325852 CPL
8858 PTE	KING	George H	CLASS Z RES
3/10971 PTE	KING	Joseph	DoW 19/11/1914 PREVIOUSLY SERVED YORK & LANCASTER REGT 8380 ABERDEEN (ALLENVALE) CEM
8649 PTE	KINSEY	Josiah	KiA 13/10/1914 PLOEGSTEERT MEM
8660 PTE	KIRBY	Herbert	ENL 11/12/1903 DIS 15/02/1915 GSW RT SIDE TRF DEPOT
11298 PTE	KITCHING	Mattew W	PRISONER OF WAR
10803 LCPL	KNIGHT	George W	KiA 20/10/1914 PLOEGSTEERT MEM
8574 PTE	KNOPP	Walter	KiA 13/10/1914 SERVED IN B COMPANY PLOEGSTEERT MEM
10784 PTE	KNOWLES	James	DoW 28/12/1915 HOP STORE CEM
5682 SGT	KRAFT	Paul	WOII CSM RENUMBERED 4437377
9141 SGT	LACKENBY	Joseph	AWOII
9449 PTE	LAING	Robert	ENL 21/10/1905 DIS 14/7/1915 TRF 3/DURHAM LI
8791 PTE	LAIRD	Laverick	TRF 15/DURHAM LI
9894 PTE	LAKE	John	ATT 6 DIV DEPOT 2/DURHAM LI DISCHARGED
7414 LCPL	LAKE	Thomas	KiA 28/10/1914. SOUTH AFRICA 1st BN, QSA CAPE COLONY, ORANGE FREE STATE, TRANSVAAL, 1901. PLOEGSTEERT MEM
11455 PTE	LAMB	George	KiA 28/10/1914 PLOEGSTEERT MEM
9036 PTE	LAMB	Robert	TRF MANCHESTER REGT 2/8th BN 44925, MACHINE GUN CORPS 157162.
9092 PTE	LAMBELL	Joseph	PRISONER OF WAR
11590 PTE	LAMBERT	Arthur	KiA 09/08/1915 YPRES MENIN GATE MEM
9702 PTE	LAMBTON	John G	ENL 23/10/1906 DIS 24/3/1916 WOUNDS TRF 3/DURHAM LI
8558 PTE	LANE	Enock	SGT TRF 19/DURHAM LI
10813 PTE	LANE	Walter	PRISONER OF WAR
8916 PTE	LARK	John	PRISONER OF WAR, SOUTH AFRICA 1st BN, QSA CAPE COLONY, ORANGE FREE STATE, TRANSVAAL, 1901
11448 PTE	LAUGHLIN	Osmond	TRF DUKE OF WELLINGTON'S REGT 30731
11360 BUGLER	LAVERTY	Thomas	LAVERTON ON STAR ROLL
11199 CPL	LAWRENCE	Archibald G	SGT
8730 PTE	LAWS	Ernest J	PRISONER OF WAR
8382 PTE	LAWS	Matthew	TRF NORTHUMBERLAND FUSILIERS 30670
7349 PTE	LAWSON	William	ENL 11/12/00, DIS 29/03/1917 TO DEPOT DLI. SOUTH AFRICA 1st BN, ORANGE FREE STATE, TRANSVAAL, 1901, 1902.
5630 SGT	LAZZARI	Joseph	TRF 3/DLI ENL 26/08/1895 CQMS, DIS 24/01/1919
11514 PTE	LEE	Allan	TRF KO YORKSHIRE LI 24863
11671 PTE	LEE	Archer	TRF 22/DURHAM LI DISCHARGED
10916 PTE	LEE	Arthur R	ENL 07/03/1910 DIS 06/07/1915 GSW THIGH TRF 3/DURHAM LI
8400 PTE	LEE	Frederick R	TRF NORTHUMBERLAND FUSILIERS 28361
8473 PTE	LEES	Henry	DoW 17/10/1916 ST SEVER CEM ROUEN
8599 PTE	LEONARD	Thomas	TRF ARMY RESERVE CLASS W 20/01/1917
11356 PTE	LESLIE	Joseph	TRF ARMY CYCLIST CORPS 1255, TANK CORPS 76045
7291 LCPL	LISTER	James A T	TRF GREEN HOWARDS 66803 LCPL,. SOUTH AFRICA 1st BN, QSA TRANSVAAL, 1901, 1902
11526 PTE	LLOYD	William	ENL 9/1/1913 DISCHARGED 12/06/1915 WOUNDED TRF DEPOT
10412 PTE	LONG	Harold	ENL 14/7/1908 DIS 23/8/1916 TRF DEPOT SICK
11685 PTE	LONGSTAFF	Frederick	KiA 21/09/1914 LA-FERTE-SOUS-JOUARRE MEM
9238 PTE	LONGSTAFF	John	TRF WEST YORKSHIRE REGT 47517
10174 PTE	LONGSTAFF	Joseph	CPL
8396 PTE	LONGTHORNE	John	PRISONER OF WAR
8631 PTE	LORD	George E	TRF LINCOLNSHIRE REGT 45176, LABOUR CORPS 31822
6240 PTE	LOVAT	William	KiA 09/08/1915 SOUTH AFRICA 1st BN, QSA ORANGE FREE STATE, TRANSVAAL, TUGELA HEIGHTS, RELIEF OF LADYSMITH, LAING'S NEK,
9075 PTE	LOWE	James	SGT

8458 PTE	LOWEN	Walter J	TRF TRAINING RESERVE BATTALION 5/1249, KO YORKSHIRE LI 41693
9206 PTE	LUCAS	James W	DoW 14/10/1914 SEC-BOIS COM CEM VIEUX-BERQUIN
10902 PTE	LYNAS	John F	PRISONER OF WAR
9657 PTE	MACKERETH	Bertie	TRF MACHINE GUN CORPS 34913, DISCHARGED 25/07/1917
11034 CPL	MADDEN	George	PRISONER OF WAR
11580 LCPL	MADDISON	Rowland E	KiA 28/10/1914 PLOEGSTEERT MEM
10657 SGT	MAKEHAM	Cyril H	RENUMBERED 4435229 WOII
7941 PTE	MALCOLM	James	DISCHARGED 17/03/1916
7958 PTE	MANLEY	Oliver	SGT ATT 6th DIV BOMBING SCHOOL
6280 PTE	MANN	Reginald W	DIED 03/03/1916 LA PUGNOY MIL CEM
11416 PTE	MANN	Thomas	TRF NORTHUMBERLAND FUSILIERS 24845
11512 PTE	MARK	William	RENUMBERED 4435528 WOII
8838 PTE	MARLEY	John	CLASS Z RES
8787 PTE	MARRIAN	Patrick	TRF ROYAL MUNSTER FUSILIERS, LABOUR CORPS 336107
9822 PTE	MARSDEN	Frederick	CLASS Z RES
6926 CPL	MARSHALL	Robert	ENL 23/10/1899 DIS 06/07/1915 WOUNDS SOUTH AFRICA 1st BN , QSA, CAPE COLONY, ORANGE FREE STATE, TRANSVAAL
8006 PTE	MARSHALL	Thomas	KiA 28/10/1914 PLOEGSTEERT MEM
7624 PTE	MARSHALL	William	TRF GREEN HOWARDS 22262, NORTHUMBERLAND FUS 56317, R ENGINEERS 315762 RENUMBERED WR/149073
10338 PTE	MARTIN	Fred	DISCHARGED
9200 LCPL	MARTIN	George	SGT
11559 PTE	MARTIN	Irvine	DESERTED STILL ABSENT DECEMBER 1920
9590 PTE	MARTIN	Michael	TRF WEST YORKSHIRE REGT 83600 ENL 24/4/1906 DIS 1/6/1917 TRF 1 GARR BN DLI
11349 PTE	MARTIN	Randolph	TRF ARMY RESERVE SECTION B
10176 PTE	MARTINDALE	Matthew	KiA 09/08/1915 LCPL YPRES MENIN GATE MEM
8788 PTE	MASON	J J	DESERTED 17/02/1915 RENUMBERED 4435046
8666 PTE	MASON	James	TRF WEST YORKSHIRE REGT 44065
11007 PTE	MASON	William C	SGT AWOII
8859 PTE	MATSON	Andrew	PRISONER OF WAR
9707 PTE	MATTHEWS	Arthur	CLASS Z RES
10049 PTE	MATTHEWS	Charles E	KiA 20/10/1914 CPL PLOEGSTEERT MEM
8986 PTE	MATTHEWS	James	KiA 23/10/1914 PLOEGSTEERT MEM
8945 PTE	MATTHEWS	Jonathan	TRF NORTHUMBERLAND FUSILIERS, LABOUR CORPS 334236
9508 PTE	MATTHEWS	Robert	
9709 PTE	MATTHEWS	William H	DoW 24/09/1914 BRAINE COM CEM
8789 PTE	MAUGHAN	Norman	TRF NORTHUMBERLAND FUSILIERS 2nd GARRISON BN 26282
8949 PTE	MAUGHAN	William	DESERTED MRC GIVES NAME AS HAUGHAN
9515 PTE	MAW	James G	SENTENCED TO DEATH BY FGCM COMMUTED TO 5 YEARS PENAL SERVITUDE SUSPENDED
8928 LCPL	MAYCOCK	Samuel	TRF ROYAL ENGINEERS TUNNELLING COY 86234
10979 PTE	MAYHEW	R T	TRF ROYAL FLYING CORPS 106564
9167 PTE	McATEE	William J	TRF ARMY SERVICE CORPS ET/49687, DISCHARGED 08/12/1917
8461 PTE	McATEER	Daniel	TRF MACHINE GUN CORPS (6th BN) 142015 KiA 22/03/1918 ARRAS MEM
11556 PTE	McATOMINEY	James	ENL 24/2/1913 DIS 11/08/1917 SGT TRF 3/DURHAM LI
9180 PTE	McCALL	James	TRF KO YORKSHIRE LI 23043 KiA 27/06/1916 BOUZINCOURT COM CEM EXT
8618 PTE	McCARTHY	Peter	KiA 09/08/1915 SERVED A COMPANY YPRES MENIN GATE MEM
9100 SGT	McCARTY	Albert A	TRF 20th, 2/DURHAM LI, CLASS Z RES
8003 PTE	McCLUSKEY	Joseph	DISCHARGED 13/10/1915
8931 LCPL	McCORMACK	Andrew	PRISONER OF WAR
9157 PTE	McCORMACK	Joseph	LSGT TRF 20th, 2/7/DURHAM LI CLASS Z RES
9089 PTE	McCOY	Henry	TRF NORTHERN CYCLIST BN 6160 SOUTH LANCASHIRE REGT 48993
10571 PTE	McCRUDDEN	Nicholas	PRISONER OF WAR
11652 PTE	McDONALD	Arthur	TRF SCOTTISH RIFLES 30848
9965 PTE	McDONALD	Edward	
8552 PTE	McDONALD	Thomas	CONVICTED BY FGCM 07/08/1916 DESERTED 24/5/1918 STILL AWOL 30/3/1920
9443 PTE	McDONNELL	Alex M	TRF MACHINE GUN CORPS 20089 LCPL
8493 PTE	McGAHAN	James A	KiA 21/03/1918 ARRAS MEM
8422 PTE	McGIRR	Patrick	PRISONER OF WAR
8725 PTE	McGOWEN	Joseph	PRISONER OF WAR
4/8995 PTE	McGUIRE	James	KiA 09/08/1915 YPRES MENIN GATE MEM
9715 PTE	McGUIRE	Peter	ENL 22/10/1906 DIS 09/06/1915 ON STAR ROLL AS MAGUIRE
8428 PTE	McGUIRE	Thomas	TRF LABOUR CORPS 702489, ARMY RESERVE CLASS P 20/04/1918 ENL 30/7/1903 DIS 1/5/1917
8796 PTE	McGURRELL	Frank	KiA 20/06/1917 MAROC BRIT CEM GRENAY
9192 PTE	McINTOSH	Hugh	DISCHARGED 12/01/1917
8946 PTE	McINTOSH	John W	KiA 21/09/1914 LA-FERTE-SOUS-JOUARRE MEM
9237 PTE	McKAGNEY	Thomas	KiA 09/08/1915 YPRES MENIN GATE MEM
8702 PTE	McKENZIE	Robert	KiA 09/08/1915 YPRES MENIN GATE MEM
11621 PTE	McKIE	Henry	KiA 10/11/1915 POTIJZE BURIAL GROUND
9169 SGT	McKINNON	Alfred	TRF MACHINE GUN CORPS 9270 WOII COMMISSIONED LIEUTENANT
9020 PTE	McKINNON	Joseph	TRF LABOUR CORPS 851 AREA EMP COY 401514 SGT
8927 PTE	McKNIGHT	John	WOUNDED AT HOOGE TRF KO YORKSHIRE LI 28984
9372 CPL	McLAUGHLIN	Peter	WOUNDED AT HOOGE DISCHARGED 11/03/1916 SGT
10473 SGT	McLELLAND	William J	AWOII RENUMBERED 4435162
8296 PTE	McMAHON	Philip	DoW 17/10/1915 HEBBURN CEM
8623 PTE	McMANN	John	ENL 10/11/1903 DIS 05/11/1915 WOUNDS TRF DEPOT
9648 PTE	McMULLEN	Alexander	PRISONER OF WAR RENUMBERED 103299
8977 PTE	McNEILL	James	TRF TRAINING RESERVE BATTALION 5/10411 SGT
9211 PTE	McNESS	David	DESERTED 04/12/1919
8039 PTE	McSWEENEY	John	KiA 21/09/1914 LA-FERTE-SOUS-JOUARRE MEM
8540 PTE	MEDDES	Alfred	TRF ROYAL ENGINEERS 37109
10246 BANDSM	METCALFE	Duncan	ENL 21/11/1907 DIS 13/9/1918
9219 PTE	MIDCALF	Thomas	TRF ARMY CYCLIST CORPS 7031, MACHINE GUN CORPS 159102

Number	Rank	Surname	Forename	Details
8782	PTE	MIDDLEMASS	Henry	ENL 24/2/1904 DIS 24/02/1917 TRF DEPOT
11345	LCPL	MILBURN	Arthur	KiA 24/07/1915 SGT YPRES MENIN GATE MEM
9566	PTE	MILBURN	James E	KiA 21/09/1914 LA-FERTE-SOUS-JOUARRE MEM
11278	PTE	MILLARD	Francis A	DoW 18/08/1915 BATH (ST JAMES'S) CEM
11008	PTE	MILLER	Henry	ENL 9/8/1910 DIS 23/01/1915 WOUNDED L FOREARM TRF 3/DURHAM LI
8032	PTE	MILLER	William	KiA 03/05/1917 SGT PHILOSOPHE BRIT CEM MARZINGARBE
7437	PTE	MITCHELL	William	TRF ROYAL MUNSTER FUSILIERS G/218 CPL
8295	PTE	MITCHESON	Robert	TRF KO YORKSHIRE LI (2nd BN) 22811 KiA 17/07/1915 VOORMEZEELE ENCLOSURE No 3
7125	PTE	MOIR	Alfred	TRF ROYAL ENGINEERS 356099 RENUMBERED WR/100273. SOUTH AFRICA 1st BN, TRANSVAAL, 1902
8884	BANDSM	MONGER	Llewellyn	SGT
9056	PTE	MONKHOUSE	George	KiA 09/08/1915 YPRES MENIN GATE MEM
5492	ORQMS	MONKS	Augustus A	TRF 16/YORK & LANCASTER REGT, COMMISSIONED CAPTAIN & QM. LSGT IN SOUTH AFRICA 1st BN, QSA RELIEF OF LADYSMITH
8466	PTE	MOONEY	John	DoW 22/10/1914 SUNDERLAND (BISHOPWEARMOUTH) CEM
8802	PTE	MOORE	Albert	DoW 21/09/1914 SISSONNE BRIT CEM
9265	PTE	MOORE	John	KiA 21/09/1914 LA-FERTE-SOUS-JOUARRE MEM
9202	PTE	MOORE	Walter	DISCHARGED 12/06/1915
10458	LCPL	MORDALL	Thomas B	TRF 15/DURHAM LI SGT KiA 01/07/1916 GORDON DUMP CEM OVILLIERS LA BOISELLE
10271	PTE	MORGAN	Benjamin	TRF ROYAL ENGINEERS 34880
10436	PTE	MORGAN	Walter	TRF ROYAL ENGINEERS 31699
9914	PTE	MORGAN	William H	CLASS Z RES
8709	PTE	MORRIS	Frederick	SGT
3/8698	PTE	MURPHY	Daniel	TRF 3/DURHAM LI DoW HOME 29/10/1914 TORQUAY CEM AND EXT
11491	LCPL	MURPHY	Frank	PRISONER OF WAR
8563	PTE	MURPHY	James	TRANSPORT SGT
8962	PTE	MURRAY	Christopher	PRISONER OF WAR
9946	PTE	NAISH	Leonard J	KiA 09/08/1915 YPRES MENIN GATE MEM
10995	PTE	NASH	Albert F	ENL 4/8/1910 DIS 11/05/1917 TRF DEPOT SICK
8567	PTE	NEAL	Valentine	DISCHARGED 22/02/1917
8405	PTE	NEEDHAM	George D	KiA 02/09/1015 CPL POTIJZE BURIAL GROUND
11653	PTE	NEVISON	John	KiA 21/09/1914 LA-FERTE-SOUS-JOUARRE MEM
8651	PTE	NEWBY	John	TRF LABOUR CORPS 531759
9485	PTE	NEWCOMBE	William	ACPL
8589	CPL	NEWMAN	William	WOUNDED AT HOOGE TRF ROYAL AIR FORCE 138470
11267	PTE	NICHOL	Ernest	TRF ROYAL ENGINEERS 79402
9891	PTE	NICHOLS	Alan	DISCHARGED 19/07/1917
8816	PTE	NICHOLSON	John	DISCHARGED 01/04/1915
11398	PTE	NICHOLSON	Robert	SGT
10230	SGT	NIGHTINGALE	James	ENL 20/4/1900 DIS 30/07/1915 WOII FROSTBITE
10401	PTE	NIXON	Ralph	SGT
8575	PTE	NOBLE	Herbert	DISCHARGED 01/09/1917
8488	PTE	NOON	Edward	PRISONER OF WAR
10038	PTE	NUTT	Charles F	ENL 8/4/1907 DIS 01/07/1915 ACPL SHELL WND TRF DEPOT
10036	PTE	NUTT	Herbert A	ENL 8/4/1907 DIS 12/11/1915 GSW R ARM TRF DEPOT
8483	PTE	OATES	James	TRF 12/dll 13/DLI ENL 14/9/1903 DIS 12/12/1918 KR para 392
9872	PTE	OLIVER	Thomas	CPL ATT MACHINE GUN CORPS
11238	PTE	OLIVER	William A	DESERTED STILL ABSENT DEC 1920
12506	LCPL	OLNEY	Ivor J	TRF NORTHUMBERLAND FUSILIERS 24624 SGT 07/08/1915, ARMY SERVICE CORPS M/443? CPL
8054	PTE	O'MALLEY	Edward	WOUNDED AT HOOGE TRF ROYAL BERKSHIRE REGT 1st GARR BN 23235
10977	PTE	ORTON	William H	PRISONER OF WAR
10156	LCPL	OXLEY	Henry	REPORTED WOUNDED 22/11/1914, SGT
11178	CPL	PADDEN	Thomas	AWOII,
7073	SGT	PADDON	Edward	CSM A COY 1918 SOUTH AFRICA 1st BN, QSA CAPE COLONY, TRANSVAAL, KSA.
9580	PTE	PADGETT	John	PRISONER OF WAR
6757	PTE	PAGE	George W	TRF LABOUR CORPS 392538, WEST YORKSHIRE REGT 58085 LCPL
10421	PTE	PAGE	William A	TRF WEST YORKSHIRE REGT 47394, ROYAL ENGINEERS 261991 RENUMBERED WR/300148
8842	PTE	PALLISTER	Walter	CLASS Z RES
9982	PTE	PARKER	Frederick	TRF LABOUR CORPS 495409
9685	PTE	PARKER	John	WOUNDED AT HOOGE
7979	PTE	PARKER	Samuel	DISCHARGED 12/09/1915
8590	PTE	PARKER	Thomas	TRF LABOUR CORPS 480 EMP COY 363602
9118	PTE	PARKES	John J	KiA 21/09/1914 LA-FERTE-SOUS-JOUARRE MEM
11070	PTE	PARKIN	William	LCPL
8777	PTE	PARRETT	William	TRF 12th & 2/DURHAM LI CLASS Z RES
8975	PTE	PARRY	Walter J	TRF NORTHERN CYCLIST BN 61048 LABOUR CORPS 632737
8756	PTE	PATTERSON	Robert H	KiA 03/10/1918 BRIE BRITISH CEMETERY
8773	PTE	PATTINSON	William	TRF EAST YORKSHIRE REGT 23237
11350	PTE	PATTON	William	KiA 21/09/1914 LA-FERTE-SOUS-JOUARRE MEM
3/7793	PTE	PAYNE	William G	ENL 26/2/1902 DIS 30/11/1915 TRF 3/DURHAM LI
8655	PTE	PEACOCK	Charles	DESERTED 26/04/1915
8471	PTE	PEARSON	James	TRF 12/DLI, 20/DLI, 1/9/DLI CLASS Z RESERVE
7853	PTE	PEEL	John R	TRF KO YORKSHIRE LI 01/05/1915 22819
8695	PTE	PERKINS	Charles E	TRF 10/DURHAM LI LCPL KiA 31/07/1915 YPRES MENIN GATE MEM
9729	PTE	PERKINS	James C	TRF LABOUR CORPS 514855
8801	PTE	PERRETT	Joseph	TRF 3/DURHAM LI DoW HOME 13/11/1914 BRISTOL (ARNOS VALE) CEM
8712	LCPL	PERRY	James E	TRF LABOUR CORPS 617140 CPL
11477	PTE	PESCOD	Richardson	TRF LABOUR CORPS 309499
11344	PTE	PEVERLEY	William	WOUNDED AT HOOGE
7059	PTE	PHILLIPS	Harry	DISCHARGED 22/08/1915
8706	LCPL	PHILLIPSON	David	TRF ROYAL ENGINEERS 86412 SGT
7580	PTE	PHILLIPSON	John	DoW 29/12/1915 LIJSSENTHOEK MIL CEM

8813 PTE	PHILLIPSON	Thomas W	PRISONER OF WAR
9718 PTE	PHILPOTTS	Frederick	TRF LABOUR CORPS 10817
11347 PTE	PICKARD	Frank E	TRF EAST YORKSHIRE REGT 23238
9116 PTE	PICKERING	William	KiA 09/08/1915 YPRES MENIN GATE MEM
11494 PTE	PINE	John W	ENL 6/11/1912 DIS 03/10/1915 NEURASTHENIA TRF DEPOT
10251 PTE	PINE	Thomas	PRISONER OF WAR
8622 PTE	PITCHER	John G	TRF EAST YORKSHIRE REGT, MACHINE GUN CORPS 124645 CPL
8551 PTE	PLEWS	Thomas	TRF LABOUR CORPS 710055
5424 LCPL	PLUMB	William	TRF 3/DLI ENL 21/08/1895 DIS 22/11/1917 DIED AFTER DISCHARGE
11010 SGT	PLUMMER	William	WOUNDED AT HOOGE
8970 BANDSM.	POOLE	H L	COMMISSIONED LABOUR CORPS
9005 PTE	POOLE	Robert	ENL 17/10/1904 DIS 09/01/1915 TRF 3/DURHAM LI
5477 SGT	PORT	Thomas W	AWOII, PTE IN SOUTH AFRICA 1st BN QSA TRANSVAAL & RELIEF OF LADYSMITH
10180 PTE	PORTER	Thomas	ENL 24/9/1907 DIS 12/6/1915 WOUNDS TRF 3/DURHAM LI
9146 PTE	POSTLEWAITE	James	DoW 31/10/1914 BAILLEUL COM CEM
11655 PTE	POTTS	Robert	KiA 09/08/1915 YPRES MENIN GATE MEM
9426 PTE	POWELL	John	DIED 24/01/1916 WIMMEREUX COM CEM
11203 CPL	POWELL	John	PRISONER OF WAR
9216 PTE	POWTON	Ralph	ENL 11/8/1905 DIS 10/07/1915 WOUNDS TRF 3/DURHAM LI
11429 PTE	PRATT	Norman	TRF MACHINE GUN CORPS 27805 CPL
10504 PTE	PREST	Benjamin	TRF MACHINE GUN CORPS 70904
8573 CPL	PRICE	Jonah	WOII
11803 PTE	PRIESTMAN	George	PRISONER OF WAR
8645 PTE	PRINGLE	George	KiA 28/10/1914 PLOEGSTEERT MEM
11717 PTE	PUMFORD	William	WOUNDED AT HOOGE SGT
8682 PTE	PUNTON	John	CPL
9073 LCPL	PURVES	Andrew T	PTE
11608 PTE	QUINN	James	KiA 13/10/1914 PLOEGSTEERT MEM
10158 PTE	QUINN	William T	ENL 19/8/1907 REPORTED WOUNDED 24/11/1914, TRF ARMY RESERVE CLASS P 13/02/1917
10943 CPL	RADFORD	Edgar W	PRISONER OF WAR
9649 PTE	RAINE	Stephen W	Croix de Guerre Belgian
11439 PTE	RAISBECK	James	PRISONER OF WAR
10004 SGT	RAND	John	AWOII ENL 02/04/1907 DIS 11/06/1919
8503 PTE	RANGER	Leonard	KiA 20/09/1914 LA-FERTE-SOUS-JOUARRE MEM
9517 PTE	RAW	Leonard	DISCHARGED
10530 PTE	RAYMENT	William	DISCHARGED 24/12/1916
8348 CPL	RAYNER	Alfred W	CQMS
11037 CPL	READ	Bertram	TRF ROYAL DEFENCE CORPS 76647
10787 PTE	READ	Herbert	PRISONER OF WAR
9277 LCPL	READMAN	Leonard	WOUNDED AT HOOGE TRF LABOUR CORPS 383846, ROYAL FUSILIERS GS/110734, DURHAM LI 4435061 WOII
4/9055 PTE	REAY	James	TRF LABOUR CORPS 382789, RENUMBERED 386047
11442 PTE	REDDEN	John	DESERTED 07/09/1915 REENLISTED 8/DURHAM LI No 4284 TRF KO YORKSHIRE LI 34599 KiA 16/9/16
7726 PTE	REED	John	TRF LABOUR CORPS 415802, ROYAL FUSILIERS GS/105598.
6541 PTE	REEVES	Albert	PRISONER OF WAR. SOUTH AFRICA 1st BN, QSA TRANSVAAL, TUGELA HEIGHTS, RELIEF OF LADYSMITH, LAING'S NEK, 1901
9493 PTE	REEVES	John S	DISCHARGED
9197 PTE	REID	William	WOUNDED AT HOOGE
6885 PTE	REILLY	William	TRF LABOUR CORPS 167337 [No ALLOTED to 25th WORKS BN DLI WHICH BECAME 7 LABOUR BN] SOUTH AFRICA 1st BN, QSA, CAPE COLONY,
9667 PTE	RENDER	Thomas	KiA 28/10/1914 PLOEGSTEERT MEM
11498 PTE	RENWICK	Ernest	DoW 31/10/1915 LIJSSENTHOEK MIL CEM
11440 PTE	REVELY	Edmund	KiA 28/10/1914 PLOEGSTEERT MEM
11376 LCPL	REVELY	Joseph	TRF 3/DURHAM LI DoW HOME 06/11/1914 NETLEY MIL CEM
11423 PTE	REYNOLDS	Thomas	TRF KO YORKSHIRE LI 22683 ARMY PAY CORPS 22001 DISCHARGED 20/09/1915
8326 PTE	RHODES	Arthur	PRISONER OF WAR
10520 PTE	RICHARDSON	Albert	TRF ARMY CYCLIST CORPS 1252, CORPS OF LANCERS L/13788
8893 PTE	RICHARDSON	Ernest	PRISONER OF WAR
8876 PTE	RICHARDSON	James	KiA 20/10/1914 PLOEGSTEERT MEM
11513 PTE	RICHARDSON	John	KiA 22/03/1918
8546 PTE	RICHARDSON	John W	TRF MACHINE GUN CORPS 27900 DISCHARGED 31/10/1916
8506 PTE	RICHARDSON	Thomas	KiA 18/10/1914 PLOEGSTEERT MEM
8358 PTE	RICHARDSON	William C	ENL 26/02/1903 DIS 25/02/1916 TERMINATION OF ENGAGEMENT.
11573 PTE	RICHES	Wilfred M	DISCHARGED 30/09/1915
8292 PTE	RICHMOND	William H	KiA 28/12/1915 POTIJZE BURIAL GROUND
8406 PTE	RIDLEY	Thomas	ENL 8/6/1903 DIS 14/12/1915 KR para 392
9168 PTE	RIDLEY	William	ENL 1/5/1905 WOUNDED AT HOOGE TRF ARMY RESERVE CLASS P 31/10/1917 CPL
11602 LCPL	RILEY	William	KiA 09/08/1915 YPRES MENIN GATE MEM
11375 PTE	RIX	Edward W	DoW 21/09/1914 VENDRESSE MIL CEM
8052 PTE	ROBERTSON	James	DISCHARGED 14/12/1915
5981 PTE	ROBINSON	David	TRF LABOUR CORPS 620523, SOUTH AFRICA 1st BN, QSA TRANSVAAL, LAING'S NEK, 1901
8794 PTE	ROBINSON	George M	ENL 7/3/1904 DIS 16/12/1915 WOUNDS TRF DEPOT
11280 PTE	ROBINSON	Robert W	RENUMBERED C/464 ON MRC
8913 PTE	ROBINSON	William	KiA 19/11/1914 PLOEGSTEERT MEM
8759 PTE	ROBINSON	William E	DISCHARGED 09/12/1915
9656 PTE	ROBSON	Charles	TRF TRAINING RESERVE 2nd BN TR5/4482 LCPL
9647 SGT	ROBSON	David T	WOII
8914 PTE	ROBSON	Geoffrey	KiA 21/09/1914 LA-FERTE-SOUS-JOUARRE MEM
8288 PTE	ROBSON	Thomas	DISCHARGED 24/12/1915
10603 PTE	ROBSON	Thomas	KiA 21/09/1914 LA-FERTE-SOUS-JOUARRE MEM
8703 PTE	ROBSON	William	PRISONER OF WAR
10274 PTE	ROCHESTER	John	KiA 24/09/1914 SERVED IN B COMPANY LA-FERTE-SOUS-JOUARRE MEM
11651 PTE	ROCKS	Edward	PRISONER OF WAR

11648 PTE	ROLSTONE	Frederick S	PRISONER OF WAR
9523 PTE	ROPER	John	TRF LABOUR CORPS 167338 RAF 148554
8299 PTE	ROSE	Alfred	TRF 10/DLI DISCHARGED 01/01/1916
11342 PTE	ROSE	John	KiA 21/11/1914 PLOEGSTEERT MEM
8901 PTE	ROSS	Michael	TRF NORTH STAFFORDSHIRE REGT 1st GARR BN 25780, ROYAL ENGINEERS 190852
8349 PTE	ROUSE	Arthur	RENUMBERED 36737 DISCHARGED 17/02/1916 TRF MIDDLESEX REGT
8430 LCPL	ROWLANDS	Harold R	PRISONER OF WAR
11384 PTE	ROWLEY	Alfred	TRF ARMY RESERVE SECTION B
9692 LCPL	RUDLIN	Albert H	TRF MACHINE GUN CORPS 11852 WOII
9727 PTE	RUFFLES	Arthur W	CLASS Z RES
11392 LCPL	RUTHERFORD	Frederick	KiA 20/09/1914 LA-FERTE-SOUS-JOUARRE MEM
7932 PTE	RUTTER	Ernest	DESERTED 26/03/1915
8534 PTE	RUTTER	Matthew	TRF WEST RIDING REGT 1st BN 30772
9006 PTE	SADLER	John	TRF YORK & LANCASTER REGT 30008
8882 PTE	SALT	Alfred	CLASS Z RES
8881 BANDSM	SALT	Harold H	KiA 09/08/1915 YPRES MENIN GATE MEM
7990 PTE	SANDILANDS	Robert	KiA 21/09/1914 LA-FERTE-SOUS-JOUARRE MEM
10316 CPL	SAUNDERS	John H	ENL 25/2/1908 DIS 08/10/1917 ASGT
10224 PTE	SAWYER	Francis	PRISONER OF WAR
9547 PTE	SAWYER	Frederick	TRF LABOUR CORPS 611357
10544 PTE	SAWYER	John	KiA 21/03/1914 ARRAS MEM SERVED IN D COMPANY
6883 PTE	SAXTON	Wilfred	TRF LABOUR CORPS 501 EMP COY 260629, ROYAL DEFENCE CORPS S/1599 SOUTH AFRICA 1st BN , QSA, CAPE COLONY, ORANGE FREE
10599 PTE	SAYWELL	Charles W	TRF NOTTS & DERBYSHIRE REGT 126117, 1/TRAINING RESERVE BN TR/6/22563. ASGT
8036 PTE	SCORER	James	TRF ROYAL ENGINEERS 274 TUNNELLING COY 86230
8044 PTE	SCOTT	Alex	KiA 08/05/1917 LCPL HAMBURG CEM
8553 PTE	SCOTT	George	DESERTED 28/5/1915
8477 PTE	SCOTT	John	CPLTRF 15/DURHAM LI
8867 PTE	SCOTT	John W	PRISONER OF WAR
5642 PTE	SCOTT	Robert	Died 03/01/1917, BURMAH MOUNTED INF COY S AFRICA QSA CAPE COLONY, ORANGE FREE STATE, TRANSVAAL, COLOGNE SOUTHERN CE
6322 PTE	SCOTT	Thomas	DISCHARGED 21/08/1915, SOUTH AFRICA 1st BN, QSA ORANGE FREE STATE, TRANSVAAL, TUGELA HEIGHTS, RELIEF LADYSMITH, LAING'S
11081 PTE	SCOTT	Thomas	TRF MACHINE GUN CORPS 149299 ASGT
7281 PTE	SCOTT	William	ACPL TRF CLASS Z RESERVE SOUTH AFRICA 1st BN , QSA, CAPE COLONY, ORANGE FREE STATE, TRANSVAAL
9879 PTE	SEARLE	John	TRF KO YORKSHIRE LI 22702
4/9027 PTE	SEATON	Nicholas	DoW 03/05/1917 STRAND MIL CEM
11489 LCPL	SEDGEWICK	John M	SGT
10269 PTE	SEERY	Albert V	KiA 09/08/1915 YPRES MENIN GATE MEM
9825 PTE	SEWELL	John E	WOUNDED AT HOOGE, TRF MACHINE GUN CORPS 16410
9112 PTE	SHALE	Richard	ENL 16/1/1905 DIS 11/09/1917
11363 PTE	SHARP	William	CONVICTED OF DESERTION, TRF YORK & LANCASTER REGT (9th BN) 39870 KiA 09/06/1917 LCPL YPRES MENIN GATE MEM
10653 PTE	SHARPE	Eli J	TRF MILITARY PROVOST STAFF CORPS ASSGT
8445 PTE	SHARPE	Robert	SGT
7864 SGT	SHAW	C	
8462 PTE	SHAW	Charles	KiA 13/10/1914 PLOEGSTEERT MEM
6934 PTE	SHEARWOOD	Luke	ENL 13/03/1900 DIS 30/03/1917 ARMY RES CLASS P SOUTH AFRICA 1st BN , QSA, CAPE COLONY, ORANGE FREE STATE, TRANSVAAL
4/6554 PTE	SHEEHAN	Charles	WOUNDED AT HOOGE, TRF SCOTTISH RIFLES 30848
11697 PTE	SHEPHERD	John	TRF MACHINE GUN CORPS 20100 LCPL
9849 SGT	SHERRIFF	Frederick G	COMM 3/YORK & LANCASTER REGT
10175 PTE	SHIELD	Andrew	WOUNDED AT HOOGE
8548 LCPL	SHIELDS	Hugh	TRF 2/9th DURHAM LI RENUMBERED 6215, 326867 SGT
9510 PTE	SHOTTON	Gordon	WOUNDED AT HOOGE, ENL 5/1/1906 DIS 10/3/1919 KR para 392xvia
10467 PTE	SHOVELIN	Thomas	TRF ROYAL FIELD ARTILLERY 285970
10978 PTE	SHRIMPTON	George	KiA 15/10/1916 LSGT THIEPVAL MEMORIAL
10861 CPL	SHUTTLEWORTH	Riley	TRF GREEN HOWARDS 1st GARR BN SGT 22206 DIED IN INDIA 15/06/1917
11609 PTE	SIDWELL	Walter	TRF LABOUR CORPS 432461
8769 PTE	SIMMONS	William J	TRF NORTH STAFFORDSHIRE REGT 1st GARRISON BN, LABOUR CORPS 309507.
8008 PTE	SIMPSON	Charles	TRF WEST YORKSHIRE REGT 46033
6325 CPL	SIMPSON	Charles S	AWOII , PTE IN SOUTH AFRICA 1st BN, QSA TRANSVAAL, TUGELA HEIGHTS, RELIEF OF LADYSMITH, LAING'S NEK
8748 PTE	SIMPSON	Robert	ATT DEPOT ROUEN, ADW HAVRE, 7th VET HOSPITAL, PB BN ROUEN, 4th ASC WKSPS, 8 CORPS REST CAMP, 7th REST CAMP, BASE.
8356 PTE	SISSON	Edward	DISCHARGED 25/02/1916
10591 PTE	SLANN	H	
8424 PTE	SLATER	Thomas	KiA 28/10/1914 PLOEGSTEERT MEM
10357 LCPL	SLIMMINGS	Richard L	AWOII RENUMBERED 4435148
8472 PTE	SLOAN	Bernard	PRISONER OF WAR 18/10/1914
11720 PTE	SLOAN	David	SGT
8686 PTE	SLOAN	Michael	TRF NORTHUMBERLAND FUSILIERS 89516, ENL 23/12/1903 DIS 21/01/1916 GSW R ARM
10043 PTE	SMEETH	Herbert	PRISONER OF WAR
8537 PTE	SMILES	Arthur	TRF TRAINING RESERVE 86th BN, LABOUR CORPS 139703
9551 PTE	SMITH	A	PRISONER OF WAR
9854 PTE	SMITH	Charles	TRF ARMY RESERVE CLASS W 22/09/1917
11405 PTE	SMITH	Edward	TRF EAST YORKSHIRE REGT 23247, NORTHUMBERLAND FUSILIERS 27014
8505 PTE	SMITH	Ernest	KiA 21/09/1914 VENDRESSE MIL CEM
11604 LCPL	SMITH	Frederick	KiA 09/08/1915 YPRES MENIN GATE MEM
10285 SGT	SMITH	Harold	TRF MACHINE GUN CORPS 9320 CQMS
11262 PTE	SMITH	Horace	PRISONER OF WAR
9668 PTE	SMITH	James	
8542 PTE	SMITH	John	PRISONER OF WAR
9687 PTE	SMITH	John	TRF 15/DURHAM LI, KiA 16/09/1916 AIF BURIAL GROUND FLERS
7956 PTE	SMITH	Ralph	TRF ROYAL ARMY VETERINARY CORPS REG/1233
8012 PTE	SMITH	Robert	TRF 10/DLI, DISCHARGED 19/10/1915
9086 PTE	SMITH	Thomas P	KiA 16/05/1915 ERQUINGHAM LYS CHURCH YARD EXT

8854 PTE	SMITH	William	ENL 4/5/1904 DIS 5/4/1916 TRF 14/DURHAM LI
11038 PTE	SMITH	William H	ATT 6th DIV SIGNAL COY RE
9639 PTE	SNAITH	George	WOUNDED EVAC SWANSEA HOSPITAL ENL 20/8/1906 DIS 5/2/1918 TRF ARMY RES CLASS W LCPL
6784 PTE	SNELGAR	Tom	TRF KO YORKSHIRE LI SOUTH AFRICA 1st BN , QSA, CAPE COLONY, ORANGE FREE STATE
9025 PTE	SNOWBALL	James	KiA 198/10/1914 PLOEGSTEERT MEM
8692 PTE	SNOWBALL	John	ENL 21/1/1904 DIS 14/7/1915 TRF 3/DURHAM LI
8576 PTE	SNOWDON	Arthur	PRISONER OF WAR DIED 23/10/1918 HAMBURG CEMETERY
9591 PTE	SORRELL	John	KiA 09/08/1915 YPRES MENIN GATE MEM
7957 PTE	SOWDEN	Edward	TRF ROYAL FIELD ARTILLERY W/5958, DISCHARGED 27/08/1915
10486 PTE	SPENCE	James	WOUNDED AT HOOGE
8733 LCPL	SPENCER	Walter	COMMISSIONED 2/DURHAM LI
11313 PTE	SPENSELEY	Richard	TRF ARMY CYCLIST CORPS(XIV CORPS CYCLIST BN) 1254 KiA 18/10/1917 TYNE COT MEM
7426 PTE	SPINK	John W	PRISONER OF WAR 01/03/1915. SOUTH AFRICA 1st BN, QSA CAPE COLONY, ORANGE FREE STATE, TRANSVAAL, 1902
9441 CPL	SPRAY	T H	SGT CLASS Z RES
9029 PTE	SPROATES	James T	TRF ROYAL ENGINEERS 32684
8357 PTE	SQUIBB	John	KiA 15/01/1918 LCPL ATT BRIGADE SIGNAL COMPANY BERLES NEW MIL CEM
8425 PTE	SQUIRES	Alfred	SGT WOUNDED AT HOOGE
7002 PTE	STANLEY	Joseph	DoW 14/10/1914. SOUTH AFRICA 1st BN, QSA CAPE COLONY, TRANSVAAL, 1901. SEC-BOIS COM CEM VIEUX-BERQUIN
6414 PTE	STANTON	James J	TRF LABOUR CORPS 369044, SOUTH AFRICA 1st BN, QSA ORANGE FREE STATE, TRANSVAAL
8389 PTE	STARK	Samuel	PRISONER OF WAR
9634 PTE	STEARMAN	Charles	KiA 18/10/1914 PLOEGSTEERT MEM
10039 SGT	STEPHENS	Harry J	KiA 10/03/1915 HARRY STEVENS IN SDGW HOUPLINES COM CEM
8894 LCPL	STEPHENSON	Alfred	CPL
9203 PTE	STEPHENSON	John C	KiA 15/10/1916 BANCOURT BRIT CEM
9486 PTE	STIRLING	James	KiA 09/08/1915 YPRES MENIN GATE MEM
11438 PTE	STOBBS	Joseph	TRF ROYAL ENGINEERS 248839 RENUMBERED WR/125795
10798 PTE	STOCKTON	Tom	KiA 31/05/1916 ESSEX FARM CEM
8764 PTE	STOKER	Frederick J	TRF LABOUR CORPS 260165
10308 PTE	STOKER	Thomas	
10994 CPL	STONE	Frederick G	LSGT COMMISSIONED 2Lt DURHAM LI
11319 PTE	STONE	Sydney	SGT WOUNDED AT HOOGE
5286 CQMS	STOREY	Harry H	COMMISSIONED POSTED BACK TO BN KiA
8390 PTE	TATE	James	DISCHARGED 10/05/1916
8800 PTE	TAYLOR	Charles	KiA 20/04/1916 ESSEX FARM CEM
8887 PTE	TAYLOR	Charles	TRF ARMY SERVICE CORPS EMT/55133 DISCHARGED 03/03/1915
8002 PTE	TAYLOR	James	REPORTED WOUNDED 24/11/1914, ENL 08/10/1902 DIS 03/07/1915 FROM 3rd BN, GSW LEFT HAND
10397 PTE	TAYLOR	Joshua	TRF NORTH STAFFORDSHIRE REGT 23785
8982 PTE	TAYLOR	Robert	KiA 21/09/1914 LA-FERTE-SOUS-JOUARRE MEM
7944 PTE	TEADER	Arthur W	KiA 23/11/1914 PLOEGSTEERT MEM
10497 SGT	TEMPLE	Thomas	MID
8945 PTE	TENNICK	James	TRF KO YORKSHIRE LI 22760 KiA 17/07/1915 VOORMEZEELE ENCLOSURE No 3
8735 PTE	TERRY	John	WOUNDED AT HOOGE, TRF MACHINE GUN CORPS 70897
6723 PTE	TEVENIN	Michael	KiA 21/09/1914 SOUTH AFRICA 1st BN , QSA, CAPE COLONY, ORANGE FREE STATE, TRANSVAAL. MEDALS FORFEITED FOR DESERTION
7930 PTE	THOMAS	Charles H	KiA 25/07/1915 POTIJZE BURIAL GROUND
8812 PTE	THOMAS	John	ATT SCHOOL OF COOKERY, 2/DURHAM LI CLASS Z RES
8607 PTE	THOMPSON	Alfred	DISCHARGED 16/02/1915
11557 BUGLER	THOMPSON	Charles	RENUMBERED 4435101
8890 PTE	THOMPSON	Henry	KiA 09/08/1915 YPRES MENIN GATE MEM
8515 PTE	THOMPSON	James	DISCHARGED 14/01/1916
4/9108 PTE	THOMPSON	John	TRF ARMY SERVICE CORPS M/324660
9224 PTE	THOMPSON	William	ENL 12/8/1905 DIS 12/06/1915 TRF 3/DURHAM LI
9721 PTE	THOMPSON	William S	TRF WORCESTERSHIRE REGT 40527
8402 PTE	TIERNEY	Joseph	DoW 30/07/1915 YPRES MENIN GATE MEM
8944 PTE	TILLEY	Edwin	ENL 1/3/1904 DIS 10/07/1915 GSW L FOREARM
10199 PTE	TINKLER	Albert E	TRF NORTHUMBERLAND FUSILIERS 24846
11544 LCPL	TOOLE	William	PRISONER OF WAR
11599 PTE	TRIGG	Harry	KiA 21/03/1918 BANCOURT BRIT CEM
9976 SGT	TUCKER	Herbert	CQMS AWOII
10721 PTE	TUGBY	Joseph W	WOUNDED AT HOOGE, TRF MACHINE GUN CORPS 25290 LSGT, AWOII DCM & BAR
8350 PTE	TUMILTY	John	DISCHARGED 12/02/1916
8351 PTE	TUMILTY	Thomas	PRISONER OF WAR
8915 PTE	TURTON	Joseph	KiA 21/3/1918 CSM C COMPANY ARRAS MEM
8532 PTE	TYE	Walter	KiA 21/09/1914 LA-FERTE-SOUS-JOUARRE MEM
8444 PTE	TYGHE	George	ENL 11/8/1903 DIS 17/04/1916 WOUNDS TRF 3/DURHAM LI
7584 PTE	USHER	Joseph	TRF ROYAL ENGINEERS 37067
11029 PTE	VARLEY	Michael W	TRF WEST YORKSHIRE REGT 47775 THEN BACK TO DLI KiA 18/10/1918
6997 CSM	VAUGHAN	Henry R	COMMISSIONED 2/CONNAUGHT RANGERS THEN ATT 2/DLI
8837 PTE	VEASEY	Arthur	TRF LABOUR CORPS 614302
8586 PTE	VERNON	Edward	ENL 10/11/ 1903 DIS 26/07/1917 GSW TRF DEPOT
8920 PTE	VERRALL	John	REPORTED WOUNDED 24/11/1914 TRF KO YORKSHIRE LI 22848 01/05/1915
9154 PTE	VINCENT	John	KiA 09/08/1915 YPRES MENIN GATE MEM
8920 PTE	WAGGETT	W	REPORTED WOUNDED 24/11/1914. MR CARD NOT FOUND
8562 PTE	WALLACE	George	KiA 20/09/1914 LA-FERTE-SOUS-JOUARRE MEM
9653 PTE	WARD	John H	KiA 28/10/1914 PLOEGSTEERT MEM
8835 PTE	WARD	Thomas	TRF MACHINE GUN CORPS 20086
8478 PTE	WARDHAUGH	Mark	CPL ENL 9/9/1903 DIS 29/12/1917 TRF 3/DLI
9581 CPL	WARNER	Charles H	ACSGT
8757 PTE	WARWICK	Jackie	TRF WEST YORKSHIRE REGT
8329 PTE	WATSON	James	KiA 21/09/1914 LA-FERTE-SOUS-JOUARRE MEM
7507 PTE	WATSON	John R	TRF LINCOLNSHIRE REGT, LABOUR CORPS 32402 RQMS

6402 RSM	WATSON	Joseph	COMMISSIONED LT & QM 1/12/1917 MID 11/03/1916
8301 PTE	WATSON	Robert	DISCHARGED 04/01/1916
8492 PTE	WATSON	Robert	DoW 03/10/1914 ST NAZAIRE (TOUTES AIDED) CEM
8017 PTE	WATT	Joseph	TRF ROYAL ENGINEERS 174 TUNNELLING COY 86235 LCPL
8123 PTE	WAUGH	John W	8123 ON 14 STAR ROLL 9123 ON W&V ROLL
4/5696 CPL	WAYMAN	Edward	DESERTED 12/02/1915
9221 PTE	WEALLANS	Thomas	TRF WEST YORKSHIRE REGT 39400
11529 PTE	WEALLEANS	James R	DISCHARGED 05/04/1915
6973 PTE	WEEDY	Thomas	WOUNDED AT HOOGE, ENL 23/11/1899 DIS 24/10/1917 KR PARA 392 SOUTH AFRICA 1st BN , QSA, CAPE COLONY, ORANGE FREE STATE,
9679 LCPL	WEIGHTMAN	William B	WOUNDED AT HOOGE
8455 PTE	WELLINGS	Samuel	KiA 21/09/1914 FORMERLY SERVED NORTH STAFFORDSHIRE REGT VENDRESSE MIL CEM TROYON CHYD MEMORIAL 48
3/11704 PTE	WELSH	Edward	TRF 20th, 2/DURHAM LI, ATT 6th DIV SNIPER COMPANY DoW 10/12/1918 GATESHEAD EAST CEM
8055 PTE	WELTON	Jack	DISCHARGED 16/12/1915
8984 PTE	WEST	Henry	KiA 05/08/1915 HOP STORE CEM
8049 PTE	WEST	James	WOUNDED AT HOOGE, DISCHARGED 11/12/195
10655 PTE	WESTBROOK	Patrick	SGT
8031 PTE	WETHERALL	Frederick	DISCHARGED 15/09/1915
9578 PTE	WHALEN	Michael	DISCHARGED 29/11/1917 LCPL
10315 PTE	WHITE	Frederick	KiA 28/12/1915 LCPL POTIJZE BURIAL GROUND
11562 PTE	WHITE	Frederick G	PRISONER OF WAR
11317 PTE	WHITE	Robert	DISCHARGED 10/10/1917
8581 PTE	WHITE	William	TRF KO YORKSHIRE LI 22855
10457 SGT	WHITEFIELD	Albert E	DoW 21/09/1914 VENDRESSE MIL CEM TROYON CHYD MEMORIAL 49
11329 PTE	WHITFIELD	George	PRISONER OF WAR
11523 PTE	WHYATT	Joseph	DISCHARGED
7993 PTE	WILKIE	Andrew	PRISONER OF WAR 01/03/1915
8675 PTE	WILKIE	James	DISCHARGED 29/03/1917
9805 PTE	WILKINSON	Frank	TRF WEST YORKSHIRE REGT 50942
10729 PTE	WILKINSON	John L D	KiA 21/09/1914 VENDRESSE MIL CEM TROYON CHYD MEMORIAL 47
10283 PTE	WILKINSON	Peter	LCPL
10143 PTE	WILKINSON	Thomas	DISCHARGED
9950 PTE	WILLIAMS	Albert H	TRF MACHINE GUN CORPS 16416 CPL
8026 PTE	WILLIAMSON	John	DISCHARGED 18/11/1915
4/7904 PTE	WILLIAMSON	Richard	ENL 28/8/1908 DIS 30/08/1915 TRF 3/DURHAM LI
7133 LCPL	WILLIS	George	SGT TRF CLASS Z RESERVE,. SOUTH AFRICA 1st BN, QSA 1901, 1902
8721 PTE	WILSON	Alfred	ENL 15/1/1904 DIS 18/09/1918
8849 PTE	WILSON	Arthur	ENL 20/4/1904 DIS 22/04/1916 NEURASTHENIA
9158 PTE	WILSON	E	TRF TRAINING RESERVE 87th BN TR/5/68525
11700 PTE	WILSON	Joseph	KiA 13/10/1914 PLOEGSTEERT MEM
7099 PTE	WILSON	Louis H	TRF WORCESTERSHIRE REGT 50283. SOUTH AFRICA 1st BN, QSA TRANSVAAL, 1901, 1902
7920 PTE	WILSON	Matthew	CPL
8714 PTE	WILSON	Thomas	
8824 PTE	WILSON	Thomas	
8886 PTE	WILSON	William	CLASS Z RES
10424 PTE	WINDLE	John W	ENL 7/8/1908 DIS 12/06/1915 WOUNDS TRF 3/DURHAM LI
11333 PTE	WINTER	Thomas	WOII
8612 PTE	WOLSTENHOLME	Joseph	PRISONER OF WAR
8746 PTE	WOOD	Alexander	KiA 28/10/1914 PLOEGSTEERT MEM
10044 PTE	WOOD	James A	DISCHARGED
6871 PTE	WOOD	John A	AWOII TRF 52/DURHAM LI, CLASS Z RESERVE SOUTH AFRICA 1st BN , QSA, CAPE COLONY, ORANGE FREE STATE, TRANSVAAL
8722 PTE	WOODROFFE	Harry	ENL 16/1/1904 DIS 27/10/1917 TRF ARMY RES CLASS W
10628 CPL	WOOTTON	William	DISCHARGED
8717 PTE	WORTON	Joseph	ENL 12/1/1904 DIS 14/12/1917 TRF ARMY RES CLASS W
8995 CPL	WRAY	Thomas	AWOII
8584 PTE	WRIGHT	Albert	TRF SOUTH LANCASHIRE REGT 63948
11024 PTE	YATES	Harry	TRF KO YORKSHIRE LI 22791
9535 PTE	YOUNG	George C	KiA 20/09/1914 LA-FERTE-SOUS-JOUARRE MEM
10638 LCPL	YOUNG	Philip	DoW 12/08/1915 SGT LIJSSENTHOEK MIL CEM
8924 PTE	YOUNGSON	James	ATT HQ 6th DIV, ATT 13 CORPS HQ, CLASS Z RESERVE.

THE FIRST REINFORCEMENTS ARRIVED IN FRANCE 19 SEPTEMBER 1914

8231 PTE	APPLETON	Thomas	TRF EAST YORKSHIRE REGT 20514
9533 PTE	ARMSTRONG	Edward J	TRF LABOUR CORPS 700593, BACK TO FRANCE 19/9/1919
7711 CPL	BARR	D	PRISONER OF WAR 25/11/1914
7425 PTE	BERRY	John	PRISONER OF WAR 20/02/1915. SOUTH AFRICA 1st BN, QSA CAPE COLONY, ORANGE FREE STATE, TRANSVAAL, 1902
6652 PTE	BIRCH	John	DISCHARGED 11/05/1916, LCPL. SOUTH AFRICA 1st BN, QSA, TRANSVAAL, LAING'S NEK. KSA 1901, 1902
7767 PTE	BIRD	J	PRISONER OF WAR 25/11/1917
7100 PTE	BLOOMFIELD	William	TRF ROYAL AIR FORCE 185293 SOUTH AFRICA 1st BN, QSA CAPE COLONY, ORANGE FREE STATE TRANSVAAL, KSA 1901, 1902
7440 PTE	BLUE	Joseph	TRF KO YORKSHIRE LI 18/08/1917 48003, WELSH REGIMENT 61851 CPL SOUTH AFRICA 1st BN, QSA CAPE COLONY, ORANGE FREE STATE
7384 PTE	BOUGHEY	James	ENL 22/01/1901 DIS 28/06/1915 GSW LEFT SHOULDER FROM DEPOT SOUTH AFRICA 1st BN, QSA TRANSVAAL, 1902
6811 PTE	BOWMAN	Albert E	PRISONER OF WAR 12/04/1915. SOUTH AFRICA 1st BN, QSA, LAING'S NEK
9616 PTE	BROWN	Joseph	TRF ARMY SERVICE CORPS 21/04/1917 T/39468
7688 PTE	BURN	William	TRF ROYAL ENGINEERS 9/10/1915 79125
7732 PTE	CALLAGHAN	Edward	DESERTED 26/09/1917
7077 PTE	CAREY	Frank	TRF WEST YORKSHIRE REGT 45785
3/6835 PTE	CARROLL	William	DISCHARGED 10/06/1916
7197 PTE	CASEY	John	DoW 28/06/1915 BOULOGNE EASTERN CEM
8729 PTE	CROOKS	Matthew	DoW 07/11/1914 NEW IRISH FARM CEM - LOMME-LA-MITERIE GERMAN CEM SP MEMORIAL 3
7528 PTE	CROWTHER	Thomas	PRISONER OF WAR 01/06/1915
7556 LCPL	CUMMINS	Archibald	KiA 02/06/1915 CPL, ON CWGC AS CUMMINGS POTIJZE BURIAL GROUND

7595 PTE	DAVIES	L W	TRF NORTHUMBERLAND FUSILIERS 23/02/1915 30663 TRF A RES CLASS W CONNAUGHT HOSPITAL ALDERSHOT
7874 PTE	DICKINSON	Andrew	TRF 8th & 18/DURHAM LI DISCHARGED
7997 PTE	DICKSON	Robert	DISCHARGED 06/10/1915
11393 PTE	DINSDALE	Albert H	DoW 06/08/1915 LIJSSENTHOEK MIL CEM
6908 PTE	DONNELLY	George	PRISONER OF WAR 01/03/1915 SOUTH AFRICA 1st BN , QSA, CAPE COLONY, ORANGE FREE STATE, TRANSVAAL
7432 PTE	DONNELLY	Peter	PRISONER OF WAR 20/10/1914. SOUTH AFRICA 1st BN, QSA CAPE COLONY, ORANGE FREE STATE, TRANSVAAL, 1902
7777 PTE	DUNN	Thomas	PRISONER OF WAR 25/11/1914
7419 PTE	FAIRLESS	James	
6463 PTE	FARRER	James	PRISONER OF WAR 18/04/1915
3/9346 PTE	FITZGERALD	James	ENL 19/10/1908, DISCHARGED 29/10/1915 GSW BACK
7474 SGT	FOSTER	Henry	WOUNDED AT HOOGE
6866 PTE	GARDNER	Frederick	KiA 21/03/1918SOUTH AFRICA 1st BN , QSA, CAPE COLONY, ORANGE FREE STATE, TRANSVAAL. ARRAS MEM
7429 PTE	GIBSON	John	KiA 28/10/1914 SOUTH AFRICA 1st BN, QSA CAPE COLONY, ORANGE FREE STATE, TRANSVAAL, 1902. PLOEGSTEERT MEM
7784 PTE	GIBSON	William	KiA 09/08/1915 YPRES MENIN GATE MEM
7537 PTE	GILBERT	Isaiah	PRISONER OF WAR 01/03/1915
7109 PTE	GOLDSMITH	Charles	TRF LINCOLNSHIRE REGT 22/03/1917 38165 DISCHARGED 26/09/1917. SOUTH AFRICA 1st BN, TRANSVAAL, 1902
7435 PTE	GOODE	George J	ATT 2/2 King's African Rifles, T/CQMS SOUTH AFRICA 1st BN, QSA CAPE COLONY, ORANGE FREE STATE, TRANSVAAL, 1902
9251 PTE	GRAHAM	Christopher	PRISONER OF WAR
7899 LCPL	GRAY	William H	TRF MACHINE GUN CORPS 01/01/1916 CQMS 27319 A/RSM
7939 PTE	GROCOTT	Isiah	TRF KO YORKSHIRE LI 01/05/1915 DISCHARGED 24/02/1916 22806
7593 PTE	GUEST	Samuel	TRF WEST YORKSHIRE REGT 24/02/1917 47790 ENL 29/08/1901 DIS 24/04/1917 WOUNDS
7715 PTE	HARRINGTON	Jeramiah	CONVICTED OF DESERTION 06/03/1916 ENL 07/01/1902 DIS 06/03/1919 FROM A RES CLASS P.
7761 PTE	HASELTINE	W	PRISONER OF WAR
6767 PTE	HATFIELD	William	PRISONER OF WAR. SOUTH AFRICA 1st BN, QSA TRANSVAAL
7870 PTE	HAYCOCK	Thomas G	ENL 8/5/1902 DIS 19/11/1917 TRF DEPOT
7695 PTE	HOBSON	George	DISCHARGED 27/03/1915 LANGLEY MOOR
7840 PTE	HOLDEN	William A	ENL 28/10/02 WND AT HOOGE TRF ARMY RESERVE CLASS W 12/03/1917
6895 PTE	HOPPER	Mark	TO CLASS Z RESERVE SOUTH AFRICA 1st BN, QSA TRANSVAAL. KSA
6783 PTE	HUNT	Alfred J	CLASS Z RESERVE SOUTH AFRICA 1st BN , QSA, CAPE COLONY, ORANGE FREE STATE, TRANSVAAL
7755 PTE	HUTCHINSON	Charles	TRF ROYAL DEFENCE CORPS 66166 ACPL
6483 PTE	JOHNSON	Thomas	KiA 09/08/1915 YPRES MENIN GATE MEM
7138 PTE	KING	Albert	DoW 19/10/1914. SOUTH AFRICA 1st BN, QSA TRANSVAAL, 1901, 1902. BOULOGNE EASTERN CEM
7185 CPL	KIRKMAN	Thomas	KiA 28/10/1914 SOUTH AFRICA 1st BN, QSA TRANSVAAL, 1901, 1902. PLOEGSTEERT MEM
7146 PTE	LARMAN	William	DoW 20/10/1914. SOUTH AFRICA 1st BN, QSA CAPE COLONY, ORANGE FREE STATE, TRANSVAAL, 1902, INVALIDED HOME BAILLEUL COM CEM
7769 PTE	LEMIN	Richard	PRISONER OF WAR
7884 PTE	LOCK	Samuel	ENL 29/05/1902 DID 02/08/1915 FROM DEPOT GSW LUMBAR
7101 PTE	LOWEN	George	TRF NORTHUMBERLAND FUSILIERS 24772 LCPL
7213 LCPL	LUMSDEN	John	PRISONER OF WAR SOUTH AFRICA 1st BN, QSA TRANSVAAL, 1901, 1902
6624 SGT	MACKENZIE	William	DISCHARGED 13/12/1915
6781 PTE	MARTEN	William	PRISONER OF WAR SOUTH AFRICA 1st BN , QSA, CAPE COLONY, ORANGE FREE STATE, TRANSVAAL
6672 PTE	MAUGHAN	John	PRISONER OF WAR SOUTH AFRICA 1st BN , QSA, CAPE COLONY, ORANGE FREE STATE, TRANSVAAL
7539 PTE	McCARTHY	Michael	SGT DISCHARGED
7538 PTE	McCARTHY	Thomas	DISCHARGED
7217 PTE	McGOUGH	William	TRF 3/DLI ENL 25/06/1900 DIS 17/04/1916
7511 PTE	McLEAN	Reuben	PRISONER OF WAR TRF ARMY ORDNANCE CORPS 10071
7671 PTE	MICHAN	John	DISCHARGED 12/06/1915
7124 PTE	MILBURN	Joseph	PRISONER OF WAR, SOUTH AFRICA 1st BN, QSA 1901, 1902
7141 PTE	MOORE	Thomas	KiA 13/10/1914. SOUTH AFRICA 1st BN, QSA TRANSVAAL, 1902. PLOEGSTEERT MEM
7011 PTE	NEWBY	Frank	DIED 26/06/1916. SOUTH AFRICA 1st BN, QSA, CAPE COLONY, TRANSVAAL, KSA NEIDERZWEHREN CEM GERMANY
8750 PTE	NICHOLSON	Robert	KiA 21/09/1914 LA-FERTE-SOUS-JOUARRE MEM
6702 PTE	O'BRIEN	Patrick	TRF 3/DLI, ENL 17/02/1899 DIS 30/10/1915 SICKNESS SOUTH AFRICA 1st BN, QSA TRANSVAAL, TUGELA HEIGHTS, RELIEF OF LADYSMITH, LAING'S
6948 PTE	OUGHTON	John	DISCHARGED 18/03/1917 SOUTH AFRICA 1st BN , QSA, CAPE COLONY, ORANGE FREE STATE, TRANSVAAL. KSA
7789 PTE	PHILLIPS	Thomas	TRF LABOUR CORPS 419957 ROYAL FUSILIERS GS/104756
9430 CPL	RILEY	Alfred	KiA 07/12/1917 RIBECOURT BRIT CEM SPECIAL MEM 13
7072 PTE	RILEY	James	KiA 09/08/1915 SERVED A COMPANY SOUTH AFRICA 1st BN, QSA 1901, 1902. PLOEGSTEERT MEM
7265 LCPL	ROBINSON	Robert	PRISONER OF WAR 01/03/1915 SOUTH AFRICA 1st BN, QSA TRANSVAAL, 1901, 1902
7142 PTE	ROBSON	Alexander	TRF 10/DURHAM LI, KiA 13/08/1916 SOUTH AFRICA 1st BN, QSA TRANSVAAL, 1902. THIEPVAL MEMORIAL
7415 PTE	RUTHERFORD	Joseph	PRISONER OF WAR SOUTH AFRICA 1st BN, QSA CAPE COLONY, ORANGE FREE STATE, TRANSVAAL, 1902
8435 PTE	SHARKEY	William	ENL 6/8/1903 DIS 06/07/1917
6983 PTE	SHAW	John	DISCHARGED SOUTH AFRICA 1st BN, QSA, CAPE COLONY, ORANGE FREE STATE, TRANSVAAL, 1901, INVALIDED HOME
7500 PTE	SMITH	Charles	PRISONER OF WAR
7295 PTE	SMITH	George	ENL 12/10/00 DIS 23/04/1915TO 3/DLI. SOUTH AFRICA 1st BN, QSA TRANSVAAL, 1901, 1902
6507 LSGT	TAYLOR	Henry C	KiA 20/10/1914 SOUTH AFRICA 1st BN, QSA CAPE COLONY, ORANGE FREE STATE, TRANSVAAL, PLOEGSTEERT MEM
7269 PTE	THOMPSON	Frederick	PRISONER OF WAR SOUTH AFRICA 1st BN, QSA TRANSVAAL, 1902
7786 PTE	WATSON	William	TRF ROYAL DEFENCE CORPS 66330, NORTHUMBERLAND FUSILIERS 98735
6132 PTE	WILSON	Fred	DISCHARGED 07/07/1916
7168 LCPL	WILSON	John	KiA 09/08/1915 LCPL. SOUTH AFRICA 1st BN, QSA TRANSVAAL, 1901, 1902, INVALIDED HOME YPRES MENIN GATE MEM
7558 PTE	WOOLLEY	James	PRISONER OF WAR 01/03/1915

THE SECOND REINFORCEMENTS ARRIVED IN FRANCE 24/09/1914

6492 PTE	BROOMAN	Frank	DISCHARGED 26/12/1914 SOUTH AFRICA 1st BN QSA TRANSVAAL, NATAL. KSA 1901, 1902
6583 PTE	BROWN	John	KiA 09/08/1915 SOUTH AFRICA 1st BN, QSA, CAPE COLONY, ORANGE FREE STATE, TRANSVAAL. KSA 1901, 1902. YPRES MENIN GATE MEM
11452 PTE	BUSHBY	William	DoW 18/09/16 GROVETOWN CEM MEAULTE
7592 PTE	CARROLL	William	WOUNDED AT HOOGE TRF MACHINE GUN CORPS 12651 SGT, LABOUR CORPS SGT 614814
7582 PTE	COULSON	James	KiA 09/08/1915 SOUTH AFRICA 1st BN, QSA CAPE COLONY, ORANGE FREE STATE, TRANSVAAL, 1902. YPRES MENIN GATE MEM
6863 SGT	COX	William	WOUNDED AT HOOGE TRF ROYAL ENGINEERS 128129, LABOUR CORPS 710798
8033 PTE	CRESSWELL	William E	DISCHARGED 09/12/1915
8625 PTE	CURRY	John	KiA 14/08/1915 LIJSSENTHOEK MIL CEM
7642 PTE	DOBSON	Harry	ENL 30/10/01 WOUNDED AT HOOGEGSW RT THIGH, DIS 15/05/1916 TRF DEPOT
8814 PTE	DONAGHY	Robert	KiA 09/08/1915 YPRES MENIN GATE MEM

6450 PTE	FARRY	Thomas	DISCHARGED 08/12/1915
11485 PTE	FRANKLIN	John	ENL 31/10/1912 DIS 11/2/1919 TRF DEPOT
6549 PTE	GLEASON	A	PRISONER OF WAR 25/11/1914
9824 PTE	HALL	Henry	ENL 22/1/1907 DIS 24/03/1916 TRF 3/DURHAM LI
6873 PTE	HANKEY	William	DOW 09/05/1917 SOUTH AFRICA 1st BN , QSA, CAPE COLONY, ORANGE FREE STATE. CALAIS SOUTHERN CEM
7772 PTE	HEAPS	Charles	TRF ROYAL ENGINEERS 05/06/1915 37065
7121 PTE	HEDLEY	William	KiA 11/07/1917. SOUTH AFRICA 1st BN, QSA 1901, 1902. PHILOSOPHE BRIT CEM MARZINGARBE
6913 PTE	HEMMING	Frank	TRF 9/KO YORKSHIRE LI 38164. SOUTH AFRICA 1st BN, QSA CAPE COLONY, ORANGE FREE STATE, TRANSVAAL, 1901, 1902, INVALIDED HOM
9760 L/CPL	HENDERSON	Richard	ENL 7/12/1906 DIS 23/03/1916 CPL WOUNDS TRF DEPOT
3/7180 PTE	IRWIN	Isaac	TRF 10/DURHAM LI KiA 28/08/1916 THIEPVAL MEMORIA
6694 PTE	JACKSON	William	KiA 07/08/1915. SOUTH AFRICA 1st BN, QSA ORANGE FREE YPRES MENIN GATE MEM
7764 LCPL	JACKSON	William	PTE
7801 PTE	JOHNSON	Alexander	SGT
3/9283 PTE	KELLY	Joseph	KiA 23/11/1914 PLOEGSTEERT MEM
3/7365 SGT	KELLY	Michael	REDUCED TO PTE RENUMBERED 74681
7004 PTE	KIMBER	Martin	WOUNDED AT HOOGE TRF LABOUR CORPS 316888. SOUTH AFRICA 1st BN, QSA CAPE COLONY, TRANSVAAL, KSA
6409 PTE	LANE	H Thomas	DISCHARGED 29/10/1915. SOUTH AFRICA 1st BN, QSA TRANSVAAL, TUGELLA HEIGHTS, RELIEF OF LADYSMITH, LAING'S NEK
7917 PTE	LINFORTH	John H	WOUNDED AT HOOGE ENL 18/7/1902 DIS 04/02/1917 TRF DEPOT
6795 PTE	MARSHALL	Frederick A	TRF NORTHUMBERLAND FUSILIERS 43278, HOME SVC AGR COY LABOUR CORPS 227221
6390 PTE	MATTHEWSON	Ralph N	RENUMBERED 36667 DISCHARGED
6907 PTE	McALLISTER	Cornelius	TRF ARMY RESERVE CLASS P 11/01/1917. ENL 17/10/1899 DIS 11/11/1917 SOUTH AFRICA 1st BN, QSA, CAPE COLONY, ORANGE FREE STATE
3/9134 PTE	McCARTAN	Hugh	KiA 06/01/1916 POTIJZE BURIAL GROUND
6623 CPL	McCARTNEY	Albert E	TRF CLASS Z RESERVE. SOUTH AFRICA 1st BN, QSA TRANSVAAL, TUGELA HEIGHTS, RELIEF OF LADYSMITH, LAING'S NEK.
7368 PTE	McDOUGALL	Michael	KiA 09/08/1915 C COMPANY LCPL YPRES MENIN GATE MEM
7285 PTE	McGHIN	Hugh	ENL 3/10/00, DIS 04/09/1917. ARMY RES CLASS W. SOUTH AFRICA 1st BN, QSA, CAPE COLONY, ORANGE FREE STATE, TRANSVAAL, 1902
7060 PTE	McINTYRE	Thomas	ENL 26/01/1900 DIS 24/01/1917 TRF 1st GARR BN SOUTH AFRICA 1st BN, QSA CAPE COLONY, KSA 1901 & 1902
8669 PTE	McKENNA	Lawrence	
6765 PTE	McNANEY	Robert	TRF MACHINE GUN CORPS 16405. SOUTH AFRICA 1st BN, QSA 1901, 1902
7147 PTE	MEARING	John Thoms	TRF DEPOT ENL 17/04/1904 DIS 03/12/1915
11639 PTE	MILLION	Joseph	TRF ROYAL DEFENCE CORPS 86903, R WEST SURREY REGT L/12076
6642 PTE	MOORE	John C	DISCHARGED 08/01/1916
3/9580 PTE	MORTON	Edward	KiA 09/08/1915 YPRES MENIN GATE MEM
7832 PTE	MOWBRAY	James	KiA 05/08/1915 YPRES MENIN GATE MEM
7926 PTE	NELSON	John J	TRF 22nd, 15th AND 18/DURHAM LI CLASS Z RES
6993 PTE	NEWTON	William	KiA 28/10/1914 PLOEGSTEERT MEM
7481 PTE	PARKER	Charles	KiA 09/08/1915 YPRES MENIN GATE MEM
8387 PTE	PARKINSON	Ernest	TRF LANCASHIRE FUSILIERS 235306, ROYAL DEFENCE CORPS 61481 DLI NUMBER 5357 ON MRC
6423 PTE	PATEMAN	William S	SENTENCED BY FGCM TO 10 YEARS PENAL SERVITUDE KiA 26/09/1915. SOUTH AFRICA 1st BN, QSA ORANGE FREE STATE, TRANSVAAL,
6952 PTE	PILKINGTON	Joseph	ENL 23/11/1899 DIS 29/01/1919 TRF ARMY RESERVE CLASS W 04/09/1916
7757 PTE	POSTENS	William	TRF NORTH STAFFORDSHIRE REGT 12/04/1916
7574 PTE	PRICE	John	WOUNDED AT HOOGE
6584 PTE	REAH	Joseph	SOUTH AFRICA 1st BN, QSA TRANSVAAL, TUGELLA HEIGHTS, RELIEF OF LADYSMITH, LAING'S NEK
11460 PTE	REDMAN	James	DESERTED 04/08/1917
8476 PTE	RENTON	William	CONVICTED OF DESERTION
6424 PTE	RICHARDS	David E	TRF SOUTH LANCASHIRE REGT 49056 DISCHARGED 13/10/1915 SOUTH AFRICA 1st BN, QSA ORANGE FREE STATE, TRANSVAAL
6903 PTE	RICKERBY	Frederick	ACPL TRF CLASS Z RESERVE SOUTH AFRICA 1st BN , QSA, CAPE COLONY, ORANGE FREE STATE, TRANSVAAL
7286 PTE	ROBINSON	William	TRF 18/DURHAM LI, CLASS Z RESERVE
7047 PTE	SINGLE	Albert	KiA 04/08/1915 SOUTH AFRICA 1st BN, QSA TRANSVAAL, 1901, 1902. HOP STORE CEM
7048 PTE	SMITH	James H	TRF WEST YORKSHIRE REGT 47704, ROYAL ARMY MEDICAL CORPS 4288. SOUTH AFRICA 1st BN, QSA CAPE COLONY, TRANSVAAL, KSA
7829 PTE	SPENCER	George	KiA 16/11/1914 PLOEGSTEERT MEM
7490 PTE	STEPHENSON	George	STEVENSON ON MRC
3/8412 CPL	STOREY	William	DISCHARGED 04/01/1918 SGT ARMY RES CLASS W
6929 PTE	SWAN	Thomas	DoW 13/08/1915 SOUTH AFRICA 1st BN , QSA, CAPE COLONY, ORANGE FREE STATE, TRANSVAAL. LIJSSENTHOEK MIL CEM
6471 PTE	SWEENEY	Michael	DISCHARGED 16/08/1915. SOUTH AFRICA 1st BN, QSA TRANSVAAL, TUGELLA HEIGHTS, RELIEF OF LADYSMITH, LAING'S NEK, 1901
6633 PTE	TANSEY	John O	ATT 19 FLD AMBULANCE RAMC, DISCHARGED 11/01/1916. SOUTH AFRICA 1st BN, QSA CAPE COLONY, ORANGE FREE STATE, TRANSVAAL
9567 PTE	TANSEY	Peter	DISCHARGED 13/05/1917
7152 PTE	TEMPLETON	Alexander	KiA 09/08/1915 YPRES MENIN GATE MEM
7449 PTE	THOMPSON	James	DoW 17/03/1915 CITE BON JEAN CEM ARMENTIERES
6465 PTE	TICKLE	Albert	DISCHARGED 20/08/1915
6835 PTE	TIERNEY	James	PRISONER OF WAR SOUTH AFRICA 1st BN , QSA, CAPE COLONY, ORANGE FREE STATE, TRANSVAAL. ON SA ROLL AS 6825
7439 LCPL	TREES	Arthur W	ENL 22/03/1901 DIS 19/06/1915 GSW RT ARM FROM 3rd BN SOUTH AFRICA 1st BN, QSA, TRANSVAAL, 1902
6661 PTE	WEBSTER	George	DISCHARGED 06/02/1916 SOUTH AFRICA 1st BN , QSA, CAPE COLONY, ORANGE FREE STATE, TRANSVAAL
6967 PTE	WEST	John	WOUNDED AT HOOGE SOUTH AFRICA 1st BN, QSA, CAPE COLONY, ORANGE FREE STATE, TRANSVAAL
7720 PTE	WIDDOWFIELD	James	SGT
6461 PTE	WILLIAMSON	John	DISCHARGED 20/08/1915. SOUTH AFRICA 1st BN LCPL, QSA TRANSVAAL, NATAL
7805 PTE	WORSTENHOLMI	John	KiA 09/08/1915 YPRES MENIN GATE MEM

THE THIRD REINFORCEMENTS ARRIVED IN FRANCE 22 OCTOBER 1914

9012 PTE	ADAMSON	G	CONVICTED BY FGCM OF DESERTION
3/9270 PTE	BARKERSS	Robert	DoW 10/01/1915 CITE BON JEAN CEM ARMENTIERES
3/9174 PTE	BENTHAM	Thomas	DoW 22/08/1916 COUIN BRITISH CEM
7098 PTE	BLACK	James	KiA 09/08/1915 CPL. SOUTH AFRICA 1st BN, QSA TRANSVAAL, 1901, 1902. YPRES MENIN GATE MEM
6777 PTE	BOYLE	Patrick	TRF KO YORKSHIRE LI KiA 15/06/1915 23050 SOUTH AFRICA 1st BN , QSA, CAPE COLONY, ORANGE FREE STATE, TRANSVAAL
3/8213 PTE	CAMPBELL	James	TRF ARMY RESERVE 22/3/1916
7659 PTE	CASEY	Peter	CPL
4/7087 PTE	CATLOW	Benjamin	KiA 09/08/1915 YPRES MENIN GATE MEM
9740 CPL	CHRISTIE	Walter	AWOII CLASS Z RES
3/9302 PTE	COLEMAN	Michael	KiA 01/06/1915 CPL POTIJZE BURIAL GROUND
11004 PTE	COWELL	Frederick	ATT 138 INF BDE HQ, 40th DIV HQ, GHQ 1st ECHELON HQ ARMY RES SECTION B
9255 PTE	CUNNINGHAM	Patrick	DISCHARGED 15/08/1915

7895 ACPL	CURRY	Martin	TRF LABOUR CORPS 22/05/1917 213978
6670 PTE	DISHMAN	Thomas	WOUNDED AT HOOGE DISCHARGED 14/02/1916 RENUMBERED 32783. SOUTH AFRICA 1st BN, QSA TRANSVAAL, LAING'S NEK
8485 PTE	DISTON	James	KiA 08/01/1915 PLOEGSTEERT MEM
3/8736 PTE	DUNN	Joseph	ENL 27/2/1907 DIS 23/07/1916 SHELL WOUND L THIGH TRF 3/DURHAM LI
9568 PTE	EADIE	Robert	TRF NORTHUMBERLAND FUSILIERS 05/07/1916 366677, SOUTH STAFFORDSHIRE REGT 34750
7085 PTE	ELGIE	John E	KiA 09/08/1915, SOUTH AFRICA 1st BN, QSA TRANSVAAL 1902 YPRES MENIN GATE MEM
8232 PTE	FITZSIMMONS	Edward	DISCHARGED 19/06/1917
3/8733 PTE	GRAY	James	ENL 30/8/1908 DIS 04/02/1916
3/8223 PTE	GREY	Thomas	TRF 10/DLI
7956 PTE	HALL	A	DISCHARGED 24/06/1916
6805 LCPL	HAYES	Albert G	DoW 23/11/1914 SOUTH AFRICA 1st BN , QSA, CAPE COLONY, ORANGE FREE STATE, TRANSVAAL. ERQUINGHEM LYS CH YARD EXT
8620 PTE	HEATH	Alfred H	ENL 23/11/1903 DIS 19/06/1915
5740 PTE	HENDERSON	Charles	TRF LABOUR CORPS 260648 23/06/1917, MANCHESTER REGT 77009
8793 PTE	HENDERSON	William	DISCHARGED 30/06/1917
3/9537 PTE	HOY	John T	CLASS Z RES
6602 PTE	HUGHES	Thomas	DISCHARGED
11383 L/CPL	HUMBLE	Richard	TRF KO YORKSHIRE LI 23041 MACHINE GUN CORPS (13th COMPANY) 16230 LSGT KiA 4/10/1917 TYNE COT MEM
9279 PTE	HUTTON	Ralph	DESERTED 28/04/1915 RENUMBERED 277288
6709 PTE	JACK	John L	DISCHARGED 11/03/1918
7500 PTE	JONES	Arthur	TRF LABOUR CORPS 384892
8894 PTE	KEGANS	John I	TRF SCOTTISH RIFLES 30828
6760 PTE	KENNEDY	William	KiA 10/03/1915 HOUPLINES COM CEM
7116 PTE	KING	Edward	TRF EAST YORKS REGT 23230 SOUTH AFRICA 1st BN, QSA 1901, 1902
8420 PTE	KIRKUP	Joseph	KiA 19/11/1914 PLOEGSTEERT MEM
9704 PTE	KNAGGS	Mark	TRF KO YORKSHIRE LI 30490
7916 PTE	LEES	Arthur	TRF ROYAL ARMY ORDNANCE CORPS S/8496
9443 PTE	LYALL	John	TRF LABOUR CORPS 397252
7628 PTE	MANN	Harry	DIED 17/02/1915 STE MARIE CEM LE HAVRE
6201 PTE	McCALLAN	John	TRF LABOUR CORPS 450905
9060 PTE	McCLUSKEY	Charles	TRF LABOUR CORPS 450900
8040 PTE	McDONALD	Thomas	DISCHARGED
6909 PTE	McGLAVE	Mark	TRF LABOUR CORPS 399788
3/9850 PTE	McPOLLAND	Hugh	CLASS Z RES
6896 PTE	MERRITT	Edward	DISCHARGED SOUTH AFRICA 1st BN, QSA CAPE COLONY, KSA
11565 PTE	METCALFE	Edward	KiA 25/05/1915 STRAND MIL CEM
6807 PTE	MILLER	George	TRF DEPOT, ENL 03/07/1899 DIS 23/05/1917 SHELL WOUNDS SOUTH AFRICA 1st BN , QSA, CAPE COLONY, ORANGE FREE STATE, TRANSVAAL
6982 PTE	MOCKLER	Thomas	KiA 05/08/1915 SOUTH AFRICA 1st BN, QSA, CAPE COLONY, ORANGE FREE STATE, TRANSVAAL. HOP STORE CEM
9486 PTE	MOORE	Nicholas	TRF MACHINE GUN CORPS 16403
6545 PTE	MORLEY	Joseph	DISCHARGED 19/10/1915
9790 PTE	O'NEIL	Michael	TRF WEST YORKSHIRE REGT 24/02/1915, LABOUR CORPS 319979
8445 PTE	SHARPE	Robert	SGT
7864 SGT	SHAW	C	
8462 PTE	SHAW	Charles	KiA 13/10/1914 PLOEGSTEERT MEM
6934 PTE	SHEARWOOD	Luke	ENL 13/03/1900 DIS 30/03/1917 ARMY RES CLASS P SOUTH AFRICA 1st BN , QSA, CAPE COLONY, ORANGE FREE STATE, TRANSVAAL
4/6554 PTE	SHEEHAN	Charles	WOUNDED AT HOOGE, TRF SCOTTISH RIFLES 30848
11697 PTE	SHEPHERD	John	TRF MACHINE GUN CORPS 20100 LCPL
9849 SGT	SHERRIFF	Frederick G	COMM 3/YORK & LANCASTER REGT
10175 PTE	SHIELD	Andrew	WOUNDED AT HOOGE
8548 LCPL	SHIELDS	Hugh	TRF 2/9th DURHAM LI RENUMBERED 6215, 326867 SGT
9510 PTE	SHOTTON	Gordon	WOUNDED AT HOOGE, ENL 5/1/1906 DIS 10/3/1919 KR para 392xvia
10467 PTE	SHOVELIN	Thomas	TRF ROYAL FIELD ARTILLERY 285970
10978 PTE	SHRIMPTON	George	KiA 15/10/1916 LSGT THIEPVAL MEMORIAL
10861 CPL	SHUTTLEWORTH	Riley	TRF GREEN HOWARDS 1st GARR BN SGT 22206 DIED IN INDIA 15/06/1917
11809 PTE	SIDWELL	Walter	TRF LABOUR CORPS 432461
8769 PTE	SIMMONS	William J	TRF NORTH STAFFORDSHIRE REGT 1st GARRISON BN, LABOUR CORPS 309507.
8008 PTE	SIMPSON	Charles	TRF WEST YORKSHIRE REGT 46033
6325 CPL	SIMPSON	Charles S	AWOII, PTE IN SOUTH AFRICA 1st BN, QSA TRANSVAAL, TUGELA HEIGHTS, RELIEF OF LADYSMITH, LAING'S NEK
8748 PTE	SIMPSON	Robert	ATT DEPOT ROUEN, ADW HAVRE, 7th VET HOSPITAL, PB BN ROUEN, 4th ASC WKSPS, 8 CORPS REST CAMP, 7th REST CAMP, BASE.
8356 PTE	SISSON	Edward	DISCHARGED 25/02/1916
10591 PTE	SLANN	H	
8424 PTE	SLATER	Thomas	KiA 28/10/1914 PLOEGSTEERT MEM
10357 LCPL	SLIMMINGS	Richard L	AWOII RENUMBERED 4435148
8472 PTE	SLOAN	Bernard	PRISONER OF WAR 18/10/1914
11720 PTE	SLOAN	David	SGT
8686 PTE	SLOAN	Michael	TRF NORTHUMBERLAND FUSILIERS 89516, ENL 23/12/1903 DIS 21/01/1916 GSW R ARM
10043 PTE	SMEETH	Herbert	PRISONER OF WAR
8537 PTE	SMILES	Arthur	TRF TRAINING RESERVE 86th BN, LABOUR CORPS 139703
9551 PTE	SMITH	A	PRISONER OF WAR
9854 PTE	SMITH	Charles	TRF ARMY RESERVE CLASS W 22/09/1917
11405 PTE	SMITH	Edward	TRF EAST YORKSHIRE REGT 23247, NORTHUMBERLAND FUSILIERS 27014
8505 PTE	SMITH	Ernest	KiA 21/09/1914 VENDRESSE MIL CEM
11604 LCPL	SMITH	Frederick	KiA 09/08/1915 YPRES MENIN GATE MEM
10285 SGT	SMITH	Harold	TRF MACHINE GUN CORPS 9320 CQMS
11262 PTE	SMITH	Horace	PRISONER OF WAR
9668 PTE	SMITH	James	
8542 PTE	SMITH	John	PRISONER OF WAR
9687 PTE	SMITH	John	TRF 15/DURHAM LI, KiA 16/09/1916 AIF BURIAL GROUND FLERS
7956 PTE	SMITH	Ralph	TRF ROYAL ARMY VETERINARY CORPS REG/1233
8012 PTE	SMITH	Robert	TRF 10/DLI, DISCHARGED 19/10/1915
9086 PTE	SMITH	Thomas P	KiA 16/05/1915 ERQUINGHAM LYS CHURCH YARD EXT

7325 PTE	O'NEILL	Michael	TRF NORTH STAFFORDSHIRE REGT 1st GARRISON BN 23807
7306 PTE	OXNARD	John	TRF ROYAL ENGINEERS 613210, ARMY RES CLASS P 13/10/1916 SOUTH AFRICA 1st BN, QSA, ORANGE FREE STATE, TRANSVAAL, 1901, 190
3/7726 PTE	QUINN	James	KiA 04/06/1915 SERVED IN B COMPANY POTIJZE BURIAL GROUND
3/9416 PTE	RACE	John	CLASS Z RES
9744 PTE	ROBERTS	Parry T	KiA 08/01/1915 FERME BUTERNE MIL CEM HOUPLINES
9336 PTE	ROBINSON	John	DISCHARGED 14/10/1915
3/8117 CPL	SHAW	Thomas	SGT
7867 PTE	SIMMONS	John	TRF LABOUR CORPS 136131, YORK & LANCASTER REGT 53427
3/9455 PTE	SMART	John	KiA 09/08/1915 YPRES MENIN GATE MEM
6639 PTE	SMITH	J	WOUNDED AT HOOGE
8702 PTE	SMITH	John G	CPL
3/8435 PTE	SOLOMAN	Robert	SENTENCED BY FGCM TO 20 YEARS PENAL SERVITUDE 30/06/1917 SOLOMON ON MRIC
9449 PTE	SPENCE	Hugh	DISCHARGED 07/06/1916
9462 PTE	SURTEES	Robert	TRF TRAINING RESERVE 87th BN TR5/68653
9334 PTE	THOMPSON	Samuel	DISCHARGED 26/10/1915
3/8824 PTE	THOMPSON	Thomas	DoW 18/05/1916 HEWORTH (WINDY KNOOK ST ALBANS) CHYD
3/8467 PTE	TYSON	Ernest	CLASS Z RES
3/8142 PTE	WADDLE	Frank	KiA 05/08/1915 HOP STORE CEM
9216 PTE	WALKER	John	TRF 12th, 20/DURHAM LI CLASS Z RES
11309 PTE	WALKER	William	DESERTED 14/08/1915
3/8611 PTE	WATERS	John G	KiA 11/07/1915 LA BRIQUE MIL CEM No 2
9581 PTE	WATSON	Frederick	TRF GREEN HOWARDS 22232
3/8132 PTE	WATSON	Joseph	KiA 22/05/1915 STRAND MIL CEM
9387 PTE	WILKINSON	William	RENUMBERED 83548 DLI NUMBERED 9389 ON MRC
9565 PTE	WILSON	Walter	TRF LABOUR CORPS 387529
8249 PTE	WOOD	James R B	DoW 09/08/1915 LIJSSENTHOEK MIL CEM
3/9469 PTE	WYNNE	David	CONVICTED OF DESERTION 23/12/1915 TRF 12/DURHAM LI LCPL KiA 08/10/1916 THIEPVAL MEMORIAL

THE FIFTH REINFORCEMENTS ARRIVED IN FRANCE 01 NOVEMBER 1914

8314 PTE	AITMAN	Thomas	ENL 14/1/1903 DIS 02/02/1916TRF 10/DURHAM LI, DEPOT
4/8022 PTE	BENNIONS	Peter	TRF TO 9th, 5th BNS, RENUMBERED 7151, 201274. MISSING 22/10/1917
8922 PTE	BERRY	Thomas	ATT 177 TUNNELING COY RE, ATT MINE RESCUE SCHOOL.
4/8000 LCPL	BETTRIDGE	Joseph	
4/8016 PTE	BEWICK	George	WOUNDED AT HOOGE TRF LABOUR CORPS 281410
4/7955 PTE	BLAIR	Joseph	CONVICTED OF DESERTION NO MEDAL REENLISTED 4436207
4/7694 PTE	BOYLE	Henry	DESERTED
9022 PTE	BOYLE	Owen	TRF LABOUR CORPS 210852 A/SGT
4/8339 PTE	BRADY	Joseph	TRF LABOUR CORPS 446342, ROYAL ARMY MEDICAL CORPS 206481
4/5806 CPL	BROWN	Charles E	TRF KO YORKSHIRE LI 16th GARR BN 27/08/1916 32885 SGT WOUNDED AT HOOGE
9141 LCPL	BURN	William	TRF LABOUR CORPS 376994
8892 PTE	BURROUGHS	Benjamin	ACPL
4/8060 PTE	CAIN	Hugh	TRF 14/DURHAM LI CLASS Z RES
4/9157 PTE	CANAVAN	Peter G	DESERTED 08/08/1916
4/7680 PTE	CAVANAGH	Peter	DISCHARGED 06/02/1916
4/8210 PTE	CHAPPELL	William	TRF NORTHUMBERLAND FUSILIERS 3rd BN 26/05/1915 20919
4/6265 PTE	CHRYSTAL	William	DoW 22/11/1914 BAILLEUL COM CEM
8391 PTE	CLARK	James	TRF WEST YORKSHIRE REGT 64345
4/8063 PTE	COLLINS	George	KiA 18/03/1915 HOUPLINES COM CEM EX
4/4409 PTE	COLLINS	Thomas	TRF LABOUR CORPS 501 EMP COY, 23/06/1917 260710, ROYAL ENGINEERS WR/300423
4/8176 PTE	CONLON	Henry	TRF 14/DURHAM LI KiA 18/09/1916 GIILLEMONT RD CEM
8791 PTE	CONVERY	Arthur	DISCHARGED 25/06/1915
4/7876 PTE	CRABTREE	Wilfred	ENL 06/08/1908 ARMY RES CLASS P DIS 02/03/1919
4/8083 PTE	CRANSTON	George	KiA 27/07/1915, D COMPANY POTIJZE BURIAL GROUND
8276 PTE	CRINSON	George W	TRF MACHINE GUN CORPS 18th MG COMPANY 25292 KiA 30/03/1917
4/6615 PTE	CULLEN	James	TRF LABOUR CORPS 07/10/1917 418501
9914 PTE	CUMMINS	A	TRF NORTHUMBERLAND FUSILIERS 01/11/1916
4/8028 PTE	CUNNINGHAM	Thomas	DESERTED 27/10/1917
8756 PTE	DALEY	John	DISCHARGED 23/02/1915
4/7743 PTE	DAVIDSON	William W	CONVICTED BY FGCM OF DESERTION 31/05/1916 COMMUTED PROMOTED SGT
4/8089 PTE	DONELLY	Patrick	TRF NORTHUMBERLAND FUSILIERS 26th BN 07/08/1915 24614 KiA 01/07/1916, THIEPVAL MEMORIAL
9002 PTE	DOUTHWAITE	Henry	TRF EAST YORKSHIRE REGT 1st GARRISON BN 20486 CONVICTED OF DESERTION
9034 PTE	DRAINES	John	TRF NORTHUMBERLAND FUSILERS 07/09/1915, LABOUR CORPS 421007
4/8927 PTE	DRYDEN	John	TRF 22/DURHAM LI DISCHARGED
4/7969 PTE	DUFFY	James A	ENL 1/10/1909 DIS 22/04/1916 TRF DEPOT
8935 PTE	EDWARDS	John	DESERTED 11/10/1915
4/8264 PTE	FAIRLEY	William	DESERTED STILL ABSENT DEC 1920
4/7725 PTE	FARRER	John	KiA 05/12/1914 RATION FARM CEM LA CHAPPELLE D'ARMENTIERES
4/8068 PTE	FENTON	John	TRF NORTHUMBERLAND FUSILIERS 3rd BN 30/04/1915 21075
4/6162 PTE	FERGUSON	John W	DISCHARGED 06/02/1915
4/7737 PTE	FERRY	John	KiA 09/08/1915 YPRES MENIN GATE MEM
8966 PTE	FISHER	Harry	
4/8066 PTE	FORD	Thomas	DISCHARGED KR para 392
4/8850 PTE	FOSTER	John	TRF NORTHUMBERLAND FUSILIERS 30/04/1915 21040
4/7988 PTE	FOSTER	John D	DISCHARGED 26/12/1914
4/5948 PTE	FOX	James Henr	DIED 19/01/1915 DURHAM ST OSWALD'S BURIAL GROUND
4/8887 PTE	GAFFING	James F	KiA 09/08/1915 YPRES MENIN GATE MEM
9106 PTE	GEORGE	James	DISCHARGED
4/7050 PTE	GIBBONS	Thomas	ENL 26/7/1908 TRF 10/DURHAM LI, ARMY RESERVE CLASS P 26/02/1916
4/9143 PTE	GIBSON	Thomas	KiA 09/08/1915 YPRES MENIN GATE MEM

7950 PTE	GILBERT	Thomas	TRF ROYAL ENGINEERS 86368 01/04/1915
4/7911 LCPL	GODDARD	Charles	DISCHARGED 25/08/1915
4/6610 PTE	GODLEY	Harry	TRF LABOUR CORPS 23/06/1917, 263791
8913 PTE	GRAHAM	James	DISCHARGED 18/09/1919
4/5969 PTE	GRAY	William	KiA 16/11/1914 PLOEGSTEERT MEM
4/8322 PTE	GUNN	James	KiA 02/08/1915 YPRES MENIN GATE MEM
7846 PTE	HALL	John W	DISCHARGED 09/07/1915
4/8292 PTE	HARRISON	Mark	DISCHARGED 26/10/1915
4/7437 PTE	HARRISON	Thomas A	KiA 12/04/1917 HOUPLINES COM CEM
4/7184 PTE	HEDLEY	James	ENL 26/7/1908 DIS 02/07/1915
8992 PTE	HENDERSON	G	TRF LABOUR CORPS 501 EMP COY, 23/06/1917 260677
4/7877 PTE	HEWITT	Thomas	BOULOGNE BASE DEPOT, 27 SANITARY SEC CLASS Z RES
4/6938 PTE	HOOPER	Thomas	WOUNDED AT HOOGE TRF KO YORKSHIRE LI 32750
8987 PTE	HOWE	J	
4/8189 PTE	HOWIE	James	WOUNDED AT HOOGE
4/7991 PTE	HUDSON	Harold	TRF TO DEPOT DLI
4/8814 PTE	HUGHES	James	KiA 09/08/1915 YPRES MENIN GATE MEM
9139 PTE	HUGHES	John	KiA 19/11/1914 PLOEGSTEERT MEM
4/6003 PTE	HUNTER	John	TRF 15/DURHAM LI
4/5716 SGT	HUNTER	Robert	WOII CSM CLASS Z RESERVE
8989 PTE	JACKSON	William	DISCHARGED 05/01/1915
4/7845 PTE	JOHNSON	Alexander	KiA 09/08/1915 YPRES MENIN GATE MEM
4/8240 PTE	JOHNSON	Edward	LCPL ENL 26/09/1911 DIS 26/11/1918
6715 BUGLER	JONES	W T	
4/8061 CPL	JORDAN	Fred	DISCHARGED 26/11/1915
4/8019 PTE	KANE	John	DESERTED 25/11/1915
4/8146 PTE	KEELIN	Francis	TRF 12/DURHAM LI, 8/DURHAM LI CLASS Z RESERVE
4/8002 PTE	KING	Edward	TRF GREEN HOWARDS 22260
4/9126 PTE	KING	James	KiA 27/07/1915 POTIJZE BURIAL GROUND
4/9005 PTE	KIRK	Henry	WOUNDED AT HOOGE KiA 22/04/1917 LOOS MEM
4/7974 PTE	KNOX	Colin C	TRF LABOUR CORPS 501 EMPLOYMENT COY
8723 LCPL	LAWSON	Thomas	DISCHARGED 25/06/1915 CPL
4/8255 PTE	LAWSON	William H	KiA 09/08/1915 YPRES MENIN GATE MEM
4/6017 PTE	LEACH	Joseph	TRF ROYAL ENGINEERS 86227 SGT
4/7480 PTE	LENG	William	TRF 14th, 19th, 14th, 18/DURHAM LI CLASS Z RES
4/7972 PTE	LIDDLE	William	ENL 10/06/1910 ARMY RES CLASS P DIS 23/04/1919 TRF 10th, ATT 35 IBD, 10TH, 15TH ATT 35IBD, 15/DURHAM LI DISCHARGED
4/8894 PTE	LITTLE	Arthur	TRF 10/DURHAM LI, DoW 09/05/1917 LSGT NEUVILLE ST VAAST MIL CEM LONDON CEM MEM PANEL
4/5811 PTE	LITTLEWOOD	Thomas	TRF ARMY SERVICE CORPS M/40439
8056 PTE	LOADER	Alexander	DISCHARGED 29/03/1917
4/9184 PTE	LONGMOOR	Thomas	WOUNDED AT HOOGE KiA 30/04/1916 ESSEX FARM CEM
4/7954 PTE	LYDON	John	TRF LABOUR CORPS 635438
4/7847 PTE	MALONE	William	TRF ROYAL ENGINEERS 204839 RENUMBERED WR/300012
4/7857 PTE	MANNION	John	KiA 11/08/1916 MARTINSART BRIT CEM
4/5541 PTE	MARKEY	Herbert	DISCHARGED
4/7898 PTE	MARRINER	T Walter	TRF DEPOT DLI DISCHARGED 19/08/1915
8790 PTE	MARSH	Charles W	TRF WEST RIDING REGT 30867, GREEN HOWARDS 39989, NORTHUMBERLAND FUSILIERS 56339.
9876 PTE	MARSH	W	TRF EAST YORKSHIRE REGT 21451
4/7739 PTE	MASON	James	ENL 6/5/1908 DIS 22/8/1916
8697 PTE	MASON	Walter	TRF LABOUR CORPS
8728 PTE	MASON	William	KiA 18/11/1914 PLOEGSTEERT MEM
4/7959 PTE	MASSINGHAM	Edwin	TRF 14/DURHAM LI KiA 10/03/1916 POTIJZE BURIAL GROUND
4/7559 PTE	McALPINE	Duncan	DESERTED STILL ABSENT DEC 1920
4/5999 PTE	McCARDLE	Henry	TRF 14/DURHAM LI KiA 22/04/1917 LOOS MEM
4/7966 PTE	McDOUGALL	George	DISCHARGED 23/02/1917
4/7511 PTE	McFARLANE	Thomas	TRF GREEN HOWARDS 8th BN 33590 CPL
8935 PTE	McGRATH	Patrick	TRF EAST YORKSHIRE REGT 1st GARRISON BN 21449
8993 PTE	McGUIRE	Philip	ENL 10/10/1904 DIS 03/07/1915
4/8043 PTE	McINTOSH	Alexander	TRF ARMY RESERVE CLASS W
4/8010 PTE	McMANN	Joseph	TRF 10/DURHAM LI KiA 28/08/1916 THIEPVAL MEMORIAL
4/6082 PTE	MIDDLETON	Robert	TRF LABOUR CORPS 451062
8961 PTE	MILLS	Samuel	DEAD ON MEDAL ROLL NO FURTHER TRACE
4/8371 PTE	MILLS	Watson	SENTENCED BY FGCM TO 3YEARS PENAL SERVITUDE, KiA 15/10/1916
4/6613 PTE	MONARCH	James	TRF ROYAL ENGINEERS 606634, ENL 20/7/1908 DIS 17/02/1917
4/9110 PTE	MORRISON	Kenneth	KiA 09/08/1915 YPRES MENIN GATE MEM
4/7616 PTE	MULHOLLAND	Thomas	KiA 19/11/1914 PLOEGSTEERT MEM
4/7895 PTE	MURPHY	John	KiA 30/04/1915 HOUPLINES COM CEM
4/8105 PTE	MURRAY	John	TRF NORTHUMBERLAND FUSILIERS 21201
3/7366 PTE	MYERS	George	TRF EAST YORKSHIRE REGT 21450
4/8329 PTE	NAYLOR	Charles	CLASS Z RES
4/7859 PTE	NELSON	John H	SGT DISCHARGED
4/9038 PTE	NICHOLSON	Thomas	TRF 15/DURHAM LI CLASS Z RES
4/8393 PTE	NIMMO	Joseph	WOUNDED AT HOOGE KiA 28/12/1915 POTIJZE BURIAL GROUND
4/8328 PTE	NOBLE	George A M	DISCHARGED 10/12/1917
4/8310 PTE	OGLESBY	Sidney A	TRF LABOUR CORPS 369541
4/7872 PTE	OLIVER	Stanley M	COMMISSIONED GREEN HOWARDS 08/1917 CAPTAIN
4/8132 PTE	OLIVER	Wilfred	TRF LABOUR CORPS 617147
4/7963 PTE	O'NEILL	John	TRF 14/DURHAM LI KiA 18/09/1916 THIEPVAL MEMORIA
4/8133 PTE	O'NEILL	Matthew P	TRF KO YORKSHIRE LI 30484, ROYAL ENGINEERS 193901 RENUMBERED WR/202625
9039 PTE	ORD	Rollins	
4/7902 PTE	PARKER	Alfred	TRF LABOUR CORPS 260042

4/8103 PTE	PATTISON	Ernest	WOUNDED AT HOOGE DISCHARGED 29/03/1917
4/8075 PTE	PEMBERTON	Nicholas	WOUNDED AT HOOGE DESERTED 31/12/1916
8788 PTE	PRINCE	Ralph A	WOUNDED AT HOOGE
4/5856 PTE	QUINCEY	Albert	DoW 13/02/1916 ETAPLES MIL CEM
4/8110 PTE	RICHARDSON	Thomas	DISCHARGED
4/8401 PTE	RICHMOND	Edward	DISCHARGED 30/05/1917
4/5816 PTE	RIDDELL	George A	RENUMBERED 103012
9111 PTE	RILEY	John	KiA 09/08/1915 YPRES MENIN GATE MEM
8881 PTE	RUTHERFORD	P	
4/8335 PTE	RUTTER	David	KiA 09/08/1915 YPRES MENIN GATE MEM
4/8613 CPL	SANDILANDS	Charles	TRF LABOUR CORPS 369123
8781 PTE	SHIELDS	Torrence	
4/8212 PTE	SHILLING	Thomas	ENL 4/9/1911 DIS 21/11/16 WOUNDS TRF DEPOT
4/7380 PTE	SIMPSON	Charles W	TRF LABOUR CORPS 481657
4/8928 PTE	SIMPSON	William	KiA 24/02/1915 HOUPLINES COM CEM
8211 PTE	SMAILES	William	KiA 06/12/1914
8918 PTE	SMITH	James	KiA 08/01/1915 FERME BUTERNE MIL CEM HOUPLINES
4/8365 PTE	SMITH	Lawrence	FRAUDULENTLY ENLISTED IN RIFLE BRIGADE No 13706 TRF ROYAL ENGINEERS 307046 RENUMBERED WR/26078
4/8311 PTE	SMITH	Matthew	TRF 10th, 1/7/DURHAM LI KiA 23/03/1918 POZIERES MEM
4/8399 PTE	SMITH	Robert	CLASS Z RES
4/7169 PTE	SMITH	William	ENL 24/4/1906 WOUNDED AT HOOGE, DIS 28/05/1917 ACPL
4/7341 PTE	SMITH	William	TRF LABOUR CORPS WESTERN COMMAND LAB CENTRE 475589
9661 PTE	STEENSON	William J	TRF LABOUR CORPS 651074
4/9109 PTE	STEPHENS	Arthur	ENL 31/8/1914 DIS 04/06/1915
9094 CPL	STOCKER	J	TRF KO YORKSHIRE LI 14th BN 41607
8978 PTE	STOREY	Thomas	WOUNDED AT HOOGE, DISCHARGED 16/07/1917
4/7989 CPL	SULLIVAN	Benjamin	TRF LABOUR CORPS 501 EMP COY 23/06/1917 260726
4/8026 PTE	SUTTON	John	CONVICTED OF DESERTION, KiA 04/05/1917 PHILOSOPHE BRIT CEM MARZINGARBE
4/8079 PTE	SUTTON	Thomas	DISCHARGED 29/03/1917
8937 PTE	TAIT	Andrew	TRF LINCOLNSHIRE REGT 45175, LABOUR CORPS 31818
4/7323 PTE	TAIT	George	TRF NORTHUMBERLAND FUSILIERS 26422
8830 PTE	TAYLOR	Edward	TRF ROYAL DEFENCE CORPS 84919
4/7757 PTE	TAYLOR	William	TRF 10/DURHAM LI KiA 16/09/1916 THIEPVAL MEMORIAL
6826 PTE	TEASDALE	George	TRF LABOUR CORPS 398550
4/8876 PTE	THEASBY	Joseph	ASGT TRF 1/7/DURHAM LI, 18/DURHAM LI
8725 PTE	THOMAS	Thomas	KiA 09/08/1915 YPRES MENIN GATE MEM
4/8736 PTE	THOMPSON	James	CONVICTED OF DESERTION 03/11/1915 TRF 10/DURHAM LI LCPL KiA 09/04/1917 NAME THOMSON IN SDGW GOUY-EN-ARTOIS COM
9108 PTE	THORNTON	Frederick	TRF ROYAL ENGINEERS 128130 SGT
4/9054 PTE	TIGHE	Thomas	TRF ROYAL MUNSTER FUSILIERS G/340 01/04/1917 SGT
4/8396 PTE	TULLOCK	George	KiA 09/08/1915 YPRES MENIN GATE MEM
4/9036 PTE	TUMILTY	Benjamin	KiA 16/10/1916 THIEPVAL MEMORIAL
4/8272 PTE	USHER	Michael	KiA 01/06/1915 POTIJZE BURIAL GROUND
4/6105 PTE	VIRTUE	James	TRF 10/DURHAM LI KiA 02/02/1916 ESSEX FARM CEM
4/8261 PTE	WALTON	Benjamin	TRF 18/DURHAM LI KiA 12/04/1918 PLOEGSTEERT MEM
4/8050 PTE	WARD	James	TRF 10th, 14th 15th 1/8/DURHAM LI DoW 15/04/1918 ETAPLES MIL CEM
4/8367 PTE	WATSON	John	KiA 30/01/1915 HOUPLINES COM CEM
10175 LCPL	WAUGH	Charles	CPL
8980 PTE	WHELAN	W	TRF LABOUR CORPS 475141, NORTHUMBERLAND FUSILIERS 89275
8685 PTE	WILSON	James	TRF 9/DURHAM LI RENUMBERED 325757
7952 SGT	WINSHIP	John	TRF MACHINE GUN CORPS 16379 SGT
4/8074 PTE	WINTER	Thomas	WOUNDED AT HOOGE, TRF LAB CORPS 599776 ROYAL DEFENCE CORPS 66341

THE SIXTH REINFORCEMENTS ARRIVED IN FRANCE 08 NOVEMBER 1914

8694 PTE	BRADLEY	David	TO ARMY RES CLASS P 23/01/1917
4/8033 BGLR	CARBRO	James	DISCHARGED 29/08/1917
4/9140 PTE	COVILLE	Charles	DISCHARGED 10/07/1914
4/5414 PTE	DALEY	Michael	CONVICTED OF DESERTION 05/01/1917 TRF 14/DURHAM LI
8733 PTE	DOCKERTY	Edward	TRF NORTHUMBERLAND FUSILIERS 2nd GARRISON BN 22/10/1915 26340
4/8248 PTE	GLENNDENNING	Thomas	ENL 3/11/1911 TRF ARMY RESERVE CLASS P 07/02/1917
4/5316 PTE	GOODMAN	Patrick	TRF NORTHUMBERLAND FUSILIERS 3rd BN 20/05/1915 LABOUR CORPS 455536
7264 PTE	HAMER	Mark	PRISONER OF WAR 25/11/1914 SOUTH AFRICA 1st BN, QSA, CAPE COLONY, ORANGE FREE STATE, TRANSVAAL, 1901, 1902
8982 PTE	HENDERSON	H	TRF LABOUR CORPS 373400 12/10/1917
4/7881 PTE	HOLMES	Thomas	DISCHARGED 20/08/1915
4/8878 CPL	HOOD	Jacob	TRF LABOUR CORPS 438001
4/8143 PTE	HORN	Thomas	ATT 177 TUNELLING COY RE
4/7026 LCPL	JOYCE	Thomas	KiA 22/08/1915 HOP STORE CEM
4/7494 PTE	KENNEDY	James	TRF ARMY RESERVE CLASS T 16/04/1917
4/6618 PTE	LYNCH	William	DISCHARGED 05/08/1917
4/8811 PTE	MARTIN	James	TRF 10/DURHAM LI, KiA 02/02/1916 ESSEX FARM CEM
10176 PTE	NEWTON	Benjamin	DISCHARGED 03/05/1916
4/8246 PTE	O'HALLERON	Michael	DoW 06/05/1915 BAILLEUL COM CEM
4/8069 PTE	QUINCEY	Edward	TRF HEAVY BRANCH MACHINE GUN CORPS, TANK CORPS 75577
9006 PTE	RAMSHAW	James	TRF SCOTTISH RIFLES 30881
8901 PTE	ROBINSON	Joseph	WOUNDED AT HOOGE TRF ROYAL ENGINEERS TUNNELLING COY 151488 LCPL
9684 PTE	ST. CLAIR	Harry	DoW 18/10/1914 FRENCH MIL HOSP ST OMER
4/6998 PTE	STOREY	Douglass	DISCHARGED 17/01/1917
8724 CPL	STRAUGHAN	John W	WOUNDED AT HOOGE, TRF ARMY RESERVE CLASS P 31/10/1916
8636 PTE	STUBBS	William	TRF ARMY RESERVE CLASS P 16/12/1916
11488 CPL	SULLIVAN	Joseph	TRF 3/DURHAM LI (D COY) DoW 5/09/1916 INJURIES CAUSED BY EXPLOSION SOUTH SHIELDS (HARTON) CEM
10023 LCPL	SURFIELD	Frederick C	ENL 4/4/1907 DIS 12/06/1915 WOUNDS TRF 3/DURHAM LI
9641 PTE	SURTEES	George W	TRF WEST YORKSHIRE REGT 40049, ROYAL ENGINEERS 310357
11614 PTE	SURTEES	John H	KiA 13/10/1914 PLOEGSTEERT MEM
8761 PTE	SUTHERLAND	John	DISCHARGED 06/12/1814
8577 PTE	SWALES	Samuel	CLASS Z RES
11581 PTE	SWITHENBANK	Roland	KiA 30/10/1914 PLOEGSTEERT MEM
8642 PTE	SYMINGTON	William	ENL 3/12/1903 TRF ROYAL FUSILIERS GS/9419, DIS 22/12/1916
8450 PTE	TARRANT	Benjamin	STILL SERVING 30/03/1920
4/8809 PTE	WILSON	Richard	DoW 13/03/1915 CITE BON JEAN CEM ARMENTIERES
4/9211 PTE	WILSON	Thomas A C	KiA 09/08/1915 YPRES MENIN GATE MEM
4/7932 PTE	WORTHY	John	ENL 27/08/1909 DIS 21/05/1915 TRF 4/DURHAM LI